32 YEARS
MAN & BUOY

IAN ATKINSON

Published by FeedARead.com Publishing – Arts Council funded

First Edition October 2013
Second Edition March 2014

A CIP catalogue record for this title is available from the British Library.

Eternal Father, strong to save,
Whose arm hath bound the restless wave,
Who bidd'st the mighty ocean deep
Its own appointed limits keep;
Oh, hear us when we cry to Thee,
For those in peril on the sea!

Civvy to Sailor

As a child, I had always harboured ambitions of becoming a fighter pilot but leaving school in June 1978, at the tender age of sixteen, with only seven CSE's of mediocre grades, I was never going to make it though I still needed to get a job.

In the fifth form at school, some of my mates were already smug with the knowledge that they had been offered the job that they had applied for. Being something of a layabout, staying on into the sixth form was never an option for me and I had long decided to leave school as soon as it was legally possible to do so.

I had always enjoyed Metalwork at school, so it was no surprise when I opted for a realistic career in metal fabrication. Dressed smartly in my recently purchased suit and shiny shoes, I attended several interviews at local factories that were recruiting. None of these were successful, but then again, I had never been for an interview before and had no idea what I was supposed to do. Getting a bit despondent, I started to consider anything.

Long before I had heard of the term 'networking', my mum, Mavis, had been chattering to her friend, Roy Benwell who, by chance, was one of the directors of bullion dealers 'Edward, Day and Baker' in Birmingham's Jewellery Quarter. Probably because he fancied my mum a bit, he invited me along for an interview. Dressed in my new suit and carrying a cloth bag containing a couple of examples of tools that I had made in Metalwork, I attended the interview at their factory on Vyse Street in Birmingham. On reflection, this must have looked quite comical to my prospective employers, so it was quite a surprise when they offered me a job as a 'Trainee Toolmaker'.

I was eager to learn and carried out every seemingly menial task that was set by the foreman with enthusiasm. One such task was to cut a perfect square of steel from corner to corner, to make two identical right-angled triangles. Persuading the saw to cut into the corner was becoming a problem as it kept slipping to one side or the other. After several attempts, in a blinding flash of inspiration, I clamped and chopped the metal diagonally using the guillotine. Chuffed with my achievement, I went to show Frank, the foreman, who promptly threw them in the waste bin, picked up another square and told me, quite forcefully, to do it again and this time to hacksaw them. It was then that I realised that he wanted to assess my skill of hand and not my improvisation. Fortunately one of the more experienced toolmakers showed me a little trick that involved filing a tiny flat on the corner of the square that would be almost invisible once the hacksaw had sawn down the scribed line.

That was day one of my short period of employment with E,D & B. During that time, I was sort of adopted by some of the ladies in the packing room. This was probably because I was a pure, sweet and innocent sixteen year old. One of the younger girls was twenty two, very slim and absolutely stunning, but I didn't have the courage to talk to her let alone ask her out. One of the lads, trying to be helpful, told me that her name was 'Clit', "it's short for Clitoris, which is a Yugoslavian name" he added "She's very friendly, so why don't you take her a coffee from the machine and go talk to her?" Geed on by the other lads, I took her a coffee and after I had succumbed unwittingly to the practical joke, I recoiled in scalded agony as she poured the hot coffee into my lap. I learned a valuable lesson that day and she never spoke to me again.

After about three weeks, Frank had had enough of my almost constant cock ups, so I was called into the office for a one-way discussion which resulted in me losing my first job. Back at home, mum was furious and after talking to Roy on the phone, she tried unsuccessfully to claim for unfair dismissal. Looking back, it was a harsh decision that arrived quite suddenly and without any warnings, at a time when I was starting to feel that I was making progress. But sacked I was, and I had to get on with it. It was a real shame, I enjoyed my first job and learned many things. How to make a wedding ring out of a sheet of gold, how to make 150 sleeper earrings on the lathe in about a minute, how to mill what looked like a very heavy crusty loaf of bread into a perfectly smooth and rectangular ingot of gold measuring about 8" x 4" x 4" and most importantly that 'Clitoris' is actually not a Yugoslavian girl's name at all, though I still needed to look it up.

The following morning, in August 1978, I was frogmarched to the Employment Exchange by my mum, Mavis, to sign on the dole before coming home with an interview later in the day for a job as a builder's mate. Amazingly, I got the job and started work the following day. I hated it from day one. I was ridiculed constantly by the small workforce. For some reason, they had decided to nickname me 'Gordon' as the one hit wonder, Jilted John was in the charts at the time with a song containing the line 'Gordon is a moron'. I hated this, but political correctness wouldn't be invented for about another twenty years and the torment was relentless. After a week of almost incessant verbal abuse, I walked out. The following morning, the boss was on the phone begging me to come back. As a sort of bribe, he offered to let me break up a garage floor using a quite dangerous Kango hammer which is a bit like a small pneumatic drill, but I had had enough of their taunting and went back to the Employment Exchange.

My dad, Lawrence, at the time, worked as a Laundry Manager at Dudley Road Hospital so to tide me over, he offered me a temporary job as a Laundry Porter collecting dirty washing from the wards and then, later in the day, delivering huge trolleys of clean bedding back onto the wards. As it was a private site, I was even allowed to drive the electrically powered truck which was a bit like a milk float with sides and a tailgate hoist.

I really enjoyed this job as I got to know all of the pretty nurses and everyone in the laundry was really friendly, though this was probably because I was the boss's son. I was keen, full of energy and loved racing around the wards crashing the clean laundry trolleys through the huge plastic swing doors. The truck was purpose built to hold nine trolleys, so the daily round saw us back at the laundry a few times during the day. At 10am we would stop for morning break and the hugely British ritual of 'breakfast'.

Before starting work, breakfast, to me, consisted of coffee, cereal and toast; but the workman's breakfast consisted of everything that you could fit onto one plate, piled high and all for the princely sum of £1.10. This was the highlight of my day. Everyone was generally happy and it was a really pleasant working environment. Unfortunately, it wouldn't last and Dad called me into the office one morning to explain that, due to job rotation, I had to move off the delivery trucks and into the receiving area working with a few lovely West Indian ladies who were all quite large and cuddly.

This job involved sorting out the dirty laundry into piles of whites, theatre greens and coloureds before loading it onto conveyor belts that would in turn feed the huge washing machines as part of an automated process. The problem was that up to that point, I had led quite a sheltered life and was not at all prepared for wet and soiled sheets, bloody theatre gowns and the occasional accidental treat of a recently amputated body part. On one occasion, to my horror, a severed finger fell onto the stained concrete floor. It seemed as if I was always reaching into a bag of laundry and coming out with something wet and squishy and sometimes smelly, so for that reason I pleaded with my dad to move me to somewhere within the laundry working with the clean linen.

After a few weeks, he eventually relented and I was moved to a point in the production line where the wet washing would fall out of the machine into a trolley bin before I was to wheel it around to the driers that I called 'Fire Eaters' as they were gas fired and had an open fiery chamber on the side. This work was ok, but once again, it was only temporary so almost daily I paid visits to the hospitals own Employment Exchange seeking a more permanent position within the hospital grounds. Within a week or so, an opening came up for a Catering Assistant in the Staff Canteen so following a brief, informal interview I was assigned to the same canteen where we ate breakfast. Things were looking up.

The Staff Canteen was on top of a huge industrial kitchen run by the Head Chef called Tony who was also something of a Karate expert. I remember being slightly scared and quite intimidated of him but without good reason as apart from a fair bit of harmless leg pulling, he was actually quite a good bloke.

I started by making teas and coffees to order in a seated area and clearing tables before graduating to serving food. I was eventually asked by Tony after a few weeks, if I would like to work in the kitchen as a trainee chef and immediately jumped at the opportunity.

To start with, of course, I got all the nasty jobs like washing up and pulling the meat off about thirty hot, roasted chickens for a curry. I spent time in various sections learning how to make Baked Alaska by Annette the puddings cook and also in butchery learning how to bone and slice a side of bacon. After some practice, I got this down to a very respectable four minutes. After a few weeks, I progressed onto making omelettes. This involved whisking up two full trays of eggs and preparing all the fillings which were presented in stainless steel serving containers before changing into clean chef's whites and transferring everything up to the canteen where I would cook omelettes to order. It was here that I met Janette who worked in the Sterile Supply Unit and after a week of seeing her every lunchtime I eventually plucked up the courage to ask her out on a date.

Janette was gorgeous; twenty two with huge dark brown eyes and matching hair. I discovered that she was a devout catholic and also a huge West Bromwich Albion fan and lived in a commune in Warley near Quinton. I used to finish work on Saturdays at midday, get the bus to her house before getting dragged kicking and screaming to the Hawthorns to watch Albion. If I was really lucky, she would also take me shopping and make me say prayers before tea. These were the sacrifices I was prepared to make, just to be with her but like all of my adult romances so far, it wouldn't last.

Mavis had long since decided that my life needed direction, so without consultation, she applied for me to join the Royal Navy. One evening, she sat me down for a serious chat to discuss my future that ended up with her asking me if I had ever considered joining the Army. At that particular time in the Autumn of 1978, the IRA were wreaking havoc in Northern Ireland and many British soldiers were getting killed and I didn't much fancy that. She then asked about joining the RAF to which I replied that they were all poofs. Undeterred, she finally asked how I would feel about joining the Royal Navy. This caused me to think. We lived about as far away from the sea as it's possible to get and my only knowledge of the Royal Navy was a drama series in the mid 70's called 'Warship' concerning the life of a fictional Leander class frigate called 'HMS Hero'. I remember sailors bringing tea and knocking on the door frame of a curtained doorway and thinking, I could do that. As it turned out, my mum had predicted my thought process and had already applied on my behalf. The following day, dressed in my suit, I was off to Birmingham Armed Forces Careers Office to take a test and have a medical as the first part of the recruitment process. The test was relatively simple and was a collection of basic English, maths, and physics psychometric tests.

This was obviously successful as I was then invited back to the Careers Office just before Christmas 1978 for an interview with a Royal Marine Warrant Officer who subsequently offered me provisional acceptance into the Royal Navy as a Junior Marine Engineering Mechanic Second Class which was actually the lowest of the low but to me sounded quite grand. I was truly delighted. After Christmas, with a degree of reluctance as I was enjoying the work, I handed my notice in at the hospital.

The day I left, a few weeks after my seventeenth birthday, we went for a celebratory drink in the Social Club on the hospital grounds. Despite being under age, I was bought a pint of lager that tasted very much like whisky which seriously affected my speech. After a couple of hours of constant drinking and having a seemingly endless supply of whisky-laced pints on the table, I was extremely wobbly. There had been heavy snowfall that day in January 1979 so it seemed logical to have a snowball fight as we left the Social Club. Due to the amount of alcohol I had drunk, I found it impossible to throw straight and ended up losing quite badly. Back in the kitchen, cold and wet, I was fed strong coffee before being invited to stand on an upturned plastic meat box in front of a small crowd consisting of just about everyone I knew in the hospital. My dad was there and also Janette had turned up to hear Tony read a non too complimentary poem that he'd written about me before presenting me with a card signed by everyone and a book entitled 'Steam and Gas Turbines for Marine Propulsion'. This was then taken from me by Tony as I tried to utter a speech of thanks to the assembled crowd. I hadn't even managed to finish the first sentence before they started to pelt me with anything to hand. I was covered in eggs, bread crumbs, food colouring, flour and just about anything else that would make a mess. Having lost the one-way food fight, I was ushered into the shower fully clothed in my chef's whites, that were no longer white to rinse off the accumulated food and to attempt to sober up.

Suitably recovered, a few days later, I started to get all of the items together that were on the list sent by the Royal Navy recruiting office. One such item was a 'Housewife'. I thought this was a bit odd as I was only seventeen and hadn't even considered getting married. On further investigation it turned out to be a sewing kit. Anne, my new stepmother, seemed to know exactly what was required so set about making me one from some old material. The result was a dark red wrap secured with a tie that had several pouches for cotton, pins, needles, and scissors. There was even a card containing several shirt buttons. My initials were finally embroidered onto the outside in blue thread. It was a work of art that I still have to this day.

We were further encouraged not to pack any civilian clothes or unnecessary luxuries as these would not be allowed and there wouldn't be enough space for anything other than the uniform I would be issued on arrival.

After much rushing around and ensuring that everything on the list was accounted for and packed, I was ready. A rail warrant duly arrived a few days before I was due to travel authorising a single journey from Sutton Coldfield to Plymouth. It was then that the enormity of what I was about to do started to sink in.

HMS RALEIGH

BASIC TRAINING
6th February to 16th March 1979

Early on the morning of Tuesday 6th February 1979 after a 'final' breakfast, Mum bundled me into the car and drove the very short distance to the railway station. After exchanging the rail warrant for a single train ticket, we made our way to Platform 2. I remember this being, uncharacteristically, a very emotional farewell as we stood on the Birmingham-bound platform waiting for the train to emerge from the tunnel. Of course, I was the big man leaving home, but inwardly, I was petrified. Mum, who had taken the day off work, presumably to make sure I actually went, was standing beside me, constantly asking if I'd got everything? Well if I hadn't, it was too late now as the train slowly approached the platform and drew to a halt.

Stepping into the nearest carriage with my bag, I sat opposite a couple of ladies who watched knowingly as I waved goodbye to my mum. No sooner was I sat down when, with whistles blowing and doors slamming, the train slowly pulled out of the station. Thirty minutes later and I was forced to change as the train arrived at the busy Birmingham New Street station.

Changing platforms, I didn't have to wait long for the Plymouth bound train that was arriving from Edinburgh. On schedule, the big diesel engine train arrived and without difficulty, I found a seat and stuffed my bag on the luggage rack above my head. Five minutes later and on time, I was finally on my way.

The four hour journey to Plymouth was uneventful as I remember but what I was supposed to do when I arrived caused me some concern. I didn't want to get into trouble on my very first day. I needn't have worried though, as I walked up the steps towards the exit in Plymouth Railway Station, humping my bag over my shoulder, I was relieved to see a sailor in uniform next to a blackboard saying 'HMS Raleigh New Entry'. After introducing myself and getting my name ticked off on his clipboard, I was told to join a group of similarly frightened teenagers who had boarded a minibus in the car park just outside the station.

When all of the scheduled arrivals were aboard, the minibus made the short ten minute journey to the Torpoint Ferry where we disembarked. Again, we had not been given any instruction, so we sheltered from the wind and the rain behind a huge wooden structure that was used to house the machinery for the chain-driven ferries.

After a few minutes, and with a fair amount of clanking from the chains, a ferry arrived. On one side of the car deck, there was a vending machine and a few orange plastic chairs bolted to the deck. Dropping our bags in a collective heap, the soon-to-be sailors, went off to explore. Up on the top deck, I saw the 'Navy' for the very first time. Anchored in the Hamoaze was HMS Ark Royal, probably the most iconic aircraft carrier of the day and although it had only recently decommissioned, she looked fantastic. It was starting to dawn on me, what I had actually let myself in for.

Arriving in Torpoint a few minutes later, we disembarked and again were forced to seek sanctuary in a bus shelter until another bus arrived and more names were taken. The final short leg of our journey then began.

My first sight of HMS Raleigh was awesome. It seemed very futuristic with white plastic-cladded walls and windows with rounded corners. It looked to me like an Earth-bound 'Moon Base Alpha' from the 1970's TV series 'Space 1999'.

After the bus had negotiated the gates to HMS Raleigh, it pulled into a small courtyard where a man in a white shirt and cap told us to line up on the pavement. So with our bags unloaded and dumped in a heap, we lined up and once again, the man, who we later found out was a Petty Officer, shouted out names like a teacher taking the register.

Satisfied that all of his New Entrants had arrived, we were told to collect our bags and follow him into the New Entry block called 'Ganges Division'.

and so it begins ...

New Entry

Inside Ganges Division, we followed the Petty Officer into a large classroom where we were instructed to sit and wait for our name to be called. With a name beginning with 'A', I didn't have long to wait. Following the Petty Officer into an adjoining room, I was faced by three uniformed people sitting behind a row of three desks. I was invited to sit on a chair that had been placed in front of the desks. Some personal details were first of all checked to ensure that I was the right chap and it was explained to me that I was about to join the Royal Navy for nine years with three years as a Reservist and if this had been an awful mistake then I could leave right now.

Ensuring them they had the right chap, I was then asked to read and sign my contract and also a copy of the Official Secrets Act that threatened fourteen years imprisonment if I divulged any of our nation's secrets to a foreign power. Fat chance of that, I thought, I didn't know anything. With the formalities completed, I was asked to re-join the rest of the class in the other room.

After everybody had been into the room to sign their contracts, one person had decided not pursue his career in the Royal Navy and was quietly ushered away. I never knew his name and we never saw him again.

One of the things associated with military life is short hair, so after the signing ceremony, we were assembled out in the courtyard again and marched as an ill-disciplined rabble down to the barber's shop on the camp. Once there, three barbers went to work on our wavy locks. When it came to my turn, I was asked the question "Regulation or quarter inch?" Without thinking, I said "Quarter inch please" as I was sure that 'Regulation' would be mega short. He then went to work with his clippers with hair flying everywhere and I was left, a very short time later, for the first time in my life, a skin head. Those that had opted for the regulation cut were allowed to keep the majority of their hair resulting in the traditional short back and sides.

Following the visit to the barber, we returned to Ganges Division where we were given a board with our name and official number on it and told to sit in a photo machine for a mug shot to be taken. After the photographs had been taken, we were all a bit shell-shocked, but it had only just begun.

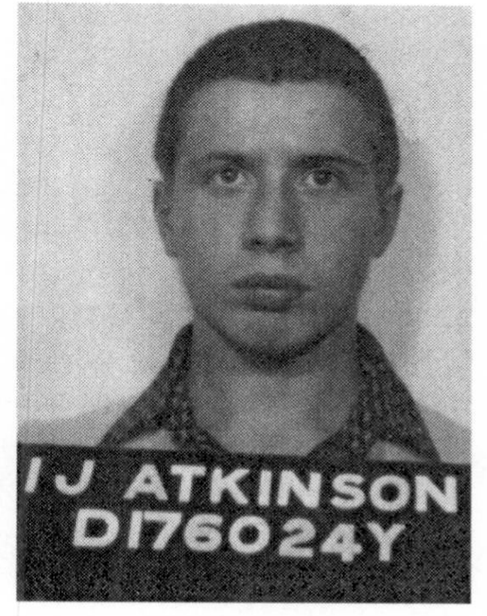

There was no time for rest though and following the Petty Officer up two flights of steps into a large open dormitory with twenty eight beds, we were told to find our bed and then to wait for instructions. On each bed was a large light brown kit bag with names and official numbers stencilled onto the bottom.

With everybody stood next to their respective beds, lockers and kit bags, we were told to empty our kit bags onto the bed. It was like Christmas, but each person had identical 'presents' and with a few exceptions, there appeared to be three of everything.

Part of the pre-joining literature that had been sent required measurements of various body parts and can I clearly remember going into a Men's Outfitters in Sutton Coldfield, and for the first time ever, trying on a hat and discovering the correct size of my head was in fact 6 $^{7}/_{8}$.

The Petty Officer went through the inventory of all of the jumbled clothing on the bed, first of all identifying everything by its correct name and secondly to ensure that it was all there. We were then invited to sign for our kit with the warning that if any item of clothing got lost, we would be responsible for buying the replacement out of our pay.

With all our kit mustered, the Petty Officer instructed us to try on all the clothing to ensure that it all fitted correctly and finally to change into a pair of dark blue trousers that he called 'No8 Trousers' and also a white T-shirt and plimsolls before putting everything else back into the kit bag. Our civilian clothing was then stuffed into our bags and taken away for storage as we wouldn't be needing those for the foreseeable future.

All of this frantic activity brought us up to tea-time and I for one, was starving. Again we assembled in the courtyard and the Petty Officer led us around the corner to Trafalgar Galley where quite literally hundreds of trainees at various levels of basic training were queued up the stairs leading into the dining hall. I can well remember feeling very intimidated as they bashed their plastic mugs against the wall in a sort of ritual initiation ceremony as we were led right to the front of the dinner queue.

The food was, at best, edible. It was largely rumoured that the bitter tasting tea was laced with bromide to counteract the effects of the early morning glory and thus keep our natural teenage hormones under control. The food also had a terrifically high calorific value to compensate for all of the intense physical activity that the next eight weeks was sure to bring.

After 'scran', we were again collected as a group and led back to the dormitory, which we were told was called a called a 'Mess'. Well at the time, it certainly lived up to its name. We were then instructed to pick up our kit bags and follow the Petty Officer down to the 'Stamping Room'. On one table against the back wall were many boxes containing wooden letters. We were told to take an initial letter and then our surname and assemble them into a name stamp with a full stop in-between them. Jostling with my new class mates for letters, I completed the construction of my wooden name stamp which now displayed the name "I.ATKINSON" backwards and with my kit bag at my feet, the class took up places next to long tables with shallow trays of both black and white paint. One item at a time, the Petty Officer held up a piece of uniform clothing, identified it and instructed us where to stamp our name and in what colour. With the shirts, it was on the shirt tail in black and with the trousers on the inside of the waist band in white. Naturally, with a class of twenty seven, somebody occasionally got it wrong, much to the amusement of those who hadn't. My only mistake at that point was to stamp the waterproof cover of my green Pay Book cover with white paint instead of black. I hastily corrected it and to this day, I still have a smudged grey "I.ATKINSON" stencilled diagonally across it.

The stamping ritual took most of the evening and understandably we were exhausted so after being ordered to take a shower and dressing in our brand new pyjamas we climbed into bed for the first time as Royal Navy trainees. With everybody tucked up in bed, the Petty Officer called "Good Night Ladies" and the lights were extinguished at 10:30pm on the dot. In the time-honoured tradition of 'The Waltons', there were a few calls in the dark in poor American accents "Good Night John-Boy", followed by "Good Night Mary Ellen" before we drifted off into an exhausted sleep.

The following morning, we were rudely awakened at 6am by someone blowing a whistle loudly over the tannoy system and shouting "Call the Hands, Call the Hands, Call the Hands". The Petty Officer arrived immediately switching on all the lights; he was already fully dressed and at the top of his voice shouted, "Wakey, wakey, rise and shine, the sun is up, the morning's fine" Well this was a downright lie for a start as it was still pitch black outside and being early February, the sun would not rise for another hour or so and to top it all, it was pouring with rain.

Almost everybody sprang into action and set about getting washed and dressed, but at the end of my aisle next to the window, one chap still remained curled up in his bed fast asleep. The Petty Officer seemingly taking pity on him, went up to his bed, gently shook him by the shoulder, "Good morning sir, would you care for some tea and toast?". He replied "Thank you, that would be ni..." as the PO roughly grabbed his bed clothes from him, and threw them out of the 2nd floor window onto the wet and muddy grass below leaving him shocked but now wide awake and on his feet.

Twenty minutes later and we were all showered, shaved, dressed and our beds made. Everything was stowed away and the mess tidied up before we were again assembled for what would become a three times daily march to Trafalgar Galley for a meal.

The unfortunate chap who was rudely awoken was a streetwise Glaswegian fellow called Cooke. We all learned a valuable lesson that morning as Cooke had now inherited some muddy, sodden bedding that he now had to wash, dry and iron before bed time. That mistake was never made again.

The rest of the week followed in the same vein. The PO, was our New Entry Instructor and he oversaw everything that we did. Nothing was assumed. We were shown everything from how to make beds to which drawer each item of kit was to be stowed in. We were shown how to wear each item of kit and even how to lace up our shoes. It might seem trivial, but it was explained that the Ghurkhas used to feel the boot laces of a potential enemy before silencing them if they were crossed instead of the regulation lacing method.

Out in the courtyard, still wearing No8 Trousers, a white T-shirt and white plimsolls, we were formed into three ranks according to size and when the squad was properly formed we were told that every time we were required to move as a class, we had to fall into exactly the same positions. From that point on, we marched everywhere. The oldest person, at the age of thirty-two, was a bearded chap called Jim Bullough. He was designated the title of Class Leader and as such, it was his responsibility to ensure that we were marched everywhere and arrived at our next class at least five minutes before it was due to begin. The penalties for being late, or adrift, in naval terminology, usually involved press-ups or running to the main gate, getting your hand rubber-stamped and running back again, thus ensuring that you'd done it.

During that first week, we were examined by doctors and dentists and put through the Royal Naval Swimming Test. This must sound quite daunting, but involved jumping off a diving board into a swimming pool wearing overalls over our swimming trunks. You were then required to tread water for forty minutes before swimming exhausted to an inflated twenty-five-man life raft and pulling yourself aboard. A tall thin chap called Crabtree seemed to have considerable difficulty staying afloat and subsequently failed when coughing and spluttering, he held on to the side of the pool. Later in the day, he did pass on his second attempt, this time encouraged by the class who were now starting to gel as a team.

On the Saturday of week one, having now been in basic training for only four days it was time to graduate from New Entry and move into Anson Division to make way for the 'sprogs' who would be joining up on the following Tuesday. In addition to that, living in close proximity to the other twenty six blokes, I had developed a bit of a sniffle that would in time, grow into a full-blown cold and would last for just about all of my training in one form or another.

Anson Division

Fallen-in for the last time at New Entry with four days of naval experience under our belts, we really felt as if we had achieved something. All of our kit was packed into our kit bags and piled high on trolleys in the courtyard. Our new Part One Instructor came up to meet us before marching us down the hill and through the camp into Lefanu Quadrangle. Retrieving our kit bags from the trolleys we struggled to hump them up the stairs and into our new mess. As it was Saturday, this gave us the rest of the day to get the mess looking lived in, beds made and all of our uniform placed in the correct drawers. If we were in any doubt as to where anything should go, all we had to do was to consult the photographs of a correctly made bed and a correctly laid out locker that had been pinned to the mess notice board as a permanent reference.

Kit Preparation

In the afternoon, after a mediocre lunch in Trafalgar Galley, our instructor assembled us in the Kit Wash Room to give us a lesson on how to wash our clothes by hand as there were no washing machines. This may sound obvious, but how many people now wash all of their own clothes by hand? As previously mentioned, all new recruits were issued with three of almost everything. This allowed for one item to be worn, one clean and pressed and in your locker ready to wear and the other one in the wash. Freshly washed kit was wrung out by twisting it around a tap or a pipe and then hung out to dry in the Drying Room which always had the aroma of smelly wet boots. Next to the Drying Room on the ground floor was an Ironing Room with about thirty ironing boards in three rows screwed to the floor. Part of the pre-joining kit list was an iron, but these could also be borrowed from your oppo or signed out from the Block Office on temporary loan.

Very early on in basic training, everyone was issued with their own personal copy of BR1938 'The Naval Rating's Handbook' this was a blue book that was slightly larger than A5 but was filled with lots of advice and instruction on how to tie knots but more importantly how to iron your kit thus ensuring that all of the creases were intentional and more importantly in the right place. The book also served as a measuring guide for folding kit. The theory was, that if everything was folded 'Book Size' then it would all fit in your ship's locker. Our instructor was seemingly always on hand to offer advice on the presentation and more importantly, the preparation of our kit.

Another skill to be developed was the ability to be able to 'bull' boots to a high gloss finish. We were issued with two pairs of marching boots, and a pair of shoes. One pair of boots were "Rubbers" and the other 'Steelys'. Both were black and finished in hard bobbly leather. The 'Rubbers' designated as daily working boots whereas the 'Steelys' were our parade boots and had a steel semi-circular insert in the heel to make a noise when we dug our heels in. Both had to have the bobbles removed and then polished and shone to a high gloss finish. As anyone, who has been through basic training will testify, this is not achieved with brush and polish alone. There are many who will gladly share their secret, but for me, it was a long hard slog, sitting crosslegged on a gash bag outside the mess listening to a cassette whilst smearing polish across the toe caps, filling in the bobbles and then attempting to gently polish using water and a duster in a circular motion. It took absolutely hours. Those that could do it, readily offered advice such as hot spooning, which is not as sexy as it sounds and melting the polish onto the boots. In my experience, there was no real substitute for sheer persistence and determination. Of all my kit, getting my boots "bulled" to a high gloss finish presented me with my biggest problem.

Towards the end of week two, we had our Petty Officer's Kit Muster. This was the first of three kit inspections and required our kit to be laid on a perfectly prepared bed, inch perfect, in precisely the right way. There were photographs in the Ironing Room and also in the Mess and also further guidance in BR1938. We took absolutely hours washing, ironing and placing everything on our bed and then checking that everything was "Book Size" by laying BR1938 on top and seeing if there was any part of the item poking out. Shorts were the biggest problem as they had short tapered legs. The boots and shoes were finally bulled and laid out in a particular pattern on the floor before we stood to attention at the end of our bed ready for the inspection and proud of our achievements.

This was a training kit muster and designed to highlight areas of kit preparation that needed improvement. It was still disheartening though to see all of my hard work undone by an uncompromising PO who dumped all of my clothing in a huge pile resembling a bonfire next to my bed. More work was undoubtedly needed. Fortunately, depending on your point of view, most of Anson 06 class suffered the same fate, but as we later learned, this was par for the course.

Learning from the list of points made by the PO, the class doubled their efforts in preparation for the Chief's Kit Muster in week five. This was always considered the 'Big One'. The standard had been set, so now everything had to be scrubbed, shone, ironed, starched and polished until the creases were razor sharp and everything was spotless and gleaming. Having now been issued with our No2 suit with red badges this could be hung on a hanger at the head of the bed, but the detachable collar had to be ironed with three vertical razor sharp creases. The centre crease pointing in and the outer creases pointing out. The idea being so it would fold in a concertina style to fit into our locker. Our PO told us a rather rude way to remember it. "Remember it as two tits and a cunt", vulgar perhaps, but effective as I have never forgotten it.

Ironing the white front was a fairly simple affair as it is simply ironed flat and then folded vertically in half before ironing a single crease in the front. During basic training, the front crease went in, but after graduating from Basic Training (Part 1) to distinguish the graduating class from those still in Basic Training, the crease would be ironed to point out.

Fortunately, I joined up just after a new style of suit had been introduced. This suit had sewn in silks on the lapels and the trousers had front and back creases instead of the older five or seven horizontal concertina style creases depending on your height. This was considered by many at the time to be not as smart as the older design of suit, but was so much easier to maintain.

After daily preparation, week five culminated in the dreaded Chief's Kit Muster. Days were spent ensuring everything was exactly right. Every evening was spent bulling boots or ironing kit until finally, the feared day arrived. My bed looked brand new. Two white starched sheets with a sharp crease down the centre. The top sheet was then turned down over the counterpane and then pulled tight and tucked in. At the foot of the bed, the bed covers were folded into hospital corners. With the bed '*perfect*', I set about accurately placing my kit onto the bed in 3 columns, each item was 'Book Size'. After checking, stepping back and re-checking, I pretended I was the Chief and looked again with a critical eye. I was ready! Looking around the mess, there was frantic activity everywhere, so with the smug satisfaction of having properly prepared, I went to assist others who were still struggling.

At 1:30pm precisely, with the entire mess ready and everybody stood to attention next to their handiwork, the Chief entered the mess carrying his clipboard. I was in the second bed alphabetically. MEM 'Darby' Allen was first as the Chief looked over the overall presentation before he picked up every item in turn, shook it out, checked creases, name stencils, sizing and overall cleanliness against a list on his clipboard. Panic started to ensue as he looked in places that I had clearly forgotten about and found dust and dirt and occasionally rust. After seemingly hours, but in reality, it was only about five minutes, 'Darby' was awarded with a satisfactory pass.

Next he came to me and casually looked at the presentation of my kit, making silent notes on his clipboard. Picking up my 'Steelys' he said "Dirt in the welts." throwing them back on the floor, my shoes were found to have rust around the metal lace holes and they joined the boots. My white and also my blue gym shorts were slightly larger than the regulation 'Book Size' and a double crease was found on one of my white fronts. I was starting to sweat. Seeing that I was getting flushed, the Chief asked me to open the huge cantilever window at the end of the mess for ventilation. Having done as he'd asked, I returned to the growing mound of my kit by the side of my bed. He ordered me to pick up my clothes off the floor, pile them onto the mattress with the rest of my kit and clean bedding and to launch everything out of the window onto the muddy grass below, "Re-scrub" he shouted. I was gutted, I had done my very best and still it was not good enough. This seventeen year old had had quite enough of this bullshit and stormed out of the mess, across the landing, and cried in the toilets. I decided there and then to jack it all in. I could never pass this kit muster with the standard set so high and now I had to start all over again.

About half an hour later, my PO came looking for me and took me down to see my Divisional Officer, a chap called Lieutenant Peter Arthur. Still very upset, sat in his office, crying was a real low point in my life thus far, but slowly, with encouraging words from my PO and also Lieutenant Arthur, I started to feel better. The PO then promised to help me improve my kit preparation by showing me where I had gone wrong. After a while, I ventured outside to retrieve my kit from underneath the window only to find that a few other kit laden mattresses had since joined it. Whilst I was not so ashamed now realising that I wasn't the only failure, there still was much to do.

That evening, the class licked their collective wounds and after evening scran and rounds, I set about scrubbing my sheets and all my kit again for the re-inspection in a week's time.

Doubling our efforts, with a real sense of teamwork, those who had passed their kit muster, smugly helped those of us who hadn't. All of the points raised by the Chief were harsh, but if a standard had been set, then it was up to us to maintain it. One by one, we addressed all of the issues until finally five of our class of twenty seven were stood next to our beds waiting anxiously for the Chief. Following a "Re-scrub" the best grade that can be achieved was a 'Satisfactory' so it was with a tremendous amount of relief that I finally passed the Chief's kit muster at the second time of asking. The carrot at the end of the kit muster was permission to join the rest of my class at the camp disco called "The Scrubbers Ball", but before doing so, I waited patiently in the phone box queue with a fist full of 10p coins to call my mum and tell her about my triumph.

That was not the end of kit musters, we still had a Divisional Officer's Kit Muster at the end of week seven, but having now achieved the standard and fully understanding what was required, this was completed without any further drama.

Parade Training

Despite failing my PO's and CPO's Kit Muster, I was starting to get used to the regime. I wouldn't say it came naturally because it didn't; I worked hard at everything I did. Marching was a particular weak point of mine. How can walking and swinging your arms at the same time be so bloody difficult? I was either out of step with the rest of the class or 'tick-tocking' that is swinging your left arm forward at the same time you move your left leg forward, which isn't natural, but somehow I managed it. After much analysis by my class mates and instructors, it was decided that I was trying *too* hard and that I needed to relax more and let it come naturally. This was of course easy for them to say, I was always seemingly falling out of step, realising the error, then taking two half steps to correct the problem but in doing so putting everyone else off behind me. Music seemed to make the difference. With the Royal Marines band or the Parade Ground speaker system blasting out 'Hearts of Oak' it seemed natural to follow the rhythm of the music. It was either that or I was listening to the music and relaxing, either way it worked.

On Friday of week three, after a week of practicing marching on the parade ground, Anson 06 took part in their first set of Divisions wearing No8's with caps as we had not been issued with our No1 Uniform yet. This is a naval tradition that sees classes from weeks three to eight assemble on the parade ground for inspection before finally marching past the assembled families of the graduating class and saluting the Reporting Officer on the dais.

I was petrified that I would screw it up for the class and as a punishment, the class would be sent around again. Fortunately, when the Royal Marine band started up with 'Hearts of Oak' everything seemed to fall into place. I listened to the music, forgot about what my feet were doing and actually enjoyed it.

Physical Training

Marching was only one of my problems. As you would imagine during military training there would be plenty of physical Training. As a slim seventeen year old, fitness was not really a problem for me. I had previously won awards for orienteering and had taken part in cross-country competitions at school, but this was altogether more archaic. I don't think the fitness regime had changed much since Napoleonic times as one of the pass/fail aspects was the ability to climb a rope and then having successfully ascended to the top of the gymnasium and touched the ring at the top of the rope we then had to do various acrobatics and let go with either an arm or both legs as instructed.

The Physical Training Instructors, having '*failed*' in their own branch, now had real power and seemingly a need to inflict misery and they wielded it. There was no walking allowed at all in the gym. Addressing them by anything other than "Staff" resulted in press-ups and the offender being sent "Down for ten". Our gym kit always had to be pristine requiring shoe whitener on the plimsolls and many *happy* hours in the Kit Wash Room scrubbing shorts, socks and divisional tops. Any slight infringement usually resulted in more press-ups or a timed run to the main gate and back. I hated it, but my fitness did improve.

The Assault Course

All of this running and climbing was a sort of diluted battle fitness test. Somebody in many years still to come would doubtless be paid millions for devising the phrase 'Fit to Fight'. In one forgotten corner of HMS Raleigh was a seemingly overgrown, marshy and muddy wilderness interlaced with high walls, taut horizontal ropes, tunnels and slippery logs. This was collectively known as the assault course.

Early on in basic training, we were double marched, or jogged, down to the Assault Course to observe a class in their final week of training take part in a timed challenge. After about ten minutes of huffing and puffing, the bedraggled and barely human contestants emerged climbing up a short vertical rope out of a drainage culvert, their overalls and boots were soaked through with mud splattered everywhere. With the brainwashing now complete, I can remember thinking that their overalls would be a devil to scrub, iron and fold back to book size. It was no consolation that we still had this to come.

So in week three after our PO's Kit Muster, we dressed in swimming trunks, rubber marching boots and overalls before doubling down to the start of the assault course. Our PT instructor walked us around the course explaining exactly how best to tackle each respective obstacle, though it was explained that much would depend on our teamwork.

Following the brief, in groups of four, we assembled at the start point. On the whistle, we were off, running down a well-trodden muddy path to a scrambling net that must easily have been 20ft high. Ascending this, albeit with difficulty, we then had to traverse the 'Leopard Crawl' that was a taut two inch rope that sloped downwards over 100ft to a height of about 6ft. So lying on top of the rope with one leg dangling as a sort of counter-balancing pendulum, I pulled myself along causing severe rope burns on my chest. Underneath there was a fine gravel pit to cushion any fall. Fortunately, I didn't fall, but I did end up hanging off the rope and pulling myself along the remainder of the length like a chimpanzee. Bumping my head on the shackle, I realized I had reached the far end and dropped the 6ft to the ground landing easily before racing off to catch up with the other members of my team who were assembling at the far end of the course, at the foot of a 12ft wall. When I arrived, two team members were positioned with their backs to the wall and their hands clasped together as a 'step' to elevate me up the sheer wall. Placing a muddy boot, I was launched upwards towards another team mate already on top of the wall who, with outstretched arms, pulled me into a sitting position atop the wall. Both of us worked together to pull the third member of the team onto the wall before the final team member took a running jump trying to run up the wall before he was grabbed my myself and my oppo and pulled up to join us.

Lowering ourselves down the other side, we continued down a muddy track to a couple of wet, slippery logs over what evidently used to be a stream. Crossing these quite fast and without incident we again had another wall to negotiate, but this was shorter than the last, so it presented no problem. After this, we slid down a muddy bank and, egged on by our instructor, we fell headlong into a slimy pond and, using our hands as claws, struggled up the well-worn and slippery embankment, sliding back into the water until, with ebbing strength, we finally made it to the top and staggered on. The next hurdle was a rope to lower ourselves back into the waist-deep water before slithering snake-like through some lengths of concrete drainage conduit and into the culvert and the end was in sight.

With our last ounces of strength, and with encouragement being shouted from onlookers, we eventually scaled the final rope, made it to the top and fell over the finish line exhausted.

I don't recall the time, but I know we didn't break any records. After getting our breath back, we analysed, as a team, how we could improve on our performance for the challenge run in week seven.

Finally, after each of the teams had completed the course, Anson 06 fell in again for the short but soggy run back to Lefanu Quadrangle. Still dripping with water and caked in mud, we were instructed to strip down to our swimming trunks and to carry our wet things barefoot into the Kit Wash Room before getting showered and into uniform in readiness for the next class. The kit washing would have to wait until the evening.

Pier Cellars

During the first eight weeks, there were a few opportunities in the training regime that allowed us to get out of the camp on what we generally call "Exped". The first time was at a small encampment on the Rame Peninsular called 'Pier Cellars'. This consisted of a small harbour, a dormitory style hut, various woodland trails and another bloody assault course but this one had taut wires directly over the water in the harbour. During the day, orienteering exercises were set around the local countryside. The class was divided into teams that would then compete against each other before the light faded. Knackered and blistered, the last exercise of the day was back at base where we tackled the assault course. The prize was beer which to this point was a) illegal, as I was under age and b) just not available. Nethertheless, we battled hard and finally, as the victors, we sat around the campfire, ate from the improvised barbeque, sang newly-learnt sea shanties and drank the prize. Life was good again.

For some unexplained reason, there were no mattresses on the bunk beds in the dormitory, so it was a very cold and very uncomfortable night huddled on bare springs in a naval issue arctic sleeping bag. The beer started to take effect, and before long I was dying for a pee, but it was too cold and dark to get out of bed, so another battle ensued. Almost before it began, I knew I was going to lose and it was therefore about an hour or so later that, freezing cold, I hobbled barefoot wearing nothing but a pair of pants, stumbling over rucksacks and wet boots that had been abandoned on the cold concrete floor and emptied my aching bladder.

We only spent two days at 'Pier Cellars', but despite being extremely weary in limb, blistered under foot, cold and wet, it was a hugely enjoyable experience and a light-hearted respite from the harsh training regime.

In the fifth week we went on another 'exped', this time to Dartmoor and we had all been looking forward to this one. A whole weekend out of Raleigh with the rumour from senior classes of pub food and beer at the end of it.

Dartmoor

On the Thursday of week five, an hour was set aside for the class to march down to the Adventurous Training Store and draw some kit. This included amongst other stuff, an orange cagoule, a rucksack, a sleeping bag, two 24 hour ration packs, a water bottle and a pair of walking boots. Nine three-man tents were also issued to accommodate the class and these would be distributed amongst the guys before we set off. Everything on the kit list was hastily checked and stuffed back into the rucksacks before staggering back to the block and dumping them back in the mess to investigate properly later in the evening.

Later that day, after checking that everything fitted and examining the contents of our rations for the weekend, we erected the tents outside the block to ensure that we had all the bits before striking them and dividing them up to even out the weight. Finally we repacked our rucksacks.

On Friday, we were given a brief lesson on how to read a map and compass. My map reading skills had always been quite good, so consequently I didn't learn much. Exercises were set to find two grid references on the 1:50,000 map of Dartmoor and then to plot a direct line course from one to the other.

Dartmoor, for the uninitiated, covers an area of about 368 square miles so it is quite easy to get lost in addition to that, the weather can be extremely changeable. We were instructed that due to the army conducting live firings on the North Moor, we would be walking on the south of the moor starting from a scout hut at Gutter Tor where we would initially camp. The Global Positioning System was at this point in time, a military contraption and the stuff of science fiction, so we only had a map and a compass and in case of emergencies, a torch and a whistle. The instruction, if lost was to head north off the southern side of the moor to intercept a road running east - west and then to phone the scout hut from the nearest phone box. There was also a television mast visible in good weather plonked on top of North Hessary Tor that could be used as a visible aid in finding our ultimate destination, the town of Princetown and the home of Dartmoor Prison.

Suitably briefed, we were dressed in No8s trousers, divisional rugby shirts and boots at 7am on Saturday morning and began loading up a three-ton truck with cooking equipment, loo rolls, gash bags, rucksacks and of course, the lads.

The ride to the scout hut in the back of the wagon was extremely uncomfortable, but we didn't care, we were excited as this was another weekend out of the camp and cheerfully sang songs and chatted amongst ourselves until the truck could go no further. We were still about a quarter of a mile from our destination, but the road had petered out into nothing more than a footpath and not suitable for a vehicle of this size. So, with everyone carrying their own rucksack and an additional item of communal kit, we trudged up the path towards the scout hut.

A little later with the camp set up and the tents pitched, we were issued route cards and sent out in teams of eight on a mission to find the answers to questions on another card. It was like a treasure hunt, but this only ensured that we visited the tops of all of the Tors on the route card. Occasionally, an instructor would pop up from behind a rock and point us in the right direction and walk with us for a short distance before disappearing again. It was about a ten mile circular walk carrying everything except the tent so it was pretty hard going. Occasionally, we would have a heated discussion about the direction we should be walking in and also about our present location. This became very difficult and usually ended up with the loudest voice winning the argument which inevitably resulted in the team trudging about a mile in the wrong direction before realising the error when the gate, bridge or stream that we'd been heading towards failed to materialise. I think they call that character-building, but after walking for seemingly ages and with the light fading we eventually got back to camp. We later found out that we had been under observation all of the time. We didn't consider it at the time, but a train of eight orange cagoules is quite easy to spot on a background of grassy moorland. Following a meal of baked beans and sausages, we slithered into our sleeping bags and fell asleep exhausted.

Waking early on Sunday morning, with stiff cold legs, we washed in cold water and dressed eager to get going if only to warm up. It also meant that we got to the pub earlier assuming the navigation did not fail us. The Sunday walk was actually a race, but more than that, there were points to be gained. Like a sort of reverse target, the further out we walked, the more points we achieved. The centre of the target was a pub called 'The Plume of Feathers' in Princetown, so heading directly towards that would give us a faster time, but also the least amount of points. So we hastily plotted a route through some high value points and generally did quite well. We had a cut-off time of 2pm back at the pub but it was easily conceivable that you could be the last back to the pub but in the time verses points calculation crowned as the winners.

Well we were neither the winners nor the losers. We collected a very respectable amount of points and were not the last back either. So, relieved to have finished, sat outside on picnic benches in the warm sunshine, I ordered a huge meal of double sausage, double egg and chips washed down with a pint of bitter and began to feel vaguely human again before being told that we still had to walk back to camp. Amidst the groans and with rapidly stiffening legs, we reluctantly left the 'normality' of the pub and headed south down a well-worn path towards Nun's Cross Farm and Eylesbarrow Mine before reaching the scout hut shortly before dusk.

The following morning, after another good night under canvas, everybody pulled their weight to pack up the tents and make the campsite look like we had never been there. After having a final skirmish for litter, we slowly walked back down the track carrying all the kit to the waiting truck for the short journey back to HMS Raleigh.

General Naval Knowledge

Despite all of this physical activity, there was also quite a bit of classroom work to do and an examination to take. The exam was simply known as the 'GNK' standing for General Naval Knowledge and as the name suggested, covered a multitude of naval orientated questions and was considered a career stopper if we failed it. Taught in modules by our PO, Chief and Lieutenant, we learned how to recognize various different classes of ship from their silhouettes, how to tie knots, practical seamanship, how to tell the difference between the various ranks and rates and their equivalent in the RAF and Army. We learned the various marks of respect, who to salute and more importantly, who not to. The different parts of a ship were also covered. I remember this as a very hard exam, but now, many years afterwards, I struggle to see what was so hard about it. Perhaps there was just a lot of new stuff to cram in and studying for exams was never one of my strong points. To graduate from Basic Training, all recruits were required to pass all aspects of training including getting more than 75% in their GNK exam.

Many happy evenings were spent sitting on the landing polishing boots and firing revision style questions at each other but some people didn't want to play this game, preferring to study on their own. It was little surprise therefore when two people subsequently failed the exam and were back-classed two weeks into the 08s.

Fortunately, with a great sense of relief and also achievement, I passed at the first time of asking and managed to complete training with most of the same people I joined up with.

Jupiter Point

Thinking about it, Royal Navy Basic Training would not be complete without a little time mucking about on the water. This wasn't so much sailing, though Jupiter Point which is annexed to HMS Raleigh does teach sailing to those wishing to learn.

The sailing centre is set predictably next to the water's edge in the picturesque back yard of the National Trust's St Antony's House. After arriving off the coach clutching a brown paper bag containing a packed lunch, we were ushered into a room where the Chief Petty Officer in charge gave us a stern warning about the need to be sensible in the boats. We were each then kitted out with buoyancy aids and split into four teams of seven. Each team had its own Petty Officer in charge and also its own rowing boat. Before lunch we had all had a turn at rowing as we got accustomed to our first time 'at sea' in the Royal Navy. The afternoon then saw a challenge issued to the teams. As a team, under the command of the PO, we had to race the other Whalers out of the small Cornish inlet, around a buoy and then back to Jupiter Point. It was hard work. We didn't win, but despite getting soaked we enjoyed the distraction. Following the debrief, still shivering, we boarded the coach for the short journey back to HMS Raleigh in time to clean up for evening rounds.

Rounds

Every evening, without fail, our personal and communal areas had to be cleaned to a high standard and then reported to an inspecting officer. The inspecting officer could be an Officer or indeed a Chief Petty Officer but the standard remained constant. Any area not coming up to the required standard was awarded a 're-scrub' and the individual responsible invited to clean it again for a further inspection an hour or so later.

The accommodation block was divided up, by the Class Leader, into areas of responsibility so everybody had a 'Cleaning Station' to look after. After scrubbing and polishing and ditching the gash, we would all would make ourselves look smart with a cap or beret and stand smartly to attention by the door to your allocated area in preparation for the ceremony of 'Rounds'.

Assuming an officer was conducting 'Rounds', he would be led by a sailor piping the 'still' on his Bosun's Call as the officer approached and came to attention in front of the rating. The rating would salute the officer and wait for the salute to be returned. He would then typically report "Kit Wash Room ready for your rounds sir, MEM Atkinson reporting" he would thank you and ask you to lead on as he then inspected your cleaning effort, ensuring that the standard had been maintained.

After conducting the inspection, the officer would then come to attention by the door when the rating, also at attention, would say "Rounds complete sir, permission to carry on?" Assuming everything was to a satisfactory standard, permission would be granted and the reporting officer would then move on to the next compartment.

Church

Never being much of a church goer, I always assumed religion to be optional, but HMS Raleigh being a law unto itself did not do 'optional'. All students in basic training on Sunday's were therefore required to attend an inter-denominational church service at 10am. This was actually not as arduous I thought it might be. We would be warmly welcomed into the church by 'The Bish', as he was affectionately known, and after being seated, with hats under the pews, a few prayers were said and a few songs sung which generally ended with the Naval Prayer followed by the Naval Hymn 'Eternal Father Strong to Save'.

After the service had finished we were always invited to stop for tea and biscuits and an informal chat with the chaplain. Naval Chaplains differ from their Army and RAF colleagues in one subtle way. Whilst they are commissioned as officers, they always assume the rank of the person they are talking to. This makes their pastoral care easier and makes them much more approachable.

The Chaplains have a true 'open door policy' meaning that should you have a problem that cannot be discussed with your Petty Officer, Divisional Officer or mess mates, then the Chaplain is always on hand with a cup of tea and a listening ear.

On a Sunday morning, after breakfast and cleaning up the mess, believe it or not, we actually looked forward to church. Having a bit of a chat and eating all of his biscuits and drinking his tea took us right up to lunchtime. We came to enjoy the peace and quiet of church on Sunday.

Military Training

At the opposite end of the spectrum to church, as a member of the Armed Forces all personnel with the exception of medics are required to bear arms. So, for that reason, there was a week-long module in basic training that taught us how to kill people.

One cold, wet Monday in week six saw us marching down to the armoury to be issued with a self-loading rifle. This weapon is a reliable, hard-hitting, gas-operated, magazine-fed semi-automatic rifle, with a maximum battle range of 300 metres and a practical rate of fire of 20 rounds per minute.

Having collected the SLR, we then marched down to the Military Training School that was situated in another far and distant corner of HMS Raleigh. All the instructors, we soon discovered, pretended to be soldiers and ran about dressed in camouflage clothing. They weren't fooling anybody.

This heralded a day of lectures, learning the parts of the SLR and how to strip down, clean it and reassemble the weapon ready for firing. The SLR was essentially manufactured in two parts; at the front the gas cylinder and at the rear the working parts. We were instructed always to strip and clean the gas cylinder first and to reassemble last as the SLR could still be used as a modified .303 single shot rifle if you were unfortunate enough to come under fire whilst cleaning it.

As I remember it, and it's been a while, first we would remove the magazine and 'cock, hook and look' to ensure that there were no rounds left in the chamber. The working parts were then allowed to go forward but the action was not fired off. Next, the nipple on the side of the gas plug was depressed and given a quarter turn to release it. This allowed the gas piston and spring to be removed. A quick twist of the spring removed it from the piston. These could now be cleaned.

At the rear, the rifle was 'broken' to reveal a 'rat's tail'. When pulled, it removed the block and carrier. The sleeve could then be slid off. The block would then be removed from its matched carrier and further stripped to remove the firing pin.

Using the dedicated cleaning kit, every bit of the rifle would then be cleaned and the barrel lightly lubricated. This was achieved by pulling a piece of oily 4" x 2" cloth through its entire length, with the appropriately named 'pull through', before the barrel was visually 'sighted' clean.

After all parts had been cleaned to the satisfaction of the wannabe soldier, the working parts were first reassembled and then the gas parts before a full functional test was carried out to ensure that everything still worked. One chap did manage to insert the gas plug upside down causing it to get jammed as the nipple disappeared into a hidden recess. This gave the instructor an opportunity to earn his wages as he struggled to remove it. Whilst he was doing this, the culprit paid for his error by doing press ups until the weapon had been repaired.

After cleaning the SLRs and lying them down out of harm's way, we were shown various items that had been 'shot at' on the range. The most impressive was a forty-five gallon oil drum that had previously been full of water. It had a perfect 7.62mm hole in one side and a huge crater in the other side where the velocity of the bullet had forced the water to follow it and ripped the back of the oil drum to bits. Apparently, this was a simulation of a bullet travelling through a human body. What a comforting thought. To cap it all, we were then shown a few photographs of injuries caused by the SLR. This was most certainly a weapon to be behind and not looking down the business end at.

The following day, after all of the lectures, we marched down to Trevol Range and with an instructor standing beside me, I fired my SLR for the first time at a plywood target imaginatively named, 'Herman the German'. This was not hugely successful; the recoil bruised my right shoulder and I also got hit in the face by hot cartridges ejected from the rifle of the person lying to my left. That said, after everyone had finished firing and all weapons had been proved empty and safe, we were taken to inspect our targets and the hits were chalked in. Mine were high and right of centre, so a small adjustment to the sights was required.

The second group of five shots were much better grouped and I dare say if this chap had actually been running towards me looking all angry, despite filling my pants, I would have slotted him and ruined his day.

The final test was to fire ten rounds standing, ten rounds kneeling and finally ten rounds from the prone position. If 28 out of 30 were on target, you would be awarded a Marksman's badge to sew onto the sleeve of your No1 Uniform. Well, I got 25 out of 30 and was mightily pleased with myself but also slightly miffed that I wasn't one of the two trainees awarded Marksman status. That said, it was another tick in the box and I was now qualified to bear arms. What a scary thought that was!

Fire Fighting

Another of the skills required, when at sea, is the ability to extinguish a fire as dialling 999 does not do a lot of good when you are several miles out to sea. So on the Monday of the final week, we again marched up to Triumph squadron in yet another distant corner of HMS Raleigh for fire fighting training.

Dressed in borrowed overalls and Wellington boots, we were taken to a demonstration area to observe as an instructor threw a bucket of diesel onto some piled up railway sleepers and then poured burning fuel over them to ignite an inferno.

This was then subsequently extinguished using a jet of water from a red fire fighting hose fitted with a heavy brass spray/jet nozzle on the end. He was protected by another instructor operating another nozzle that projected a huge wall of water, allowing him to get closer to the fire without getting too toasty.

Following this, as an example of what not to do, the instructor then poured burning fuel into a huge metal tray of diesel igniting a fierce oil fire. Standing back the fire fighter then attacked the fire using the same method as before but this time it resulted in a spectacular fire ball. We could feel the searing heat from where we were safely observing. With the fire still burning, a different nozzle was used, called an FB5X. This nozzle incorporated a suction pipe that sucked up the foam called AFFF and mixed it with water. The resultant foamy mixture was then sprayed on top of the burning oil effectively cutting off the air supply and smothering it.

Following the impressive demonstrations, we were then taken into the classroom to learn all about how a fire is caused and how best to extinguish it. We were told all about the 'fire triangle' and that by removing any single element would result in the fire being extinguished. In simple terms, we are surrounded by oxygen in the form of air and fuel in the form of anything else that will burn. If the fuel is heated up to its own ignition temperature, then the three elements of the fire triangle come together and fire will start. It does get a bit more complicated than this, but for the purpose of this course, this was sufficient knowledge to prevent our already overloaded brains from self-combusting.

Following a well-earned cup of tea, we had a lesson on ICABA which was a duel cylinder breathing set designed to allow fire fighters to be inside a smoke filled compartment without succumbing to smoke inhalation. This took us up to lunch that consisted of a sandwich, drink, NAAFI No3's and an apple.

In the afternoon, we got introduced to the 'Smoky Joes' which were blackened steel mock ups of ships that could be set on fire time and time again for training purposes. After a tour of the three deck unit, we were able for the first time to attack and extinguish a fire using a portable nine litre fire extinguisher. It was brilliant fun and as we got more and more confident, the fires became bigger and much hotter culminating in the whole unit being set alight which then had to be systematically extinguished working from the top to bottom.

At the end of the afternoon, we were soaking wet and covered from head to toe in soot and despite many showers and hours with a scrubbing brush we still looked like we had borrowed some makeup as we all had black eyes and nails. This was most definitely a highlight of basic training. No wonder they saved the best stuff until the last week.

The end was now in sight, we only had one more hurdle and that was our 'Passing Out' parade.

Passing Out Parade

The culmination of eight weeks of purgatory was finally drawing to a close. There had been tears, lots of them, and a few smiles. As a class we had lost a few of our members. Two people had decided that life in the Royal Navy was not what they had expected so had opted for Premature Voluntary Release. Two others had failed their GNK exam so had been back-classed, but for the rest of us, Friday 16th March 1979 would be the day we completed our Basic Training.

Of all of the graduating classes, the best at marching had been awarded the coveted honour of being the Guard. This meant that that they got to wear white gaiters and belts and more importantly, they were the last class to march onto divisions and the first to march off. It barely needs to be said, but it wasn't Anson 06. My marching would never be anything other than adequate. Fortunately, I wasn't the worst, so I couldn't be entirely blamed for us not winning the Guard.

So, after a week of parade training for what would be our Passing Out Parade we were ready to show our families what eight weeks of gruelling training had transformed us into. Friday finally arrived and the weather was bloody awful. Wet weather routine meant that Divisions would be held in the drill shed rather than on the parade ground to prevent the assembled families from getting soaked. There was worse to come though. As it was close to freezing, our instructor made the decision that instead of wearing the traditional naval white fronts, we would have to wear our sea Jerseys that were made of dark blue scratchy wool and most uncomfortable. Despite our pleading, the decision had been made and there was nothing we could do about it.

So at about 1:30pm, we assembled outside the block in the rain and marched down towards the parade ground feeling as proud as punch. With our heads up, digging our heals in and swinging arms in unison, there was no chatter as everybody concentrated on our final performance. This was our first opportunity to show off to our mums and dads.

As we marched into the drill shed, the Royal Marine band started up with the theme to 'Warship'. We located our tallest classmate stood on his spot and formed up on him as the right hand marker. This was followed by the usual dressing and open order march before the inspecting officer looked everyone over from gleaming cap to shiny boots. He would stop occasionally and make small talk to every other recruit to prolong the agony. The ceremony would take about an hour for every sailor on Divisions to be inspected before those who had excelled during the last eight weeks were awarded prizes. I wasn't amongst them, but frankly, I was just happy to have graduated.

After the prize giving and prayers, the order was given to march past with the Guard leading, so with the band starting up with 'Hearts of Oak', the order was given "Divisions, into line, left turn". The Chief Gunnery Instructor then came up to us and at the correct moment shouted, "Anson 06, by the left, quick march". Opposite the dais, the Class Leader, Jim Bullough, called "Eyes Left" as he saluted the reporting officer. Eight weeks after joining the Royal Navy, everything now clicked into place. "Eyes Front … Left Wheel" as we turned to exit out of the far door of the drill shed.

We were quickly halted and to my lasting relief, dismissed before being reunited with my Dad, Step-Mother and Step-Brother. After a graduation reception where I got the opportunity to introduce my parents to my instructors, I was granted leave for only the second time during basic training, so I went out to Millbrook with my parents for a lovely evening meal. As they still had to drive back to Birmingham, it was never going to be a late night, but it was a wonderful evening nevertheless.

After waving farewell, I returned to the block where everyone was jubilantly in the process of packing suitcases and kit bags. Early the following morning we were to board a coach for the journey to HMS Sultan in Gosport to start the next phase of training: learning how to be a Marine Engineering Mechanic.

HMS SULTAN

Part 2 Training
17th March 1979 to 23rd June 1979

Following the excitement of our graduation day, the remaining members of Anson 06 were packed up shortly after breakfast on a sunny Saturday morning for the journey down to Gosport. All kit bags and cases were piled high in Lefanu Quadrangle awaiting the coach that would finally see the class leave HMS Raleigh and transport us to HMS Sultan for our trade training as Marine Engineering Mechanics.

With all of the luggage safely stowed away on the coach, we bade farewell to Raleigh with a unanimous cheer as we finally pulled out of the main gate for seemingly, the last time.

The coach headed out into the Cornish countryside before crossing the Tamar Bridge about half an hour later and heading east towards Portsmouth.

After about two hours of uneventful travelling, the coach pulled into a coach park in the centre of a small market town called Dorchester where the driver gave us thirty minutes to stretch our legs and to use the loo. One of the chaps, after a brief exploration of the town, reported a fish & chip shop that was soon overwhelmed by the onslaught of a load of hungry matelots all wearing their best uniforms.

Returning to the coach park triumphant, arms laden with small paper parcels, we were sternly informed by the driver that no food was allowed on the coach, which then gave us only a few minutes to consume our food and retake our seats on the coach.

Leaving Dorchester and continuing our journey through Dorset's towns and villages we finally arrived at HMS Sultan around the middle of Saturday afternoon.

Inside the camp, the coach slowed to a stop outside a rather tired old, red-bricked, two storey accommodation block with a flat roof. This was Grenville Block and would be our home for the next fifteen weeks.

The building had evidently been constructed in the 1920's and was one of many similar looking accommodation blocks in Sultan. Unlike the futuristic accommodation in HMS Raleigh, this was cold, uncomfortable and basically unloved. The floors were bare lino tiles with no rugs or carpets and the windows were of the box sash type that rattled in the wind. The block had been sub-divided into messes with six beds in each. Each bed then had a bedside table and a battered wardrobe and in the centre of the mess was a square table and a few hard-backed chairs.

Having identified and retrieved our luggage from the mound of bags piled up near the road, we struggled to negotiate the narrow doors and stone steps before claiming our pre-allocated beds. The rest of the afternoon was taken up with unpacking and preparing our uniform for the start of the course on Monday morning.

At about 5:30pm that evening, which is usually the time for scran, not knowing where to go, we got together as a class and sort of followed other people carrying plastic mugs who seemed to know where they were going. The assumption was correct and for the first time, I enjoyed naval food. The quality and the quantity was far better than had previously been served up in HMS Raleigh; even the tea lacked the bitter taste of bromide. Things were most definitely looking up.

After tea, I went off to explore the camp and get my bearings before it got dark. Next to the main gate was the Regulating Office with the Officer of the Day keeping a watchful eye over trainees entering and leaving the camp from within his glass-fronted office. Across the grass was a newish block that housed an automat with a queue of people outside waiting to use one of the two phone boxes. The ground floor of the block also contained some clerical offices which I would later discover was the MACCO and the Pay Office. Climbing the stairs I discovered the Junior Rates bar although it was still shut. Across the road was the Dining Hall, Jack Blair's and Louis Bernard Naval Tailors as well as the NAAFI. Despite the accommodation, everything else seemed considerably more relaxed than the strict regime we had recently endured in HMS Raleigh.

Back at the block, someone had discovered a TV room with some comfy chairs; also a Kit Wash room and the usual heads and bathrooms. With the heating now turned on, it started to feel more like home, even the beds felt more comfortable, but maybe it was because I was knackered after the day's travelling.

On Sunday morning, we were visited by a Petty Officer who introduced himself as John Baty, our instructor. He had brought along a timetable for the next fifteen weeks and some basic dos and don'ts that, if followed, would make life in Sultan considerably less painful.

He seemed a nice bloke, who allowed us to call him John providing that there were no other officers or senior ratings within ear shot. Failure to abide with that first rule would result in the culprit being 'down for ten'. Following the introductions, John took us for a tour of the 'Accommodation Side' of HMS Sultan. First of all, he took us into a seemingly identical accommodation block that had been transformed into a youth club. It was called 'The Tankies Club' and had a table tennis table, a fruit machine, Space Invaders and also an Asteroids machine. It was run by more senior trainees who also sold cans of pop and packets of crisps. Essentially, it was somewhere for the under 18's to chill out in the evenings.

Walking around the perimeter road, we came across a footbridge over the road. John said that HMS Sultan used to be an airfield during the Second World War. He went on to explain that 'Military Road' used to be a runway which accounted for it being a perfectly straight and a potentially fast road. For that reason, we were not allowed to cross the road to get to the 'Technical Side' and had to use the footbridge at all times. We were also instructed to march to the foot of the bridge every the morning, fall out, cross the bridge and then fall in again at the other side before marching off to class.

With the promise that he would pick us up in the morning, John took us off to the dining hall for lunch before leaving us to continue settling in.

After a fairly decent roast dinner and a visit to the NAAFI to replenish essentials such as washing powder, starch, boot polish, soap and of course a big bottle of fizzy pop and some sweets we moseyed back to Grenville Block and knowing no different, sat in the TV room polishing boots and shoes whilst watching the traditional Sunday western.

At about 8pm, the previously quiet camp suddenly started to come alive as other trainees who had been allowed home for the weekend started to return. Ironically, the songs of the era were Dire Straits, 'Sultans of Swing' and also Meatloaf's 'Bat out of Hell'. Despite the chill of an evening in mid-March, everybody seemed content to want to share their music from open windows across the camp. This would continue late into the evening until the Duty Petty Officer, doing his bed checks at 10:30pm, would order music off, windows and curtains shut and everybody to bed. Over the following weeks, this would become a reoccurring theme and part of the evening ritual.

We were awoken at the comparatively leisurely time of 6:30am by 'Call the Hands' and after the usual scramble to get all of the trainees through the bathrooms and dressed in clean uniforms, under the command of Class Leader, Jim Bullough, we followed the example of other classes and fell in to three ranks on the roadway and marched off to breakfast.

With the camp now full of trainees again, the dining hall was packed with people queuing for toast or cereal or simply opting for the 'normal' breakfast fry-up whilst tea or coffee was vended from huge urns. Breakfast was far a more hurried affair and after ditching our dirty dishes into the pot wash, we scurried individually back to the block and ensured our beds were made and that the mess was tidy and all lockers were locked.

A frantic hour after been awoken by the tannoy, the occupants of Grenville 06 were again mustered on the roadway and marched through the camp towards the footbridge. Falling out in front of the steps, we ascended the wrought iron and wooden structure to cross Military Road.

On the other side of Military Road, as promised, Petty Officer Baty was waiting for us in the 'Technical Side' of HMS Sultan. Falling us in, he marched us down a straight road inside the perimeter fence before coming to a halt outside a huge grey corrugated building called 'Newcomen Hangar'.

This was day one of the course, so there were many formalities to complete. After falling out we were ushered into a classroom and instructed to sit down behind an empty desk. When we were all seated and settled, we were brought to attention by PO Baty calling "Class Ho" this involved sitting up straight with arms folded and looking straight ahead as a Lieutenant Commander strode into the class. He introduced himself as Lt Cdr Roberts'. He was our Training Officer otherwise known as 'TO2'. Lt Cdr Roberts appearance was quite striking; he was tall with piercing blue eyes and short ginger hair. He invited us to relax as he formally welcomed us to Part Two training. He explained that in order to pass the course, we had to achieve a pass mark of 70% in all of our exams and that any infringement of the regulations would see us in his office being read the riot act. The Warning System was explained to us in full; basically three strikes and you are looking for another job. In practice it was not as simple as that. There were three very different warning systems; Training, Discipline and Personal Standards. Each subsequent warning was more severe until the Navy decided that an individual was a lost cause and chucked them out. This was all a bit scary, but in hindsight necessary to ensure that we were properly motivated.

After TO2 had left the room, in fitting with the nature of the training, grey canvas tool bags were handed out to use as satchels and would in due course contain all of our text books. These were subsequently decorated with names and numbers to aid in identification before being filled with pens, pencils, a ruler and coloured pencils for drawing diagrams. It was like Christmas as books and all manner of new stuff was handed out to ensure we were adequately prepared for the forthcoming instruction.

At 10am on the dot, we were sent off for 'stand easy' which is naval terminology for a morning break. An oggie van would turn up and sell tea, coffee or bacon rolls and pies to the noisy queue of hungry trainees. Smokers would assemble around a large silver 'ash tray' on the floor called a spit kid whilst others wandered around the hangar looking at mysterious tools and bits of machinery contained within glass cabinets. There were cutaways of gas turbines, steam turbines and also a huge Y100 boiler. Of course, at this point, we only knew this by reading the placards. In one glass-fronted cabinet was a lump of curly metal with a placard posing the question "What is it?" Well it looked for all the world like some sort of medieval surgical implement. On further investigation, it turned out to be called a 'wheel spanner' which is a lever to assist in opening and shutting stiff valves. Every week, on Monday, a new tool would be placed in the cabinet and the answer revealed the following morning during daily prayers.

Back in class, we were issued with a personal copy of 'Naval Marine Engineering Practice Volume 1' and this would prove to be our engineering bible as we systematically worked through it during the course of the next few weeks. It covered many subjects including warship construction, boilers, steam systems and turbines, propellers and shafting, lubrication, auxiliary machinery and diesel generators.

Being naturally inquisitive, but not a born engineer, I found the subject very interesting but also quite difficult to comprehend. I remember sitting at the back of the class one day getting very distressed as the instructor was explaining with the aid of a model how the ship's wheel managed to turn the rudder and in particular how the 'hunting gear' worked. The rest of the class appeared to have understood this at the first time of explaining. Was I the only one who didn't understand how it worked? Scared to be revealed as the class thicko, I kept quiet hoping to pick it up as the class progressed, but it only compounded my misery. I wanted to understand, but it was beyond me at that point so I spiralled downwards into despair until, plucking up the courage, I just got up and walked out of the class ending up in TO2's office in tears whilst he tried to explain in simple terms how the hunting lever connected to the rudder and when the desired rate of turn had been achieved, would stop hydraulic oil from reaching the steering rams by taking the pump off stroke. It is actually a very simple mechanical process but it took a little while to sink in before I could fully understand what was happening. Fully recovered from my little upset, I returned to the class finding that it now all made sense. During the next stand easy, it turned out that nobody else had understood it either and that none of us had had the courage to say so. For that brief moment in time, I had the advantage over my peers and wallowed in my newly-found knowledge.

I vowed quietly to myself, that I would never ever find myself in that situation again and would always ask questions so as to fully understand my subject. Stuffing all this knowledge into my head was one thing, keeping it there was another thing altogether, so I often found myself working long evenings revising to consolidate the day's lessons and to stay ahead of the game.

Classroom theoretical work was one thing, but all engineers need practical experience to become effective so after discussing the theory in class, the instructor would then take us into the hangar where various pieces of machinery had been installed. Under supervision, we would run through the checklist and start a bit of kit, carry out running checks and then stop it again, consolidating the theory. The practical aspects were far more interesting than the classroom work and I found that actually opening valves and watching gauges move made the understanding process so much easier.

In the workshops, we were all assigned a toolbox containing exactly the same tools including spanners, hacksaw, knife, ruler, callipers and hammer. Each came with a muster list and like our initial kit issue several weeks previously, the instructor held up each tool in turn to identify it before telling us what tray to stow it on until he had ensured that everyone had all of the correct tools and they were all in the correct place. We were each then assigned a work station that had a steam valve held in a jig. Like an episode from The Generation Game, the instructor would demonstrate how to undo the two nuts on the valve gland before sliding the gland follower up the valve spindle. Selecting a packing extractor from the toolbox, he inserted the corkscrew end and after some difficulty managed to remove about five rings of asbestos packing. Having done this, he showed us how to measure and then to cut the replacement packing before using the gland follower to push it down into the recess. When fully home, another ring was added and the process repeated ensuring that the chamfered cuts were 180° apart so as to provide a torturous path for the steam and thus prevent it escaping up the valve spindle. After the demonstration, we each pulled our respective valves to bits and had varied success cutting the asbestos packing to the correct length.

Every Tuesday and Thursday, before instruction, as a class, we were instructed to 'fall in' inside Newcomen Hangar for morning prayers. This was far more formal than in Raleigh but 'The Bish' would come along nethertheless and say a couple of motivational prayers before leaving us with a thought-provoking pearl of wisdom. Sometimes it was utter bollocks, other times, it appeared as if he actually knew what he was talking about. Everybody liked the padre as we could talk, seemingly in confidence, about just about anything whilst following the convention of eating his biscuits and drinking his tea.

Every second Thursday was another day in the calendar that we all looked forward to. Pay day! Not that we got paid a lot of course, but something is always better than nothing, so by classes, we would line up alphabetically with caps on (so we could salute) and with our pay books in our left hand. The routine was simple. Your name was called; you would march forwards towards the Paymaster coming to attention in front of a counter window. Salute as you held your left hand out containing your pay book and clearly quote your ship's book number "024Y sir" The Paymaster would then tell you how much you were getting paid before placing it on top of your pay book. The notes would then be clamped in place by your left thumb before saluting again and exiting stage right to count it. Having been paid, this usually heralded a trip to the NAAFI to stock up on goodies or perhaps a burger when the oggie van turned up at stand easy.

The Marine Engineering course, on the whole, was very interesting. Everything was new to me and every day threw up a fresh challenge. One such challenge was guard duty. With my name being one of the first alphabetically in the class, it should have been no surprise that I was amongst the first to get stitched-up for a duty. I was simply told to muster at the Guard House at the back of the Regulating Office at 5pm for a briefing on what I was supposed to do.

So, after instruction and marching back to the bridge, much to the amusement of the rest of the class, I tootled off to the Guard House and joined about seven equally pissed off trainees from other classes and a Leading Hand. We were fallen-in and after names had been taken, the Duty Petty Officer explained that we were to be split into four watches of two and armed to the teeth with a wooden stick and a tin hat and detailed to patrol the perimeter of HMS Sultan following a pre-designated route card. This type of patrol became known as "Wandering Willy" and was cold, boring, very tiring and sometimes quite scary. We had to walk around the route checking doors and windows and generally defending the camp from terrorists. Fortunately, I never found out what two weedy seventeen year olds armed with battered truncheons would have done when faced with the IRA or armed bad guys. If I was lucky, I would be given the added '*protection*' of a wrist band with NP on it standing for Naval Provost. I dare say that would have evened the balance of power if I had been faced with an armed intruder.

The obvious down side to being duty was sleeping in a flea-infested, skanking bed for about three out of the usual eight hours. Consequently, the following day never got off to a good start. Fortunately, everybody got a go so I only ended up doing Wandering Willy every two weeks or so.

Back in the mess, things were quite relaxed. This was a contrast to the strict regime of basic training. Night leave was granted allowing us, when not on duty, to explore the town of Gosport or make the short ferry crossing to Portsmouth. Having not yet been granted permission to wear civilian clothes ashore, any night leave had to be taken wearing No1 uniform and before being allowed to set foot out of the gate, the Officer of the Day would inspect all liberty men to ensure that we remained a credit to the service. Obviously, this was a real pain in the arse. Despite it being a naval town, everybody still stopped and stared at this group of brand new young sailors strutting down Gosport High Street.

Having a blue identity card with a line drawn diagonally across it identified me first of all as a serving member of the Royal Navy, but more irritatingly, as under eighteen, so the challenge, when in uniform was to try to buy beer at a pub, when it was clear to all that I was under age. Barmaids and landlords would routinely ask to see ID cards as they all knew that they had to be carried at all times. I considered the law to be ludicrous at that point. I was old enough to join the armed forces, old enough to leave home and get married and old enough to go to war, old enough to drive a car, but not old enough to drink a pint of lager and lime, and the problem was that we stuck out like proverbial sore thumbs.

The incentive, therefore, was to pass our Chief Stoker's Kit Muster. He was a seriously scary bloke but a fair disciplinarian. The couple of times that I was stupid enough to cross him resulted me carrying out some trivial punishments, such as spending a Saturday morning with some rags and a tin of Brasso polishing the two big brass propellers mounted at either side of the parade ground.

So, in week three, after much washing, scrubbing, polishing, starching and ironing, my kit was laid out on my bed in the traditional fashion along with my other mess mates. All of us then stood to attention to report our kit ready for inspection. The Chief dutifully inspected every bit of kit, sniffing under arms checking collars for tide marks before finally, with much relief, awarding me a pass and the privilege of being allowed to wear civvies ashore.

After being in the Navy for approximately ten weeks and halfway through my trade training, a rash started to develop in the trouser department. Like most blokes, I scratched at it and basically tried to ignore it until it became so inflamed that I was left with no alternative than to visit the sickbay.

Missing any training at this point was obviously going to have a detrimental effect, but I needed to go and get it sorted out. I still had the same cold since joining up, but more painfully, I now had two huge sores at the top of my inner thighs where my underpants had been rubbing. Waiting at the sickbay, I tried to ease the boredom by reading a copy of People's Friend that had been brought in by one of the staff before I was finally called into see a Medical Assistant in the treatment room. Dropping my trousers and holding my tackle to one side, he immediately saw what the problem was and went to get a doctor.

The doctor took one look, ordered me to take my underpants off before deciding, without consultation, to use me as a teaching aid. He then ushered in about ten student medics, some of them female. This was about as humiliating as it got. The doctor then went on to explain that the bright red and weeping sores were known in the Navy as 'Dhoby Rash' and a result of either poor personal hygiene or not rinsing out my knicks thoroughly enough. After almost total embarrassment, I was prescribed some cream to apply with the direction to wash thoroughly and to change my underwear twice a day before applying the cream.

I was also asked how long I had been sniffling like that. When I replied that it was since joining up, another appointment was made to determine if I was allergic to anything.

Hobbling back to class, I resumed instruction for the day, managing to copy the notes that I had missed from a mate at stand easy. The problem was that I simply couldn't walk fast enough to march as it was just too painful, so when marching between classes or going to lunch, I had to hobble behind my class as fast as I could.

My classmates found this hilarious, but as I couldn't do any of the physical stuff and was missing quite a bit of instruction, spending more and more time in the sickbay, it was a huge disappointment when I was inevitably back-classed and set back by two weeks into the 08's.

Leaving the guys I had joined up with was quite hard, the advantage was that I now had two week's knowledge of what was coming up, so I was made very welcome by my new classmates who were trying to get a head start. Doing the same lessons all over again also helped to consolidate my understanding which meant that when the weekly progress test came around on Friday, I whizzed through it.

Back at sickbay a week later I was tested for allergies by having spots of different liquids dropped onto my inner arms which were then pricked with a needle to see if I developed a reaction. The doctor struck gold when he eventually tested me for house dust discovering that I was allergic to it. I was subsequently sent to RNH Haslar where the tests were confirmed and I was injected with the first of a course of six injections which would hopefully clear up my 'cold'.

Early in April 1979, HMS Sultan closed down for Easter leave. Going home for the first time in two months was very exciting. As with everything in the Navy, there were hoops to jump through before being allowed to proceed on leave. First of all, the CMEM's Kit Muster had already been passed, all exams passed, I was not under punishment and basically I was up to speed on everything. There were a few anxious moments for a couple of the lads, who had to retake exams, but hey, I'm alright, Jack! There was a coach laid on that for a nominal fee would take me and the other Brummies' to Digbeth Coach Station in Birmingham.

Despite having the privilege of being able to wear my civvies ashore I wanted to show off my new uniform to my mum who had been unable to attend my passing out parade at HMS Raleigh, so with my naval issue suitcase packed up, I bade farewell to my new oppo's and joined the utter confusion outside the gate as seemingly, the entire camp was catching a bus home. There were several different coaches departing to distant corners of the country, so you can imagine the chaos. It was therefore vitally important to get on the right one before potentially slumping in a seat, falling asleep and ending up in Cardiff.

On the correct coach, I did sleep and after an uneventful journey, the coach pulled into Birmingham's Coach Station where my mum was waiting for me. My emotions were all over the place. I was so relieved to be home.

Pleased to see my mum, my brother, Simon and Georgie, the cat. I was also proud of what I had achieved so far. I felt like I had been in the Navy all of my life, though in reality it had only been a little over two months and now I had two whole weeks of nothingness to look forward to.

Strange though it might seem, I actually missed the routine. I had, in my short service life, been institutionalised. So for the first few days, found myself out of bed at 0630 and quickly washed and dressed. Mum commented that if the Navy taught me nothing else, it had taught me to stand up straight and to walk without slouching.

During the course of my leave, due to industrial disputes, the petrol tanker drivers had gone on strike meaning many petrol stations had run dry. This had the possible consequence of me being adrift if I couldn't make it back to HMS Sultan on time. Mum decided that despite the lack of petrol, she would drive me back to Gosport in her relatively new Fiat 127. So, loaded up with clean washing, and a huge bag of sweeties, we set off South towards the A34 which in turn would lead into the A33 north of Southampton. We were making good progress, but every petrol station we passed displayed a 'Sorry, No Fuel' sign. As the Fiat's petrol tank was approaching the point of no return, Mum said that if she couldn't find any petrol by Newbury, then she would have to abandon me at the railway station so she had enough fuel to get home. Fortunately, we were in luck and following a top up, Mum managed to drop me off at the main gate to HMS Sultan before spinning around and heading back home to Sutton Coldfield.

As most of the training was classroom or workshop based, there was no substitute for actually working and sleeping on-board a real warship. For this reason HMS Sultan had two old decommissioned ships, HMS Diamond and HMS Russell which were tied up together in Gosport. They were collectively known as the Harbour Training Ships and although decommissioned and not fit to return to sea, the accommodation and machinery still worked and would hopefully add another piece into the mechanical jigsaw in my mind. Moving on-board HMS Russell for the week was quite exciting. The mess deck was very spartan and there were absolutely no frills. Each member of the class had their own bunk and a small metal locker to stow all of their kit. As HMS Diamond, a Daring-class destroyer, was in a poor state of repair, we were not allowed into the boiler room as it was considered too dangerous for trainees who frankly knew nothing about machinery.

On-board HMS Russell, in the boiler room, dressed in overalls and steaming boots, PO Baty instructed us how to flash the boiler and with steam now being raised by the Y100 boiler, he showed us how to flash the turbo alternator and evaporator using the steam generated by the boiler. This was extremely interesting and served to consolidate a lot of the classroom instruction. I found that in this environment, I could '*see*' how all the various systems worked together. For example, the boiler created the steam to drive the TA and evap. The TA then supplied electrical power to the entire ship and the evap supplied fresh water to the ship's tanks and more importantly to supply the boiler with water to boil into steam. The steam would then turn the turbine which in turn after being reduced in the gearbox, would turn the shaft and the propeller. The steam would subsequently be cooled in the condenser and returned back to the boiler in a big mechanical loop. Theoretically, there would be no wasted water, but steam has the ability to escape through the tiniest of gaps meaning that there was always the need to replace the lost water. We stayed on-board HMS Russell for the whole week but by the end of the week, it was good to get back to the relative comfort of HMS Sultan again.

The following day, we started, arguably, the best part of the course and the first qualification of my career. Junior Basic Diesel. At one end of 'Watt Hangar', there were about twenty small Foden diesel engines connected to a group exhaust system to prevent the operators from being gassed by the noxious carbon monoxide emissions. Following some instruction and armed with a toolbox full of spanners, we set about stripping the top down and cleaning the component parts before refitting valves, collets, rocker arms and push rods. When it was all back together and there was nothing left over, the instructor would check it over and then attempt to start the engine. If it ran, you passed. Mine ran at the first attempt and for probably, the first time, I realised that I was actually enjoying this engineering lark.

The course was now drawing to a close. Little by little, lads in the class were getting assigned to ships. Everybody wanted to get the Type 21 frigate HMS Arrow as it was generally known that she was deploying around the world. The CMEM, later that day, came into the class and informed us that eight members of the 08's were being drafted on loan for six months to the County-class destroyer HMS Fife and that it was not a topic for discussion. He then read out the nominated trainees. The last name on the list was 'Atkinson'. I was ecstatic, HMS Fife was going to the States before sailing around the Caribbean as the West Indies' guard ship and I was going with her after only having been in the Navy for a few months.

That Friday, we prepared for the end of course. Certificates were distributed before everyone got dressed into their best uniforms and shiny shoes for the Passing-Out parade. We were quite blasé about Divisions now, so it was no surprise that we actually got sent around again for being out of step. It didn't matter though, the course had finished and as a class we were all going to Southsea for an all-day celebratory piss up. After being in the Royal Navy for about 4½ months, we were now off to sea for the first time. It seems strange looking back, but we were all incredibly excited about the adventure.

The following day, despite the worst hangover ever, vowing "Never Again" and seeing most of the previous night's beer for a second time, I started to pack my kit bag and suitcase for the journey to join HMS Fife. She was paying a visit to Cardiff so myself and the seven other stokers nominated by the CMEM said our goodbyes to the lads and headed off on the coach that would drop us at the Gosport Ferry.

HMS FIFE

24th June 1979 to 14th September 1979

Exchanging rail warrants at the station for single tickets, we took our seats for the three hour journey to Cardiff where, HMS Fife, was paying a visit. Travelling in No1 uniform was the custom back in 1979 so we largely had to behave ourselves. As we were still feeling slightly jaded, apart from a couple of lads chatting, most, including myself, slept off the previous night's excesses and the three hour journey went by in a flash.

Arriving at Cardiff, it slowly dawned on us that we had no idea where the ship was or indeed how to find it. We considered getting in a taxi in the hope that the driver would know where our new war canoe was parked. We didn't have to worry for long though. Waiting for us was this massive chap who introduced himself as LMEM 'Dad' Duffield and was the Killick of the Mess. Picking up a kit bag in each hand as we struggled with the rest of our luggage, he led the way to a waiting Land Rover with 'HMS Fife' and the ships crest stencilled on each side door. Piling our entire luggage on the floor, we clambered up over the top of it and within minutes of arriving in Cardiff, we were doing battle with the city centre traffic.

Arriving at the docks, the first glimpse I saw of HMS Fife was the massive framework on the back of the ship that we knew from training was the 'Sea Slug' missile launcher. Following 'Dad', we struggled with bags as we managed to negotiate the steep and narrow gangway and following his example, saluted at the top before following our leader through a myriad of narrow passageways and steep ladders until we reached an open hatch leading down to 3Q mess towards the stern of the huge ship.

With teamwork, we formed a human chain and finally managed to get all of our kit into the mess square where 'Dad' allocated us bunks. There were cosy, more private areas of the mess called gulches, but as new joiners, we had no say in the matter and did as we were told. Of course if there was a mess party in progress, my bed along with others around the mess square would be folded down to use as a seat, so going to bed early was simply not an option. We were instructed to unpack, look around the ship and then to muster on the 'Iron Deck' at 8am the following morning.

Some of the lads in the mess were very helpful, showing us where to hang suits and stow suitcases. My brown canvas kit bag when it was empty was concertinaed flat and stowed under my mattress. Having unpacked, the eight of us went off to explore our new home as a small gang of baby stokers.

A warship of HMS Fife's size, was like a floating town. Almost everything that you could possibly need for a crew of about five hundred sailors could be found on-board. There was a Chinese laundry and tailors shop; a police station, a fire station, a shop, a TV studio, a hospital, a galley, dining halls, a pay office, an airport, a generating station, a church and of course a bar in every mess. HMS Fife could therefore remain self-sufficient for days on end, requiring only diesel fuel to keep a flame in the boilers and food to keep a flame in the crew.

After getting lost a few times, we managed to figure out where all of the important stuff was, like where to get washed, where to go to the loo and more importantly where to get fed. Having explored as much as we dared, we returned to the mess and went to bed, absolutely knackered.

The following morning, didn't start well at all. After climbing up two steep ladders wearing just a towel and flip flops, I showered and dressed before going off to the dining room for the traditional cooked breakfast which was served on a 'prison style' steel tray. Back in the mess after breakfast, we all changed into overalls and boots and went off to muster as previously instructed on the 'Iron Deck'. This is where, on day one, things started to go wrong.

In training, we were taught that the 'Upper Deck' is often known as the 'Weather Deck' or 'Iron Deck', so after wondering around the 'Upper Deck' for a while and not seeing anybody that looked vaguely like an engineer, we continued to explore the ship looking for a friendly face. After about half an hour of wandering about, a loud Scottish voice startled us "Where have yee fucker's bin?" The voice belonged to LMEM 'Jock' Begg whom I took an instant dislike to. We explained about the misunderstanding before he screamed at us that *this* was the 'Iron Deck'. Looking down, we saw what he meant. As this was the passageway that was directly above the boiler room it had the potential to get quite hot so the deck tiles had been removed leaving the deck as bare steel with welded treads. Conceding the mistake and learning the valuable lesson, Jock pointed aft and shouted "Cooks" at us so off we went to the galley. A few minutes later, standing at the door to the galley, the chief cook asked us what we wanted; I told him that we had been sent to do 'Cooks', so pointing us in the direction of some cleaning gear, he told us to scrub the deck. Twenty minutes later, an incensed 'Jock' appeared screaming at us again. This was to become a reoccurring theme during our time on-board HMS Fife as we struggled to come to terms with life on-board ship. When he had calmed down sufficiently to be able to speak without shouting, Jock explained that the term 'Cooks' is a shortened version of the term 'Mess Cooks' and was a traditional name for those who clean the mess in the morning. Another valuable lesson learned; and it wasn't even 9am.

Things did get better though; the ship was undergoing some trials and exercises around the UK, which gave me the opportunity to start learning my job. Promotion at that stage of my career was based around completing numerous day to day tasks and recording their successful completion in my task book. All tasks would need to be witnessed by a Chief or a Petty Officer to ensure they had been carried out correctly before they would endorse my task book with their signature. In addition to this, I also had to prove myself competent in four specialist subjects. These Auxiliary Machinery Courses or 'AMC's as they were known were: steering gear, diesels, fire pumps and motor boats and each had its own docket to learn from, so I had plenty to be getting along with.

As new joiners are generally not trusted to do anything unsupervised, I was assigned to double bank an already endorsed watch keeper in the steam room who was supposed to teach me his job including how to operate various bits of machinery. The reality was quite different and initially I spent a lot of time making tea, cleaning and painting. If something interesting appeared to be happening, my inquisitive nature always ensured that I was watching, learning and then asking questions to fill in the gaps. After I had been shown how; I used to love checking and filling oil boxes. Some of the rotating machinery was fitted with a small reservoir designed as an automatic lubricator and they had to be checked regularly to ensure that the machine didn't seize up. This was 'sold' to me by the Chief of the Watch as '*A very important job*' and if it wasn't done right, then the engines would seize up and then the ship couldn't go to sea. The Captain would then want to know why I hadn't done my job properly, so consequently; I took my only responsibility at that time very seriously indeed.

Whilst I was conducting my rounds, checking the oil boxes and taking readings one day, there was an almighty bang followed by a mechanical clunking noise that even my inexperience deducted something bad had happened. This was immediately followed by quite a bit of intense activity by the 'tiffs' before it was discovered that one of the TWL feed pumps had decided to shed its turbine blades quite explosively. In hindsight, it's a wonder that nobody got killed as fragments of turbine blading pierced the casing and one piece shot through the MCR and embedded itself into the roof of the compartment narrowly missing the watch keepers. Of course, I got the blame and then got quite upset and asked if I could help to fix it. This was apparently a wind-up and the feed pump was buggered, so we headed back to Portsmouth to have it replaced.

A couple of weeks later, with the new pump installed and final phone calls made, the ship slipped quietly out of Portsmouth and headed west, bound for the States. This is most definitely why I joined up. I was starting to make slow progress with my task book but it was hard work and there was always something more interesting going on around the ship.

It appeared to me that the whole ship was designed around the Sea Slug missile system mounted on the back of the ship. There was a central trunk from the magazine some way forward that transported the missile to the launcher. At each stage, something would be added to the missile in preparation for flight. It would 'grow' wings or get fuelled until, when it was fully prepped; it would pop out of some doors onto the trellis like launcher on the back of the ship. Live firings were rare occurrences, so sprogs were encouraged to observe from a safe area, high up towards the front of the ship. Dressed in overalls with anti-flash gloves, hood and for some strange reason, a tin helmet, the goofers assembled to watch the launch. Apparently, over the horizon, our sister ship, HMS Kent, was steaming a parallel course about twenty miles away and an aircraft towing a target was flying on the same course down the middle of the channel. The idea was for both ships to launch their Sea Slug missiles simultaneously and obliterate the same target. There were a few false starts before finally the missile erupted from the launcher in a bright fiery streak of flame. In the distance, although the ship itself was not visible, HMS Kent's Sea Slug missile could be clearly seen converging on the target until the plan finally came together and the target was destroyed. I imagine the pilot of the towing aircraft was having a few bottom clenching moments with the adrenalin running brown. Not a job I would ever wish to apply for.

With the live firing completed, HMS Fife converged on HMS Kent for final goodbyes and an occasional moon from the braver more adventurous sailors. My pants stayed firmly in place on this occasion though we did chuck a few potatoes at them as we bade them farewell. With the traditional ceremony complete, HMS Fife then continued westwards for another week before calling into Ponta Delgada on the Portuguese island of Sao Miguel in the Azores for fuel and my first ever foreign run ashore in the Navy. Only being granted two hours leave, this was not enough time to explore much more than the port area and with no local currency, I contented myself with a walk around the harbour, soaking up the atmosphere and more importantly, the sunshine.

Not being used to the effect of a tropical sun, I got horribly burnt in no time at all. That in itself is quite painful, but getting sunburnt in the Navy is an offence under Naval Law as it was considered to be a self-inflicted injury. If I decided to report to the sickbay, I would first of all get treated and then reported, so I was advised by my mess mates to suffer in silence. In a sadistic attempt to reduce the stinging, it was also advised that I take a hot shower. God, I screamed like a little girl and worse still, it didn't even work; I was in total agony. This forced me to wear a T-shirt under my overalls in the hot engine room to prevent them rubbing on my inflamed shoulders for a few days whilst the pain subsided. Another valuable lesson learned.

A week out of Ponta Delgada and the weather was getting steadily warmer. The ship called into Bermuda overnight for another fuelling stop. Fantastic, I was really looking forward to getting ashore and exploring this seemingly beautiful and British island on top of a sea mount and about a thousand miles from anywhere, but guess what? I was duty! We were only alongside for one day and I was duty. Not happy! I had to content myself with looking at the aqua blue waters of the harbour from the confines of the ship. I even volunteered to take the gash ashore, just so I could say I had actually set foot on Bermuda.

The following morning, the ship continued steaming on its merry way towards Florida. As the ship was programmed to be in Port Canaveral for a couple of weeks, myself and the other young stokers had been stitched by the Chief Stoker to do a double boiler clean, but it couldn't start until the boiler had been shut down for a day and given sufficient time for it to cool properly. For that reason, we had been granted leave from the moment the ship had fallen out from Harbour Stations. So, early on the morning of HMS Fife's arrival in Florida, I was washed, dressed in my civvies and waiting with my oppos behind a screen door for the "Fall Out from Harbour Stations" pipe. We didn't have long to wait and before 9am, we were off the gangway and ashore looking for the way out of what turned out to be a massive naval dockyard. Fortunately, a pick-up truck stopped, took pity on us and offered us a ride to the gate which still took a good fifteen minutes bumping about in the back of the truck. Obtaining directions to the nearest beach, we again started walking down the highway before another truck stopped and, determining that the nearest beach was in fact Canaveral Beach, he gave us a lift about five miles down the road.

Thanks to the good Samaritans, we were on the beach before 10am finding immediately that the sand was too hot to walk on. Laying down towels like stepping stones, we quite literally hot-footed it into the relatively cool Atlantic Ocean. Splashing around like silly school children, life was good again but it was short-lived. One of the guys, looking quite frightened, noticed a dorsal fin circling fairly near to us, so in a mad panic we struggled to get out of the water as the 'shark' approached. We must have made quite a racket as a couple who had been observing all of the commotion came over to us and the woman asked in a broad Brummie accent, what the problem was? Quickly getting over the shock of hearing an English voice three thousand miles from home, we told her about the '*shark*'. Grinning, her reply was "Them's not sharks luv, them's dolphins" and on cue, three dolphins started leaping out of the water. I could swear they were taking the piss out of us.

Following a good relaxing day, we managed to scrounge a lift back to the dockyard and eventually found the rest of the lads playing pool and eating burgers in 'The Green Room' which was a sort of American NAAFI. Burgers were made to order and came open, looking frankly a bit odd. There was a beef patty on one side with lettuce, tomato, gherkins and onion piled up on the other bit. On a side counter there was a choice of ketchup, mayo and relish to build your burger how you liked it. I decided there and then that I needed to emigrate to Florida, this was heavenly and knocked the socks off Wimpy.

Out back, like a scene from the yet to be produced 'Top Gun', US Navy sailors were playing volleyball, drinking beer and eating BBQ burgers and chicken. Like all good matelots, this looked far more exciting than playing pool, so we gate crashed their party. With typical American hospitality, we were made very welcome and following many beers and making fools of ourselves falling about trying to play volleyball, they invited us back to their mess at Patrick Air Force Base "just down the road" for beers and also for the remainder of the evening.

After cramming about five people each into four Corvette Stingrays we were off on a magical mystery tour where I couldn't see a thing as someone was sat on top of me. I finally managed to untangle myself out of the jumble of sweaty bodies and was truly amazed by what I saw. Inside the base, near the CPO's mess were about ten rockets all stood up on end like a huge mechanical clump of trees. Quite what they were doing or why they were there, I never found out as no sooner had we arrived, we were ushered into the CPO's mess and given four glasses and a jug of beer called a pitcher. This was all very nice, but one pitcher of lager only amounted to one small glass each. When it came to my round, I asked for six pitchers and no glasses causing some eyebrows to be raised. The reasoning was that the jugs were not much bigger than a pint pot and there were large queues forming at the bar. Inevitably, this led to a rather messy evening and later in the evening I was revisited by the earlier burgers.

Remembering that many of us were still under eighteen, we had to be back on-board the ship by midnight. It's what is referred to, in the Navy, as 'Cinderella leave'. So, at 11:30pm, the Yanks were persuaded to drive us back to Port Canaveral. The problem was, that everyone was drunk and they sort of got lost. With five minutes to spare, we ended up at the gates to John F Kennedy Space Center at Cape Canaveral, a good twenty miles by road from where we needed to be. We could actually see where the ship was berthed but the Banana River was preventing us from driving in a straight line. This required us to back-track to a bridge and by the time we got back to the ship, it was well past 1am. The Officer of the Day, stood at the top of the gangway, was anxiously looking at his watch and clearly not impressed. Fearing the worst, the driver climbed the gangway, saluted the Officer of the Day and explained that it was all his fault that we were adrift and fortunately he believed it.

The following morning, very hungover, the boilers were cool enough to start work. There are two types of boiler clean: internal and external and as *luck* would have it, we would be doing both. Working under the instruction of the boiler room POMEM, starting from the top, we wire brushed the economiser, brushing each rusty surface clean of soot and rust before moving down. After this, all of the nuts and bolts securing the plates to the outside of the boiler had to be removed. This exposed the generator tubes which then had to also be wire brushed. Inside the furnace, the bricks had to be checked before the plates were then re-secured with new CAF gaskets. With the external clean now completed and all the plates properly buttoned up, the steam drum's baffle plates had to come off before one by one, a bullet brush was fired down the tubes into the water drum using low pressure air. There was one brush for each tube and when all of the brushes had been fired, the tubes were then 'sighted' by ball bearings with each ball being collected into a numbered tray until all tubes had been cleaned and then proved clear.

With the first boiler nearing completion, some of the team started work on the other boiler. It was hot and dirty work. To be honest even by the end of the afternoon, I was still suffering from the excesses of the previous night. I was not in a very good mood at all. Noticing this, the Chief Stoker seemed a bit concerned and came down into the boiler room to see me. Acknowledging that the team was doing some good work, he tried to gee me up a little. As the Chief Stoker in charge of training, he knew I still had to do my Motor Boats AMC and knowing that the boats were due to be launched in the next few weeks, asked if I would like to train as a motor boat driver? This had the desired effect. The thought of driving a motor boat in the crystal blue waters of the Caribbean Sea was a dream come true.

It took us about two days to complete the clean on both boilers meaning that we were again given some time to explore Walt Disney World and also the Space Center before the ship sailed from Port Canaveral and headed out to sea to conduct the duties of the West Indies guard ship.

After being at sea for about a week, I went to see the CMEM and asked about the promised motor boat driver's course. As *luck* would have it, the motor boat was being launched that very evening and as it turned out, he was glad that I'd come to see him. I was given a form that needed to be stamped by seemingly everyone on the ship including the Captain and the Commander. I was sent to see the divers to get a black rubber drysuit with first a white and then another green thermal inner suit. I was also given a diver's face mask and a pair of fins. Next I saw the buffer where I was also given a tin helmet, painted white with a red cross and the word 'COX'N' scribbled hastily on the front. The sailors also gave me a safety harness and an assault life jacket. In the Radio Room, I was given a hand-held radio and a heliograph, which is essentially a mirror for flashing signals. I asked about how I would be able to signal the ship after dark. This was apparently a very good question and I was then issued with a torch to flash should the need arise.

With the stamping routine complete and loaded down with kit, I went back to the mess to prepare for what was certainly going to be a night to remember.

At around 6pm, as I was getting kitted up in preparation for the launch, when the mess's 'gobby cockney' called 'Ginge' told me he had organised for me to be interviewed on the ship's own TV station. After I had finished dressing, he escorted me up to the SRE compartment for my interview.

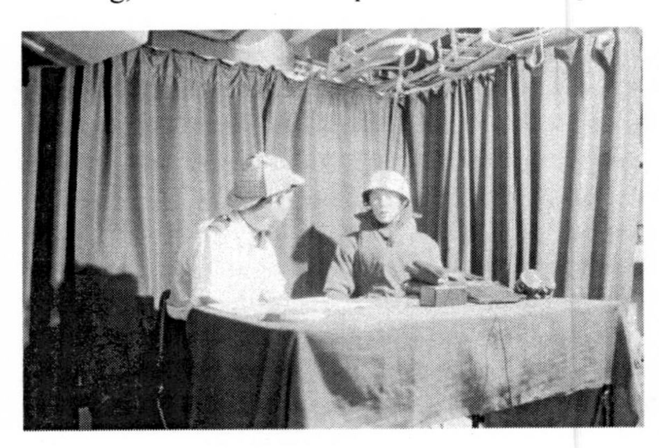

Waiting outside the SRE compartment, sweating buckets with all the clobber I was wearing, the ship's chaplain came to see me, asking if I really wanted to go through with this. I thought this was probably because it was a bit dangerous, but being very young, very foolish and somewhat gung-ho, I was actually looking forward to it. He then told me that it was all an elaborate wind-up and I didn't have to go through the humiliation of the TV interview if I didn't want to.

First of all I found it very difficult to comprehend that the Captain and the Commander would have been part of a practical joke and then, considering all the trouble that the Chief Stoker had gone to, just to wind me up; I simply had to play along with it. Appearing behind me quite suddenly was the Education Officer wearing a huge 'Robin Day' style spotted bow tie and a deer stalker hat carrying a copy of Navy News under his arm.

We were then ushered into the compartment where I was told by the operators to remove all of my ancillary items and lay them out on the table. When it was time, the operator, using his fingers, signalled a countdown before finally the red light came on and we were live on Fife TV. The Education Officer was reading his paper and not paying the slightest bit of attention, so I nudged him gently in the ribs and in a stage whisper muttered "Sir!"

Clearing his throat and folding his paper, he started "Good evening, gentlemen and welcome to another edition of ... '*Authentic Sweat*', where we highlight the difficult, sometimes dangerous jobs carried out by the ship's company of HMS Fife. Tonight we welcome JMEM Atkinson. JMEM Atkinson, welcome." I was then asked to explain the purpose of some of the elaborate kit placed on the desk in front of me and after spending about five minutes answering his questions, I was wished the very best of luck before being whisked back down to the mess by 'Ginge' and bought way too many beers for being such a good sport.

The following day, I was feeling particularly groggy and distinctly hung-over from the previous evening's party. Taking some advice from one of the more senior lads in the mess, I snuck away in the boiler box and climbing up a long vertical ladder into the uptakes had a rejuvenating snooze in the tropical temperatures of the funnel on some bags of rags and boiler compound. This became a favourite hideaway as it was rarely visited by anyone. By lunchtime, I was feeling much recovered and descended back into the boiler box paying careful attention to get a bit dirty in the process so it would appear that I had been working. Unfortunately for me, Jock Begg had been looking all over the ship for me. Although he had no idea where I'd been loafing, I still got a bollocking for not working in my part of ship.

A few weeks later whilst HMS Fife was transiting between ports, the ship conducted a ceremony called 'Crossing the Line'. This is a naval tradition dating back a hundred years or more where all new sailors who had not previously crossed the equator would have to pay homage to King Neptune and his lovely 'bride'. Obviously, being my first time away from home, this was all a bit new to me and apart from some advice about the possibility of getting soaked, I had absolutely no idea what to expect.

Dressing in tropical shorts, sandals and my No8's shirt, I joined the majority of the ship's company standing behind a rope on the flight deck. A makeshift stage had been erected whereupon, 'King Neptune' was dressed in a large white sheet with an improvised golden crown on his head carrying a trident in one hand. Sitting next to him was his lovely 'bride' Amphitrite who was in fact a Chief Petty Officer dressed up with improvised makeup, false boobs and looking, after a few weeks at sea, really quite good. Also on the stage was a surgeon, a barber and a master of ceremonies. The King and his bride sat on their respective thrones facing a chair for the victims. This was hinged on the back legs so if the 'accused' were subsequently found guilty; as indeed they always were, they could be pushed backwards into an improvised swimming pool full of salt water to be met by 'The Bears' in the guise of other members of the Chief's Mess. The Master-at-Arms took the logical role of Head of Police and ably assisted by the Chief Stoker, hunted down officers and ratings on their 'Wanted' list.

The Captain, Sam Fry, was first on their list. I assumed that nobody would dare find the Captain guilty, but after being apprehended by the police, he was, none too gently, forced to pay homage to the 'King' before a list of jumped-up charges were read out. He was subsequently found guilty on all counts, fed a laxative laced biscuit, squirted up the bottom with some green goo and given a mock haircut using a pair of oversized comedy scissors. He was then forcibly sat down and finally pushed backwards into the pool where 'The Bears' dunked him and roughed him up a bit. It was great fun. The Commander was next on their list followed by all of the Heads of Department who all had a similar 'punishment' administered. I considered myself quite safe as I was a) the youngest rating on-board and b) virtually unknown amongst the five hundred strong crew. What I had failed to consider was that recently, the whole of the ship's company had witnessed my total humiliation on the ship's TV system. Even so, it still came as a total surprise when after all of the Lt Cdr's had been found guilty, the next name called from the list was "JMEM Atkinson." Bugger!! All of a sudden, I was being chased around the flight deck by the 'Police' being whacked with batons made out of masking tape before being apprehended and manhandled up onto the stage in front of a cheering ship's company. Seemingly everything I had done wrong in the couple of months since first coming on-board was documented on the charge sheet and even I had to concede that I was guilty as charged. I was then fed an iced gem that tasted very, very spicy. A huge syringe was then poked into the waistband of my shorts and green gunge was squirted into the back of my pants. The 'barber' then ruffled my hair up a bit before without warning, I found myself being pushed backwards getting a mouthful of salt water in the process. The 'bears' wearing hessian sacks, wasted no time in beating me up before I was allowed to exit the pool feeling like I had just come out of a washing machine. After my humiliation, I drew cold soggy comfort in watching from the side lines as quite a few other members of the ship's company were also apprehended and found guilty. All in all, everyone had a fantastic afternoon.

During that first deployment, we called in to many ports for visits; one of the more memorable ones was Antigua. Walking away from the harbour in the capital, St John, we were instantly accosted by taxi drivers vying for a fare. During our stay, this was to become a reoccurring theme until four of us decided to hire a Toyota Corolla for the week. Of course, I didn't have a driving licence at this point, but I was quite content for someone else to drive and to just sightsee from the back seat as we explored the island.

One of the places we visited was 'English Harbour'. Apparently, the deep sea diver, Jacques Cousteau had recently been doing some exploration and a lot of his kit was still stored in one of the warehouses. We didn't get to see him, but it was still a bit of a thrill to be swimming the same harbour as the celebrity diver. Sunk in the harbour and lying on its side was a large sailing boat. One side of the hull was still visible above the aqua blue waters but just beneath the surface, a hundred foot steel mast was causing an underwater obstruction. In an effort to win favour with the islanders, HMS Fife had volunteered a team of our ship's divers who, as we watched, were on the boat trying to cut away the mast and sink it to the bottom of the harbour. Not part of the operation, but because we knew some of the diving team, we swam out to the boat and had a very pleasant hour or so bronzing on the capsized boat in the middle of the harbour whilst the divers did battle with lifting and cutting equipment. They eventually succeeded and lowered the severed mast onto the sea bed where I expect it still is.

The following day, we drove up one of the most westerly points on Antigua and whilst stopping to admire the view, were joined by some Pongos who had sailed to the island with us on the ship. Somebody decided it would be a brilliant idea to have a car race to see who could get to the other side of the island the fastest. I don't remember much of the race except for the fact that we won! After waiting about half an hour for the Pongos to turn up, we decided to back track at a more sedate pace to see if we could find them. One of our guys noticed some bushes on a tight bend had a fairly big car shaped hole in them and stopping for a closer inspection, we saw the four Pongos at the bottom of the hill, examining the damage to their rental car. Fortunately, nobody was seriously injured, but it did cause us much hilarity.

Having been away from the UK for several months, we were all now looking forward to getting home, but there were rumours on the grapevine about a hurricane building in the middle of the Atlantic and heading for Barbados. We did in fact have several crates of hurricane relief stores already stowed on-board the ship. To add some substance to the rumour, the ship's radio started playing the 'Typically Tropical' song 'Barbados' just to wind everybody up. We could see the swirling cloud forming hundreds of miles away on the ship's main long-range radar so the ship's communication centre contacted Portishead Radio near Bristol who confirmed the progress of 'Hurricane David'. It's charted course was indeed the Caribbean island of Barbados, but these things are notoriously unpredictable. HMS Fife duly changed course to ride out the imminent storm at sea and warned Barbados to prepare for the inevitable devastation.

Following the warning, the Barbadian's wasted no time in battening down the hatches and securing the island for what was a fairly regular event at that time of year. With preparations in place and the islanders sheltering, they prepared to be battered by the worst storm of the century.

On-board Fife, the sea was certainly getting lumpy. The ship's securing for sea was starting to get severely tested whilst the Captain tried to position the ship on the most comfortable course for his crew. Those not actually required for work were ordered to strap themselves into their bunks as this was considered the safest place to be. Monitoring the collision course of the storm on radar we could see hurricane David change course at the last moment and head straight for the Leeward island of Dominica. There was simply no time to prepare, the Dominicans left the capital of Roseau and hurried for the hills away from the approaching tidal wave. It was too little, too late!

Hurricane David ravished the island with a hundred and fifty mile winds for over four hours and immediately the storm abated, they needed help and quickly. Fortunately, HMS Fife was only a few miles off shore and the powers that be went into action immediately mustering all non-essential personnel and forming them into six specific rescue teams. As I wasn't trained or trusted to do anything else, I was assigned to 'Light Rescue One' and formed part of the first team ashore.

Flying over the island in 'Humphrey' the ship's Wessex 3 helicopter, the devastation looked like a scene from News at Ten. Everywhere you looked; debris was scattered. Most of the buildings had no roofs, many trees and telegraph poles were down; the place was a mess. As the power lines were down, the island was without electricity, gas, water, and fuel. The government buildings had been totally wrecked, the hospital was not functional and the airport runway had huge holes in it preventing aid reaching the stricken island. They were in a bad way.

Despite debris littering the town, the ship's helicopter pilot, skilfully managed to land safely in a large open area in Roseau and as we disembarked, we were immediately inundated with young able-bodied Dominicans rushing to the helicopter to assist us in carrying our kit. Captain Fry liaised with the locals prioritising what we needed to do first and where help was most needed. It was decided that getting the nearby hospital operational was going to be our top priority because it may prevent further people from dying.

A short walk up the hill from the landing site and we arrived at what until recently had been a hospital. Everything in the two storey building was sodden and caked with mud. The first task was to completely empty the ward before scrubbing it from top to bottom with disinfectant. It was intensely hard work in the tropical heat, but by the time we stopped for lunch, I am proud to say that the first patients were now coming onto the re-designated General Medical Ward. New mattresses had been flown out from the ship and the original iron bedsteads had been scrubbed and disinfected. It was simply, the best that we could do.

After a lunch that consisted of a tin of pineapple chunks, Light Rescue One moved upstairs onto the children's ward where at the tender age of seventeen I was faced with the most horrible sight of my life; under the weight of water from the tidal wave, the roof had caved in and many bed-ridden children had just perished in their beds. Using sheets of corrugated iron as improvised stretchers, we gently carried the dead to the mortuary before myself and a few others climbed onto the roof beams and started re-securing the corrugated iron; rendering the ward weather-proof again. At some stage during the afternoon, I gashed my knee with some rusty corrugated iron sheeting, causing it to bleed quite badly. Seeing this our team leader, Colour Sgt Baker Royal Marines, ordered me to go and get it seen to by the medical team. I tried to argue that there were many more injured people in far greater need of patching up than me. The counter argument simple; if it went septic, then I would be no use to them at all and just another casualty. This was my first experience of triage in the field.

I still felt quite bad about pushing in, but I worked my way past many seriously injured and dying Dominicans to the front of the queue where a huge black nurse took pity on me and told me to sit down. After cleaning and examining my wound, she explained that it would need a couple of stitches and as I was a big boy, I wouldn't need an anaesthetic. Despite my protests, she carried on regardless and by the time I had finished whimpering, she had stitched me up and bandaged my knee allowing me to go back to work.

With the hospital now operational, our attentions were centred on getting the generator working for the petrol station. The generator turned out to be a simple diesel generator that, when working, allowed the petrol station to be self-sufficient. The boss was a large black chap wearing a dirty T-shirt and baggy linen trousers and sandals. I was somewhat shocked to see that he also had an old revolver poking out of one pocket. I asked him, rather naively, why he carried it. After telling me of the looting on the island and being quite friendly towards me, he went on to ask me where I came from. "England, mate," I replied, "Where in England?" he asked. "Birmingham," I answered, wondering where this was going. "Where in Birmingham?", "Sutton Coldfield, mate, why, do you know it?" "Yes," he replied, "I own the Esso station at Six Ways Aston." Well, this just about blew me away. Despite his outwardly scruffy appearance, he was actually a multi-millionaire and claimed to own a chain of petrol stations all over Europe. In hindsight, perhaps we should have charged him for fixing his generator?

During the course of the following ten days, we drove a three ton truck out to the airport, stopping at every pot hole and fallen tree and clearing the road as we went. Another team air-lifted into the airport did good work repairing the runway in preparation to receive a Hercules transport plane flying out from 'RAF Brize Norton'. The first aircraft apparently had to turn back due to hurricane 'Frederick' forming in the wake of hurricane David.

After a week of repairing the island's infrastructure, HMS Fife was finally alongside after the ship's divers had cleared underwater rubble from the harbour. The Venezuelan Army had now arrived and set up camp on Humphrey's former landing site and the French Navy had also arrived. HMS Fife formally handed over responsibility for repairing the island to the French and sailed from Dominica, turning east and heading home. This gave me about a week to take my first exam on-board ship. So, just before we got back into UK waters, I managed to convince the diesel chief that I knew enough about his engines for him to pass my Diesels AMC. At least I wasn't going home empty-handed. HMS Fife arrived back in Portsmouth on 14th September 1979 to a hero's welcome, flying her paying off pennant from the main mast.

Fife manoeuvred alongside her sister ship, HMS Kent on South Railway jetty where TV cameras and families were waiting and waving. With our kit all packed and with fond farewells, the eight original trainees from HMS Sultan after nearly three months on-board, left HMS Fife for the final time and staggered the short distance to the railway station to catch the train home for a well-earned Summer leave.

In the wake of the disaster, the President of Dominica, paid tribute to the ships company of HMS Fife, by sending a telegram to Queen Elizabeth. "*They arrived on our ravaged shores at our darkest hour and lit the first beacon of hope. Their relief efforts were ceaseless and untiring, their devotion to duty a shining example of true friendship in our hour of need*"

Many people were recognised for their efforts on Dominica with Commendations, OBE's and MBE's being given out like sweeties. Personally I got just two lines on my report from the Captain "Worked hard at the hospital during the recent hurricane relief effort on Dominica".

I had enjoyed my first ship and learned much. I was sorry to leave HMS Fife, but she was coming to the end of a long and distinguished career and as I was just starting mine, it was time to part company with this old lady of the sea. I found that I had been drafted to the Fleet Maintenance Base in Devonport for a couple of months of respite before joining my next ship.

FMB DEVONPORT

15th September to 16th December 1979

Following a very enjoyable Summer Leave relaxing at home, I joined the Fleet Maintenance Base at Devonport in Plymouth for a short spell as I already had a draft chit to join my second ship, the Leander-class frigate, HMS Bacchante in January 1980.

After a joining routine and dickey induction period, I was assigned to work with the Craft Support Unit, a small workshop at the back of the main workshops in Devonport Dockyard. CSU, as it was known, looked after the maintenance of mine sweepers and small vessels based at Devonport, carrying out diesel engine changes, rectifying mechanical defects and a fair bit of cosmetic repair to the lagging and painting.

As a Marine Engineering Mechanic, I was part of the Engine Change Team and having recently passed my Diesels AMC, I was able to assist in the main engine change on a couple of tiny inshore mine sweepers and also HMS Sandpiper and HMS Petrel both of which were slightly larger patrol boats.

Changing an engine on these small boats, involved removing a lot of the upper deck fittings before actually hoisting the upper deck off using a crane to expose the engine room. After uncoupling the engine from the gearbox and all of its systems, the engine could then be lifted straight out of the craft. It sounds simple, but actually involved quite a lot of spanner work.

If a smaller repair was needed, this would be done in situ. For example, some engines required a top overhaul which was less time-consuming than a whole engine change. Having removed the cylinder head from an engine, it then had to be stripped down and cleaned. This was done back at the workshop and usually involved a few happy hours scraping away with a wooden scraper and squirting loads of Ardrox, which consists largely of trichloroethane. The net result of using Ardrox in a confined space usually meant that the day flew by and by the evening I had a raging headache. That said, it was also fairly therapeutic, sat crosslegged on the floor in the workshop, chattering to the other stokers scraping the compacted carbon from our respective cylinder heads whilst listening to Radio 1.

All young sailors are assigned a 'Sea Dad', usually a vastly experienced man in the same branch. My 'Sea Dad' was LMEM 'Shady' Lane who was absolutely ancient. He had already served more than twenty two years and was a recovering alcoholic. I am not sure that he was the best choice of mentor for me, as he used to tell me stories of being in a hospital bed in Netley recovering from alcohol poisoning and seeing little green men climbing over the end of his bed. I absorbed every word. 'Shady' was full of tall stories. Anything I had done in my short career, he had done quicker, deeper, faster and in short, better. At 8am on most mornings, he would take me for a dockyard bimble that usually ended up with us visiting a floating canteen at the north end of 5 basin. He would then purchase us both a bacon and egg sandwich and a pint of cider just to kick-start the day. The bacon and egg sarnie was most welcome, I must say, but I struggled with the cider at that time of the morning. As the weather was frequently cold, wet and windy, the floating canteen did always offer warmth, shelter and as 'Shady' often pointed out, a place to 'hide'.

Not long after joining the CSU, I was working with the team on HMS Sandpiper whilst the PO Stoker, Chris Willoughby, was manning the phones back in the office. At lunchtime, Chris asked if he could borrow my huge Hitachi 'ghetto blaster' so he could listen to the cricket on the radio. At that time, most portable appliances only ran on batteries and they were running a bit low so the radio was sounding a bit crackly. No matter, after lunch, I left it with him before catching the dockyard bus back down to South Yard. Returning to the office just before 4pm, Chris thanked me for the loan my radio and said that he'd replaced the batteries. Brilliant! That would save me a few quid. Walking through the dockyard on my way back to my mess in HMS Drake with it playing on my shoulder in true Rastafarian style, I was stopped at the North Barrack gate by a MOD plod. Believing I had purchased the radio/cassette player abroad, he asked me the usual 'where I'd got it from' questions. This wasn't an issue as mum had ordered it from a catalogue, but on further examination, he discovered that my fading Duracell batteries had been 'kindly' replaced by six government property green batteries. This was not good at all. Mr policeman was looking all serious and I was in a real danger of being charged with stealing them when I had absolutely no idea that Chris had stitched me up. The copper pondered for a bit before telling me cryptically to do what I wanted with the batteries. In a rare flash of inspiration, I picked them up off the table and dumped them in a large empty oil drum that was being used as a rubbish bin inside the gate. The oil drum had about six inches of collected rain water in the bottom, so they landed with a hollow sounding splash. The plod, standing at my shoulder said "Good choice, son, if you had taken one step through the gate, I would had been forced to charge you with theft." Breathing a huge sigh of relief, I collected my now powerless radio and walked back up the hill to my mess in Hawkins block vowing silently to myself never to make the same mistake again.

Occasionally, the team was required to visit vessels outside of the Devonport area and this was generally regarded as a perk. During my short time at CSU, I was sent with Chris, Shady and the rest of my team on one 'mobile' to Cardiff to work on the Royal Naval Reserve Mine Sweeper, HMS St David. Normally on this type of visit, when there was no naval accommodation available, subsistence would be paid on a daily basis and with a bit of imagination, could work out to be quite lucrative. However on this occasion we didn't qualify for subsistence as our boss had rented us rooms above a pub in Cardiff's dockland. The deal was that the landlady would provide us with two cooked meals and a packed lunch each day of our stay. I dare say she made a fair bit of cash out of the deal, but we had to buy our own beer on this trip.

The accommodation was still rather squalid, but it suited the purpose. Three rooms were shared between the team with Chris, as the Petty Officer, demanding his own. All the rooms led out onto a large landing that had a communal settee and TV which we used as a sort of improvised mess. The food was of the pie and chips variety and extremely hearty, but there seemed to be an overwhelming aroma about the place. It was a common smell, but it took us a day or so to actually identify it. The whole place smelt faintly of stale urine like a gent's public toilet. It became quite a talking point amongst the team until Chris commented one day that it always smelt the strongest when the landlady was about. He was right, as she left the room; the odour seemed to go with her.

On-board the RNR Mine Sweeper, as she only had a part-time crew, it fell to CSU to maintain and preserve her. Being very junior and not too experienced, I was assigned with another lad to paint the main mast. Health and Safety had yet to be adopted by the Royal Navy and as common sense is usually lacking in your average seventeen year old, it should come as no surprise that without a safety harness I was hanging onto the top of the mast with one hand and painting with the other. It was quite windy and apart from overalls and boots, I had no protective clothing. Loading up my brush with grey paint, a gust of wind caught the brush causing my face to get splattered with paint, gluing one eye shut. Not having a rag or a cloth to hand, I gingerly climbed back down the mast to get help. HMS St David's part-time Leading Seaman, not famed for his intelligence, tried to clean the paint from my eyes and face using a cloth soaked in white spirit. To cut a long story short, within half an hour, I was in agony being treated at Cardiff Royal Infirmary after being dumped in casualty by the ship's Fleet Chief.

Once I had been cleaned up by a lovely young nurse and examined by a non-sympathetic doctor, I was fitted with an eye patch and given instructions to return the following day for a check-up. Back at the waterfront later in the day, I received so much piss-taking from the lads for my total stupidity; but basically, they didn't give a toss about the fact that I could have lost an eye.

The following day, as instructed, I got a bus back to the Cardiff Royal Infirmary where, not for the first time, I witnessed triage in action. This time, I was at the opposite end of the medical spectrum and sat bored to tears for four hours only to be briefly examined and sent on my way.

Completing our work by the end of the week, all of the team buggered off home for the weekend. Not wishing to stay on my own in a pub stinking of piss where I couldn't even get a beer, I also packed my bag and caught the train home for the weekend before returning back to Plymouth on Sunday evening.

Back in Plymouth on Monday morning, I found out that my draft to HMS Bacchante had been cancelled and replaced with a draft to a similar Leander-class frigate. I subsequently left FMB Devonport in mid-December and joined my second ship, HMS Ajax on the 19th December 1979, just in time for Christmas leave.

HMS AJAX & ARIADNE

17th December 1979 to 24th March 1981

Having now been in the Royal Navy for nearly a year, I was starting to feel a bit like an old hand. I had deployed across the pond to Florida and the West Indies, assisted in the hurricane relief effort on Dominica and had also been part of a Fleet Maintenance Team working in Plymouth and Cardiff. Joining HMS Ajax I considered to be my first proper sea draft as my previous loan to the destroyer, HMS Fife, was only ever meant to be a temporary job.

Having left FMB Devonport just before Christmas leave I only had a short time to unpack and settle in before going home. The first person I was introduced to on-board HMS Ajax was the Chief Stoker who explained straight away that I would live with the rest of the stokers in 3 Kilo Mess Deck and for the first three months would be employed as a member of the Communal Party. After showing me where to go for Action Stations on the Watch and Station Bill, he took me down to the mess and introduced me to the rest of the lads. Once he had an audience, he then asked me a strange question "Are you in the shit?", "No Chief", I replied. "We'll soon change that" he countered as everybody laughed. This didn't sound too good at all.

3 Kilo mess was located immediately aft of the engine room and above the deep Seacat magazine. On a Leander-class frigate, I learned that this was the traditional home of the stokers. The ladder from 2 Deck descended into the mess on the starboard side of the ship to a row of lockers. At each side of the mess was a gulch that was the privileged home of the leading hands on the starboard side and a detachment of Royal Marines on the port side. Between these gulches, there were two mess squares with rows of triple bunks on each side meaning that the mess squares alone could accommodate up to twenty four stokers. Top bunks were a sort of status symbol as they could be used at all times of the day and night. The middle bunk and the bottom bunk folded down like a caravan bed to make a settee that would be used as seating during the day. I had a middle bunk to start with, but later moved into a top bunk when someone left the ship and went on draft.

As I mentioned earlier, my first job on joining the ship was as a member of the Communal Party which is basically washing up and maintaining the cleanliness of the dining rooms. This is most definitely not what I joined up to do. As Communal Party, I was essentially divorced from the Marine Engineering Department and worked during the day only, which meant I always got a good night's sleep. Everyone had to do it, and usually it was a job for the most junior of lads as they found their way around. Let's not pretend that this was a good job, but I made the best of it and true to his word, within three months of joining, The Chief Stoker had moved me to a '*real*' job in the boiler room as a 'Boiler Front Stoker'.

The guy in charge of my watch in the boiler room was POMEM 'Mick' Jagger, who whilst being an all-round good egg and a snappy dresser had a bit of a reputation for being a panic mechanic. Mick would stand in front of his operating panel in the middle of the boiler room and, due to the noise, would issue hand signals to myself on the port boiler and my oppo MEM Boak on the starboard boiler. As the ship increased speed, it needed more steam. This could only be created by 'punching' sprayers which would then spray fuel into the furnace. Likewise, if the ship needed to slow down, less fuel was needed to spin the turbines, so hand signals would be issued to remove a sprayer.

As a boiler front stoker, there was no formal qualification required to do the job. Each new joiner was required to understudy or double-bank a more experienced stoker until he was convinced that you could carry out all of the required boiler operations and routines for that watchkeeping position without being baby sat; it was all rather daunting to start with. At my watchkeeping position in front of the port boiler, I was standing in front of a huge Babcock and Wilcox Y100 boiler with a seemingly huge array of valves and slides. I always assumed that as a stoker I would be shovelling coal, but thankfully those days had gone forever.

The boiler front was fitted with six sprayers, or 'burners' that allowed diesel fuel to be sprayed into the furnace. Each sprayer had two air slides and one fuel cock. The process to put another burner on was simple. First the burner was pushed into the furnace, then the two air flaps were pushed in and rotated to lock them in position and finally the fuel was opened carefully. To take a burner out of service was an exact opposite of the procedure, so it wasn't rocket science.

For the most part, a four hour watch would consist of sitting in front of my boiler facing inwards, watching 'Mick' for hand signals to change the sprayer configuration. Should he wish to talk to you, he would beckon you forward. On one occasion, I wasn't looking when we needed more speed. There was no time to muck about so 'Mick' attracted my attention by throwing a small wheel spanner into the boiler front with the intention of making a noise. It did just that and as I turned to see where the clang had come from, was hit in the face by the rebounding 'wheelie'. Lesson learned!

There would always be lots to do to keep us amused during the night watches when the ship would usually be steadily steaming from one place to another. During the middle watch, it was traditional for us to blow soot, eat pot mess and to do our dhobying. Blowing soot was essential to maintain the efficiency of the boiler and the ship would conduct it daily during the middle watch. Due to watch rotation, I would only have to do it about once in every four days. The soot blower valves were cammed valves and as I recall, usually quite stiff. As a soot blower valve was opened, it would admit dry, high pressure steam into the boiler and as the name suggests, it would then blow soot progressively higher up the boiler until finally it was blown out of the funnel. As this was carried out in the middle of the night, nobody got to see the cloud of black soot issuing from the funnel, but if the Officer of the Watch got the course wrong, then the upper deck would be plastered in sooty deposits.

Whilst we were busy blowing soot, the leftover meat and potatoes from that evening's scran would be boiled up with some gravy in a big pot using one of the steam drains to create a sort of stew that we called 'pot mess' which was a savoured a middle watch delicacy. Occasionally, potatoes would also be baked on the steam-driven fuel pumps for a couple of hours and enjoyed with lashings of butter and cheese straight out of the foil. It rather depended on what the chefs had left over and if we had upset them or not. One of the golden rules of ship-borne life is not to piss off the chefs or they will put you onto an involuntary diet. Traditionally the relationship between the chefs and the stokers was always good and long may it continue.

With the pot mess devoured, it was then time to do my dhobying. Generally, I only took my overalls, pants and socks into the boiler room to wash on watch and allowed the Chinese dhoby wallah to wash the rest of my kit. My washing would be put into a clean bucket of cold water with 'dhoby dust' and placed under another steam drain to boil up for a couple of hours. After a while, the dhobying would be agitated thoroughly with a broomstick before everything was thoroughly rinsed in salt water to prevent dhoby rash and finally rinsed again in fresh water. My now clean overalls would be hung over a ventilation blower until they inflated like a Michelin Man to dry and my knicks and socks hung over a guard rail. In the heat of the boiler room, it didn't take long for them to dry so when the watch changed at 4am, I was ready with a nicely scrubbed pot mess 'fanny' to return to the galley and my dhobying under the other arm.

As I have already mentioned, there was little need for speech in the boiler room due to the ambient noise levels being so high. For that reason, we were issued ear defenders that looked like a huge pair of head phones albeit, without the music. In another blinding flash of inspiration, I attempted to remedy the situation with my newly-purchased state of the art Sony Walkman. With a little bit of modification, the smaller earphones fitted nicely inside my huge ear duffs and the player, not really much bigger than a compact cassette, slipped comfortably into my overalls' trouser pocket. With the headphone lead running up the inside of my overalls to the earphones, I should have been able to listen to my music on watch. The design was one of pioneering innovation and in trials, worked perfectly. In the boiler room however, I was rumbled within the first half an hour. Whilst boogying to Queen in front of my boiler, 'Mick' wanted to roll the sprayers up and when I didn't respond, another wheel spanner came hurtling in my direction. My Walkman, which was the iPod of its day, was subsequently confiscated and I got a bollocking for wrecking a perfectly good set of ear duffs and for not paying attention. Well it was good while it lasted.

It wasn't all work and no play though as the ship visited Amsterdam for a civic visit. Having never been to 'Amsters' before, it was decided that, for safety, we would go ashore in a group and go in search of the fabled 'Canal Straza' the infamous red light area for a 'shopping trip'. According to the seventies band 10cc, everybody goes window shopping in Amsterdam. Unfortunately, when leave was granted, I was busy shutting the boilers down and not wishing to wait for what could be hours whilst my watch secured the boilers, I said I would meet my run-ashore oppo's on Canal Street after I had been secured.

So, after finishing work, I got a shower and dressed in trainers, flared jeans, a shirt and my favourite black bomber parka jacket. I was now ready to go off in search of my mates who had at least an hour's head start on me. My jacket was similar to a parka jacket with an orange quilted lining and fur around the hood but mine had ribbed cuffs and waist and looked totally cool unlike the other version that made you look like a sack of spuds.

Looking at a street map, that had been brought onto the ship, I knew roughly which way to go, so set off walking away from the ship. I thought I must be getting close as the road I was walking down had a canal in the middle of it. This proved to be wildly inaccurate as anybody who has been to Amsterdam will testify; most roads have canals running down the middle of them.

Having been walking for about half an hour along deserted streets and not passing anybody to ask directions, I became aware that an orange Opel car was following me at walking pace. I thought he might be lost and wanting directions but as I had no idea where I was anyway, I carried on walking. Periodically, I would look back and found that the car was keeping pace with me which was starting to become a little worrying. I stopped walking and looked back at the driver before continuing down the road. The car then pulled ahead of me and stopped. After I had walked past the car, I looked back again and whilst doing so, walked slap bang into a tree causing my parka and jeans to get covered in green moss. The driver beckoned me towards the car and wound the window down. Apart from feeling rather foolish after walking into the tree, I remember thinking that I couldn't help him as I was lost too. Perhaps he was about to offer me a lift into town? Bending down at the open window, he asked in heavily accented English "Are you from the ship?" "Yes mate" I replied. He then said, "You come with me for six?" "Six what?" I naively questioned. He apologised for his English and rephrased the question, "You come with me for sex?" "Er, no mate!" I recoiled, quite shocked. "You can get twenty five guilder" he persisted. Mentally working out the exchange rate, this worked out to be approximately five pounds. I again declined his kind invitation and now feeling somewhat vulnerable and alone I decided that I had had enough excitement for one day and hurriedly retraced my steps back to the ship. I was not about to get anally invaded by anyone for a measly fiver.

Back on the ship, still quite shocked, I told the lads in the mess about the encounter. The response was varied. One chap was quite concerned and supportive, a couple of lads, worryingly, wanted to know where they could earn some quick cash, but most just found it hilarious. I vowed there and then never to walk alone in a foreign port again.

Recovered from my earlier near sexual encounter, a group of us later went ashore and finally found the fabled street of windows. Not having the nerve to purchase, I contented myself with sightseeing which was entertaining in itself. Later in the evening, we bumped into the Chief's Mess who were stood in front of a sex shop discussing rather disgustingly whether or not to buy a mess head. Leaving them to their deliberations, we crossed a bridge over the canal when a Rastafarian chap, without looking at me, and in a stage whisper, offered me all manner of drugs. This was one seriously scary place that I wasn't yet mature enough to deal with. After a few drinks with one of the Killicks, 'Brigham' Young in the Scottish Bar we decided to go back on-board. 'Brigham', having been to Amsterdam before, knew his way around the city; guiding me down the back streets on a shortcut back to the ship.

Walking down one street, three black chaps emerged from the shadows announcing that we were friends and offered their hands in the international gesture of friendship. 'Brigham' quite forcefully told me to keep my hands in my pockets and to keep walking. Safely back onto the main road that was well lit, he told me that if I had shaken hands with them, then my arm would probably have been twisted into a half nelson and my wallet lifted, possibly at knife point. Scary stuff indeed.

It wasn't all bad though. The ship had received some complimentary tickets for the Ajax v Feyenoord league game. Having always been a long-suffering Burnley supporter, I was excited at the proposition of seeing an international league game. Forget corporate hospitality, I don't think it had been invented yet, we were just given free tickets and as a souvenir, I bought a scarf that said 'Ajax - Cup Fighters'. Well, I am sorry to say, the standard of football was dire. The game finished in a one-all draw and frankly, I am glad I hadn't paid for the privilege.

After four days alongside, we were just about ready to leave Amsterdam. A few of the lads, it turned out, were bringing home some infectious souvenirs that they'd paid for on Canal Straza and I had been scared to death on numerous occasions. The learning curve was almost vertical.

It was decided by the grown-ups in the wardroom that the ship would conduct a ceremonial departure from Amsterdam and as such everyone was dressed in their best uniforms lining the decks in what was, and still is, called 'Procedure Alpha'. One of the stokers, MEM 'Scouse' Donegan had failed to return on-board and if he missed the ship would face an expensive trip back to Devonport and subsequently face the consequences of being adrift. With the ship's company fallen-in and a handful of local ladies waving goodbye, HMS Ajax had already let go aft and was moving off the berth when, in front of everyone, a taxi came hurtling up the jetty and screeching to a halt by the head rope, 'Scouse' got out, threw a handful of notes and coins at the driver and shimmied up the rope. Having successfully scaled the rope and climbed onto the focsle, a pipe was made over the Main Broadcast, "MEM Donegan's on-board now sir" "Roger, let go forward". So, with 'Scouse' now on-board, we left the Netherlands and headed back to Blighty.

A few days after leaving Amsterdam, the ship made a visit to Newcastle for a few days. The ship was given a berth on the Tyne right near the centre of town very close to the railway station and a pub called the 'Pig and Whistle' that was extremely friendly and became out 'Duty Watch Bar'. The local lasses were also quite friendly and showed few inhibitions as some of HMS Ajax's finest may well testify. Late one evening, shortly after arriving alongside, the Chief Petty Officer's mess hosted a social evening with the sole intention of networking with the locals. I was asleep in bed in 3 Kilo mess when I was rudely awoken by somebody shouting to see if anyone was awake. Making the mistake of switching on my bunk light, the intruder homed in on the beacon. It was the engine room chief who was clearly quite squiffy. He ordered me to get out of bed and to get dressed in my best trapping gear. Apparently, he had been chatting to some young local lady who had evidently not been about to jump into bed with a married, drunk, fat, balding chief in his mid-forties and had asked him to find her some young blood. Ten minutes later, I had hastily dressed in my best going out gear that embarrassingly included a brown velvet jacket, flowery shirt and flared trousers and was ushered into the CPO's lounge, given a pint of CSB and introduced to a rather chubby girl called Linda who had quite a pretty face. Whilst I was trying, through bleary eyes, to make conversation, the Master-at-Arms decided that my presence at a Chief's Mess function was not very appropriate, so I was asked to finish my pint, leave the mess and take the lovely Linda with me. As my mess was still in near total darkness, I showed her round the ship, visiting some very small unoccupied compartments where we got to know each other a little better. The following evening I met her again and after a very pleasant night out, she invited me back to her place on the 'Walker' estate not far from the town centre with the promise of a bit of naughty stuff. Unfortunately as the taxi drew up outside her house, it appeared that her entire family was at home and as a result, she got a free taxi ride home and I was sent back to the ship sexually frustrated. After the ship had sailed, she did send me a letter addressed to:

Ian (Plug)
HMS Ajax
BFP Ships

The letter miraculously arrived on-board the ship but I was summoned to the Regulating Office by The Master-at-Arms. He handed me the letter and asked if I was the intended recipient. When I assured him that I was, he gave me a bollocking for not giving the sender the ship's correct postal address. When I told him how I had met Linda, he quietly smiled and let me off. He was a nice bloke really. Despite my explorations, I had never really got to see her in the flesh, so it came as a pleasant surprise when I found that she had sent me some naughty photos of herself. Strangely enough, the only thought that occurred to me was, who had she got to take them? I never heard from her again and consequently, the photos got consigned to the mess 'Gronk Board'.

Continuing north, the ship called into Aberdeen a few days later where seemingly the entire ship's company was invited to a civic reception hosted by the Lord Provost. This was a truly lavish affair and started with everybody dressed in our best uniforms being ushered into a reception room for aperitifs. Facing us on entering the room were literally hundreds of glasses of whisky already decanted from various Scottish distilleries. There were labels next to the glasses identifying which glasses contained which golden firewater. Not being a great fan of whisky, I asked a waiter if there was anything else to drink. He pulled a disapproving face and swiftly disappeared. He returned a few moments later with a glass half-filled with an amber liquid and asked me to try it. Surprisingly, the drink tasted really good before he admitted that he'd mixed a dash of lemonade with it to soften it a wee bit. After a couple of these, I was sufficiently relaxed and ready for my dinner. Fortunately, I didn't have to wait long before some chap bonged a gong very close to my starboard earhole and announced that dinner was now served.

The Captain and the Lord Provost went in first, followed by the officers who, after finding their place settings, all stood behind their respective chairs. We were then called into the huge room and placed, by mess, at long tables before the Lord Provost who then invited us to be seated. The delicious soup starter was quickly followed by Aberdeen Angus Beef Wellington which was simply delightful. Waitresses dutifully toured the tables with bottles of red and white wine ensuring that everyone remained topped up. I am sure that the wine was of a decent vintage, but to me, it was just plonk. After dinner came the brandy, cigars and speeches. Without even being asked, I was handed a huge Castella cigar irrespective of the fact that I had never smoked. I thought that I might save this for my dad and stuck it behind my ear like you would a pen. It must have cost the local council an absolute fortune and I still have no idea why we were invited, but it was a really good reception and we all left, more than a little squiffy.

Outside in the fresh air, the lads from 3 Kilo mess decided to stay in town in uniform for a few more quiet ones. As we were quite drunk already, this ended up getting quite messy. England apparently were playing Scotland in some competition or other so there was quite a bit of friendly banter with the natives in the pub as we watched the game on the TV. Our lives were undoubtedly saved that night by the fact that Scotland eventually won the game, but by the final whistle, I was so pissed I couldn't really have cared less. Somehow, that night, we ended up in a Chinese restaurant with some nice Scottish people eating duck a l'orange that somebody else had evidently paid for. All in all, it was rather a splendid day. I had been fed twice, well watered and it had cost me very little. Life was indeed good.

Fully recovered from the excesses of Aberdeen, HMS Ajax called into Stockholm a couple of days later for yet another port visit. This turned out to be a lovely city surrounded by literally hundreds of tiny little islands. My big boss, Cdr E, asked me if I would like to join him and some of the other stokers on a Gemini boat ride around the harbour and islands. This sounded like brilliant fun, so with a small ensign flying from the bows and powered by a big Johnson outboard motor, we set off with Cdr E initially at the helm. Cruising around the many small islands was very scenic in more ways than one. In the warm weather, some of the more adventurous Swedes had chosen the relative privacy of the islands for a bit of nude sunbathing, totally unaware of the boat full of pervy sailors approaching. A bit later on with LMEM 'Milly' Millington driving, he noticed a very beautiful young girl sat on the harbour wall wearing a skirt that had ridden up as she sat with her chin resting on her knees. 'Milly' exclaimed quite suddenly that the girl was wearing hairy knickers before it dawned on us all that she was going commando. Without the need for any instruction, 'Milly' held the tiller hard over as he steered the boat back for a closer inspection. Unfortunately, after a couple of passes, she cottoned on and swiftly disappeared. I am sure she shouted some obscenity or other but over the sound of the engine noise, her insults were lost. We each took a turn on the helm before I inched us slowly under a very low bridge before beaching the inflatable craft at a waterfront bar for a beer to round off an extremely pleasant afternoon. On the return journey to the ship, I was again helming and in my inexperience, motored at speed across the wake of another craft causing the inflatable Gemini to nearly take off. This brought an immediate flash of anger from Cdr E, "Fucking slow down, somebody could get killed..." Shutting the throttle immediately, the small boat came instantly to an almost full stop, wallowing in the lumpy water. Expecting Cdr E to continue with his bollocking, I waited for further instructions. He just continued with a smile saying "...but they didn't did they?" This completely defused the moment of tension which could easily have marred a brilliant afternoon. As it was still my 'turn', I carefully, and this time slowly, steered the Gemini back alongside the Ajax without any further incident. My moment of madness aside, it was a lovely afternoon of mucking about on the water in the sunshine.

After all of this sea time, in such a short period of time, Ajax was starting to look a bit tired. She was in desperate need of a refit. The current trend back in eighties was to put one ship into refit in Gibraltar and for the crew to transfer to the ship just completing her refit. It was therefore in the late summer in 1980 that HMS Ajax entered Gibraltar for her refit. HMS Ariadne was just completing her refit so within a matter of weeks, the ship's company would move lock stock and barrel from one ship to the other and after trials, sail the refitted ship back to Plymouth. It sounds simple enough, but as always, it wasn't all plain sailing. As a ship's company, we were all looking forward to spending three months alongside in the Mediterranean sun. Ajax's refit would then be carried out by naval personnel of the Gibraltar Refit Group who were based on the 'Rock'. On arrival in Gibraltar, HMS Ajax berthed on the South Mole to de-store and prepare all the machinery for the forthcoming maintenance. To make the most of the weather, the ship operated what was known as a 'Tropical Routine' which saw us start work at 7am and apart from a short break for stand easy at 10am, we worked straight through lunch finishing work for the day at 2pm. The idea was that we could still do our work but also get ashore and enjoy the weather. If you believe that, you'll believe anything. Gibraltar was, and in some respects, still is, every matelot's dream. There used to be about two hundred and fifty bars in roughly two and a half square miles of usable land. Some, like 'The Hole in the Wall' are infamous and Charlie, the rather camp landlord made *his boys* very welcome indeed. Arguably, the smallest pub in the world was also in Gib and was called 'Seven Steps Down' this had, obviously, seven stone steps from the road into the pub, a bar and a usable floor space of about four square foot. Whilst we were effectively based in Gib, everybody on the ship found a 'local'. Tucked away up a narrow side street behind the Cannon Bar and next to a theatre was my local. It was called 'The Birmingham Arms' and was run, not surprisingly, by a Brummie ex-pat called Dennis. The 'Birmingham Arms' had everything we needed; beer, a toilet, a state of the art table top Asteroids machine, a TV, a pool table, a really good atmosphere and not least, Dennis' homemade burgers. The lads from the mess adopted the pub as our local and came to treat it like a living room and popped in just about every day for a couple of beers and a burger. As regulars, Dennis would allow credit for his regular punters as we often became skint towards the end of the month.

As the Spanish border was still firmly shut, Gibraltar remained a British garrison and as such had just about everything the self-respecting tourist could wish for. There was a forces family's lido called 'Nuffield Pool'. This was a salt water filled swimming pool surrounded by a large flat area of paving slabs with deckchairs and a refreshments bar. The rock of Gibraltar is also honeycombed with a myriad of tunnels which lead to a hospital, generating station, a reservoir, some Second World War gun emplacements and ammunition stores. From the Naval Dockyard, there was, or probably still is, a perfectly straight tunnel through the rock to 'Both Worlds' beach. For a bit of exercise, I would blaze a trail through it, quite fast on my racing bike, emerging on the other side into dazzling sunshine and then follow the road left, up the hill past the Caleta Palace Hotel on Devil's Tower Road past Eastern Beach and the airport before heading back to the dockyard on Queensway. The whole circuit used to take about fifteen minutes, not that I could do that now of course.

After a few weeks of refit preps and de-storing, HMS Ajax cold moved alongside HMS Ariadne. The changeover day had been set as Saturday 23rd August 1980 and we were under strict orders not to board our new home before then. It was, strangely, very exciting to get a clean and shiny ship straight out of refit. Quite a few of Ajax's ship's company were leaving the ship in Gibraltar which meant there was a lot more scope to get a good bunk in Ariadne's Stokers Mess. So despite the regulations, myself and a few of the lads snuck on-board one evening and bagged our new bunks. I chose a top one in the corner of the port side mess square.

Eventually the changeover day arrived and all hell broke loose. With all hands in, everybody including the Captain was employed carrying boxes of stores and personal kit from one ship to the other. The theory was that the contents from one locker would be taken from HMS Ajax and replaced in the same corresponding locker on-board HMS Ariadne, but like most ships of the same class, they look identical at first glance, but the more you look, the more subtle differences you notice. Some lockers were simply not there or were just located in a different place. Like moving house, it is initially utter chaos with boxes everywhere, until eventually, everything finds a home, but it was still several days before Ariadne looked anything like ship-shape.

Once everything was pretty much stowed away, attentions were focused on ensuring that the boilers, engines and auxiliaries were all ready for steam.

Ariadne was fitted with a Babcock & Wilcox Y160 boiler which was a later variant to that on Ajax, so it took a little while getting used to it and finding where all of the valves and cocks were located. Eventually we managed to get a flame into the boilers and started to gingerly warm through the systems and raise steam.

Whilst we were still alongside in Gibraltar, there was the unusual requirement for us to blow soot. I was on watch for this evolution and take my portion of the blame for the resultant mess in Gibraltar Dockyard as months of accumulated soot was blown out of the funnel over Gibraltar.

After finally getting the boilers lit and turning the main engines by steam, Ariadne would sail every day for a short time, proving all of the systems and rectifying the resulting defects until finally after being alongside in Gibraltar for about three months, we bade farewell to Dennis and the other friends we had made and steamed back home towards Devonport.

After getting home and taking some well-earned leave, the ship then had to prepare for Basic Operational Sea Training that was eight weeks of simulated fires, floods and famines that would progressively increase in intensity whilst the Captain continued to fight the ship. BOST, was conducted at the Naval Base on Portland and everybody, without exception, dreaded it. We learned that when things were going badly, to adopt a forced toothy grin that we called 'The Portland Smile' with the sole idea of proving to the staff that they couldn't break our spirit.

The examining team were called FOST staff, and for identification, they all wore white overalls. The one thing I came to hate about the FOST staff was that they were never wrong (even if they were). I should introduce them to my wife, they would get along famously. They became known, privately, as 'The White Mafia'. It was not unusual for them to suddenly initiate a 'FOST Funny' to test the ship's teamwork and resourcefulness. An example of this was when the ship was given twenty minutes' notice to host a volleyball game on the jetty with two teams, a few cheerleaders, a crowd of supporters and a hot meal for all. The game was therefore preceded by some frantic activity by the Physical Training staff and the chefs. The Stokers mess were told to get into fancy dress and act as cheerleaders. What fancy dress can anyone come up with given only minutes' notice? A decision was taken by the Leading Hand of the Mess, LMEM 'Jan' Towsey, to dress in togas. This was easy as it only involved a clean bed sheet and a uniform issue money belt to hold it all together. Flip flops or sandals would be worn as footwear whilst to protect the lad's modesty, shorts or underpants were optional. To save my blushes I opted to wear mine. The chefs managed to conjure up some lumpy soup or watery stew, depending upon how you looked at it with bread rolls whilst the club swinger sorted out the net and refereed the game. The result was unimportant, it was just about getting everything organised and everyone involved in the allotted time.

One of my other jobs whilst on HMS Ariadne, was as part of the IS Platoon. In a nut shell, this was just sailors playing at being soldiers. A stoker with a 7.62m Self Loading Rifle is a dangerous combination, but the third team was comprised entirely from the lads who lived in 3 Kilo mess. One of the exercises whilst at Portland was called 'Operation Awkward' where the ship had to pretend that we were in a foreign port and under attack from all kinds of naughty bad guys. Divers were sent down to check the ship's hull for limpet mines and the landing party were put ashore to secure the jetty. It was tremendous fun and we even got to *shoot* people with blanks if they failed to respond to our code word challenge. Whilst all this was happening, an intruder somehow managed to get on-board the ship unchallenged and ran into the Wardroom with a big black rubber ball with a piece of string protruding from it. The word 'BOMB' had been written on it in chalk. He placed it down on the deck and then ran away. About five minutes later, an officer brought out the 'Bomb'. The string had been removed and he reported that the 'Bomb' had been safely defused. I dare say, if this had happened in the Stokers Mess, then we would all have been *killed* and got our heads down for the remainder of the exercise.

There were lots of other FOST induced 'funnies' to contend with. On one occasion, a man was pretending he was riding an imaginary motorcycle up and down 2 deck passageway, making the sounds himself and twisting his right wrist to accelerate his imaginary motorbike. A FOST instructor told a passing stoker "Stop that man!" the stoker replied, "Right Sir" and promptly kick started his own imaginary motorcycle and ran after him.

On another occasion, one of the Leading Hands was walking towards an instructor who had drawn a large white circle with chalk on the deck. "That's a large hole in the deck, laddie, what are you going to do about it?" Quick as a flash, the LMEM replied "Can I borrow your chalk please sir?" he then drew two parallel lines across the 'hole' and handed the chalk back "That's a plank sir" and walked over it. I think you get the idea. They appeared to be doing everything to break us, and we just had to smile and get on with it.

At the end of the 8th week, there was a final inspection to contend with, where the ship would finally be tested. All the joking and the funnies were over, this was serious and there was also a serious 'carrot' dangling in the form of a foreign deployment if the ship passed. If it failed, then a few more weeks of FOST-induced misery beckoned. Fortunately, the training had been beneficial. By mid-afternoon, after the weekly 'Thursday War' which was full of action damage, fires and floods, Ariadne had seemingly singlehandedly won the 'war' and gained a 'Satisfactory' pass. Hurrah!

This heralded the end of BOST and following the final inspection, as a sort of reward, Ariadne visited Hamburg in company with HMS Euryalus where we managed to sample some German hospitality. In Hamburg's Reeperbahn, one of our lads got arrested for walking down the middle of the red light district, pissed as a fart, chanting "Two World Wars and One World Cup do dah, do dah". Later the same evening, I was propositioned in a heated underground car park called the 'Eros Centre', which, turned out to be a sort of prostitute's supermarket. There were conical concrete planters dotted about all filled with complementary condoms. As a pure and innocent nineteen year old, I knew all of the theory, but hadn't yet put it into practice. Unfortunately for me, Hamburg's Ladies of the Night all had master's degrees in extorting cash out of naive nineteen year old virgins. Consequently, I was essentially conned out of about twenty four pounds ending up with nothing more than a red face and slightly tight jeans.

One of HMS Euryalus' ship's company did manage to get himself shot during the visit. I didn't see the incident myself, but apparently, a policeman, who'd obviously been watching too much Starsky and Hutch on the TV, screeched his car to a halt, rolled over the bonnet of his car and parted this guy's hair with a single shot. The bullet just managed to break the skin and he was taken to hospital with a slight graze to the top of his swede and presumably soiled pants. I am not sure what he had done to provoke this reaction from the law, but there was generally quite a lot of drunken silliness going on with people shouting loudly in a 'Basil Fawlty' voice "Don't mention ze vor" so it was no surprise when some of the lads got into bother.

On the day before the ship sailed from Hamburg, there was a planned anti-nuclear demonstration on the jetty. When asked if we carried nuclear weapons on-board, the Captain instructed us to neither confirm nor deny the fact. As a precaution against any trouble, we rigged fire-fighting hoses on the upper deck to squirt any less than peaceful protestors. As it was quite cold, the feeling was that cold and soggy protestors might just give up their right to protest and waddle off home. Tempted though I was, I was never given the opportunity to soak the Germans as unfortunately, they were all on their best behaviour.

Back in Devonport for a maintenance period and some leave, HMS Ariadne finally prepared to deploy westwards towards the United States and the West Indies. Unfortunately for me, I had completed all the hard work and now it was my time to leave the ship and a lot of good mates. I had received a draft chit to join the Fleet Maintenance Base in Devonport

So I reluctantly left HMS Ariadne as she sailed off into the sunset towards America on the 24th March 1981 a bit miffed that I was missing the opportunity to go back to the States, but also looking forward to a bit of shore time in Plymouth.

FMB DEVONPORT

24th March 1981 to 2nd June 1982

Two years into my Royal Navy career and I was still a lowly MEM(M)2. Nothing was happening fast on the promotional front. I had just about completed my task book for promotion, but to be eligible for advancement, I still needed to gain two more AMCs namely in Steering Gear and Switchboards.

Having now completed a full sea draft, I could look forward to at least a year and a half in a shore job with the expectation of a relatively stable social life. After completing the Joining Routine, I was employed in the Lagging Section which, whilst being a really dirty job was actually quite interesting. Due to the hazardous nature of the work, a lot of it could only be carried out at night. For that reason, we were organised into five shifts that rotated weekly within a twelve week cycle. Due to the unpleasant and anti-social nature of the work, the shift pattern allowed each shift to get three weeks leave in every cycle. Any budding mathematician will tell you that that is close to a quarter of a year on leave. For this reason, the lads would happily put up with working in a dirty and dusty environment.

I was assigned to 'B Shift' under the supervision of a quite serious Petty Officer called 'Paddy' McLaughlin. Working shifts during the night was great as the office and workshop were very quiet. This meant as there was generally nobody else about you could pretty much work your own system, provided that the work got done. The usual routine would be to come into the office in civvies with a sandwich box containing your 'lunch' at least ten minutes before the scheduled start of the shift.

Without wishing to state the obvious, lagging hot and cold pipes was essential to keep the internal fluid or vapour at the correct temperature. This prevented heat loss and condensation and also made the work place much safer. Trust me when I say that touching a hot, unlagged steam pipe is a most unpleasant experience.

Asbestos had been outlawed long before I joined the section, so most of our lagging was now preformed calcium silicate or fibreglass. The calcium silicate was a white powdery pipe-covering that came in varying lengths, diameters and thicknesses and would be measured, cut, and secured using seizing wire and pliers. Sometimes it could be quite a fiddly business securing small pieces of lagging around the bend of a pipe and it became a real labour of love to cover every inch of the bare pipework. Once all the preformed lagging had been secured around the pipe, any gaps were then filled with a sloppy mixture called 'slackers' which was mixed in a bucket with water to form a creamy coloured paste. This would then cover all surfaces, sealing all the gaps and ensuring that the heat did not escape. When the 'slackers' was dry, the job would then be finished off by applying another mixed compound called 'armouring' that did exactly what it said on the tin and dried like cement protecting the lagging beneath.

The downside to this type of work was that despite all of the protective clothing, I always ended up with my forearms itching with the lagging fibres. We were required to wear special nylon zip-up green overalls over the top of our normal cotton overalls. We then wore Marigold gloves to protect our hands and these were taped at the wrists using masking tape, but somehow the fibreglass still managed to get through, causing me to need a really hot shower and a good scrub at the end of each shift.

I had been in the Lagging Section for about three months when, as a nineteenth birthday present from my mum, she had bought me a load of driving lessons. Anxious to pass my test and buy a car, I took my driving lessons in a block and passed my test a few weeks later, at the first attempt, in August 1981. As the Royal Wedding between Prince Charles and Lady Diana was all the rage, after passing my driving test, I celebrated in the Ark Royal pub in Devonport with a bottle or two of 'Royal Ale' that had been brewed specially for the occasion.

Despite not having a car, I wasn't entirely without wheels. My mate, LREM Steve 'Pincher' Martin, who was still deployed in the States on-board HMS Ariadne, loaned me his motorcycle for safekeeping. At the time, I could legally ride a 250cc motorcycle on the strength of my car licence and had ridden his Yamaha RD250LC on a few occasions, usually to transport Steve back from the pub after he'd had a few.

The bike was chained up in a cycle shed in HMS Drake and, being bored one afternoon, I decided to take it for a couple of circuits of the camp. All was going swimmingly until, after deciding that I'd had enough fun for the afternoon and rode back to the cycle shed, I realised that I had a kerb to mount to get the bike back into its parking position in the cycle shed, but when I gently opened the throttle and released the clutch, it caused the bike to lurch forward, up the kerb where it subsequently crashed into the corrugated back wall of the shed. Being off-balance and with me a little shocked, I couldn't prevent the bike toppling over onto another one in a domino effect before both bikes ended up on their sides.

Fortunately, there was nobody about, so I quickly righted Steve's bike and then the other bike before examining both vehicles for damage. Apart from a couple of superficial scratches, I thought I'd got away with it. On Steve's return a few weeks later, he noticed the damage instantly which was considerably worse than my initial assessment so he hunted me down like a dog. Although I could not see it, apparently crashing into the rear wall had caused the front forks to twist. Whoops! I offered to pay for the damage, but he was too annoyed with me to take any money. Fortunately we can laugh about it now, but it was not a happy time.

One of my mates from Ariadne, Steve Pratt, offered to sell me his 1966 'D' registered Mini 850 for £180. I wouldn't say I actually *needed* a car as I had managed perfectly well without one since joining the Navy, but in the search for more comfortable living accommodation, I had moved into a flat in a house with my mate Gary 'Ginge' Charman in the Stoke district of Plymouth. As luck would have it, our flat-mates were four girlie students from the local Polytechnic. We each had our own rooms, but shared the kitchen, dining room and bathroom.

I decided to buy the Mini from Steve, and as it was so old and potentially unreliable, I also bought a year's membership with the AA. I loved the car and made a point of driving it absolutely everywhere, even just up the road to the post box. Without any mod-cons, I bought and fitted a self-adhesive heated element for the rear window that worked really well at keeping my hands toasty when I needed to push it. Unfortunately, it didn't last long and fell off. In an attempt to customise my Mini and make it look cool, I bought a racing steering wheel and bucket seats and a cassette player that blew up as soon as I switched it on. Not knowing the finer points about electrickery at that point, I had wired it in accordance with the instructions, but as the car's battery was earthed from the positive terminal, I had effectively reversed the polarity. I took it back, explained that it was faulty, and amazingly, they took pity on me and exchanged it for a new one. I didn't make the same mistake again.

My AA membership turned out to be worth every penny as I got to know the local AA Man 'Inch' on nickname terms. On one occasion in early November 1981, I had worked a night shift the previous evening and, having slept all morning, I was wide awake and bored by mid-afternoon. For want of something to do, I decided to take the Mini for a drive. I planned to head out towards Princetown in the centre of Dartmoor, see the prison and then return to Plymouth on a different route via Tavistock. All was going well, it was a bitterly cold day up on the moors and by 4pm, I was a few miles away from Princetown heading home on the Tavistock Road when things started to go badly wrong. Losing power, struggling up a steep hill, I progressively changed down the gears until in first gear the Mini died just before the crest of the hill. All attempts to restart it failed and the whirring of the starter motor confirmed that I was going to flatten the battery. As I was facing up hill, bump starting was just not an option.

With the light fading fast and fine flakes of snow beginning to fall, this was all starting to become rather tedious. I had no means of contacting anyone and the alternative to staying with the car on this lonely stretch of road was to walk a few miles back down the road to Princetown to summon assistance. Deciding that this was my best option, wrapping myself up in my black parka I started the lonely walk back towards Princetown. Fortunately, after walking a short way back down the hill, I saw a light on in a workman's hut in a roadside quarry. Knocking on the door, I was greeted with "Christ, where did you come from, son?" Before I could even ask for help, I was dragged in, sat in front of a pot-bellied stove and given a mug of tomato soup to warm me up. The good samaritans then phoned the AA and told the control room where I could be found as they took real pity on this teenager stranded in the middle of nowhere.

After about an hour, there was a knock on the door and a smiling 'Inch' said, "I recognised the registration number and came as quickly as I could." After thanking my saviours, I got a lift back up the hill with 'Inch' in his AA van to the poor little Mini. The snow was now starting to drift into the verges and it was bitterly cold. Fortunately, 'Inch' knew his way around a car and after crawling under the back axle; he banged away for a moment before shouting "Try it now" and on the first turn of the key, the little car burst into life. 'Inch' explained that the fuel filter had become clogged with dirt and rust and that he had managed to dislodge it. He offered to follow me back to Plymouth in case of any further problems and he was as good as his word, but fortunately, it didn't conk out again.

Towards the end of November 1981, I had, what could only be described as an epic journey as I drove home to Sutton Coldfield for the very first time. Heavy snow had fallen during the night as I was preparing to go home on shift leave for two weeks. Nothing short of a natural disaster was going to prevent that happening. Calling the AA for travel information revealed that the A38 and M5 were passable with care. So the following morning I left Plymouth around 10am with a little difficulty and headed out of town towards the main roads that I was sure would have been cleared and gritted. Learning from my previous experience on Dartmoor, I carried a flask, a blanket, some tools and a goodly supply of WD40 which would hopefully be sufficient to see me home in safety. Out of Plymouth on the A38, I started to make decent progress listening to my music whilst heading towards Exeter. Around Buckfastleigh, bad luck and sheer lack of experience combined causing me to spin the car and end up in the central reservation buried in deep snow facing the other way. Everything had died; the car, the lights and also the music. Recovering from my near accident, I prioritised and got the music working first as I discovered that the tape had come to the end. It also turned out that in the confusion, I had stalled the car and when I restarted the engine, the lights came back on. It was then I realised that I was stuck in deep snow and with no shovel in the boot, I was forced to dig the car out with my bare hands until they were grazed and numb. Eventually, I managed to free the Mini from its icy tomb and after turning the car around continued with my journey home. Braking in slush, as I found out, was not such a bright idea.

Continuing with my slow journey, I made it to Bristol by mid-afternoon when the traffic finally ground to a halt. With no radio, I had no idea what the holdup was, but seeing other motorists out of their cars discussing the grid lock, I decided to join them. It became apparent, that an articulated lorry had overturned on the M4 slip road and this was causing a tailback that was affecting the northbound M5 as well. After about an hour and following the example of other motorists, I turned around on the M5 and drove the wrong way back up the hard shoulder and up the Junction 18 slip road onto the A4. Crossing the bridge and following the stream of traffic, I joined the M5 southbound carriageway that was clear and made it the mile or so over the Avon Bridge back to Gordano Service Station at Junction 19 where I abandoned the Mini in a parking space and sought sanctuary in the cafeteria as it was again becoming bitterly cold.

Inside was reminiscent of the London Underground during the Blitz. Families were huddled together around cases and personal belongings, children were running about screaming and there was a real sense of determinedness. Some people were helping each other whilst others' were trying to keep warm in their sleeping bags having already given up hope of continuing their journey. There was a group of people attending to a man laid on the floor. He was covered in coats and blankets in an effort to keep him warm. As it turned out, in an attempt to prevent the diesel in his truck freezing, he had wrapped himself around the tank in an attempt to transfer his body heat and promptly got stuck to it. Silly man! He urgently need hospitalisation, but the ambulances just couldn't get through and it was still snowing hard.

News was starting to filter in of the road conditions on the motorway; it was not good. There was only one lane open in each direction with the middle and the fast lane now under several inches of snow, and it was still falling. A large bowl of soup revived my spirits somewhat, though in the confusion, I failed to notice that I had only received change of a tenner from my £20 note. I got chatting to some lorry drivers who were heading up to Scotland. Their suggestion was to take it slowly and to stop at each service station for a break. Thawed out and with renewed confidence having heard that the traffic was again moving, I went out and started to excavate my little Mini from its own personal snow drift.

Back on the M5 heading north, I managed to get up to about 20mph, unfortunately the little car didn't much like driving in wet weather. The problem was that the distributor and the coil were situated right behind the grill and 1966 Minis were not fitted with any protection from the elements. Every now and then it would just die, requiring me to get out and dry the electrics with a rag before giving everything a liberal squirt of WD40. After about two hours, the road signs told me that I was approaching Michael Wood Services where I had every intention of stopping for a break. As I got closer though the queue waiting to pull off the motorway was longer than the signs advertising its approach, so with gritted teeth, I pressed on towards the next services at Strensham.

A little later, sensing the car was dying again, I swung the Mini into the snowbound and deserted fast lane and stopped. Getting out with my trusty WD40 and rag, I noticed that in the dark, a queue of traffic that had been following my tail lights had stopped behind me like a big white snake of head lights. A lady leaned out of her window and shouted against the wind "Are you in trouble? Sorry can't help," and slowly crawled past me. This was no matter as I was an old hand at this now and was on my way again inside five minutes. Back on the carriageway, I continued onwards and amazingly about five hours after leaving Gordano, I finally arrived at Strensham Service Station, dying for the loo and completely knackered. I decided there and then that I had had enough and made the command decision to spend the rest of the night as a refugee inside the service station.

Walking into the cafeteria, I heard a voice calling me "You made it then?" It was one of the lorry drivers that I had met at Gordano Services in Bristol. Sitting down with another bowl of lifesaving soup I told them I had given up and was staying here for the night as it was now about 10pm and I was absolutely knackered. When they asked where I was headed, they told me that Sutton Coldfield was only about thirty five miles away and easily achievable. So with my bladder drained and myself properly defrosted, I made an update phone call to Mum and set off for hopefully the final leg of the journey. With a lorry ahead blazing a trail and another behind me, they shepherded me with their huge wheels. Now making much better progress, after an hour or so, we approached the turning for the M6 southbound. With lots of honking and in my case, pipping of horns, I dropped out of formation, eternally grateful for their assistance. Approaching midnight, the southbound M6 was unusually quiet and as my tape had come to the end I became aware that the Mini's engine was not sounding too good at all; a bit like a baby tractor. It was obvious that not all of the cylinders were firing. As I was still moving and close enough to home to abandon the car and continue on foot if need be, I pressed on. Thankfully, the little car kept on chugging until sometime after 1am, with the snow still falling, I eventually arrived home pipping the horn triumphantly, announcing to my undoubtedly annoyed neighbours that I had finally made it. My relieved mum was waiting on the door step for me holding a huge glass of sherry to warm me up. Despite being completely exhausted, I found that I couldn't sleep and for the next couple of hours just lay in bed replaying the events of the journey.

It was a few days later before the snow had thawed sufficiently enough for me to be able to excavate the car. Amazingly, it started on the first turn of the key. Discovering a design fault with the positioning of the Mini's electrics, I manufactured a sort of shield out of a cardboard box, plastic bags and Sellotape to protect the distributor and coil from the wind and the rain. After a wee bit of trial and error and subsequent modification to allow for the horn cable, it worked perfectly.

The journey back to Plymouth two weeks later, in contrast, was far less eventful and I managed to get back to my flat in a little under four hours which shaved a massive ten hours off my epic return home.

Back at work the following morning the shift pattern resumed, but it wasn't long before I was called into the office and told that my job was being changed. It appeared to my superiors that I wasn't progressing fast enough up the promotional ladder. There was some concern that in my two and a half years, I had only managed to pass two AMCs and still had to complete two more before I could be promoted to .

After a rather uncomfortable one way chat with the Captain, I was placed on 'Captain's Warning' giving me three months to improve or I could be looking for another job. To assist me, I was taken away from the comfortable shift pattern of the Lagging Section and loaned to the Leander-class frigate HMS Sirius, where I virtually camped in the tiller flat with a mug of tea, watching the steering gear operate. After a little while, I started to see how the hunting gear was moving in reply to the movements of the ship's wheel and suddenly, in a blinding flash of logic, it all became clear. Amazingly, switchboards didn't take long to master and within the week, I was sitting in the workshop being questioned by an officer and two chiefs on basic stokering tasks. For me, this was all 'old hat' and after about half an hour of questioning; they got bored and passed me for promotion. Later in the week, I was summoned back in front of the Captain who was much nicer this time. He accused me, probably quite rightly, of being lazy and after a little pep talk, promoted me to MEM1. This meant that I got a star above my badge and could be considered by some to be a useful member of society for the first time in my naval career. As a

newly promoted MEM1, I was moved to join the D5 Engine Change Team as they were short-handed.

The Type 21 and Type 22 frigates all carried two Olympus gas turbines and two Tyne gas turbines that only had a certain amount of running hours in them. They were fitted inside acoustic modules and were designed to be changed relatively easily as they approached their required amount of running hours. As part of the Engine Change Team, I was essentially a spanner monkey; unbolting and then refastening parts of the exhaust trunking and rigging sets of rails to guide the engine as it was hoisted out of the module.

So in the spring of 1982 I found myself changing a starboard Tyne engine on the Type 21 frigate, HMS Ardent. As part of the team, I was required to unbolt and remove the 'top hat', the 'transition piece', the 'cascade bend' and also the 'soft patch' before rigging the rails on either side of the module all the way up to the hangar. Whilst this was happening, the 'Tiffs' would be disconnecting all of the fuel systems and other pipework inside the module, preparing the engine to move. Finally, a series of chain blocks were used to draw the engine horizontally aft out of the module before using the rails as guides; it was rotated vertically and pulled up through five decks until finally it was rotated again back to a horizontal position and lowered onto its trolley. The replacement engine would then be lowered slowly into the module, reversing the procedure. Once it was safely in the module, the 'Tiffs' went to work connecting all of the systems back up and my team replaced all of the exhaust trunking, spending literally hours tightening up all the hundreds of nuts and bolts. Finally by Friday evening, the job was complete. The technical types were having some difficulties setting up the clutch, so we were sent home with strict instructions to remain by the phone at the short trail and if required we would need to come back in over the weekend to replace the engine again if the 'Tiffs' could not align the clutch correctly to the gearbox.

Whilst we were doing battle with a Tyne gas turbine, some South American meat packers had decided to wage war on a tiny group of islands that we all thought were somewhere off the top of Scotland. It occurred to us that it seemed a long way to come to claim the islands for themselves. The Falklands Conflict was all over the news and a task force was hurriedly being assembled to sail halfway around the world armed slightly better than the island's sheep farmers to give the Argies a moment of pause. This was very exciting, but nobody took it too seriously as it wasn't exactly on our doorstep and frankly most people hadn't even heard of the Falklands before.

HMS Ardent was named as part of the task force so it was no surprise when the phone rang as Frank Bough was reading out the football scores off the Grandstand teleprinter. The artificers had failed to get the clutch correctly aligned, so a new engine was being dispatched from Lee-on-Solent, near Gosport. We were therefore required to go back into work on Saturday evening, to undo everything that we'd previously tightened up and replace the engine with a new one. Fortunately, as all the nuts and bolts had been greased, removing them was a doddle. Working throughout the night, breaking only for cups of tea and piss breaks, we smashed all records taking only fourteen hours to remove and replace the engine. With the Tyne now correctly aligned and run up, I managed to scam a bit of breakfast from the ship's galley before hearing HMS Ardent's captain make a broadcast to the ship's company informing everyone that the ship would be sailing in fifteen minutes and all personnel not intending to sail with the ship were to leave immediately. This concentrated the mind as I quickly finished my free breakfast and hurried off the ship. When I appeared on the flight deck, the dockside crane already had the gangway airborne, hovering slightly above the flight deck, so dodging the wire strops, I joined my workmates on the jetty and within five minutes the gangway was hoisted skywards allowing HMS Ardent to leave Devonport and sail off to war.

As Ardent made the turn to port and disappeared from view, my chief asked me where his tool box was. In my haste to finish my breakfast and to get off the ship, I had completely forgotten about it. It was still in the after engine room and it was now on its way to the Falkland Islands. Not a happy chief.

With the Falklands Conflict now occupying most of the emergent work, we didn't do any more engine changes, but instead helped load coffins and body bags onto the requisitioned container ship, 'Atlantic Conveyor'. This had the effect of convincing us that what was happening in the South Atlantic was really quite serious. People could actually get hurt. Up until this point, it was almost like a scene from a war film, but we hadn't stopped to think that the conflict could actually kill people. It was quite a sobering thought.

About a week after HMS Ardent had sailed, I got called into the office to read a draft chit. Unusually, I was given a choice; I could fly down to the Ascension Islands to form part of a Forward Maintenance Base or if I preferred, I could join the County-class Destroyer HMS Kent that was now the Fleet Training Ship at Whale Island to complete AMC Course. As a newly promoted MEM(M)1, I opted for the AMC Course as it was a much faster track to getting more cash. Granting my wish, I subsequently joined, HMS Kent in Portsmouth a few days later.

As I arrived on-board HMS Kent, the Falkland's conflict was beginning to gain momentum. The Type 42 Destroyer, HMS Sheffield had been sunk and the news was full of exciting grainy footage of aircraft whizzing around the sky.

Getting straight to work, I started tracing the systems of HMS Kent's water distilling plants called Evaporators but a few days later, before I had even managed to complete the exam, I was summoned by the Chief Stoker with some good and then some bad news.

The good news was that I was being sent home on extended weekend leave from Thursday, but the bad news was that I was leaving the six week course after only four days and was being crash drafted the following Monday to join HMS Tartar, a Tribal-class frigate, that was being brought out of mothballs to replace the ships that had already been lost in the conflict.

Still reeling from the shock but also needing to get something out of the course, I hurriedly took and passed my Evaporators exam at the end of May 1982 before going home on weekend leave.

HMS TARTAR

2nd June 1982 to 5th June 1984

The following Wednesday, after a whole weekend of interrogation from Mum who was convinced I was going off to war, I presented myself to the MACCO at the Fleet Maintenance Base in Devonport to get my joining instructions for HMS Tartar. When I asked where she was berthed, the chap behind the desk swivelled around and pointed out of the window towards a ship berthed on 7 Wharf. Compared to my other three ships, HMS Tartar was considerably older and still in mothballs, having been decommissioned some years previously.

An hour later and I had joined a large group of apparently lost sailors on 7 Wharf adjacent to our new ship. Never before, in my experience, had the entire ship's company all joined a ship on the same day. Reporting to an official-looking chap with a clipboard, I was ticked off and told to report to Chief Mechanician 'Taff' Leader who was to become my engine room Chief.

After getting his lads together, we boarded HMS Tartar for the first time and after dropping bags, were escorted down to the engine room for a familiarisation tour of the ship where we met POMEM 'Harry' Hawkes. My first impression was that the engine room seemed considerably smaller than any other ship I had been on. This was primarily because the gearbox, like the County-class Destroyers, was in its own compartment. The engine room, we learned, had a single steam turbine and next to it a big silver blob, called a G6 Gas Turbine. On the starboard side, there was an evaporator and two air compressors as well as various other smaller pumps. The main access to the engine room was on the port side aft with the ladder rising up to join the port side passageway on 2 deck. In the middle of the engine room, there was also another manhole up into the MCR that was situated above and between the engine room and boiler room.

Following the quick tour, I went aft to discover where we were going to live. The stokers, I discovered, were all going to be accommodated in '10 Mess' that was located in 2 Romeo section and was the furthest mess aft, just forward of the tiller flat and underneath the after 4.5" gun. The mess was huge and comprised two mess squares on the port side with a ladder leading up, through a hatch onto the quarter deck amidships. Around the back, on the starboard side, there were five gulches. Mine had nine beds and as I was pretty much one of the first inhabitants. I managed to secure myself a nice top rack.

After unpacking, I changed into overalls and steaming boots and headed back to the engine room later in the morning. As four Royal Navy ships had recently been sunk and the Falkland's Conflict was still raging, there was a real sense of urgency to get the ship ready for sea.

As it had been laid up in Chatham and towed to Devonport as a 'dead' ship, everything was caked in a thick preservative grease and that had to be cleaned off and every piece of rotating machinery turned by hand and lubricated. On the upper deck, the old wooden decks had seen better days and were now considered to be beyond economical repair so these were ripped up to expose the metal decks underneath which were then preserved and repainted.

Everywhere you looked, people were busy painting, greasing, fuelling or storing ship. Simultaneously, sister ships, HMS Gurkha and HMS Zulu and also the Whitby-class frigate HMS Torquay were also being brought out of mothballs so there was a certain amount of competition amongst the Tartar's to be the first of the four ships to be declared fully operational.

A week after joining, we finally managed to get a flame into the single Babcock & Wilcox Y111a boiler and eventually turned the steam turbine and single shaft first of all by hand and then by steam power thereby winning the 'race'.

A week later, HMS Tartar recommissioned on 17th June 1982 and left Devonport to concentrate on moulding the raw ship's company into an effective fighting unit. At Portland, the FOST staff, worked us hard until finally about four months after joining the ship, Tartar was finally passed as fully operational and ready for deployment. As one of the oldest Royal Navy ships afloat, there was little danger of us being deployed to the Falklands but she would instead carry out the duties of ships that had already been sunk or were fighting the war in the South Atlantic.

Now fully operational, the four newly recommissioned ships acted as 'trouble shooters' ready to go anywhere in the world as the political situation dictated. As a Fleet Contingency Ship, we were once ordered to sail at very short notice to intercept and shadow some Russian ships exercising north of Iceland. I wouldn't say I fully understood the politics of the day, but it was the era of Lech Walesa and the Polish Trade Union, Solidarity. It was therefore extremely interesting when a convoy of Soviet ships steamed past us on a mutual intelligence-gathering exercise followed in close company by a Polish diving vessel who decided to dip her ensign as a salute to us. As a mark of respect, a pipe was made by our Officer of the Watch "Attention on the upper deck, face to starboard, Polish Warship" thus returning her salute. We spent about a week chasing the Soviet Navy around the North Atlantic and the Arctic Ocean keeping a watchful eye on what they were up to. Quite what we would have done if we'd have spotted any misdemeanors', I never found out. The Cold War was still very much being *fought* so a lot of time was spent watching you, watching us, watching you. I am sure they were just as cold and as pissed off as we were.

Back in Portsmouth a few weeks later and with no cash, I had remained on-board one evening. My run ashore oppo, Gary 'Buck' Taylor, had gone home to his married quarter to see his lovely wife Jackie and three year old daughter Kelly-Anne who knew me affectionately as 'Uncle Flug'. On the face of it, he was living the dream; he had a lovely wife and daughter and a house to call home but, all was not as well as it seemed at chez Buck as he had a great deal of trouble keeping it in his pants and unfortunately, his pants seemed to sneak down occasionally when Jackie was nowhere to be seen. On one such occasion, he was drinking in a pub in Gosport called the 'Green Dragon' with two ladies whom I shall refer to as Sharon and Tracey to protect their blushes.

'Buck', it appeared was getting on famously with Sharon, but Tracey was understandably feeling somewhat left out. 'Buck' mentioned that he had a friend who, as far as he knew, was still sweet and innocent and desperately needed teaching what goes where. This apparently appealed to Tracey, so 'Buck' gave me a call on the ship. "Mate, get your arse over here pronto as this bird wants to shag you." Well, I had known 'Buck' for a couple of years and was well versed with his optimism with regards to the fairer sex, but as I had nothing better to do, within the hour, I was being introduced to Tracey.

She was quite a well-proportioned lady as I remember and after asking if I wanted to see her tattoos, she scooped an ample boob out her top and flopped it on the pub table revealing a horse's head tattoo which was frankly hideous, but when you're on the pull, a definite turn-off is to say it looked awful, so I made all the right noises and after several beers, we were invited back to her place in the concrete jungle of Rowner's Married Quarters for *coffee*. Whilst Sharon and Tracey were in the kitchen preparing the *coffee*, 'Buck' confirmed that I was about to get laid. Frankly, he seemed more excited than I was. Philosophically, I concluded that I would believe it when I saw it.

The ladies both reappeared wearing very little indeed. Both were wearing skimpy night shirts and it was clear that neither of them had any knickers on though oddly, Tracey kept her bra on under her nightie. Each carried two cups of coffee before Tracey plonked herself on my lap and strangely started to spoon-feed coffee from the cup ensuring that I drank every last drop, even some suspicious looking black treacly gunge in the bottom of the cup.

Before long, Gary and Sharon, wished us a good night and disappeared upstairs. Tracey magically produced a couple of blankets and pillows from behind the sofa and made an improvised bed on the floor. Climbing in, she invited me to get undressed and join her, where after a wee bit of fumbling to ensure I was equal to the task, she jumped on top of me and stole my cherry. Over the course of the night, I became quite an enthusiastic student as this lady showed me many techniques that I had, to this point, only read about. In fact the lesson went on for most of the night as we explored every nook and cranny of each other … three times! Thoroughly shagged out, I fell into an exhausted sleep sometime after 4am only to be awoken by 'Buck' sometime around first light reminding me that we needed to get back to the ship.

Promising to ring Tracey, we jumped into my car and made good time getting back to Portsmouth where I woke up my mate 'Rattler' Morgan, who slept in the bed under me to tell him my news. 'Rattler' was a good bloke and congratulated me on becoming a man. He promised not to broadcast the fact before wanting to know all of the gory details. Fortunately, I didn't have time to give him chapter and verse, as I had to get changed into uniform and attend the Duty Watch muster on the upper deck.

A few minutes later, fallen-in at the Duty Watch muster; the Chief Stoker, who was also the Officer of the Day, read out the names on his list to ensure that everyone was present who should have been and that they all knew their fire fighting responsibilities. Satisfied that he could tackle any ship-borne emergency with the twenty or so assembled ratings, he addressed the group with a couple of parish notices before I died on the spot of total embarrassment. "…and finally congratulations to MEM Atkinson, who lost his virginity last night" and started everybody clapping. My humiliation was now complete; then again, had the situation been reversed, I dare say I would have done the same.

Towards the end of 1982, HMS Tartar deployed to the States to carry out the duties of West Indies Guard Ship. As we were going to be away from home over Christmas, the Floridian local papers had been publicising our visit for weeks requesting that if any American families wished to host a British sailor, then they could, in effect, 'Dial a sailor'. When we eventually arrived in St Petersburg on the west coast of Florida for a maintenance period, a US Coast Guard came on-board and set up shop in the Combined Technical Office on the starboard side of 2 deck. As a Liaison Officer, his job was to answer the phone and write all requests and invitations into a book. Periodically, I would check the book, and if an invitation took my fancy, I would take the phone number and write my name in the book next to the invitation. In doing so, this now became a duty and I was obligated to attend. I had accepted an invitation to go for dinner with an elderly lady and her daughter that was very pleasant. They were extremely good hosts but also quite religious. As Christmas was approaching, everyone that was not duty on Christmas Day had arranged to spend Christmas with a family as their guests. Choosing an invitation from the book, I contacted a chap called Guy Seletic on behalf of myself and my buddy, Tony Francis, and arranged to go to their house on Christmas Day. Guy told me that his son, Phil, would drive by the ship and pick us up at 11am on Christmas morning.

Myself and Tony were up, showered and dressed in trousers, shirt and tie by about 10am and drinking beer in the mess. We had acquired a photo of the ship and a ship's crest mounted as a wall plaque as gifts when, at precisely 11am, we were piped to the gangway to be greeted by the scruffiest individual we had ever seen; he was dirty, unshaven and had holes in his T-shirt and jeans. This was not looking good at all. He seemed friendly enough though and we had signed up for it, so there was no backing out.

Phil told us that his truck was parked on the jetty. Looking down from the ship, we saw a scruffy looking battered, red pickup truck with clearly only one passenger seat. Tony and I looked at each other, mentally asking the other who was going in the back. Deciding to make the best of it, I offered to go in the back and as I was about to jump into the trailer, Phil said "Not that one, *that* one" as he pointed to a customised 'passion wagon' with a very pretty lady sat in the passenger seat. This 'truck' was fantastic. In the back there was a round table with holes to put drinks into. The swivel chairs were like those found on an aircraft, there was a settee on the back wall and a fridge full of beer. The walls and roof were carpeted with a TV suspended from a bracket. This was like a mobile living room. The lady in the front, swivelled her chair around to face us. Her name was Patrice, she was Phil's sister, very beautiful and as luck would have it, unattached.

Making ourselves comfortable with a beer for the short ride, Phil drove the luxury RV back to their home in nearby Clearwater, whilst we got better acquainted with Patrice. As we pulled up on a residential road outside a large house, Phil asked us if we could wait in the RV as about fifty people filed out of the house and lined up on the lawn. Phil opened the side door for us and we were greeted by a smiling elderly man. "Hi, my name is Guy Seletic; welcome to my home. There is beer in the garage; there are cocktails in the living room. My house is your house. Merry Christmas." With that, he then introduced us first to his wife and then to his entire family which was very humbling, but they really could have done with name badges as it was too much information to retain all in one go.

With the formalities completed, we were given beer and shown into the living room whilst Phil and Patrice went to change into something a bit smarter. It appeared that all of the family adults had been allocated an area of responsibility. Phil reappeared a few minutes later having transformed himself into a Tom Selleck look-alike cocktail waiter. Patrice though had been tasked with looking after us and I must say she did it very well indeed.

Lunch was soon announced and Patrice ushered us to our places around a huge table. Christmas dinner in Florida was not like a traditional English Christmas dinner. The turkey had been shredded in the kitchen and placed in a huge foil dish. There were also quite a few sweet and savoury dishes, one of which contained cream and grapes. It was different, but also very delicious. Towards the end of the meal, Guy Seletic at the head of the table, stood and made a speech, during which, he announced how honoured he was to have Ian and Tony from the Royal Navy, grace his table.

Following dinner, there was a traditional present-giving ceremony. As we had already handed our gifts to Guy on arrival and considering this to be a family affair, myself and Tony decided to get a beer and sit around the pool to allow the family space to exchange their gifts. Guy, however, was having none of it and we were summoned to witness the giving of presents. It soon became apparent why, as we were handed about ten presents each from different family members. These ranged from aftershave to tool kits and were fantastic. These people had only known us for a few hours and previously knew nothing about us other than gender. I was incredibly humbled by their kindness and generosity.

After all of the gifts had been exchanged and opened, the family then prepared for an afternoon of traditional party games, whilst some of the more senior members of the family indulged in a well-deserved snooze.

Later in the evening, Patrice gave us the choice of going back to the ship or staying at her house for the night and being dropped back at the ship the following morning after breakfast. This was a no-brainer as we unanimously chose the latter option. Patrice then drove us around the corner to her equally impressive house. As she was feeling quite tired, she quickly showed us how to operate the cable TV, where the beer was stored and the option of sleeping on sofas or spare rooms. We decided to flob out on a sofa each with a beer and fell asleep watching 'Stir Crazy' on cable.

The following morning, Patrice woke us with fresh orange juice and coffee and asked us if we'd like to take a swim before breakfast. How the other half live. Not having a lot of time and not wishing to be adrift for our Boxing Day duty, we declined her kind offer and after breakfast, she drove us back to the ship arriving on-board before 8am.

A couple of days later, Guy called me on the ship to thank us for spending Christmas with his family and also to invite myself, Tony and eight of our friends on his motor yacht as he sailed from Tampa Bay down to the Florida Keys. Guy did however request one favour from us. He would supply all of the beer on-board, but he requested a case of English beer for himself. Unfortunately for me, I was unable to go as I had already booked a flight the following day from Tampa to see my Uncle Simon and Auntie Penny in Austin, Texas. Tony was therefore able to handpick nine of his closest mates from the mess to join him and Guy on the yacht. The price was set at one case of Courage Sparking Beer per person. Guy Seletic consequently had ten cases of CSB secreted aboard his boat. I hope he enjoyed them.

The next day, I was all packed and ready to fly to Texas on seven days station leave. As the ship was about twenty miles from Tampa Airport, I had taken advice and booked a Limo to take me to the airport. There is nothing quite like travelling in style. The reality, however, was quite different and the 'Limo Service' was basically a door to door minibus service, crammed in with about ten other passengers with their luggage, but it really didn't matter so long as I got to the airport in good time.

I have always had a fear of missing a plane, train or bus and have always strived to arrive at the embarkation point well before the advertised check-in time. In this instance, I needn't have worried as I arrived about an hour before the domestic flight to Atlanta Georgia on the first leg of my journey to Austin, Texas.

On arrival at Atlanta, I discovered the airport to be seriously huge. Apparently, there were five concourses, each seemingly identical and since I had the better part of four hours to wait between landing and departure, I decided to go for a walk. There seemed to be the same clump of shops and cafes every hundred metres or so. There was a coffee shop, a newsagents, a pharmacy and a snack bar. Continuing down the concourse and in a déjà vous moment; passed an identical group of outlets further down. The only clue was the gate number. Grabbing a drink and some Bonjela for an emerging wisdom tooth, I sat down to read a book adjacent to my departure gate.

The flight to Austin was quite pleasant, but it was well after dark when I arrived in Texas. I had no idea how far my uncle lived from the airport and considered hammering my Access card to get a taxi. I just hoped they were still awake.

I needn't have worried, because as I emerged from the baggage reclaim area, the whole family were there to greet me. Uncle Simon, Auntie Penny and cousins, Yvette, Jason, and little Camille who was wandering round aimlessly pondering who was this stranger keeping her out of her bed at this ungodly hour. Back at their house a short time later, the family went to bed whilst I chatted to Uncle Simon for a few hours over a couple of glasses of whisky.

As ET the Extra Terrestrial had just been released in the United States, it was suggested that I take Camille to the cinema in the local shopping mall as she was apparently dying to see it. I also went along with Auntie Penny and purchased three seats. What a waste of money! As soon as ET showed his face for the first time, Camille screamed, jumped on my lap and buried her face into my chest for most of the film. Well, I enjoyed it.

After the film, we looked around the shopping mall. As I wanted to get a souvenir of my visit, I decided to buy a real cowboy hat from Texas, where else? The array was vast, but the assistants were, as always, extremely helpful and it wasn't long before I was the proud owner of a huge, wide-brimmed cowboy hat that everybody decided was the perfect style, colour and fit. Of course, they could all have been winding me up in attempt to take the piss out of the visiting Brit. It was suggested that I wear it home as it was too big for a bag. So, with hat purchased and with the shop assistant wishing us all a pleasant day, we went home for lunch where Uncle Simon produced a large present which, turned out to be a pair of genuine light tan cowboy boots that perfectly matched my newly purchased hat. All I needed now to complete the transformation was a shirt to wear with jeans. Fortunately, my auntie and uncle knew exactly where to find such an item and the following day, I was the proud owner of a red checked shirt with genuine mother of pearl buttons, thus completing the ensemble.

It was a short, but also very enjoyable visit to Austin. Early on New Year's Day in 1983, as I had to get back to the ship, I was deposited at the airport, dressed in my new outfit for the return trip to Tampa. Walking around Austin airport as a 'cowboy' did not even raise an eyebrow until I opened my mouth. The Texans in the airport just assumed I was one of them. The story when I arrived back in Florida however was very different where I was, without doubt, the only 'cowboy' in town. Needless to say, the piss-taking as I arrived back on-board the ship was relentless as my new outfit was hastily consigned to the fancy dress hamper.

In my absence, the lads in the mess had discovered a night club which was just around the corner to the ship called 'Ten Beach Drive' that was subsequently nicknamed '10 Park Drive' after the cigarette brand. This was a bit like going to a rather lavish party in somebody's huge front room. There were plush sofas to sink into around the room, the lights were dimmed and the venue had a generally very relaxed atmosphere. Similar to a casino, punters were required to exchange money for different denomination chips at the door and then use these to subsequently purchase drinks at the bar. I can only assume this was to reduce the amount of people with their hands on the cash. Pretty girls, wearing aprons and very little else, would tour round the club enticing people to exchange more dollars for chips thus ensuring the trade. On one memorable occasion, drinking a Bacardi and Coke, I was standing with a group of lads from the mess, listening to a chap playing the piano and belting out an Elton John song. An American chap next to me commented on how good he was, when I agreed, he offered to buy me a drink. No harm in that, I thought, as we struck up a friendly conversation. When I was empty, I asked him what he was drinking, to return the favour. He was having none of it and purchased a further round of drinks. He introduced himself as 'Griff' and said he was a local businessman. He was just a generous, friendly Floridian chap and actually very good company. As the evening wore on, the music became louder and the conversation became more difficult. Griff suggested going on somewhere else, as he knew an equally good club not too far away.

We arrived at the ABC in 4th Street North a short time later, where, as it turned out, 'Griff' was a member. This club was much livelier. The bar was circular and actually rotated around an illuminated dance floor. The girls serving behind the bar were all wearing very short red miniskirts and matching knickers that were visible most of the time. As I toured the room, sat on a bar stool, I got chatting to a barmaid called Sara who was seriously gorgeous and slowly rotated around the dance floor getting to know her. 'Griff', sensing that I fancied her, went up to the DJ and requested that he play 'Sara' by Fleetwood Mac for me and dedicate the track to Sara behind the bar from the English sailor. Smooth Git!

After an hour or so, 'Griff' asked if I was hungry as he knew a good burger joint just up the street. Saying my reluctant goodbyes to Sara, we left the club and, as Americans never walk anywhere, jumped into his car that was seriously impressive. Remembering that this was 1983, his car had every conceivable accessory, a radio/cassette player, an eight track cartridge player, a CB radio and even electrically controlled seats that moved in any direction. Everything was covered in shiny chrome. As the yanks might say, this was a 'nice ride'.

This burger joint was, as 'Griff' had promised, just up the street; about twenty miles, up the street to be exact and we had long since left the lights of the town behind us. Pulling into a roadside diner, 'Griff' told me that these were the best burgers in town. I thought, we're not in town, in fact, we cannot even see the town. Nethertheless, we were shown to his usual table where he ordered for both of us. The burger, salad and fries that arrived very quickly were, as promised, delicious. 'Griff' seemed to be a really nice bloke; the conversation was easy and he appeared to be very well known around the area. When he asked for the check, all attempts by me to pay were thwarted by 'Griff' who seemingly had an account. I had been eating, drinking and chatting to this bloke for about four hours and he had not let me pay for a thing. It was now well after midnight as we headed back towards civilisation. 'Griff' suggested that he show me the sights before dropping me back at the ship and before long, we were touring an area called 'Treasure Island' that was a local tourist resort. Stopping to admire the view, 'Griff' confessed that he actually preferred the company of men. Shit! I explained that although I had really enjoyed his company, I actually preferred the company of women. Whilst confessing to being a little disappointed, he said that he respected my honesty and enjoyed my company. Back at the ship a bit later, we parted as friends with a formal handshake.

That was not the end of the story however. A couple of days later, 'Griff' called me and told me that he'd set up a date between me and the pretty barmaid called Sara and generously offered to pick me up later that day. 'Griff' was a real friend. Although he was gay and I was not, he respected my wishes; he just valued genuine friendship. My relationship with Sara, however, continued very well indeed. She was a single mother living in St Petersburg and managed two jobs in order to make ends meet. Her little boy was a lovely little chap who we would collect from school each day and whilst he was happily playing in his room, we would be playing a different sort of game in the living room. After a short while, she asked me if I would like to move in with her. This was awkward; despite being single, I was still under contract with the Royal Navy and I simply could not just leave. It was with great reluctance, therefore that we parted when the ship sailed from Florida for the last time. We continued to write for a few months before it sort of fizzled out. Long distance relationships are never very easy and I just didn't have the money to fly backwards and forwards to Florida on a date.

Later in the deployment, the ship visited the island of St Croix in the US Virgin Islands where we were berthed alongside in the town of Frederiksted opposite a huge ocean-going liner. Due to the perceived dangers of muggings by the Rastafarian population in the town, we were told only to go ashore in groups of five or more. Our LHOM, Dave Mchale, decided to go ashore alone on a hunting mission. Dave used to boast that he had a black belt in Aikido and none of us really wanted to question the fact. Dave had decided that if someone was silly enough to try and mug him, then he would win the contest and nick his woolly hat as a prize. Well that was the theory, he came back some time later unharmed but also empty-handed.

Sailing from St Croix, we tootled around for the week before calling in to the nearby island of St Thomas, berthing in the picturesque capital city of Charlotte Amalie. Five of us decided to hire scooters for the day and go off to explore the island. Having not ridden a motorbike since my little prang on 'Pincher's Yamaha RD250 I was a little shaky, but the small 50cc scooter was fairly easy to master and it wasn't long before we were heading out of town in convoy. One of the lads in the group, a young stoker by the name of Andy Tutchings, was telling us all about his younger days as a mod back in his native Solihull. Apparently, he claimed to have been the leader of a scooter gang. Knowing Andy, we didn't think this was very likely as his dad was a local well respected copper and crashing his scooter within the first couple of miles only confirmed the lie. The scooter only sustained minor damage so he was able to continue, though with bent handlebars, grazed knees and slightly dented pride.

The rest of us fared much better and had a wonderful day exploring the various beaches and coves around the island. As we had only rented the bikes for the day, they had to be back to the waterfront hire shop by 3pm so after returning them and Andy had lost his deposit, we found a bar on the boardwalk where we could recount the events of the day and take the piss out of a rather crestfallen Andy.

In the bar, we met a chap who had just opened a health spa just down the boardwalk. He invited myself and my best mate 'Buck' Taylor to come along and have a sauna, a massage and to generally relax from the rigors of a dusty day in the saddle. This sounded great and 'Buck' was all up for it. The chap escorted us to his health spa and introduced us to the receptionist and told them that we were very good friends and needed to be looked after. Happy Days!

We were shown into a changing room by a very lovely lady before a short while later, a naked 'Buck', wearing only a towel, was taken for a full body massage. Whilst he was in the treatment room, I was invited to relax in the jacuzzi and sauna until she had finished with 'Buck'. In due course, he returned with a beaming smile on his face. The advice he gave me was to feign a groin injury from playing rugby as apparently he had received a rather sensual massage centred on the groin area. Either 'Buck' was again massaging the truth or she just didn't believe me, either way all I received was a standard massage with no extras.

After we had both been massaged, we were invited to take a dip in their icy cold plunge pool before relaxing in the bar over a glass of wine. This seemed all very civilised. As there were no bar staff around, we helped ourselves to a couple of bottles of Mateus Rosé and settled in for the rest of the evening. The staff, wishing to get rid of us, eventually asked if there was anything else we needed. Taking the hint, we got dressed before being landed with a huge bill as we were leaving. The bill was well over two hundred dollars for both of us, which was about two hundred dollars more than we were expecting to pay. Rummaging in pockets, we managed to scrape together about forty dollars in notes and change but that didn't even come close to satisfying them. Fortunately, or unfortunately, depending on your point of view, I had my Access card in my wallet and ended up footing the entire bill. Gary did pay his share eventually after much prompting as my plastic card was starting to melt from its excessive use over the past few months.

During the visit to St Thomas, the ship organised a banyan to nearby Tortola in the British Virgin Islands. This was an excellent opportunity to get off the ship and visit another island for a barbeque and a piss up on the beach. Using the ship's Cheverton boat, a number of the lads, each armed with beach gear, sun tan lotion and a case of McEwan's Export were lowered from the boat deck onto the inky blue sea. Steered by one of the killick dabbers, after clearing the harbour, we motored away from the ship on a north easterly course towards Tortola, though, in reality, we had no real idea where we were heading, just trusting the dabber with his compass.

A few hours later, when most of us were a few cans into the case and feeling quite merry, he slowed the boat and inched closer to a seemingly deserted beach. Getting as close as he dared and not wishing to beach the sea boat, he dropped the small anchor before we each stripped off to our trunks and waded, chest deep, up onto the beach, holding a gash bag of beer, clothes and towels above our heads.

The beach was idyllic. There was nobody in sight and the decision to bring beer was well founded as there was absolutely no sign of civilisation. Somebody came up with the bright idea of burying the beer in the sand, near the shore to keep it cool. Digging a sizable hole, all but one of the cases of beer was buried and a palm frond used as a marker. Making a camp, a few of us then headed back out to the boat and brought ashore the barbeque gear and a plastic tub of meat to cook and set about lighting the charcoal.

With the barbeque still getting hot, towels were thrown down for goalposts and a game of Murderball ensued. This is like a cross between rugby and full contact football … with no rules. This was quite good fun and distracted us for about an hour until we were all knackered, had run out of beer and the food was ready.

It was at this point that we noticed that the tide had come in a bit, the palm frond marker had floated away and the beer was now buried, a good eighteen inches deep under the breaking surf and we had absolutely no idea, for sure, where to start digging first. It was a cock-up of biblical proprortions, but that didn't stop us trying to find it. The problem was, in that hour, everything about the beach had changed. The boat had moved position and the tide had come in, reducing the width of the beach by another two feet.

After a further hour of intermittently coming up with 'good ideas' and digging in another place, we were forced to admit defeat. The sea had claimed a total of nine whole cases of 'Red Death' otherwise known as McEwan's Export. Two hundred and sixteen 'grenades', as we called them, probably even now, lie rotting undiscovered under that beach in the British Virgin Islands. What a waste. After digging for the remainder of the afternoon in vain, we were forced to call off the search and endure a long, cold voyage back to the ship in the dark, sober.

On arrival back in Portsmouth a few weeks later, I was duty on the Friday meaning that I wouldn't be allowed to go home on short weekend leave until Saturday morning at the earliest. One of the killick stokers was also in the same situation. After calling the railway station, I learned that the best train to catch on Saturday morning was at 6:20am. We were not due to get relieved until 8am, which meant we both had to get a stand-in to cover our fire-fighting responsibilities for the remaining couple of hours. My mate, 'Rattler' Morgan who slept in the bunk below me was duty on the Saturday and Sunday and offered to assume the duty at 6am thus giving me time to make the train. I cleared this with the engine room POMEM who made the stipulation that 'Rattler' had to be awake, sober and dressed before I left the ship.

So, after completing an uneventful middle watch at 4am, I took a long shower and quietly packed my bag before waking him up with a cup of tea at 5:45am. 'Rattler' was dressed and sitting in the mess square drinking his tea as I handed over the duty to him. Following my brief, he simply said "I've got it, mate, have a good weekend." With that, I high-tailed it the short distance to the railway station before managing a few hours of sleep on the train.

On Monday morning, I was given an almighty bollocking by POMEM 'Harry' Hawkes for leaving the ship without his permission. When I explained that he had granted permission the previous night, he countered by saying that I hadn't woken him up to say that I was leaving the ship in the morning. The upshot of this was that myself and the killick were both getting trooped for being absent from place of duty. We both considered this a bit harsh but there was no arguing with him.

To this day, I still don't fully understand the reasoning, but we were both subsequently marched before the Captain and I was awarded an £18 fine, whereas the killick was awarded a £24 fine for the same offence. The difference being, because he was a higher rank he should have known better.

After a spot of real leave, Tartar was berthed in Portsmouth on Fountain Lake Jetty and once again Fleet Contingency Ship. I had arranged to meet a girl in Cox's Bar, which was a short walk outside of Unicorn Gate. She was a barmaid there, but on this particular Thursday, it was her night off. She had agreed to meet me there and then to go on to somewhere else. Where we went became irrelevant as she shot through, so there was I, Billy no-mates, standing in the corner of the bar drinking by myself and listening to the Juke Box. The lonely tranquillity was broken by a noisy drunken group of sailors clearly stopping for a couple of pints on their way into town. The Falklands Conflict was now over and the victorious troops and ships had returned home to a hero's welcome.

The ringleader was a big bloke wearing an HMS Glamorgan rugby jersey. He challenged the entire occupants of the bar to place a beer bottle standing upright further than he could without touching the floor. He then proceeded to demonstrate; standing on the oche in front of the dartboard and with an empty beer bottle in each hand, he 'walked' out on them like stilts until he was almost at full stretch. Placing one of the bottles, he transferred his now free hand to the neck of the other bottle and slid it back along the floor until he was able again to stand up. He promised to buy a pint for anyone that could better his impressive effort. It looked easy enough, but I thought I would watch some other efforts quietly from the relative safety of my barstool first before making a complete prat out of myself. Most of the younger lads had tried and failed miserably, until finally, the challenge was issued to me. With nothing but my pride to lose, I had a go. The first couple of times I ended up losing my balance and rolling about on the floor until I figured out what was going wrong and in a gargantuan effort managed to place my bottle further forward than his. True to his word, he first congratulated my persistence before going to the bar and buying me a pint. He introduced himself as Ken Gillard from HMS Glamorgan and said he had recently returned from the Falklands.

Sitting down with my new friend, I discovered that he was a Radio Operator from Cornwall and this was a rugby team run ashore. Whilst deep in conversation, one of the lads came over and said that they were moving on to another pub. Ken said he would catch up with them later in the evening. I told him to go with his shipmates, but he was having none of it and we continued to drink and chat. Approaching closing time, Ken asked if I would like to go to Beastie's with him. 'Beasties' was the nickname for an infamous night club in Southsea called the Bistro Club. Agreeing to the suggestion, he called a cab from the phone on the bar and off we went.

As the taxi pulled up outside the club, Ken asked for the fare to be put on his account and when I went to pay the entrance fee, Ken said he was a member and that I was his guest. Walking up the stairs into the club, Ken seemed to know everyone and we had a really good friendly evening of drinking and talking. Leaving the club quite drunk in the early hours, we decided to get a kebab and walk back to the dockyard along Southsea sea front, when all of a sudden, Ken said "Let's fight!" so with bits of salad and kebab flying everywhere, we wrestled on the ground drunk for about ten minutes. No punches were thrown and there was no animosity, just two blokes seemingly beating each other up ... For a laugh! When we got knackered, one of us called a truce before continuing, back towards Victory Gate. Outside HMS Vernon, the same thing happened again and also in the dockyard. It was really good fun to have a fight where nobody gets hurt.

As HMS Glamorgan was berthed behind HMS Tartar and because I was duty the following day, I invited my new-found friend on-board for a few drinks the following day, before I watched him wobble up the gangway and disappear inside the County-class Destroyer on the next jetty.

The following morning, I could barely function, but gradually recollections of the previous evening came back to me. At about 10am, as my hangover was starting to subside, I decided to call Ken and remind him of his invitation for lunchtime drinks often referred to as a DTS. The Quartermaster answered the phone on the Flight Deck. The exchange went something like this:

"Gangway HMS Glamorgan, Quarter Master speaking, can I help you?"

"Can I speak to RO Gillard please?"

"We don't have an RO Gillard on-board."

"Yes you do. I was out with him last night and saw him walk back on-board."
"Can you describe him?"
"Big bloke, blonde hair wearing an HMS Glamorgan rugby jersey."
"Hmmm …we don't have an RO Gillard on-board, but we do have a Lt Cdr Gillard."
"Er ... can I speak to him please?"
"Who's this speaking?"
"MEM Atkinson from HMS Tartar."
"…and you want to speak to Lt Cdr Gillard?"
"Yes please."
"Hmmm … please hold the line and I'll see if he wants to talk to you."

I then heard him pipe "Lt Cdr Gillard is requested to take a shore telephone call on the Flight Deck." Shortly afterwards, I heard the internal phone ring on Glamorgan and the QM say "Yes sir, ok, I'll tell him."

The Quartermaster came back on the phone. "He's in bed and will call you later on." Thanking the QM, I hung up thinking that was that. What appeared as jolly japes last night would look very different to a Lieutenant Commander in the cold light of day. Officers are not really supposed to socialise with damn ratings.

Shortly before midday, I answered a phone call. The voice simply said "I'm hung over!" "Serves you right ... Sir!" I replied. "Ah! You found out about that did you? Does it make a difference?" Frankly, it didn't. I had long hated the naval class system so this was quite refreshing.

Ken agreed to come into the mess for a few drinks on the understanding that I didn't expose him as an officer. The reason being, that ratings tend to behave very differently around officers and he wanted the lads to be their natural selves. This was agreed; Ken came into the mess and stopped for quite a few hours spinning dits, getting quite squiffy and generally having a really good time. We remained friends for many years, occasionally meeting up for a drink and a scrap.

The following day, we were activated as Fleet Contingency Ship. This meant amongst other things that my weekend leave had been stopped, so nobody was particularly happy. Apparently the conventional submarine HMS Otus had lost both diesel engines and was unable to dive. She was in a force 12 sea, limping back across the Bay of Biscay on the surface and we were assigned to support her and provide emergency assistance if it was required.

Two days later and we had sort of rendezvoused with HMS Otus. She was apparently about half a mile off the starboard beam, but with the rough weather, we couldn't see her and with all the surface clutter, didn't hold her on radar either.

In the south west approaches, it was incredibly lumpy; everyone not required to work was told to strap themselves into their bunks. The upper deck was out of bounds and just moving around the ship was becoming extremely hazardous. I was starting to feel a little queasy with the constant movement of the ship. One of the best remedies for seasickness that I have discovered is to focus on the fixed horizon. So with that in mind, I requested permission from the Officer of the Watch to look out of the window on the bridge.

The ship was having great difficulty making way in the rough seas. One minute the window was full of a grey overcast sky and in the next the sea filled the window as Tartar plunged into the depths of the trough. One of the lookouts suddenly shouted "There she is!" pointing out of the starboard bridge window. Looking to where he was pointing, I saw nothing but a rough sea. He kept on pointing and after a few seconds, as we were on top of one wave, HMS Otus was cresting another wave about half a mile away. It was only a fleeting glimpse, but I could clearly see people on the bridge, instantly feeling sorry for them, but I still failed to see why we were there and what good we could possibly do as they struggled home on battery power.

The following day, if anything, the storm had got worse. I came on for the morning watch in the gear room at 4am and wedged myself into my chair. An hour later, myself and the boiler room stoker were summoned to the MCR. The tiller flat bilge alarm had gone off meaning that sea water was somehow entering the compartment. Knowing the tiller flat as I did, I remembered that there was a vertical ladder leading through a round hatch up onto the quarterdeck. This was spring-assisted and held back by a spring clip. So, together with the boiler room stoker, we went aft, grabbing hand-holds as we went as the sea strived to throw us from our feet.

In the tiller flat, our assumptions were proved correct. The hatch was indeed open and every time the ship plunged into a wave, a full bore of water would pour through the hatch. Discussing the plan of action, we agreed that timing was everything. Immediately the water stopped, as I was senior, I would rush up the ladder and unclip the hatch whilst 'Smudge' grabbed my ankles from the bottom of the ladder. At the agreed signal, I quickly clambered up the ladder, getting my arms around the hatch and looping a finger into the retaining spring clip. I couldn't budge it; maybe it was panic, but it just wouldn't move. Then I felt the ship lurch, there was a tremendous shudder as Tartar effectively fell off the wave and came crashing back down into the sea again. Looking behind me, I saw a vertical wall of grey water and, clinging onto the hatch cover for dear life, I buried my head in my arms as the water hit me. Whilst I was effectively still underwater, I was hit in the side by something solid that knocked the wind out of me but strangely, despite it being dark, the water felt warm and I had the sensation of being pulled out of the ship. Clinging on, I still wrestled with the hatch until finally, as the ship lurched again, the clip came free. I realised that in the confusion I had wrapped my legs around the back of the ladder and 'Smudge' had disappeared. Soaked to the skin, I virtually fell down the ladder, clipping the hatch as I came. With the hatch now shut and clipped, the bilge level in the tiller flat was well above plate level, but the bilge eductor appeared to be slowly pumping it out. Leaving the compartment, I realised that the whole of the stokers mess were now out of bed. A lot of the light fittings had come down and everywhere I looked, there were books and cassettes lying on the deck having been thrown from their respective shelves by what later became known as the '5:30 shake'. The General Alarm had been sounded bringing the ship to 'Emergency Stations' which explained why the ship was now a frenzy of activity. Freezing cold, I resumed my watch in the gear room, still aching and shaking from my life-threatening experience. Dropping my cold and wet overalls in the machinery space, I investigated the pain in my right side, only to discover I had a huge bruise forming. I had no idea what had clobbered me, but it had caused me considerable pain.

Falling off the wave had broken the ship's back. We were now taking in water in three compartments and later discovered that we had a eighteen foot split in the ship's hull and one of the vertical deck stanchions amidships was now 'S' shaped. Breaking off from our escort duty, HMS Tartar limped back into Portsmouth as the perfect storm slowly abated.

Safely alongside in Portsmouth and duty one night. I was on watch during the Middle which was usually very boring punctuated on the hour with rounds of any running machinery. To ease the boredom between rounds, I would usually take a book to read, some biscuits and a cup of tea and put my feet up in the MCR on 2 Deck. During my three o'clock set of rounds, in an effort to hand over the watch in a good state, I started both HP air compressors to re-pressurise the high pressure air system up to the top of the band at 4000psi. All was going according to plan. I would shake my relief at about 3:40am and then do a final set of rounds, shutting the air compressors down in the process.

At about 3:30am, with my feet up, trying to finish a chapter in my book, there was an almighty bang, shortly followed by some black smoke pouring out of the engine room manhole into the MCR. Instantly realising that this was not good, I quickly secreted my book behind the panel and rushed down through the manhole where I discovered the starboard HPAC had burst into flames. This was not good at all. Worse still, it was still running and spewing hot oil around the area. Picking up the Machinery Space Broadcast I shouted "FIRE FIRE FIRE, fire in the engine room!" hoping that the Duty Electrical chap who I had seen wandering about would hear my pipe and come to assist. I needed first of all to shut down the machine, but realised, not for the first time, that the designers had erected a cat walk above the burning air compressor to the starter box. Fortunately, all 'Stop' buttons were shaped like mushrooms, so I was able twat the starter box with a broom head and at the third attempt managed to shut down the compressor. Instinctively I picked up an AFFF extinguisher and squirted foam all over the burning compressor. As this ran out after about forty seconds, I realised that I was still on my own and could easily be overcome by smoke. It goes against the grain, but coughing and spluttering, I ran away! Leaving the engine room I leapt up two ladders to the upper deck and seeing the sentries screamed at them "I've got a fire in the engine room!", The Boson's Mate turned to the Quartermaster and said quite calmly "I told you I could smell something!" Shouting something unrepeatable at them, I legged it back to the scene of the fire as I heard the Quartermaster make a main broadcast pipe alerting everyone on-board.

"FIRE FIRE FIRE, Fire in the engine room, location marking 4H, Attack Party muster at the scene of the fire, Support Party muster at the After Section Base."

Back in the engine room, I continued to fight the fire with another extinguisher. The black acrid smoke was becoming a real problem, but I seemed to be winning the battle. Within a couple of minutes, I was joined by my Chief, CMEMN 'Taff' Leader wearing overalls and flip flops having just rolled out of bed. He was shortly followed by the Attack BA wearing an ICABA set and very little else. Fortunately the fire was now under control.

Needless to say there was quite a bit to discuss at the watch handover. I got a bit of a Spanish Inquisition from 'Taff' Leader, but later got praise for my actions from the Marine Engineering Officer and the Captain for raising the alarm and fighting the fire single-handed.

There was a lot of political rhetoric going on at the time concerning the future of Portsmouth Dockyard. The morning after the fire, the Captain cleared lower deck to explain the situation that Portsmouth Dockyard could well be closing and as a result, the dry dock repairs to the hull would now be carried out, under contract, in Blackwall Dock in London's East End.

Due to the need for drivers whilst we were docked in London and because I had a civilian driving licence, I was sent to the Dockyard Garage in Pompey for a MoD Driving Test. This involved driving a three ton Bedford truck around Southsea until the instructor's heart or nerves couldn't stand it anymore. The award of the Admiralty Driving Permit meant that I could legally drive virtually any service vehicle. This was like having the use of a company car except not quite so grand but it came in very handy when the ship sailed in to the port of London a week later for repairs to the hull.

After docking down in London, I was placed into a Duty Driver's watchbill which was brilliant as it meant I got ashore every day. Ok there was a catch, I had to be in uniform and driving a dark blue minibus with Royal Navy plastered down the side. As Satnav and mobile phones hadn't been invented yet, I had the use of an A to Z road map of London and an ancient Clansman radio fitted under the seat so the ship could call me if I was needed.

Apart from dropping the lads to the pub, one of my first real jobs was to pick up a bus load of Admirals from Queen Anne's Gate at 1pm and bring them back to the ship. Setting off in good time, I drove down the East India Dock Road and then onto Commercial Road before getting to Aldgate where I tried, unsuccessfully, to turn right. Selecting the inner lane on the huge roundabout, I made my way round the roundabout before indicating left to leave at my exit but nobody would let me out. Having completed three circuits of the roundabout without success, I finally lost my rag and whilst indicating left, stopped in the middle of the road.

A uniformed policewoman who had heard the vehicles honking their horns at me, dodged the still moving traffic and tapped on my window "What's the problem, Jack?" Virtually at the end of my rope, I explained that I had fourteen admirals to pick up in a few minutes and couldn't get off this *fucking* traffic island. She replied quite sympathetically "Don't worry, mate, watch this," and holding out her arms, she stopped two lanes of traffic before pointing at me and waving me through the gap with a smile and a wink. I learned a valuable lesson about driving in London that day. Never give an inch.

Despite getting a bit lost and not being able to get off the roundabout, I arrived at my destination, in true naval fashion, five minutes before the allocated time. About twenty minutes later, when my passengers were good and ready; they emerged from the building and squeezed themselves into the minibus. The First Sea Lord, climbed into the passenger seat, moving my map to take his seat. "Afternoon, stokes," he said, noticing my branch badge, "Know where you are going?", "Sort of sir," I replied, pointing to the map. "No problem, you drive, I'll navigate." What a nice man. Despite the heavy traffic, we made good time back to the ship and I learned a few shortcuts into the bargain.

Most of my errands involved taking people to the pub or to the local tube station and picking them up at prearranged times. Usually, there would be a pint waiting for me on the bar as this was most definitely a cheap taxi. All in all, HMS Tartar spent a couple of months in dry dock at Blackwall before we were finally deemed seaworthy again. During that time, we were unfortunate enough to lose one of our shipmates. Leading Seaman 'Streaky' Bacon who somehow managed to miss the gangway as he was returning to the ship. He also missed the net that was slung underneath the gangway and fell headlong into the dry dock. By the time anyone reached him, sadly there was nothing that could be done.

One of the traditions in dealing with the tragic death of a shipmate is to auction off his kit and Streaky's was no exception. The sailor's mess organised the auction and arranged for a crate of free beer to entice people from other messes to come along and bid with their hard-earned cash. Each piece of kit was held up in turn and the bidding would usually start low at around 50p for a pair of steaming boots. It would then, usually, rise meteorically to thirty pounds, fifty pounds or sometimes even a hundred pounds depending upon the chap's popularity. Let's face it; nobody actually wanted a mouldy old pair of boots but the idea was one of compassion dating back hundreds of years to raise some money for his family or his widow. Personally, I bought the 3rd button down on a pair of 8's trousers for twenty pounds thus representing an increase in value of about £19.97, but it was all in a good cause. The mess would then raise a glass privately and toast their fallen shipmate. He was a nice bloke and the accident was indeed a tragedy.

Leaving Blackwall Dock with all compartments watertight again, we headed out of London steering a westerly course back towards Portsmouth. Watchkeeping in the gear room during the forenoon, I became aware that 'KATY' was sounding rather rough and up in the Switchboard, it was noticed that the gas TA was having difficulty holding its load. Shutting it down, I was soon joined by a handful of 'tiffs', who after checking the evidence of the readings and where the noise was coming from, decided, as 'tiffs' do, to take '*her*' to bits. By the end of the day, it was clear what the problem was; 'KATY' had shed all of the blades on '*her*' HP Turbine. The rotor looked to me like a huge corn on the cob that had been eaten and the blades that had been shed were all chewed up in the bottom of the turbine casing looking like little golden corn flakes, clearly this was not good and needless to say, it couldn't be repaired as we didn't carry a spare on-board.

This was obviously going to put us alongside in short order. So, after some frantic signals ashore and calls to the shore procurement agency we arrived back in Portsmouth where a new turbine turned up and the 'tiffs' set about installing it. It took quite a while as the old turbine had to be painstakingly reconstructed to ensure that all the bits of turbine blading had been found and accounted for. It was explained to me that a tiny piece of blade left in the casing would be thrown around the casing like a ball in a pinball machine causing the new turbine to suffer the same fate as the old one. After a week of constant work, the new turbine was installed and when 'KATY' was finally flashed up, she worked like a dream.

Having been on-board now for over a year, strong friendships had been formed. Steve Dormer and his gorgeous wife Jenny used to regularly invite me around to their house for tea, Sunday lunch, a haircut or simply just to watch the TV as a welcome break from staying on the ship in the evenings. As I could drive and had a car, it was easy to get around to their married quarter in Rowner. To repay their hospitality and also to save them a taxi fare, I often used to take them shopping. Jenny was very bubbly, quite short and very cuddly with a squeaky southern accent. As a home hairdresser, she would occasionally, if she thought I needed it, just get a towel and start cutting my hair. Unfortunately, her husband, Steve, although bearded, was quite follicly challenged on top, so Jenny needed to recruit me as her haircutting test bed. It suited me as I then didn't have pay to go to the barbers and she was actually rather good. In short, I became part of their family.

Jenny originally came from Hayling Island where her parents still lived and this is where her twenty first birthday party was due to be held. Of course I received an invitation and also a request to drive them the twenty miles or so over to her dad's place. The plan was to dump the car, enjoy the party and then crash at Jenny's dad's place when we were all suitably pissed and incapable after the party.

The party was actually hilarious; Jenny was very drunk probably before the party even started. Grabbing hold of Steve in one hand and me in another, she proclaimed, very loudly, to all that would listen, in her squeaky Barbara Windsor voice, "I'm going three in a bed tonight." Of course, I didn't actually think it would happen, but Jenny was very drunk and Steve had consented to let her enjoy her birthday how she wished.

Well it didn't turn out quite like that; in fact there were four of us eventually crammed together under a king-size quilt on the floor. In fairness, I actually started out fully-clothed in a chair with Steve sandwiched between Jenny and her sister Sarah on the floor. Jenny told me to come and join them, as it would be slightly more comfortable on the floor than curled up in a chair. Getting the nod from Steve, I took position at the right hand side with Jenny on my left. At that point we were all fully-clothed until Jenny tugged at my belt and, after struggling for a bit, removed my trousers. She then instructed both Steve and myself to unclip and to remove a stocking each. After I had dutifully obeyed her order, she then told me to remove her suspender belt, but whilst doing this, she grabbed my hand and thrust it inside her panties. At the same time, she had worked her hand inside my pants. I was a bit worried about Steve's reaction, but he was totally oblivious to his wife's naughtiness as he was also *busy* entertaining Sarah who didn't seem to mind too much either. So for the next half an hour or so, we kissed and cuddled and mutually pleasured each other until we were all too knackered to continue and fell asleep.

I awoke on the Sunday morning with a seriously baggy head. All four of us were largely naked with panties, bras, trousers, shirts and stockings littering the lounge floor. I must say, in the cold light of day, I felt quite awkward with my mate still sleeping the other side of his slowly stirring wife.

Grabbing some pants, I trudged off to the kitchen to make tea for everyone and by the time I got back, everyone had at least got their underwear on and were slowly identifying and retrieving clothes from around the room. I had a quiet word with Steve to see if he was ok and unbeknown to me, this was part of his birthday present to his wife who had apparently long fantasised about a threesome. I was flattered that she chose me to indulge her fantasy. Steve also confessed later, that he had always fancied his sister-in-law and although it never happened again, we all agreed that it was a brilliant party.

Shortly after the party, we sailed to Gibraltar as the Guard Ship. It was nice to get back to Gib and my old stomping ground and it wasn't long before I was ordering a pint in my local, 'The Birmingham Arms' and reacquainting myself with Dennis the landlord.

Whilst in Gib, HMS Tartar entered a period of Assisted Maintenance called an AMP. This was good news for us as the ship again adopted 'Tropical Routine' meaning that we would be finished by 2pm allowing us the rest of the afternoon to enjoy the weather.

In the engine room, we had the main condenser open at each end and were busy sighting and cleaning the many tubes. To save water, all steam turbines have a condenser slung underneath them to condense the used steam and turn it back into clean usable water which the boiler could in turn boil back up again into superheated steam. The steam enters the condenser at the top and passes over banks of tubes that carry cool sea water thus condensing it back into water. Occasionally a tube would block up with seaweed or perhaps a trapped fish but more often than not, they would corrode allowing sea water to contaminate the clean condensed water. These tubes would then need to be identified and plugged at each end as changing the condenser was almost impossible.

It was for that reason in the summer of 1983 that I was in the forward end of the condenser systematically sighting the many small bore tubes with a torch. My oppo was at the other end of the condenser peering down the tube looking for the light. After successfully confirming that a tube was intact and clear, it would have a lump of chalk ground into it to mark it as complete before we moved onto the next tube. It was long and uncomfortable work working in the close confines of the condenser dome with the added disadvantage that I might lose my footing and fall into the sea water inlet that was about two feet in diameter and full of seawater. The only human access was a small manhole that I had previously wriggled through after I had removed the door.

The job was going quite well. We decided that it would be better for us to work through 'Stand Easy', and get the job finished. The promise was that when we were finished and the doors were buttoned up, we could knock off work a bit earlier. However, shortly after 10am I heard a muffled pipe "D'ya hear there, Captain speaking..." I couldn't hear the detail from inside the condenser, but it was a long broadcast by the old man himself, so it must be serious. Poking my head out of the hole, I asked the engine room killick who was overseeing the job "What's going on mate?" His reply was a curt "We are going to sea, mate, so if you don't get your arse out of there pronto, I'm going to seal you in." I didn't need telling twice and with some difficulty I managed to slither out. "Taff Leader," the engine room chief, was now in the engine room "Right Plug, get yourself into the gear room, flash the donkey boiler, flash the evap on live steam and get 'KATY' on load; quick as you can lad."

From the serious look on his face, this was not open to discussion. With wet, slimy and smelly overalls, I left the engine room at the run and slid down the ladder into the gear room. The first job was to get the Stone-Vapor donkey boiler flashed so we would have steam. This was a relatively simple process and within minutes I was making low pressure steam. Whilst this was happening, I was starting the various pumps and filling the evaporator with sea water sufficiently slow enough to allow it to boil. Opening up the steam to the evaporator, it was now a matter of time waiting and tweaking here and there whilst the sea water heated up, and the vapour created was condensed into fresh water.

While I was waiting, I climbed over the catwalk aft of the gearbox and prepared 'KATY' for flashing. Obtaining permission from the MCR, I slowly turned the control wheel that started the process which would quickly bring the Allen's 500kw gas turbine alternator into service.

Elsewhere in the ship, everyone on-board was bustling around doing something positive to get the ship to sea. In the engine room, the G6 gas turbine had been flashed and the engine brought to immediate notice for sea. The dabbers were busy preparing to let the ropes go that were holding us to the wall.

In the gear room, everything was going according to plan. 'KATY' was flashed and on load providing electricity to the ship. The donkey boiler was making steam and the evaporator was now making good clean water. POMEM 'Harry' Hawkes popped down the gear room to see how I was progressing and told me what the problem was.

Apparently, some Spanish criminals had illegally crossed the border into Gibraltar carrying guns and drugs, they had stolen a motor cruiser and were heading out to sea. Flag Officer Gibraltar, on receiving the request from the Gibraltarian Government, had sent a signal to HMS Tartar's Captain ordering the ship to give chase, intercept and board her before apprehending the criminals and returning them back to Gibraltar.

This was quite exciting. Following receipt of the signal, the Captain made the pipe that I had missed and twenty-eight minutes later, Tartar passed through the breakwater in pursuit of the stolen boat. In all of the excitement and due to the time of day, many of the ship's company were ashore queuing up for pasties and pies and failed to either hear or understand the significance of four blasts on the siren. We therefore sailed with only about half of the crew on-board not knowing when we would return.

In the boiler room, the watchkeepers already had a flame in the boiler and were working as hard to raise steam and in turn bring the steam turbine into service. The condenser I had been working inside had now been resealed but it was still about four hours before the boiler was making sufficient steam to spin the steam turbine and in turn assist the G6 in driving the ship.

Meanwhile, with Tartar now at sea and well out of sight, the remainder of the ship's company were sporadically returning to an empty jetty. We later heard there were comments such as "I'm sure I parked it here," and other dry witticisms were muttered amongst those that had been left behind.

With steam now raised, HMS Tartar continued the chase at full speed. The ship's 'Wasp' helicopter was launched to visually acquire the motor cruiser and to radio back her exact position, course and speed. The chase continued well into the afternoon until we received intelligence that the motor cruiser had now entered Portuguese territorial waters. Without the diplomatic clearance to follow, we were reluctantly forced to abandon the chase and hand over jurisdiction to the Portuguese Navy. Returning back to Gibraltar, arriving back alongside sometime after 7pm, we were greeted with, amongst other things, "Where the fuck have you lot been?"

During our time in Gibraltar, we had many good run-ashores. It was customary for a small group of us to do what we called 'A Set of Rounds'. This would typically start in 'The Birmingham Arms' where we would just have one drink before walking around the corner to the 'London Bar' for another drink. Then we might wander down to see Charlie at 'The Hole in the Wall' before getting back onto Main Street and having a drink in 'The Barrel House'. Walking back up the street, we would call in to 'The Bat and Ball' for a swift one and finally up to 'The Horseshoe' before going back to 'The Birmingham Arms to start all over again. There were so many drinking houses to choose from, but these were our favourite watering holes. Whilst conducting a set of rounds, we never stopped for more than one drink before moving on but drinking could go on late into the night or even into the morning. It was conceivable in Gibraltar that someone could get a full twenty four hours of drinking in, if they had the constitution for it. This would usually finish up at a bar called 'Loopys' that would happily serve a pint with breakfast as early as 6am.

During one such set of rounds, I was out with 'Buck' Taylor and after putting the world to rights over several hours decided to finish the night off at 'Buccaneers', which was a night club near HMS Rooke's football pitches below the Piazza. Uncharacteristically, the place was dead. There was only a handful of people in the club and the dance floor was deserted except for one solitary woman dancing by herself. In typical form, 'Buck' said "Don't wait up," and got up to dance with her. Whilst admiring his confidence and courage, I couldn't help but notice that a chap sitting to my right was getting increasingly annoyed. Asking him what the problem was, he replied that 'Buck' was dancing with his wife. Getting his attention, I beckoned him over and after informing him of his obvious mistake, he didn't bat an eyelid, simply went to the bar, bought a pint of beer and placing it in front of the chap said "Sorry mate, no hard feelings."

The free beer had the desired effect of pacifying the chap and before long, the four of us were getting along like old mates. He was called Raymond Blunt and his wife was Rose. He claimed to be a Company Sergeant Major with the Duke of Yorkshire Regiment that was currently on detachment in Gibraltar. As the evening wore on, we learned that they lived in the married quarters not too far away. Excusing myself to go to the loo, I noticed that the club had now filled considerably from the time we had entered; but when I returned, 'Buck', Rose and Raymond were nowhere to be seen. After spending some time looking around the club, getting annoyed at being deserted, I decided to go back on-board. Leaving the club, I noticed some way off, Rose & Raymond walking back towards the married quarters, but there was no sign of 'Buck'.

The following morning, I was still very annoyed with 'Buck' for just buggering off without me. Playing the innocent, 'Buck' asked me where I had disappeared to as he had gone back to their place and shagged Rose whilst Raymond had watched. Believing this to be utter bollocks, I ridiculed him as a liar in front of the entire mess at stand easy. This obviously pissed him off so 'Buck' said "Right, tonight we will have a carbon copy run-ashore and we will see who is lying!"

Later that day, childish as it sounds, we did everything exactly the same as the previous evening even down to getting the same 'Big Eats' from the greasy spoon in the Piazza. Everything was going according to plan. 'Buck' was getting more and more excited as the evening progressed until we finally paid to enter Buccaneers for the second night in a row only to find the place virtually deserted again. Getting a drink, we settled down to wait for them to arrive. It just never occurred to us that perhaps they might not have two nights out in a row. By 2:30am, I was ready for bed and wanted to go back to the ship, but 'Buck' was adamant that he wasn't lying and *needed* to prove it to me. He finally said, "Look, I know where they live, so let's go and knock on the door?" This seemed like a crazy idea, but there was no stopping him in his quest to prove his innocence to me.

Half an hour later and he was knocking on doors at the married quarters in Edinburgh House. At the third attempt, he struck lucky when Rose answered the door in a nightie, having clearly just woken up. She reluctantly let us in and showed us into the living room where she explained that Raymond was still asleep in the bedroom.

Fetching a bottle of Cinzano Bianco from the kitchen we sat and chatted for a while. Rose leaving nothing to the imagination in her skimpy nightie, said after a short while that she'd better go and wake Raymond up. Leaving us alone in the lounge, she went to wake Raymond whilst 'Buck' told me the plan of action. I was well versed with 'Buck's ambitious plans as they never worked out anyway. As usual, I would just go with the flow and see what happened.

Raymond entered the room a short while later looking very bleary-eyed and frankly a bit confused. Following the formalities, 'Buck' asked him to step out into the hallway for a quiet word. I wasn't privy to the conversation, but surprisingly, I heard Raymond say "It's alright with me, mate, but we'd better ask Rose. Rose, love, can you come here a minute?" Left on my own in the living room, I heard Rose say "I don't know, I can take two, but not three." With this apparently agreed, 'Buck' came back into the lounge to appraise me of the situation, "We are going into the bedroom now, mate, give it twenty minutes and then come in, she won't know what's going on by then anyway," before leaving me alone with the remainder of the bottle of Cinzano Bianco.

Within five minutes I was waiting at the door, watching the clock tick by awfully slowly whilst listening to sounds of lovemaking from the bedroom. The door was slightly ajar, and I was trying to nudge it open ever so slightly when abruptly, the noises stopped and I was beginning to think that I had missed the boat. Without warning, the bedroom door was suddenly opened wide and there was Rose, absolutely stark naked except for a pillow held in front to spare her blushes. She simply said "Excuse me!" and pushed past me followed by two naked blokes apparently competing in a flagpole competition.

In the lounge, with the main light switched off, the only illumination was the orange glow from the electric fire. Taking the initiative, 'Buck' laid on the floor with his head on the pillow before Rose straddled him. Raymond opted to try the rear entrance, whilst noticing me standing at the door with gaping mouth, Rose invited me to join the party by using me as a lollipop.

After a short while, she simply said "All change" as we changed position at the start of a round robin. After qualifying in all disciplines over the course of an hour, I was completely shagged. Rose and Raymond invited us to get cleaned up and finish our drinks whilst they went back to bed.

About twenty minutes later, fully dressed, we dropped the latch before walking back to the ship in the early morning light, thoroughly pleased with ourselves. I also vowed to clear 'Buck's name in the mess as it was now clear he was not bullshitting.

Back on-board and grabbing a quick shower, we both went to bed to enjoy a lazy Sunday morning sleeping off the aftereffects of too much drink and lack of sleep. Unfortunately, that was not the end of the story. I was rudely awoken by the Leading Hand of the Mess shortly after 8am, "You're wanted in the Reg Office, get up and get dressed!" The Regulating Office was our on-board Police Station and manned by the Master-at-Arms and his Leading Regulator. Getting up, I quickly dressed in my No8 uniform consisting of dark blue trousers and a lighter blue long-sleeved shirt with the sleeves rolled up to above the elbow. I was then escorted to the Regulating Office by the killick of the mess and told to wait outside where 'Buck' was already waiting.

After about five minutes, the door opened to reveal the Master-at-Arms and two gentlemen in civilian suits. One of the chaps walked out and said to 'Buck' "Follow Me," and off they went. I was invited into the Regulating Office and told to sit down. The Master-at-Arms then left, shutting the door behind him. This was getting scary as I had no idea who this bloke was or what I had done wrong. The remaining gentleman identified himself as a Lieutenant Colonel in the S.I.B; this is like an armed forces version of the Police's C.I.D.

I was immediately asked by the Lt Col to account for my movements during the previous evening. I was hardly about to admit to this senior officer that we had been up to naughty stuff with another bloke's wife whilst he watched, so, lying through my teeth, I just said that myself and 'Buck' had gone ashore for a couple of drinks before popping back to a friend's house for a coffee. The Lt Col peered over his glasses, clearly not believing a word of my cock and bull story. After I had finished my fabricated version of events, he simply said "Now then, let's have the truth shall we? We know exactly where you were, exactly what you were doing and exactly who with. What we don't have is a transcript of the conversation." I was absolutely flabbergasted; I didn't know quite how to respond. He tried to help me out by asking if Raymond had questioned us about our ship or its armaments. I thought this was quite amusing as we were members of one the oldest ships afloat in the Royal Navy. Unfortunately for me, Mr S.I.B blokey was deadly serious. Apparently, they had had their flat under video surveillance for some time now recording the various comings and goings. Apparently Sergeant Major Blunt was suspected of being a Russian spy and also of selling information to the Soviets. Shit! This was serious. He warned me that if I was convicted of passing over sensitive material, I could spend years imprisoned in Moorish Castle, in Gibraltar. It wouldn't be an understatement to say that I was shitting myself and after learning the consequences of aiding a Russian spy, I decided to spill the beans. Of course there was no conversation other than sexy stuff to discuss, but like the true pervert he most probably was, he wanted to know every little detail with questions such as "...and did you get a blow job too?" Of course he already knew the answers to these questions having seen the movie, he just needed the soundtrack.

Back in the mess, myself and 'Buck' were absolute heroes. Somebody was singing the theme song to the James Bond movie 'The Spy Who Loved Me' in the background and everybody wanted to know all the gossip. At the end of 'Buck's interview, apparently he asked "I suppose that means we cannot go back?" Surprisingly, the reply was "Of course you can go back, but be aware, we will be watching and we will need to talk to you again." We never went back.

On another run ashore with 'Buck' Taylor and another mate 'Jan' Burge, they spent seemingly a whole evening persuading me to get the remainder of my AMCs completed with the promise of elevated status in the mess and a few more shillings in my pocket. After much badgering and having worn me down, I agreed that I would see the Chief Stoker and start my HP air compressors AMC having recently extinguished a fire on one of them.

True to my word, I knocked on the CMEM's door and after asking, received a thin booklet that would give an introduction and then set tasks on learning about the Revell's 4000psi HP Air Compressor. Having operated them on numerous occasions, it didn't take me long to complete the small exam that I sat in mid-August 1983.

This success spurred me on and a week later, I had completed the AMC on 'KATY', the 500kw gas turbo alternator.

My watchkeeping position was in the gear room but not actually on the gearbox. Having now recently passed my Evaporators AMC, I was trusted to make water using one of the ship's two twin shell distillers and though I do say so myself, I did it rather well making about a ton and a half of fresh water per hour. I also operated the Stone-Vapor 'Donkey' Boiler when it was required and also on the starboard side of the gear room, an Allen's 500kw Gas Turbo Alternator called 'KATY' or K TA standing for the Turbo Alternator in Kilo section. It was a fairly lonely existence as I had to spend four hours alone on watch only reporting to the MCR on the hour with readings for the Master Log and to get a cup of tea. Whilst on watch, I took the opportunity to learn the systems in the gear room and was consequently the only stoker to gain the coveted AMC on 'KATY'.

Having gained the AMC, this didn't stop me making an embarrassing cock up during a middle watch. One of the watchkeeping routines, during the hours of darkness was to clean the gas turbine's compressors and power turbine, by introducing a kilo bag of walnut chippings called 'Carboblast' which would subsequently fly out of the after funnel as carbon blackend grit. There was a convenient hopper sited on top of the machine with a screwed cap that allowed me to funnel in the 'Carboblast'. With permission once the ship was facing into wind, I would then open up the outlet valve and then introduce low pressure air into the hopper to force the chippings through the gas turbine.

After a few minutes, I isolated the air and opened up the hopper to check that all of the 'Carboblast' had gone. Noticing that a third of it still remained, in a moment of absent-minded stupidity, thinking that I'd watch it go down, I opened up the air again.

The 'Carboblast', however, had other ideas though and taking the path of least resistance, it shot upwards, sandblasting my face before covering the starboard side of the gearbox with thousands of light brown chippings that took me ages to sweep up. Admitting to the fuck up during my hourly visit to the

Machinery Control Room, caused much laughter from the Chief of the Watch and the other lads.

On another occasion, I had sneaked a book on watch with me, secreted in my overalls to help pass the time. Once my rounds were completed, I had the better part of thirty minutes to kill so out came the book from its hiding place. I was soon sat on my box seat, deeply engrossed in my book when "Gear room, MCR" came over the broadcast. Without thinking, I reached behind me for the microphone "Gear room" I replied. "What you doing?" "Reading a book" was my instinctive and truthful answer before it dawned on me what I had just admitted to. "What are you reading?" Never being very good at thinking on my feet, I replied "A Bridge Too Far." There was a pregnant pause of a couple of seconds before I was ordered "Report to the MCR and bring your book with you." I got a bollocking, the book was confiscated so the Chief of the Watch could read it and I was then sent back down my hole with orders to do a full set of rounds without my cup of tea.

Concentrating on learning my trade, I now found myself in an unspoken competition with my peers, working hard on my training for perhaps the first time in my career subsequently saw me elevated to the dizzy heights of AMC Stoker in September having completed another seven AMCs.

I was now on a roll, so when the Chief Stoker asked who wanted to sit the latest round of promotion boards for Leading Hand, I volunteered. Studying hard, I gave it a gargantuan effort. I had nothing to lose but my pride. It is a standard practice for promotion examinees, to sit a dummy board first of all as failure is not recorded and any shortfalls can then be rectified before sitting the actual written examination and subsequent oral board.

The dummy written paper a few weeks later was my first formal examination, but despite not being able to answer a question about the operating parameters of an Air Conditioning Plant, I didn't waste much effort, doing just enough to pass. The subsequent dummy oral board was horrendous; I was asked loads of questions that I simply couldn't answer. I came out of the dummy examination totally crestfallen; my confidence took a major hit as I questioned if I was ready for this big step. Surprisingly however, the CMEM took me to one side to tell me how well I'd done and how impressed he was.

Learning many lessons from the Dummy Board, I was much better prepared for the real thing. A week later I sat and completed a good written paper with a percentage mark well into the eighties. Knowing full well that I would be hammered on the things I had got wrong a week later in the Oral Board, I spent every hour revising and asking questions of those around me.

The Oral Board for promotion to LMEM finally took place on 13th December 1983 as we transited away from Gibraltar and headed back home for Christmas leave. Sitting in the MEO's cabin with his deputy and the CMEM was a nerve-wracking experience, but they did their best to put me at ease. With sweating palms, I tried to answer everything to the best of my knowledge, applying educated guesses when I didn't know or couldn't remember the required answer. After about an hour, as is customary, I was asked to wait outside the cabin whilst my fate was discussed.

After what appeared to be ages, but was in actual fact about five minutes, I was invited back in and asked to sit. The MEO asked me how I thought the board had gone. What do you say to that? If I said "Really well, sir," and then he told me that I had failed, I would look quite stupid. Alternatively, if I said "Terrible, sir," and I had passed, that would leave them doubting my own suitability. In the end, I opted for a neutral statement "I think it went ok, sir. I tried to answer everything to the best of my knowledge." He responded by saying that the board could not agree and that a 'tie-breaker' question would decide my fate. Bloody Hell! How unfair is that! Left with no option, the MEO turned round and looking out of the porthole in his cabin, he asked "What country is that?" gesturing toward the thin stretch of coastline that was barely visible on the horizon. Shit! I had a choice of three, France, Spain or Portugal. Having only recently departed from Gibraltar, we couldn't have got far. Reasoning that we would not see a lot of the Spanish coast and would only see the French coast of Brittany as we crossed the Bay of Biscay, I opted for Portugal. "Congratulation's, lad, we are pleased to tell you that you've passed." I have no idea to this day, what would have happened if I had given a different answer.

It is traditional on these occasions to buy beer for the mess to celebrate and as all of the candidates that day had passed, there was much celebrating to do. I am afraid to say that I got a little squiffy.

After Christmas leave, I learned that there had been a cancellation on a ship's divers course and was asked if I would like to earn some extra cash. Ship's divers, after spending so many minutes underwater each month, were awarded a considerable bonus in their pay packets. The job appealed to me anyway, but the extra money would always come in handy, so I agreed.

The following week, with a few other lads from HMS Tartar, we were transported by bus to the Royal Navy Diving Training Centre at Horsea Island near Port Solent. As it was January and seriously cold, I didn't much fancy the idea of getting immersed beneath a frozen lake. In fact a couple of chaps were out in a boat as we arrived, smashing the thin ice with oars to break it up before the sun rose onto the lake.

After the introductions, we were ushered into a classroom for a quick overview of the Aquarius diving set and the programme for the day's diving aptitude. Clearly, not all volunteers are suitable for the training so the day was designed to weed out the unsuitable candidates. I didn't know it at the time, but I would be the only failure of the day.

Striping down to my pants, I was given first of all a thin white thermal suit followed by a thicker green fleecy suit. With these in place, I now had to squeeze into a grey thick rubber dry suit with neoprene cuffs and also a removable neoprene neck seal that was finally attached to the diving suit by a large metal band that dug into my shoulders. We were also issued diving fins and ordered to climb to the top board of the diving platform overlooking the freezing cold lake and await further instructions.

Forming a line, with my left hand holding on to the metal ring around my neck and the right hand grasping the wrist of the other, I was ordered to stand at the edge of the abyss before being ordered in a loud commanding voice "Facing Portsmouth, one pace forward... March!" as I complied, I instantly plunged feet-first twenty feet down into the icy water below.

After getting totally immersed in the sub-zero salt water, I bobbed to the surface like a cork as the air trapped in the suit aided my buoyancy. With all of the class eventually in the water, we were instructed collectively to sit up in the water using the buoyancy of the suit and put the fins on our feet. That done, we were then told, using only our legs, to power backwards across the lake to the other side and after removing the fins climb out and run around the edge back to the start point. Knackered, we were again ordered back to the top of the diving platform to do it all again until we had each been across the lake three times. Despite being quite fit at the time, I was still exhausted, but everyone managed it.

After a brief rest to get our breath back, we were each given an Aquarius breathing set but this time entered the water slowly by means of a rusty metal ladder on the side of the lake. Putting the fins on whilst wearing the diving set was more of a challenge but once done, we could easily tread water whilst breathing off the set. The next instruction was to raise our left arm high out of the water and with the right hand pull the neoprene seal away thus allowing the trapped air in the suit to escape, essentially vacuum-packing us into our own rubber packages as we then started to slowly submerge for the first time on air.

As I became aware of my surroundings, I also noticed my left arm getting steadily wetter. I had now reached the bottom of the lake at a depth of about twelve feet and whilst my colleagues were swimming around the various objects placed on the bottom to explore, I had to clumsily walk around as my suit gradually became heavier as it filled with water. Whilst being uncomfortable, I wasn't particularly worried as I had a tank full of air on my back and if needs be, I could just wander across the bottom of the lake and up the far rocky slope. A diving instructor swam over and, noticing that I appeared to be anchored to the bottom of the lake, motioned me towards the metal ladder before I started my slow, heavy ascent out of the water.

It transpired that whilst venting my suit, I had inadvertently put my fingers through the neoprene cuff seal causing my suit to flood. This caused quite a bit of laughter as I was slowly emptied out before I could finally get out of the suit. As a result of this, I failed the diving aptitude and frankly, I was never gladder to fail anything than I was at that particular time.

Back at the ship the following week, we learned the sad news that the three Tribal-class frigates, HMS Tartar, HMS Zulu and HMS Gurkha were to be decommissioned and sold to the Indonesian Navy. So, the following week, we sailed again for one last trip before coming back to Portsmouth in early March 1984. We arrived back into Portsmouth in Procedure Alpha with the ship's company lining the decks in full dress uniform before the MEO made the immortal pipe "Total Steam Failure, Total Steam Failure; The flame has gone out in the boiler for the last time," to rapturous cheers from the ship's company. After a few weeks of de-storing and de-fuelling the ship, HMS Tartar finally decommissioned on Thursday March 29th 1984.

There was still much work to do until she was formally handed over to the Indonesians. The Captain left the ship and the MEO took over command whilst we got the ship ready to sell.

At the time, I was lodging in the spare room of my old mate Steve 'Pincher' Martin and his lovely wife Diana. Steve had recently been discharged from the Navy on medical grounds but still lived in Gosport. I therefore travelled into work each day on my racing bike. Going to work in the morning, I would cycle down Forton Road and into Clarence Yard where I would lock up my bike and catch a PAS boat across the water, finally walking the short distance to where the ship was berthed. Reversing the route, one evening, there was a Ministry of Defence policeman waiting for me next to my bike that was chained up to a fence near the landing jetty along with many others.

"Is this your bike, sir?" he asked. "Yes," I replied, "is there a problem?" "I don't know sir; can I see your padlock?" Unlocking my bike, I handed him the small padlock which he quickly examined. "There is a Naval Stores Number on this lock; can you tell me where you got it from?" After I had answered, he told me to cycle up to the main gate and to wait for him there.

As I approached the main gate, another MoD policeman called out "MEM Atkinson?" "Yes that's me" "Put your bike there, sir and please come with me." I was shown into an interview room and told to wait until the first policeman joined me.

I was asked the usual, name, rank and serial number questions before he said "Right! Tell me where you got this padlock from?" "The stores on board," I replied. "Did you tell them what it was for?" "No!" I replied. "If you had have told them what it was for, would they still have given it to you?" Knowing full well that they would have given it to me and not wishing to incriminate anyone else, I replied with a question "Do I have to answer that?" "No you don't lad. I used to be in the Navy myself, so I know how it works." This struck me as rather odd, as matelots either in the job or retired tend to look after their own.

After my grilling, I was eventually allowed to cycle home without my padlock and chain, so when I got home and told Steve of my adventures, he simply said "I'm a civilian now and this is a civvy house, so they will need a civvy search warrant to come in here."

As it turned out, that wasn't needed, though it did worry me for a bit as the house was a bit like an annex to Naval Stores; with all manner of 'borrowed' spanners and tools. The following day, I went and confessed to the MEO, who thanked me for bringing it to his attention and told me not to worry.

About that time, after much consideration and discussions with my mum and dad, I had decided to volunteer for service in submarines. They had always fascinated me, but the added draw was a sack full of cash on successful completion of the Submarine Escape Training Tank. As it happened, there were two of us, myself and MEM 'George' Pringle that both applied and received manning clearance for submarines.

I left HMS Tartar on Tuesday the 5th June 1984 with the padlock incident seemingly forgotten about. I was only on there for a little over two years, but it was my most memorable sea job to date. I had a great many adventures and achieved a great deal. I doubted at the time that I would ever enjoy a draft as much as my time on the 'Good Ship Tartar'.

FMG PORTSMOUTH

6th June 1984 to 22nd October 1984

Leaving HMS Tartar, already passed for promotion to Leading Hand and a volunteer for submarines, I was now getting quite experienced having been in the Navy for over five years. I had visited many countries and experienced many adventures. Whilst awaiting a submarine course to start the next chapter in my career, I was drafted to the Fleet Maintenance Group at the North Corner of Portsmouth Dockyard.

The joining routine was now becoming a familiar dockyard run--around. The idea was quite simple; I was handed a sheet of paper with my name on the top and a series of boxes that all represented a different department, each had to be visited and the box rubber-stamped. Only when the sheet had all the boxes stamped by the correct departments was the joining routine considered complete. I was required to visit the Sickbay, the Dentist, the Car Pass Office, the Accommodation Office, the Bedding Store, the Pay Office and finally the MACCO. Whilst in the MACCO, I had been assigned to a duty watch when the Wren behind the counter said nonchalantly "Oh, you've got a charge outstanding; I will put you on Defaulters on Thursday." Bugger! It had been a few weeks since the padlock incident on HMS Tartar and naively, I assumed it would have been forgotten about. No such luck.

The following Thursday morning after spending most of the night pressing my white front, and suit and polishing my shoes to a high gloss finish, I presented myself to the Regulating Office in HMS Nelson at 8am looking as smart as a Guard's Van for a briefing before seeing the Commander. Apparently, I would be told to do everything, all I had to do was to listen and follow the instructions.

Standing smartly to attention outside the improvised courtroom where the Commander would hear the case, I was quaking in my boots. I had only met my new Divisional Officer about two days previously, so it would be fair to say he was going to cuff any character reference he would read in my defence.

Finally, the door was opened and my Divisional Officer was called into the room and the door shut behind him. After a few moments, the door opened again:

"MEM Atkinson!" the Leading Regulator shouted

"Sir," I replied in a loud and seemingly confident voice, before marching into the room, halting about two feet in front of the Commander who was holding onto a lectern and gazing at me from under his cap.

"Salute … Off Caps!" as I followed the Leading Regulator's order.

"MEM Atkinson, sir, charged with the misappropriation of government stores, namely a one inch brass padlock."

"How do you plead?" the Commander asked

"Guilty, sir," I replied

"Record the plea of guilty," the Commander ordered. "Divisional Officer's report, please."

My newly acquired DO then, as predicted, tried to defend me, but as he had only known me for a matter of hours it went along the lines of "Atkinson has a promising career in the Royal Navy, keeps good kit and works well when cornered."

During my Divisional Officer's citation, the Commander continued to give me a withering glare and after my DO had finished, the Commander said "Well, young man, what have you got to say for yourself?" before I could answer, he continued "Do you think you can just borrow naval stores when you feel like it? I mean, where will it end? Today it is a padlock; tomorrow it could be a Harrier. Where will it end?" his voice got steadily louder as he reached a crescendo. Finally, he paused for a few moments, thinking, before saying "Admonished! If I see you here before me again, young man, you will be in serious trouble, do you understand?" "Yes, Sir" I replied.

"Admonished, Sir," the Leading Regulator confirmed. "On Caps … Salute… Right wheel quick march ... Wait for me outside."

Outside of the makeshift courtroom, I breathed a huge sigh of relief and removed my cap. The Leading Regulator followed me out of the room. "You got admonished, son, do you know what that means?" "No, Leading Reg," I replied honestly. "It means, you're guilty as sin, but we'll let you off."

Following my second brush with the naval law in as many drafts, I decided not to push my luck. Royal Naval Detention Quarters was a small prison situated just inside the dockyard and after hearing stories from some of my mates that had spent twenty-eight days there; it was not something I wished to try.

Back at work, I was assigned to Chippy's Party, which is generally working with wood, but most shipwrights tend to be a master of all trades. One of the big jobs I was assigned to was replacing the old ICABA breathing apparatus with the newer single cylinder version called BASCCA. As the Type

42 destroyers carried thirty-two sets, it was long hard work removing the old ICABA lockers and then drilling and replacing them with the new BASCCA lockers.

At the time, just to see if I could do it, I decided to grow a beard. We are not talking designer stubble here, this was more like a privet hedge, but crucially, the bit under my bottom lip refused to be part of the deal, so the resulting 'beard' looked more like a chin strap. Naval regulations meant that I had to keep it for at least four weeks, during which, as it made me look considerably older than my twenty-two years, people were calling me 'Chief' and asking me questions that were far too technical for me at that point in my career. I subsequently got a bollocking when one evening; I decided to shave it off without authorisation.

Still lodging with my old mate, Steve and his lovely wife Diana at their house in Gosport, I was really starting to enjoy naval life. I had passed my exams for promotion to killick and was now playing a waiting game in a roster. As a mate, Steve had offered me his spare room for the bargain rent of £50 per month including full board. Even in 1984, this was very cheap, so it was no real surprise when after about six months, that I was asked to find alternative accommodation. There was no argument and Steve clearly did not like asking me to move out, but their marriage was starting to suffer, so I had to go. It is not easy having a permanent house guest especially as the only loo was at the far side of their bedroom forcing a semi-naked blinkered dash in the middle of the night. More than once, I caught them in the middle of something naughty, much to my embarrassment.

Having tasted independence again, there was no way I was moving back into barracks if there was an alternative, so I started looking around for suitable digs. After visiting a few squalid, dirty and damp rooms, I was offered a room with a young married couple who had three children, a dog and a mischievous cat who had learned how to open doors. This looked brilliant, Rob and Di were extremely friendly and I got on well with all of the kids, so moving in, my rent quadrupled overnight to a more realistic two hundred pounds per month. This still included all my meals; my washing, ironing and Di even cut my hair. I was treated like one of the family. Di would cook all of the meals and in the evening, Rob would make my sandwiches for work. They really spoiled me, but I am sure if they did not need the rental income, I wouldn't even have moved in. It was during my tenancy with Rob and Di, that one evening I met my future wife Anita.

My long-time friend and run-ashore oppo Gary 'Buck' Taylor was experiencing, not for the first time, some marital difficulties. In short, his estranged wife, Jackie, had put a court injunction on him preventing him from returning home. He called me one Friday evening in 1984 needing a friend to drain down over whilst getting drunk somewhere. So changing my plans for the evening, I drove out to pick him up and then motored to Fareham, about four miles up the road and slowly started working our way down the street on a pub-crawl whilst he explained how unreasonable his wife was being. I did not argue with him, he needed a mate right then, so I played the part of the proverbial sponge and allowed him to get it off his chest.

All of this changed when we entered a pub called the 'Old Coach House' in Fareham. 'Buck' saw two young women by themselves, so immediately went over to introduce himself. Offering them a drink and then dispatching me to the bar, he started chatting up the pretty quiet girl whilst I was left to chat to the other girl called Lesley who was far more adventurous but not a patch on the pretty Anita who 'Buck' was chatting up.

Later in the evening, he asked the girls if they would like to come back for coffee, clearly wishing to close the deal. I quietly asked him where he was planning to take them, as going back to his house was not an option. Luckily, it appeared that he was housesitting in Gosport for a family whilst they were on holiday. Reluctantly, the girls agreed to come back with us to Gosport where 'Buck' opened a bottle of homemade wine that was disgusting and tasted like anti-freeze. To liven up the party, he then put on a porn video. This scuppered his chances completely as Anita did not like this at all and pleaded with Lesley to go home. Being chivalrous, I offered to drive them back to Fareham whilst 'Buck' promised to cook me a fried breakfast at 2am on my return.

As it turned out, Anita was stopping the night with Lesley, so, after seeing the girls safely back to her house in Fareham; I drove back to Gosport looking forward to my cooked breakfast. Unfortunately, and true to form, 'Buck' had fallen asleep and there was no evidence of anything having been cooked so I just crashed out on the sofa in the lounge, feeling really quite jaded.

Hung over in the morning, coffee and bacon sarnies revived my spirits sufficiently enough to discover where I had left the car. Checking that everything was as I had left it, I noticed a small brown envelope sitting on the back seat. Investigating further, it contained about seven ten-pound notes and a wage slip. Deciding what to do with it changed my life forever. The moral dilemma of whether to keep it or return it would depend on me being able to find the road and then the house where I had dropped the girls off the previous evening. Therefore, after another coffee and leaving 'Buck' to fully recover, I retraced my steps back to Fareham until I was relatively sure of having the right house. Knocking on the door at 10am, I was confronted by a rather angry looking man. Feeling sure that I had the wrong house, I explained that I had dropped two girls off the previous evening and wished to return something left in the car. Hearing this, two girls dressed in dressing gowns appeared at the top of the stairs and a very relieved Lesley came to greet me. After handing over the cash, I also gave her my number and offered to take her out for a drink if she wished before leaving, feeling very pleased with myself for returning her wages.

The following Wednesday, the phone rang and Lesley asked if I fancied that drink. Not being overwhelmed with offers, I jumped at the chance and about an hour later, I was pulling up outside her house for the third time in a week. This time the angry foster parent was not nearly as grumpy as before and Lesley promised faithfully that she would not be late. Clearly, Lesley had already explained everything to Mr Grumpy.

In the car, Lesley said, "Shall we go and pick Anita up?" Surprised, I replied, "If I knew Anita was coming, I would have brought 'Buck' with me."
"It's ok; she doesn't want to see 'Buck' anymore."

Anita, as it turned out, lived in a children's home about four miles away in Wickham. Having picked her up, the three of us then walked into the village square where I bought the drinks and we all sat down to chat. Most of the conversation centred on our previous meeting and the honesty I had shown in returning Lesley's wages.

After finishing her drink, Lesley made her excuses and left me in the pub with Anita. It was then that I realised the two scheming women had set me up. Recovering from the slight deception, we drove a short distance to Bishops Waltham for another drink where the underage Anita would not be recognised.

Later that evening, after agreeing to see me again, I returned Anita back to the children's home in Wickham before driving back home to my digs at Rob and Di's place in Gosport.

This was about the same time that my submarine course dates came through. Despite finding a new girlfriend, I was still determined to embark on this new adventure, so a few days after receiving my course dates, I left FMG Portsmouth and joined HMS Dolphin at Fork Blockhouse in Gosport to commence my six weeks of initial submarine training.

HMS DOLPHIN

23rd October 1984 to 18th February 1985

The day I joined HMS Dolphin for basic submarine training was, understandably, quite worrying as I had no idea, really, what I was letting myself in for. The attraction, of course, was the extra pay. Once new submariners had completed a successful ascent in the Submarine Escape Training Tank, they would receive in the region of another two hundred pounds in their pay packet and this was, to tell the truth, the main reason for me volunteering. Another reason was the sheer fascination of what makes a five thousand ton lump of metal submerge under control and then miraculously surface again. In addition, after five years in the Royal Navy I was now looking for a new challenge.

Cycling the short distance into HMS Dolphin from my digs in Gosport for the very first time, I was faced with the usual first day dilemma of where to get changed out of my sweaty cycling kit, showered and then dressed into naval uniform before finding someone to report to.

In the MACCO that I located in a cluster of buildings called 'Alecto Colonnade' I was handed a Joining Routine that consisted of the traditional whole camp stamping routine and told to report to the Royal Naval Submarine School by 8:15am to start my submarine course.

Before leaving the MACCO, I requested and was duly allocated a locker in the RA's changing room, which would make changing in the morning considerably easier. Having still got about fifteen minutes to spare, I set off like an orienteer, trying to collect as many stamps as I could before reporting to the Submarine School.

HMS Dolphin, as I discovered was long and thin with a submarine base at the one end, the Royal Naval Submarine School in the middle and the accommodation much closer towards the main gate. The historic base also formed part of the sea wall, affording gorgeous views across the Solent to the Isle of Wight. The downside to this, of course, was that it wasn't at all sheltered and suffered everything the sea, wind and rain could throw at it.

Reporting into the main entrance of the Submarine School, I was directed along corridors lined with pictures of submarines and into a classroom that was already half filled with similarly nervous students. When everyone was seated, the instructor introduced himself as POMEM 'Billy' Wass and giving us a brief précis of his experience, we learned that he had served on submarines for many years. With the introductions over, 'Billy' went on to tell us that over the next six weeks we would learn how the submarine's many systems all work together to make the boat float, move and fight efficiently under the water. The course, UG200, was streamed towards the Swiftsure-class of submarine and we were told that we would all eventually join one of the six Swiftsure-class submarines that were based in Devonport.

'Billy' handed us all a Swiftsure Course Handbook and an exercise book in which to write up our notes and then got going straight away on the course syllabus. Before learning about the any of the systems that make the submarine function, it was important to learn how submarines are generally constructed and what allows them to submerge to great depths without crushing and afterwards return safely to the surface again.

We soon learnt that the pressure hull of the submarine was a cigar shaped tube with domed ends that was strengthened by 'T' Frames about every eighteen inches apart and these were numbered sequentially from stem to stern which, whilst adding rigidity to the boat, also provided a reference as to where everything was fitted. We learned that this strengthened cylinder was sub-divided by using four hydraulic watertight doors and these were fitted at frame numbers 29, 58, 65 and 74; that were designed to section the submarine should one compartment sustain damage.

There were various hatches fitted into the pressure hull and all of these were of a very similar construction. At the front, there was the weapons embarkation hatch and quite close by was the forward escape tower. In the middle was the conning tower hatch. The conning tower, contrary to popular belief, is actually fitted inside the fin, which is the big black lump in the middle. The main access hatch is just aft of the fin and then some way aft, the after escape hatch is fitted next to the engine room hatch. I found all of this new information incredibly interesting and absorbed every word whilst frantically scribbling down notes. Being an inquisitive sod, I found myself asking questions about anything that I could not understand.

In the evening, back at Rob and Di's place after tea, I would write up my almost illegible notes neatly into a fair book and replicate the drawings into something vaguely legible that I could use for revision prior to the final exam at the end of the course.

'Billy' would set us a short consolidation test at the start of each day to ensure that the class was keeping up the pace of the instruction. It quickly became apparent that the three senior students were learning faster than the rest of the class who had recently joined straight from training.

Having mastered the layout of the compartments, the main ballast tank fittings and what makes the submarine submerge and surface again; we then started to concentrate on the essential systems that allow the boat to function. 'Billy' decided to start with Electrical Distribution.

Prior to the course, I was mechanical and electrics had always been considered 'white man's magic'. Flick a switch and the light comes on ... Magic! However, 'Billy' went into detail to describe how the steam created by heat from the reactor as well as propelling the submarine, also drove two turbo generators that could each generate enough wigglies to power a small town. The flavour of this particular type of electricity was 440v AC and as I said, we had stacks of it. The problem with this is that if ever the reactor broke down, not only would the lights go off, but also the lack of steam would make the submarine stop in the water. Therefore, for that reason, a battery is fitted to store the spare wigglies. The problem with this is that all batteries store electricity in DC and since the turbo generators only make AC another machine was required to convert it from AC to DC. This was called a motor generator and was actually quite clever; not only does it convert AC into DC, but also when the reactor breaks down; it then takes the stored DC in the battery and converts it back into AC, which allows, amongst other things, for the lights to stay on. Should the battery now run low, the submarine was fitted with a diesel generator that would make more DC power at 250v and top it up again. As AC powered most of the pumps and stuff, there was a requirement to transform it down into usable voltages and distribute it using load centres. Of course, it was a bit more complicated than this, but I am starting to confuse myself, so let us leave it there.

As it was described, the submarine was like a huge set of scales the weights being quantities of water or fluids that could be transferred between various tanks by operating a series of switches on the Systems Control Console and starting the pump. The operator could then alter the trim of the boat by transferring water either aft or forward to balance the submarine.

After learning about the Trim System, we then had to master the understanding of Archimedes' principle to appreciate how the bodily weight of the submarine could be changed thus making the submarine positive, neutral or negatively buoyant depending on whether the submarine was surfacing, submerging or simply operating under water.

This was not an easy principle to understand, but I shall briefly try to explain it. Imagine for a second, that there is a huge tank, full to the brim, holding exactly ten tons of water and a submarine weighing about five tons is dunked into the tank. The weight of the water that overflows will equal the weight of the submerged submarine. If the submarine is lighter than the weight of the water it displaces, it will float. If water is then allowed into the internal tanks and the submarine becomes heavier than the water it displaces, it will submerge. The trick, for a submarine to effectively operate under water is to achieve neutral buoyancy where the weight of the submarine is finely balanced against the weight of the displaced seawater.

Having completed teaching us all about the intricacies of the submarine's water systems, POMEM Wass started to describe how the air systems were the life blood of the submarine. Without high-pressure air blowing into the ballast tanks, the submarine could not easily surface. High-pressure air has many other functions, including torpedo discharge and starting the diesel generator, but not being able to surface, renders the submarine a pretty inefficient mode of transport.

A basic diagram of the HP air system looked vaguely like a football pitch; with goals, goalkeeper, corner flags, touch lines and even a halfway line. That is the way the system was explained to me and frankly, it was an easy way to understand how two HP air compressors could maintain the system at a constant pressure and like most of the submarine's systems with redundancy built in. This meant that if a valve should fail on one side, then the other side of the system would supply HP air to the various services. The watertight bulkheads each had valves close to them to quickly isolate parts of the system for repair.

In the event of an emergency, as we later learned, another eighteen bottles of stored high pressure air would enable the submarine to surface should the HP air system fail completely or we had a desperate need to get onto the 'roof' quickly. The principle scenario would be if there was uncontrolled flooding in the boat.

Along with HP Air, the submarine could not easily operate without the hydraulic systems. Three separate hydraulic systems were almost identical with a few subtle differences. These, as we were taught, were the Main, External and After Hydraulic systems. The Main, as the name suggests, did the lion's share of the work, but could also be cross-connected to do the work of the other two systems should there be a failure of some sort.

After a total failure of electrical power, we were largely buggered. The first noticeable effect would be that the lights went off, but also the hydraulic pumps could not be operated and neither could the air compressors. Without power, the submarine would continue to propel forwards only for a short time as the residual steam spun the turbines, which in turn rotated the shaft. The problem was that the submarine could not easily steer or indeed surface. These contingencies had been considered many years before and batteries and DC motors had been introduced to enable power to be restored for a limited time. If the submarine was at periscope depth or actually on the 'roof', the diesel engine could be run which would then generate sufficient electrical power to keep the main battery topped up. If the reactor was knackered, there was a large electric motor fitted on top of the gearbox to basically turn the shaft relatively slowly using DC power. Which, if nothing else, could put the boat on the surface and probably get the submarine home.

If this all sounds a bit gloomy, it must be stressed that these were emergency measures. Steam was essentially the key. We needed it to turn the engines and also to generate the electricity, so where does it come from? Frankly, as anybody with an elementary knowledge of physics knows, if you heat water enough, it will boil and steam is given off. Back in the First World War, the K-class submarines were fitted with boilers and funnels, which produced the steam to turn the turbines. The idea was very innovative, but at the time technology hadn't advanced sufficiently for these unique submarines to be very effective. From the order to dive, the boilers had to be shut down and the furnaces raked before the funnels could then be lowered and 'mushroom' ventilators sealed the hole. This all took a considerable amount of time, so the term 'Crash Dive' didn't really apply. They were also seriously huge for their day; on the ill-fated submarine K13, the Captain famously asked the engine room "My end's diving, what's your end doing?"

The theory of steam propulsion was sound, but the method of producing it on a submarine was seriously suspect. Fast forward forty odd years to the 1950's and the Americans unveiled the USS Nautilus a revolutionary new nuclear powered submarine that could propel a submerged submarine around the world.

All vessels previously known as 'submarines' were in fact only submersible craft. Nautilus' nuclear plant enabled the boat to remain submerged for weeks, even months. Thus Nautilus was the world's first true submarine.

The details of pressures and temperatures within the nuclear steam raising plant are highly classified, but essentially the reactor is just a means of heating water. As the system is pressurised, it remains as water although it is much hotter than the traditional boiling point of water. This is known as the Primary Loop. Main coolant pumps circulate the water through a steam generator which is in fact a huge heat exchanger. The heat is transferred to water in the Secondary Loop which, because of the much lower pressure, immediately flashes off into steam which then spins the main engine turbines and turbo generators. The turbines then feed into a huge gearbox which reduces revolutions of the single output shaft to an efficient speed for the propeller.

After the steam has done its stuff, it is condensed back into water and then fed back to the steam generator for the process to start all over again. In an ideal world, this cycle of steam and water would go on for ever, but there would always be some leakage requiring the submarine to make its own water in order to remain self-sufficient.

The water was made by boiling up seawater and then evaporating the steam vapour. The vapour would then be condensed into pure fresh water as the salt would not evaporate. Presumably this is why we don't get salty rain. The main reason for us distilling the water is to boil it into steam for propulsion. Any that is left over is then sent to the ship's tanks for washing, cooking and making cups of tea etc. Consequently, all submariners are quickly conditioned to conserve water.

We were taught, that a shower should only last two minutes from start to finish. For those with delicate sensibilities, look away now. At odd times of the day and night, submariners would traipse off to the shower wearing nothing but a flimsy towel. The procedure was simple but effective: Get in, turn on the water and get wet. Turn off the water, soap up and wash thoroughly. Turn on the water and spin on the spot to rinse off the soapy lather. Turn off the water and exit. Job done!

There would generally be a queue to use the two showers and anybody using more than their fair share of water would be rudely reminded by those waiting in the queue. 'Billy' used to tell us his own personal experiences and how he used to take lengthy 'Hollywood showers'. When he was reminded of the time, he would forcibly reply, "Fuck off! I make it, so I'll use it."

We spent a good six weeks learning the systems, hearing personal experiences from 'Billy', and sitting weekly progress tests. I loved the course and found it to be extremely interesting. Some members of the class had difficulties, but as a stoker, this was not simply engineering, but it also answered quite a lot of my unspoken questions about how submarines do what they do.

At the end of the Swiftsure Class Basic Submarine Course, we had to sit a final exam. This would test all of our accumulated teachings and cover all aspects of the course. Despite being in the top five in the class, it still required nightly revision to prevent me slipping on the potential banana skin of failure. There were seven drawings that needed to be learnt as well as the emergency procedures and stopping and starting routines that all had to be committed to memory before we finally sat the exam.

I needn't have worried though, all of my revision paid off and I ended up getting 98%, coming second in the class to a chap called 'Whisky' Walker. I did however, get awarded the course prize for being a girlie swot and the best all-round student. The Captain of HMS Dolphin subsequently presented me with a certificate of achievement, which was nice.

Despite passing the course, in order to qualify for my submarine pay there was still the small matter of completing the Submarine Escape Training Tank. This is a hundred foot cylindrical tank of water with various airlocks and chambers positioned at various depths. The tank enabled trainee submariners to perfect their submarine escape techniques in the relative safety of a warm water-training environment.

After a week of stringent medical examinations, I reported to the SETT the following Monday for escape training. Just to make sure that I had not contracted something nasty over the weekend, I had another brief medical examination before being ushered into a classroom for a very boring day of lectures and films all of which demonstrated the correct procedure and explaining the sometimes fatal consequences of not getting it right.

Obviously, safety was paramount and before we could be allowed to carry out a pressurised ascent, we had to prove to the instructors at the tank top that we had mastered the exhalation technique. The following morning, donning my best speedos, I rode the lift to the top of the structure, where, as a class, we witnessed different instructors demonstrating all of the ascents that we would shortly be doing, whilst the tank top chief, gave a running commentary.

There was a good bit of discipline and what we like to call 'gun drill', which was to ensure that everything was essentially done by numbers until it became second nature. It would be comparatively *easy* in a tank full of warm swimming pool water with all the lights on, but in the pitch cold darkness of the North Atlantic, only the instinctive actions of a trapped crew would save their lives. After the demo, it was time to get wet, so, holding onto the top of the ladder, in turn, we ducked our heads in the water and pursing our lips, blew out hard, trying to expel all of the air out of our lungs, which is harder than it sounds. Only when we had perfected this technique would we then be allowed to carry out the first free ascent from the airlock at a depth of thirty feet.

It had already been rigorously explained that in the thirty-foot airlock, we would be breathing air at fifteen psi above atmospheric pressure so, as we ascended, we would need to blow out all of the way to the surface to prevent the air expanding and bursting our lungs, which was not a cheery thought.

Following all of the briefings, demonstrations and practical tests, we were directed down several flights of steps and into the thirty-foot airlock with an instructor who shut the door behind us. Donning goggles and a nose clip, the instructor informed us that he was now going to flood the lock befo
opening a valve to allow the lovely warm water to rapidly fill the
compartment up to chest level. Trapped in the tiny chamber it

claustrophobic and a little scary. Communicating with the tank top, the instructor warned us that he was about to pressurise the airlock to equalise with the tank at thirty feet and to stay ahead of the pressure. Once he had finished, he was able to open the inner door and now there was now nothing to prevent us 'escaping' for the first time. As per usual, alphabetical order meant I was called first and told to stand with my back to the open door. When I was in position, an order was shouted by the instructor "Take a good deep breath," which was my signal to bend forward and offer my bottom out of the door into the tank. A waiting instructor then pulled me in slow motion through the door and as I straightened up, immediately went into my pre-rehearsed blow routine before I was released and natural buoyancy took over rocketing me towards the surface. All the way, 'Swim Boys' accompanied me. These chaps were specially trained instructors who would gently encourage us to continue to blow out hard by thumping us in the stomach if we stopped exhaling.

Well, what can I say? It was fantastic and easily the best fairground ride the Navy has. Having successfully surfaced unscathed at the top, we were like excited children pleading with a favourite uncle "Again, again." So, to prove it was not a fluke, as a class, we all went back down and did it again from the same airlock and later in the morning proved the technique once only from twice the depth in the sixty foot airlock.

There was one more ascent still to do, but this was the big one. This would be a suited ascent from the bottom of the tank via the one-man escape tower and this was causing more than a little anxiety. In fact, I was crapping myself. We had seen the video and the practical demonstration, sat through the lectures and knew all of the component parts of the tower, but still, it was bloody scary.

In the changing room at the bottom of the tank, we dressed in the bright orange Mark 7 Submarine Escape Suit. This had an integral life jacket with two relief valves in the top. There was also a dildo-like yellow charging valve that ran down the left sleeve and by plugging this into a connection in the tower, this would fill the life jacket and the excess pressure would exhaust into the hood, giving the wearer a bubble of clean air to breath.

As the escaping submariner ascended through the water, the pressure in the life jacket would constantly expand giving the wearer a continuous supply of air all the way to the surface. The golden rule was simple:

Head in Air: Breath normally
Head in Water: Breath out hard

After yet another briefing, I climbed in to the claustrophobic single escape tower. Once clear of the bottom hatch, it was closed beneath me and now the only way was up. My heart was pounding like a drum and the feeling of panic was starting to well inside me. Remembering the training I plugged in the yellow 'Stole' connection and air immediately started to fill the integral buoyancy aid causing the suit to tighten around my chest. Over the panic, I became aware of a hand on my leg before realising that I was actually not alone in the narrow escape chamber. There was a side compartment for an instructor to monitor my progress. He now shouted that the tower was starting to flood, as once again warm water swirled around my ankles and rapidly rose, the pressure increased as I struggled to keep ahead of it. When the water level reached my chest, the pressure in the tower equalised with the tank, instinctively I looked up and was amazed to see 'rain' falling on my head for a split second before suddenly I was engulfed in water and buoyancy took over as I shot out of the tower on my way to safety.

Two instructors wearing only trunks, goggles and a nose clip immediately arrested my ascent, in quite a surreal experience. They were intent on speaking to me, but unusually, I was in no mood for a chat. Whilst one of them fiddled with my suit, the other one shouted in my ear, "What's your name and official number?" I shouted quickly back "ATKINSON, D176024Y." Not satisfied with my answer, he shouted again "What football team do you support?" "BURNLEY!" I shouted back not comprehending why these two marine boys without their oxy-gum were preventing me from escaping. Shouting one more question, he asked "Name the team?" before I told him to fuck off and suddenly I was on my way, rocketing to the surface. A few seconds later, after a brilliant ride, I shot out of the water like a champagne cork out of a shaken bottle. On the surface, two other instructors immediately grabbed me, pulled me towards the ladder, and assisted my climb out of the tank.

I was breathless, wobbly, exhilarated and relieved all at the same time. Thank god, that was over. I was now qualified in submarine escape and as such my pay packet was about to increase by about three-thousand pounds per year. This was my prime motivator for transferring to submarines in the first place. Despite the now ebbing fear, it was a superb experience, the only downside was that I would now have to wait another four years before I could have another go.

Having finally completed my basic submarine training, the stokers in the class were sent off to HMS Sultan for Nuclear Short Course where we would learn in much more depth what actually made the reactor tick and more importantly, not go pop.

Ian Atkinson

HMS SULTAN

19th February 1985 to 15th April 1985

Rightly proud of our newly-elevated status, the class left HMS Dolphin and marched into the naval engineering school at HMS Sultan as a class of submariners. I will be the first to admit that submariners are quite a rare breed. Despite now being paid an extra three grand per year for having completed the Submarine Escape Training Tank, the paperwork and more importantly, the submarine pay would still take a couple of months to come through.

A minor technicality like that would not stop us spending the money that we did not have. It became a bit of a game to throw loose change at the poor skimmers and use Harry Enfield's alter ego's catchphrase "Loadsamoney" in a fake cockney accent.

This had the double effect of alienating us from our General Service colleagues and making us poorer than we already were, but it was quite a lot of fun all the same.

We had joined HMS Sultan to complete our Nuclear Propulsion Course that was designed to teach us the intricacies of the Nuclear Steam Raising Plant. As already explained, the Nuclear Reactor was just a means of heating water to a very high temperature, but the process of splitting the atom was previously something of a myth to me. I mean how can you split something that you cannot see?

In nuclear physics we were taught how a single tiny little neutron would be fired into an atom of enriched Uranium 235, this will release fission products as well as another couple of neutrons and an awful lot of heat. These other neutrons then whizz off and crash into other atoms of U235 which then give off even more heat and a couple more neutrons and as such the previously fabled chain reaction begins.

It occurred to me that having all of these neutrons whizzing about willy-nilly is a bad thing as the reaction just keeps getting hotter and hotter until, if left unchecked, it could potentially explode or melt through the bottom of the boat. This thought caused me to momentarily doubt my new career direction. I had evolved over my six years in the job into something of an inquisitive sod. Demonstrating my understanding of the process, I asked how the reaction was stopped or at least controlled. This apparently, was a very good question and involved a series of control rods that apparently, when lowered into the reactor, form barriers to stop the neutrons hitting the uranium and as such slow down the reaction, which in turn reduces the amount of heat given off. This all seemed bloody clever to me and made me wonder vaguely which bright spark had first decided to fire a neutron at a radioactive atom; just to see what happened. It seemed to me to be a bit like hitting a bullet with a hammer and trying to make it go pop!

Believe it or not, what I have endeavoured to describe in a few words over a couple of minutes, actually took us a couple of weeks to really absorb in sufficient enough detail to sit and pass the nuclear physics exam. The exam, when it came, was bloody difficult and required the class to reproduce several diagrams and to list the many pressures and temperatures. The relationship between pressure and temperature, we learned, was crucial. When the reactor is fully started up and running at the correct pressure and temperature, it is termed ‘Critical’. This did not sound too good to me at all. Surely, if it is critical, that is a bad place to be, but apparently not. There are a few graphs to plot the progress as the reactor warms up, but like many things in the nuclear engineering world, it is classified as confidential-atomic, so you will have to take my word for it.

Having generated all of this heat, it was then used to warm up a system full of water called the primary loop. In theory, this was the same water, going round and round the same circuit forever and ever; and as it was under a lot of pressure, it remained as water.

This high temperature, high pressure essentially glowing radioactive water was circulated around the system by six main coolant pumps into two steam generators that more accurately emulated a domestic kettle. The primary and secondary loops met inside the steam generator. The secondary loop entered the SG as cool water at the bottom and after having a brief meeting with the primary loop, left a bit higher up as high pressure-saturated steam. This would then be used to spin four steam turbines, two of which were main engines and the other two were generators used to generate all of the submarine’s electrical power.

After the steam had done its job and lost most of its energy, it took the easiest path through a couple of huge sea water condensers where, under a near total vacuum, the steam would be turned back again into cool water. Using huge pumps, this was again fed back into the steam generator to start the process all over again.

From the back of the main engines, an output shaft, turning extremely quickly entered the single gearbox where, clutches and a series of cogs, wheels and bearings reduced the speed of the single output shaft by a ratio of 50:1. So, assuming a turbine speed of around 5000 rpm, the output shaft speed would be only 100 rpm if my secondary school maths has not let me down.

From the gearbox, the shaft went through a big rubber coupling that would allow for any misalignment before entering into a thrust block. This lump of wizardry which looked very unimpressive on the outside was to prevent the shaft being pushed back into the gearbox by the propeller's thrust. There were a few other lumps and bumps on the shaft before it finally left the submarine via a stern seal, which was actually a very clever bit of kit as it always 'knew' what the outside seawater pressure was and adjusted itself to seal the shaft and prevent the green crinkly stuff coming into the boat and ruining everybody's day. At the end of the shaft the propeller or in some cases, the propulsor pushed the boat through the water.

There was much more to learn than on the Basic Submarine Course, so my earlier cockiness had largely worn off. I revised hard for this exam and I needed to. Just getting the drawings perfect would reap a massive 50% of the available marks. Spelling your name right might gain another valuable mark whilst some class members would try quite different but also ingenious methods of cheating such as scribing the start and stop routine along with the alarm parameters of a given machine onto a clear plastic ruler. This could then only be seen by holding the ruler in a certain way. Brilliant! Of course, when the reluctant academic had spent literally hours with a scriber scribbling down formulas and routines, he had learnt the information anyway. The same principle was applied to hexagonal biros and calculator cases. Someone even managed to draw all of the diagrams and stick them onto the rectangular plastic ends of the fluorescent light fittings; the plan being that a struggling student would gaze skyward 'trying to remember' whilst cribbing from the tiny drawings on the ceiling. Many other innovative ideas were considered, but ironically, this actually aided in the revision process. So much so, that in the exam, I actually managed to reproduce all the required diagrams unaided and did enough of the written work to pass the final exam at the first time of asking, though there was only a slight margin of error and very little wasted effort.

Having now passed the exam and completed the course, we were all looking forward to getting drafts to Swiftsure-class submarines. The prize at the time was a draft to HMS Spartan, which seemed to flit backwards and forwards across the pond to the United States. So much so, most submariners dubbed her USS Spartan.

The Swiftsure-class of submarines were largely identical with apparently only a few internal distinguishing differences, so it did not really matter which boat I got. I was therefore quite pleased when I was subsequently drafted to HMS Sovereign. She was the second boat in the class and was based along with all the 'S' boats in Devonport.

My relationship with my girlfriend Anita had now lasted for about six months and was considered quite serious, though not serious enough for me to drive back to Portsmouth every weekend. This caused a problem. Do we split up or what?

My landlord Rob, mentioned casually one evening, "Why don't you ask her to move to Plymouth with you?" For some reason, I had not even considered that as a viable option. I was seriously skint at the time, though my submarine pay and a couple of months of back pay was promised quite soon and would go some way to pacifying my grumpy bank manager.

A week later, after convincing everyone who had an interest, we loaded all of our combined meagre possessions into a hired Transit van and took a leap of faith by driving to Plymouth with the sole intention of renting a flat when we arrived.

Arriving in Plymouth after an uneventful journey, I managed to track down one of the girls I used to share a flat with in Stoke a couple of years previously. She had now got flat close to Plymouth Hoe and took pity on our new homeless status by offering a mattress on her living room floor for a couple of nights.

The following morning, the search for a flat began in earnest and after scouring the local Evening Herald and circling some adverts, armed with a fist full of loose change and a bag full of optimism; I trekked down the road to the nearest phone box. After making about five calls, I was talking to the property owner of a flat in the Plymouth district of Stoke. He was a little suspicious at first, after telling him that I was joining my first submarine very shortly, he proclaimed submariners to be a passive lot and so we got the flat for the princely sum of fifty pounds per week. That was the funniest thing I ever heard him say.

He met us later that day at 124 Pasley Street in Stoke where he showed us round the first floor flat. It was nothing special, it was very expensive but we were desperate. Two lads of dubious sexuality shared the downstairs flat and we shared the same front door. Our living room was huge with a big bay window and was really light and airy. In contrast, the bedroom was small and dark and disturbingly, the two single beds that had been pushed together were different heights forming a height difference of about two or three inches. An attempt had been made to hide the discrepancy with a chunky eiderdown. It was hardly ideal as each door leading out to the landing had its own key, but we were not in a strong bargaining position. Parting with two hundred quid as a month's deposit, we were handed the keys and set about emptying the Transit van.

With everything moved in, which frankly didn't take long, we celebrated with a bag of fish and chips from the chippy a little further down the road.

The following day saw me driving back to Gosport to take the van back and to retrieve my car whilst Anita stayed in Plymouth to play house and to make the flat as homely as possible. When I got back in the evening, Anita had made a list of the essential household items that we needed to buy very quickly if only to survive, this included a washing up bowl, kitchen bin, bedding, cutlery, oh and some food. The grand total was well over a hundred pounds. As I was skint, at the supermarket I tried to pay with three cheques as these would be guaranteed by my Cheque Card, but the jobsworth from ASDA wasn't having it and we left the store with two trolleys of food and supplies having parted with a single cheque of nearly one hundred and forty pounds knowing full well that it was likely to bounce.

Well I wasn't wrong and after ASDA had presented the cheque twice more costing me a total of twenty pounds, they gave up. What a result!

After a couple of days' leave and with the flat now looking quite homely, with a mixture of excitement and trepidation, I joined HMS Sovereign, my first submarine.

HMS SOVEREIGN

16th April 1985 to 19th November 1989

After spending most of my leave settling into the flat and racking up a huge overdraft on essential household stuff, I joined my first submarine, HMS Sovereign on Tuesday 16th April 1985.

The training courses at HMS Dolphin and HMS Sultan only went part of the way to preparing me for the cramped, musty confines of what was, essentially, a steel tube. After the introductions, I was shown to where I would sleep in the Weapon Stowage Compartment next to a Mk24 Tigerfish torpedo. My bed was actually a fibreglass cot, specially designed to attach to the torpedo loading rails. A mattress had been plonked into the cot and a pillow accompanied a rather thin green nylon sleeping bag. There was a lot worse to come though, as there were more trainees than beds, I was forced to 'Hot-Bunk' with my oppo. I must say, this struck me as a rather gay thing to be doing, until it was explained that we would not be sharing the bed at the same time. Phew! Later in the week, HMS Sovereign sailed for a couple of days to test some recent repairs, which gave me the perfect opportunity to get used to the sleeping arrangements.

The shift-pattern was simply arranged as six hours on followed by six hours off which rotated around the clock. I shared my bunk with a chap called Gerry Lipscombe who was even greener than I was. As I got up to go on watch at around a quarter past twelve, I would drag Gerry's sleeping bag out from under the mattress and lay it out for him along with our shared pillow. My sleeping bag was then stowed away under the mattress. Six hours later, he would then extend the same courtesy to me. Therefore, in an ideal world, coming off watch tired and in the dim-lighting of the 'Bomb Shop', I would undress down to my pants and slip into my sleeping bag. Unfortunately, on one horrible occasion, Gerry forgot to change over the sleeping bags and knowing no different, I slipped into *his* sleeping bag before I discovered, to my horror, his 'sock of love' which was somewhat crusty and not at all pleasant.

After ejecting myself onto the cold metal deck, I retrieved my sleeping bag from under the mattress and tried to banish all thoughts of the encounter as I attempted to get to sleep. Sleeping in the WSC was not at all comfortable; there was the constant noise from the 'fore-endies' bustling about and it wasn't dark as some of the lights needed to remain on all the time. Some of the 'Bomb Shop' residents, desperate for darkness, would attempt to drape the other sleeping bag as a sort of improvised curtain, but after finding my oppo's sperm-encrusted, I was not keen to even touch it and contented myself with burying my head deep inside my own sleeping bag.

Space, as I am sure you may appreciate, was severely limited. Receiving some intelligence before we sailed, I only arrived on-board with one set of civilian clothes that were stuffed into the bottom of a locker. As for uniform, all I brought with me were two sets of No8's, two pairs of overalls and three pairs of pants and socks. My towel, wash-bag and flip-flops completed my sailing kit. As I was still training, there was not much time for reading books or listening to music, but I did take my trusty Sony Walkman with me with a box of well-worn cassettes, so I could listen to some music in bed. The trouble with that was, I usually fell asleep and ended up being garrotted by the headphone cable. The kit that I was not wearing needed to be stowed away into a small metal locker that was about twelve inches square.

Despite the cramped and uncomfortable living conditions, I did not have much time to sleep, as there was much work to do. Sleep therefore, became a luxury as eighteen-hour days became the norm whilst I strived to complete the BSS. The Basic Submarine Safety exam, as the name suggests, involved anything to do with safety on-board the boat. This covered compartment layout, knowing the quickest way out in the event of an emergency and identifying all of the big lumps of machinery. I also needed to familiarise myself with the location of all of the fire-fighting equipment and more importantly how to use it. Once this was complete, I was considered safe to wander around the submarine unsupervised. The next part of my submarine training was the 'Part 3', which involved me learning just about every system on-board, and assumed no prior knowledge at all. This was truly a level playing field for submarine trainees of all ranks and rates.

During my 'Part 3' training there were quite a few memorable events, one of which was 'Navy Days'. HMS Sovereign was one of two Swiftsure-class submarines that had thrown their doors open to visitors. Being able to tour a nuclear submarine was considered quite an attraction and huge queues formed on the jetty in the hope of invading our 'home'. Submarines are cramped at the best of times, so to facilitate a flow of visitors; an improvised entrance, in the form of a set of steps, was erected near the forward gangway for visitors to gain access through the weapon embarkation hatch. After a whistle-stop tour of the forward escape compartment, they were herded down onto 2 Deck, past the bunk space, messes and galley, before climbing another ladder into the control room with a chance to view the outside world through either the search or attack periscopes. The visitors were then directed aft towards the main access hatch, where I was stationed as a sentry. This was partly to prevent visitors straying aft into the tunnel and the restricted areas around the reactor compartment and to assist members of the public in negotiating the vertical ladder out of the boat.

Quite by accident, to start with, I ended up looking up the skirts of many of the female visitors. This, as it turned out, was a fringe benefit of being a Navy Days sentry. Many of the repeat visitors to the submarine knew the form and wore trousers, most however, did not. So, over the course of the day, I was treated to a vast array of ladies' undergarments, from knickers and tights to stockings and suspenders. Two women seemed to prefer to go commando, choosing to wear nothing at all, as a running tally was kept on a chit stuck behind the ladder. There really was no way of getting around the moral dilemma as the health and safety of our visitors was, of course, paramount. Further forward, near the embarkation point, Les Meek, the leading torpedo engineer, with even fewer morals, had made himself a flask of coffee and a pile of sandwiches and had positioned himself in the fridge machinery space underneath a circular grille, which would then afford him unhindered upshots as the ladies concentrated on stepping over a rather unforgiving hatch coaming. His experience, certainly paid off, as unlike me, he was never caught.

Another event worthy of mention, in the middle of 1985, was marrying Anita. Never very romantic, moving into the flat in Pasley Street was a considerable drain on our combined resources, so in a blinding flash of inspiration, I proposed by saying "Shall we get married, as it's cheaper?" The reasoning was that, as a married man, I would then qualify for a married quarter and a married man's tax allowance. To my surprise, she agreed so following a whirlwind engagement; we married early in June 1985.

We didn't have much money, so everything was done on a budget. Rings were purchased from Argos and Plymouth Registry Office was booked for the short ceremony. Our neighbour, a barmaid at the nearby 'Millbridge' pub, chatted with the landlady and agreed to host a small wedding reception. As an afterthought, I called my mum, my dad and my brothers to see if they had anything planned, before inviting them to the wedding. Mum had met Anita previously, but Dad had never had the pleasure.

With seemingly everything arranged, my mate Karl, who thought of himself as a bit of a local playboy, managed to persuade the landlord of 'Trader Jacks' in Plymouth to open his doors for us at 8am for a couple of swift nerve-settling pints before I got married.

My dad, stepmother Anne and stepbrother Ian arrived at Plymouth Registry Office and before we all went in, Dad then asked if it was possible to meet his future daughter-in-law before the ceremony. It was not an unreasonable request, under the circumstances, but it was all a bit hurried.

Following a simple ceremony and not being able to afford a photographer, we had photographs in the registry office garden taken by another neighbour who was famous in his own right. His name was Peter and he was the Royal Marine Corporal in the iconic photograph from the Falkland's conflict with a Union Jack poking out of his bergan.

In the evening, as a family, we went for a meal at 'Old Mother Hubbard's Cottage' a rather nice restaurant in Yealmpton before spending our wedding night in the Smeaton's Tower Hotel near Plymouth Hoe. On Monday, it was back to work. In comparison to today's prices, it all cost next to nothing. I think we did the whole thing for less than two-hundred pounds. Nowadays, you could easily add a couple of noughts to that figure.

A week later, we moved out of the rented flat in Pasley Street and into a two-bedroomed married quarter in St Budeaux, which was infinitely better than the rented flat, it came furnished and more importantly, it was about a fifth of the cost.

Back at work, as a recently married stoker, qualified for Leading Hand and with more than six years' experience, I was asked to work in the Senior Rates mess as a Messman. I was initially disappointed with this arrangement as I considered it a backward step. It was, however, brilliant! As it transpired, the job had quite a few perks. As a 'Part 3' scumbag, I was only allowed into the Junior Rates mess to make and drink a cup of tea. I was not allowed to watch TV, listen to music, watch reel to reel movies or engage in other mess activities as all time out of bed should be devoted to completing the course and gaining the coveted 'Dolphins' submarine badge. Drinking a cup of Bournvita, early one morning, I had a surreal experience. I had come on watch two hours previously and was sat in the mess head bowed into my steaming drink contemplating why I was hundreds of miles away from my pretty new wife, six hundred feet under water and out of bed in the middle of the night, when suddenly the sound of a car raced past my head from left to right. This caused me to instantly question the contents of my drink but then I realised that it was a sound effect from the music playing on the mess stereo system. One of the chaps had purchased a brand new CD player and was playing 'The Pros and Cons of Hitchhiking' by Roger Waters. Now, whenever I hear that track, I am immediately transported back to that period of sheer-loneliness and fatigue whilst grabbing a drink in the forbidden mess. As a Messman, I was elevated to the temporary status of Senior Rates mess member and as such, in addition to cleaning-up and laying the tables for meals I could sit and relax in the relative tranquillity of their mess and even pour myself a beer if I desired. To prevent any misunderstanding, I would generally be pretending to read a work-related manual or studying a system diagram as I relaxed. Another fringe benefit was that I got to know the petty officers and chief's quite well, which came in bloody handy when I needed to ask a question or request a walk-round of a particular system. Consequently, I made rapid progress with my systems and within five months of joining the submarine, I had completed all of the task book and had demonstrated my knowledge by showing the 'Wrecker' around the submarine, pointing stuff out and answering his questions about the stuff I had missed. Like most oral exams, this was a two-way process and as long as I was speaking more than he was, there was a good chance of passing the board.

The final part of the 'Part 3' qualification was to sit an oral board in front of the Chief Stoker, Wrecker and AMEO(S). This was a gruelling test of all of the knowledge I had gained and involved me drawing a couple of diagrams and explaining how most of the systems worked. Fortunately, I had done enough and passed my 'Part 3' a little over five months after joining the submarine and instantly became a useful member of society again.

The subsequent celebration was quite messy as I was now allowed into the mess and the very same chaps who had previously banned me, now demanded free beer to help me celebrate joining the brotherhood of submariners.

A week later, Flag Officer Submarines paid the submarine a visit. This was generally a really good excuse to scrub-out and make the boat clean and sparkly again. The reason for his visit, apart from chatting to the Captain and scamming a free lunch, was to award myself and the other successful 'Part 3' graduates with the sought after and highly-coveted little gold badge that sets submariners apart from other lesser mortals.

The ceremony took place at sea, in the Junior Rates mess whilst we were submerged. All of the graduates were lined up in the mess looking as smart as our meagre clothing and washing facilities would permit. Sitting on the table in front of us were six very large glasses of 'Pussers' rum. Each had a pair of 'Dolphins' *swimming* in the bottom. Flag Officer Submarines first made a speech about welcoming new submariners into the brotherhood before presenting us, in turn with our glass of rum. The convention was, to down the drink in one large swallow, catching your 'Dolphins' in your teeth. With Flag Officer Submarines, the Captain, Commander Gavin Lane, and my Divisional Officer, Lt Hall watching, I gulped down the firewater, nearly gagging in the process, before receiving my prize.

Having now received my 'Dolphins', my training was still not complete. The last hurdle was to qualify in my watchkeeping position as a Forward Stoker. There was no actual task book as I remember for this final part of my submarine training. Essentially, it was another far more detailed 'Part 3', but concentrating on the HP air, hydraulic and water systems. The board also encompassed a practical exam with the 'Wrecker', a chap called Tony Yalden or 'TY' to his mates. When he considered I was ready for the exam, he knocked on the mess door one morning and in a gravelly London accent, demanded to know, quite aggressively, "Where's Plug?" He was wearing a naval uniform raincoat, called a Burberry, a pair of steaming boots and apparently, very little else. As a weapon, he was also carrying half a broomstick, covered in yellow insulating tape with the label 'TY's Training Aid'. I was roughly escorted up into the control room where I was then 'bagged-up' with a white muslin gash-bag that essentially blindfolded me. I was then ordered to touch, but do not operate valves and switches, as I proved that I could competently find them all in the correct sequence without the benefit of sight. Fortunately, my training and hard work had paid off and within thirty minutes, 'TY' had seen enough and the bag was removed. I could finally breathe a sigh of relief. This final exam, of course, heralded me buying another crate of beer for my freeloading messmates.

After patrolling the high seas for a couple of months, HMS Sovereign finally returned to Devonport in the winter of 1985. Arriving alongside after so many weeks at sea, everyone was anxious for leave to be piped so we could spend some time at home with our loved ones; but of course, there was always work to do. Whilst other teams rigged telephone lines and shore supply cables

to the submarine, I assisted a couple of other members of the forward mechanical team who were responsible for rigging freshwater hoses. After flushing the hoses and attaching them to the freshwater system, we waited patiently for the other sections to complete their immediate work before leave was finally announced at about 7pm.

After waiting in the queue for one of the two dockside phone boxes, I tried to call Anita, but she wasn't answering. I eventually decided to share a taxi with Tony 'Oz' Osborn and a couple of the other lads who lived locally and travelled the short distance from where the submarine was berthed to our newly acquired married quarter in the St Budeaux area of Plymouth.

I could see our flat from the dockyard, and I sensed that something was wrong. I couldn't quite put my finger on it, but the scene didn't look right. After dropping me off outside the flat, the lads continued further down the road towards their houses. From the front, the flat still seemed strange. Due to being extremely weary, my tired mind was just not computing everything I was seeing, so it was with shaky hands that I turned the key in the door.

The door, which normally brushed stiffly against the doormat, swung freely and banged against the wall. The entire flat was in darkness. All of the carpets had gone and the lights, when I tried them, did not work. Panic started to set in. All of the curtains had been removed and what remained of the furniture was now piled up in the middle of the living room like a huge unlit bonfire. In the kitchen, some previously frozen food was now thawed and rotting in the sink. In the glow from the streetlights outside, I could see our old Trimphone sitting on the floor in the lounge; picking up the receiver, I was amazed to get a dialling tone when all the power appeared to be off.

This was all too much for me to comprehend, I was convinced that Anita had left me, but this did not answer the questions about the food and the furniture. What had happened here? I called my brother, Simon, whose initial words were "Don't panic! You've had a flood. You've moved, but I don't know where." Brilliant! Now what? I then decided to call Anita's friend Fran. She answered with the same "Don't Panic! You've had a flood. You've moved ..." "Where's my wife!" I shouted, rapidly losing patience with the unfolding situation. "Oh, you've only moved a few yards down the road to number thirty-nine," Fran replied. Thanking her, I hurriedly left the flat and walked down the road counting the numbers until I saw the number '39' across the road.

Hoping that I had the right address, I nervously knocked on the door. A meek voice answered, "Who is it?" I replied with "Do I live here?" before the door swung open and a mightily relieved Anita crushed me in a backbreaking hug, before recoiling from the unmistakable smell of the submarine. Despite recently showering and wearing clothes that had been sealed in a polythene bag, I still apparently stank of the musty odour of the submarine. Ordering me to strip naked on the doorstep, she led me to our new bathroom to be bathed.

A few minutes later and smelling sweetly again, Anita showed me round our new home. I noticed that the flat was an exact mirror image of the flat that Anita had hurriedly vacated a couple of days previously. Over a coffee, she explained that one morning, after a particularly cold night, melted ice from a burst water tank in the loft had cascaded down through the flats and as such, the naval authorities had deemed them unfit for human habitation and re-housed all of the residents. Well, they could have at least told me. As she had only just moved in, the new flat was still full of unpacked boxes. Unable to find plates to cook me a meal, my ever-dutiful new wife served me baked beans on toast on the breadboard for my homecoming meal.

The following morning, I was required on-board the submarine as I was duty. Relating the story of my shock and subsequent relief from the previous evening, carefully editing some of the more intimate details, my mate, Tim Marstan, offered to assist with unpacking and hanging pictures and shelves. Therefore, the following morning, I took him home for breakfast with the intention of working all day to make the new flat look like 'home'. Opening the door, I was met with yet another surprise, Anita had unpacked everything. All of the cupboards were filled and despite the strange feeling of living in a mirror, we were almost back to normal again.

The new flat, however, did present a few unique problems. Despite being seemingly identical, everything was the opposite way around, meaning that a carpet that had somehow survived the deluge of water, now only fitted if it was turned upside down and some shelves that I had lovingly crafted to fit into alcoves, now needed some technical adjustment before they fitted. I also became rather annoyed at having to have a new telephone line installed at a cost of well over a hundred quid. A telephone was something of an essential item, unless I wanted the naval provost knocking on my door every time I woke up late for work.

My time-keeping was generally not too bad, but on one occasion, I did oversleep. Anita, thinking that I had the day off and forgotten to mention it, brought me a coffee at around 8am saying "Are you not going in today?" Bleary-eyed, I asked what the time was. She replied that it was a little past eight. Shit! I was late. Throwing off the quilt and jumping out of bed, I knew I was adrift and already in the poo, the only question that remained, was how deep.

Remembering a previous instruction, I telephoned the boat's control room and spoke to my Petty Officer, a nice chap by the name of Hughie Porter. Hughie, having already realised that I was not on-board, was first of all relieved to learn that I was not lying in a gutter somewhere before asking how long it would take me to get washed, dressed and into work. Mentally working out an abbreviated morning routine, I said that I could be there by 9am; an hour late. Hughie then asked where my overalls, boots and beret were stowed. I replied that they were on my bunk having now moved into my own bed in the bunkspace. Hughie then said my mate Tim would meet me in a dockyard toilet at 9am, with my working clothing in a gash bag. Looking back, this sounds quite dodgy and a bit gay, but it was an attempt by Hughie to prevent me getting into trouble and also to prevent him having to do a lot of unnecessary paperwork.

Arriving at the convenient rendezvous, somewhat flustered, Tim was waiting with my working clothes. Hurriedly getting changed and stuffing my civvy clothes into the bag, Tim and myself walked back on-board to be met by the Coxswain who, having not seen me that day, asked where I had been. "Over stores," I lied, before disappearing down the hatch and locating Hughie. Naturally, he was not too pleased with me and as a punishment, I was ordered to give him two hours extra work at the end of the day. Grateful for the admonishment, and wishing to make amends, I worked hard that day. I appreciated Hughie's style of management and quietly vowed to adopt the 'sensible' approach myself, if the situation dictated.

As this period alongside was designated as a maintenance period, there was much to be done including preparing the sewage and slop drain tanks for an internal inspection. I didn't relish the thought of entering either tank. As the name suggests, the sewage tank was full of human waste and naturally quite unpleasant but as the medical profession would no doubt agree, "It's only poo." The slop drain tank however, was far worse. This was the collection tank for greywater including sinks, showers and food waste, so it was a slimy, stinky mess of soap scum, pubes, potato peelings and dirty water from scrubbing-out which really made you want to retch. Therefore, to prevent disease, periodically, both tanks had to be emptied, flushed and disinfected with some potassium hydroxide granules called 'Elkol'. Flushing this stuff down the loo, was my first job. Clad from head to foot in a green plastic suit, plastic hood, rubber gloves, boots and breathing apparatus, I was taped up with masking tape as the stuff, when mixed with water, was extremely harmful and could cause nasty burns.

With both tanks pumped dry and then half-filled with clean water, I cordoned off the bathrooms and blocked all of the scuppers and set about flushing the lilac-coloured granules down the loo. Unfortunately, the reaction when the granules came into contact with water, was quite violent and some of the mixture foamed up and splashed out of the pan onto my boots. I wasn't too concerned about this at first, as I could rinse off in the shower after I had finished. The 'Elkol', however, had different ideas and started to burn its way through the leather until the tops of both of my feet started to sting. Realising what had happened, I squirted my feet with cold water, which only made matters worse as the reaction intensified and the solution continued to eat its way through my feet. Shouting for help, one of the on-board Medical Assistants, Dave Arnott, came to my rescue and on discovering that 'Elkol' was in fact one of the strongest alkalis, rushed to get a gallon container of vinegar out of the mess. I was initially horrified as I was sure this was going to sting even more, but as any budding chemist will tell you, mixing an acid to an alkali reduces the pH towards neutral and as vinegar is, in effect, acetic acid, the reaction was slowed and although they were severely burned, my feet were saved. That's not to say it didn't hurt, my feet were on fire and after some remedial treatment to ensure the reaction had stopped, I was sent home to rest.

The following morning, as I got out of bed, the pain was so excruciating that my legs buckled under me and I collapsed into a snotty heap on the bedroom floor. Working through the agony, I attempted to get dressed and off to work, but Anita had other ideas and phoned the boat to say I was ill and not coming in.

I had a wound about the size of a 50 pence piece on top of each foot. It was black and shiny like onyx and about two millimetres deep and on top of that, I discovered that I could not walk. My right foot was a lot worse than the left, but both were bad. Later that morning, a Royal Navy minibus turned up outside the flat. It appeared that the boat did not believe Anita and had requested that a doctor come and check me out. In short, he ended up taking me back to HMS Drake's sickbay where an in-depth examination was carried out. I was then told that the prompt actions of the medic had probably saved one, maybe even both of my feet from amputation. This was scary stuff, but fortunately, after about three weeks of sick leave, I was able to wear shoes and walk again. Being laid up enabled me to completely strip down the knackered engine of my aged Fiat 127 in the kitchen of the flat. Unfortunately, only one of us would ever work again and it was not the Fiat.

HMS Sovereign's ship's company numbered around a hundred and fifty officers and men, but there was only sufficient accommodation for about a hundred and ten. Therefore, whilst the submarine was at sea, a fifth watch remained behind to take leave and attend necessary courses. This allowed certain jobs to be rotated, but obviously, the Captain and other key players had nobody to rotate with. Most jobs, however, had spare capacity allowing a proportion of the crew to be landed.

I joined Sovereign having already passed my exams for Leading Hand, but I needed to attend the Leading Rates Leadership and Qualifying Courses, which would see me off the boat and studying for a total of about seventeen weeks. This was good news as it would give my feet more time to properly heal and frankly I could do with a bit of break. The reality was that it was like returning back into training again. At the beginning of 1986, I re-joined HMS Sultan on-loan to complete the fifteen week LRQC. Half of this course was entirely dedicated to workshops, where I successfully managed to remove my fingerprints after hours and hours of incessant filing. We were each given a toolbox, a technical drawing and a lump of mild steel and instructed to fabricate the object in the drawing, to a tolerance of plus or minus five thousandths of an inch. Included amongst our tools was a micrometre and a set square so we could constantly measure and remove high-spots. The task appeared, at first glance, to be easy. We had to first of all square off the lump of rough chopped steel to the specified measurements, make a smaller one-inch cube of metal and finally make a hole in the larger block for the smaller one to fit exactly. The problem was, it all had to be done by hand. On a lathe, it is a doddle requiring only a couple of hours of swarf generation, but using a series of files, a hacksaw and a hand drill it took considerably longer. In fact, it took weeks of constant measuring, marking, cutting and filing until my fingertips were almost worn away and remained numb for months afterwards. The task, as it turned out, developed useful skills, and by trial and error, I eventually managed to complete the project to the instructor's satisfaction. I was however, mightily pissed off after watching him measure my work with his vernier callipers and eventually grade my efforts into a percentage mark. After he had completed marking my work, he turned around, launched my couple of weeks' worth of blood, sweat, and sometimes tears into the scrap metal bin, to join those that had already been graded.

My prize, was another lump of metal and another drawing. This time we were to manufacture a G-clamp using the same principles and skills. This was the start of another few weeks of measuring, marking, cutting and filing until I successfully managed to manufacture a working G-clamp that I was quite proud of. Learning from experience, after the instructor had marked it, I stamped my name on it and stuffed it into my pocket. There was no way this was being consigned to the scrap metal merchant.

With the workshop module complete, the class moved on to the academic modules where, in the classroom, my grey cells were stretched to breaking point as we were taught first of all maths to O-level standard, Engineering Science and Electrotech. Both of the latter subjects involved memorising about thirty different equations and applying them to whatever the question required to calculate the answer. The pass-mark for the academic stuff was thankfully only fifty percent, but even that required a good deal of creativity for us to pass each of the thirty-seven separate exams. There was a need for some sort of innovation and after discussion with a class, several weeks ahead of us; the answer lay in the ability to scribe the formulas onto the end of a clear plastic ruler or onto the six sides of a cheap biro. This took many hours of patience and to the casual observer, the end result was invisible. However, holding the pen or ruler at the required angle allowed the user to be 'reminded' of the many different formulae. The irony was, after spending hours of painstakingly blatant cheating, I had memorised them all and although nobody will believe me, I passed all of my exams at the first attempt, on my own merits. It is an unorthodox method, but it worked for me. I can now only remember one formula from electrotech because we were taught a bit of rhyme to assist us; "One over two Pi root LC equals the Resonance Frequency." I have no idea what it means as I have never since had a use for it, but it seemed important at the time.

The carrot dangled at the start of the course, was selection for Mechanician. This was sure and fast-track promotion to Chief Petty Officer, and arguably a better career. To be selected, all candidates needed to have achieved an average course mark of more than seventy-five percent. The Mech's course, as it was known, represented another three years of purgatory and threatened to make my brain explode. At the time, I think I had reached my intellectual ceiling, so I was not too bothered about even trying for it, but I still strived to make the selection board. I had this hankering to pass the selection board and then to tell them to "Shove it!" Unfortunately, I never got the opportunity, my average mark from the course was in the seventies, but less than the required percentage. At least I had passed the course.

Re-joining the submarine, it was not long before we were off to sea again. HMS Sovereign was equipped with all manner of special communications equipment and as such was termed a 'sneaky boat'. With the cold war still quietly raging beneath the waves, we spent most of our sea time patrolling in the Arctic Circle somewhere north of Russia. For the most part, it was quite boring, punctuated with the odd bit of excitement, and occasionally, it was just plain bloody scary. Whilst transiting some way north of Iceland towards the permanent ice-pack, our sonar operators detected a possible submerged contact. After interrogating the contact for a little while, it was eventually classified as a Russian Delta 4 submarine. This presented us with quite a bit of excitement as the tactical types started a track on it. The Delta 4 was a missile submarine and therefore a contact of significant interest. Edging ever closer over a few days, we tracked the contact that appeared to be 'patrolling' the same area. Assuming it was in its designated area, we recorded all the information we could about it. The Captain was very excited and spent many hours in the control room, analysing the tactical picture, as we tracked the 'submarine'. After about four days of *chasing* this contact, the sonar operators, with egg on their faces, reclassified the contact as the island of Spitsbergen. We later found out that the island is quite well known for its ability to emit strange noises. Having spent quite a bit of time, taking the piss out of the sonar operators, we resumed our transit to our designated patrol area within the Arctic Circle.

A lot of the time on patrol, absolutely nothing happened at all and is barely worthy of note. All the time we were in our patrol area, the submarine would remain submerged and covert maintaining radio silence. In an effort to keep the noise down, I used to wear training shoes, as they were soft-soled and more comfortable than our clumpy steaming boots. Occasionally, somebody would accidentally drop something and make a noise. This would be immediately admonished by everyone else by shouting "Banging in the boat" which no doubt made more collective noise than the original incident. If there was a requirement to use a hammer, permission would first need to be granted from the officer of the watch who would generally grant permission to "Bang quietly". This always puzzled me, as hitting metal onto metal admittedly emits quite a lot of noise but by muffling, it lessened the effect but prolonged the activity.

Communication with home, in the mid-eighties, was virtually non-existent. We were, however, permitted to receive familygrams. This was a forty-word message from home, designed to reassure us that all was well. Bad news was not allowed so the Captain vetted all messages before the intended recipient was allowed read it. There was nothing private about the familygrams as many eyes would first scan them, looking for coded meanings. A typical message from Anita would read something like "Hi darling. I am fine, car fine, house fine, cat's fine. Videoed Coronation Street, missing you and love you. Anita xxxx." These small strips of typed white paper became potential lifesavers. The recipient would read and reread the text hoping to analyse it and find some hidden meaning, not that there was any. These would typically be Sellotaped into the back of a notebook and read again during the moments of inevitable homesickness.

Anybody who says they don't miss home is a liar. Many people tried to brazen it out but, privately they worried. When isolated from the outside world, the mind plays devious tricks on you. Occasionally, without any form of justification, usually when trying to sleep, I would convince myself that my wife had died in a horrific car accident and coincidentally, the house had burnt down as well. These were of course irrational thoughts, but with no evidence to either prove or more importantly disprove the feelings, you would inevitably spiral downwards into depression until you eventually dropped off to sleep. The following morning, in the fluorescent light of day, it would all seem a little silly. I found that the best way to suppress these depressing thoughts was to keep busy which generally ensured that when you did go to bed, you slept.

In January 1987, after waiting for about four years in a roster, I was eventually promoted to Leading Hand. This obviously meant a pay rise and elevated status on-board the submarine. I still needed to complete the Leadership Course at HMS Raleigh to be confirmed in the rate. This was nearly two weeks of running, kit preparation and presentations that was apparently designed to character build. I approached this with the 'It's only twelve days, so let's play the game' mentality and it appeared to be the right attitude as I excelled at everything and achieved an excellent report. One chap didn't do too well, and was, shall we say, 'invited' to stay a bit longer and do it all again. This was a major tick in the box for me as this now meant that I could get confirmed as a Killick Stoker.

Rejoining Sovereign again, we sailed back to our familiar stomping grounds, for another eight weeks of total boredom. We were stooging around our patrol areas around Easter but I think the Soviet Navy had decided to have a holiday, as there appeared to be nothing at sea apart from ourselves. I expect the Murmansk to Vladivostok train was full of vodka-fuelled Russian matelots off to the dacha for the holiday.

After Sovereign had been relieved in her patrol area by another submarine, we would quietly leave our allocated patrol area and slowly make our way south, over the course of about a week, eventually surfacing, due to the increase in fishing traffic once we had rounded Land's End. On the surface, the main vents would be cottered, preventing the submarine from submerging again, and the navigation lights including an orange flasher would warn all visible shipping of a submarine on the surface.

On the bridge, the officer of the watch and a lookout would pass all conning orders down to the helmsman in the control room. As a bit of a treat, with the permission of Ship Control, members of the ship's company were allowed to venture up to the bridge or the radar mast well for a goof and to get a breath of fresh air. After weeks of breathing recycled air and living under fluorescent light, it was quite exhilarating to feel the wind and the rain on your face, however one day, approaching Plymouth Sound, on our way home, it nearly went very badly wrong for a young stoker called Sam Fry.

When the submarine was on the surface, I kept my watch, sitting in front of the Systems Control Console next to the helmsman. I had been on the SCC for six hours and relieved at 1am. After a swift beer and a quick wash, I had gone to bed, looking forward to getting home the following day. At roughly the same time, Sam had come off watch back aft. Wishing to cool off in the night air and look at the distant lights of Plymouth, he had requested permission to go to the bridge for 'freshers'. As the radar mast shutters had not been hydraulically isolated, he was granted permission to go to the bridge. Sam had only been on the boat for a short time and had only visited the fin on one previous occasion, so retracing his steps, he ended up underneath the radar mast that was still turning and burning. In a classic cock-up, the officer of the watch, concentrating on navigating the submarine around fishing boats, had failed to realise that Sam hadn't arrived on the bridge.

A few minutes later, to compound the cock-up, my relief on the SCC, Tim Marstan, was ordered to secure and lower the radar mast. The usual procedure to check the fin clear, was seemingly ignored as the radar mast stopped rotating and slid back down into its recess.

Things then went from bad to worse for the hapless Sam. When the radar mast completed its lowering sequence, it triggered a microswitch and like a huge pair of pincers, the mast shutters, operated by three-thousand pounds of hydraulic pressure, started to close. If, noticing his impending execution, he had chosen to collapse his legs, he may well have got away with a few bumps and scrapes as the shutters closed above him. Instead, he opted to jump up on to the top of the fin as the shutters closed around his waist.

The first I knew of the emergency was when the Wrecker, Kev Mullord, shook me roughly at around 3am. "Plug, you've got to get up." "I'm off watch, Kev," I replied, not really comprehending why I was being awoken in the middle of the night. Kev persisted, quite urgently, "Plug, I need you to get on the SCC now, we're talking dead men in the fin." Well this had the desired sobering effect as I quickly rolled out of bed, jumped into my overalls and slipped my feet into my boots. As Kev followed me up to the control room, he filled me in on the events that had left one man, seemingly, fatally injured.

Poor old Tim, on the SCC, was a gibbering wreck when I arrived in the control room. It was not his fault, but he was convinced that he had just killed one of his shipmates and was in no fit state to resume his watch; hence, I was called, as the senior watchkeeper to take his place.

Fortunately, Sam was still alive, but not in a good way. Communications for assistance were being transmitted ashore and before long, a Sea King Search and Rescue helicopter out of the Naval Air Station at Culdrose was hovering above the fin. Quite a few of the dabbers were required to assist in getting the unconscious Sam into a stretcher, before he was hoisted into the hovering chopper, that then bee-lined for RNH Stonehouse in Plymouth. With the excitement now over, HMS Sovereign entered the western breakwater and tied up to Charlie Buoy where we would ride out the night before the confidential records could be disembarked later that morning.

After the masses of records had been safely bagged, tagged and off loaded, Sovereign could then proceed up river before eventually tying up to one of the submarine berths on 8 Wharf. Popping the hatch and seeing for the first time in eight weeks, the returning fifth watch, I was amazed to see in their ranks, the previously injured Sam Fry. Stood next to him, holding a huge file, was my oppo, 'Taff' Austin who shouted over to me, "I'm going to sharpen up those shutters so we get the bastard next time." Such was naval humour. Luckily, Sam suffered no more than a few bruised ribs and a bit of dented pride.

Occasionally, following a period of back-to-back patrols, as a sort of reward, the submarine would zip off to somewhere sunny for a bit of R&R. In 1987, following some extensive sneakiness in the cold waters of the Barents Sea, HMS Sovereign sailed westwards towards the Caribbean island of St Croix in the US Virgin Islands. The bad news was, it was now my turn to be left behind. Bloody typical! Do all of the hard work and receive none of the perks. Fortunately, the Captain, Commander Gavin Lane, was having none of it and arranged for the crew to rotate in St Croix. This ensured that most, if not all, of the crew got a bit of sunshine on the back of their necks.

Therefore, after a couple of weeks of well-earned leave, I rendezvoused with nine other shipmates who had also been left behind. We piled our collective luggage into a minibus and left Plymouth on the start of our journey to re-join Sovereign in St Croix. Prior to departure, we were each given one hundred dollars subsistence. Apparently, there was a ruling preventing immigrants from entering the United States without sufficient means. The routing had us flying first to Boston and then down the eastern seaboard of North America to the US Virgin Islands.

On the journey to London Heathrow, the airline tickets were handed out. Whilst I was checking the important stuff like name, destination and flight details, one of the lads exclaimed that we had been booked into Club-World. For the uninitiated, this is Business Class, where, if it turned out to be true, would result in some serious in-flight pampering. Personally, I could not believe that the navy would pay something close to seventeen hundred pounds for a single ticket. A late addition to our group was the PO Chef, called Steve, who, in the days before e-mail, was told to collect his ticket, on arrival, at Heathrow Terminal 4.

Four hours after leaving Plymouth, we arrived at Heathrow in good time and set about finding the right check-in desk. I immediately saw a British Airways desk, announcing Boston as its destination. Seeing no queue, I presented my passport and ticket to the lovely girl behind the desk who, after examining my ticket, redirected me to check-in, seemingly about five miles down the concourse, with the rest of the Club-World passengers. Gathering up the lads, we trudged past dozens of check-in desks, passing First-Class, Club-Europe and Club-Concorde before eventually finding Club-World. Selecting the Boston flight, I again presented myself at the desk with an 'I've made a terrible mistake, send me on my way' look in my eyes. I was greeted with a polite "Good morning sir, smoking or no smoking?" Successfully completing the short quiz, I was presented with a boarding-card and invited to take advantage of the hospitality in the Club-World Lounge.

After we had all checked-in, we needed to find Steve who, after finally obtaining his ticket, had learned that Club-World was full and that he was to be seated in Economy or 'Scumbag Travel'. This, of course, caused much hilarity as we waved goodbye and disappeared through Passport Control in search of considerable freebees.

Following signs, we rode a lift upwards and were greeted at the door to the Club-World Lounge where our boarding-cards were duly checked. Travelling in jeans, training shoes and T-Shirts was not the usual dress code for Club-World, so we did get a few disapproving looks from businessmen wondering if we were in the right place.

The lounge was fantastic. There was a plate-glass window along one side of the room with the pointed nose of Concorde only inches away from the glass. Along another wall, there was a bar. Imagine walking into a well-stocked pub without the counter or the barmaid. This was a help yourself free bar, complete with nuts and nibbles. Bloody brilliant! We quickly established a base on some comfortable seats before I disappeared to load up a plate of complimentary sandwiches, nuts, crisps with a pint and a Bacardi and Coke to chase it all down. Along another wall, stands displayed complimentary newspapers, magazines and even books that could be taken to read on the flight. Unfortunately, we only had a very short time to enjoy the lounge before a woman appeared at our table requesting that we follow her as our flight to Boston was now boarding.

To the undoubted relief of the other occupants, we left the lounge and rode the lift down to the concourse where a train, being pulled by what looked like a milk float, was waiting to transport us to the gate. As Club passengers with priority boarding, we were introduced to a very effeminate steward, called Jonathan, who immediately presented us with gifts of a complimentary wash bag and a tub of mixed nuts, before taking orders for pre-flight drinks.

Safely in the air, we established a routine where one of us would press a 'magic' red button in the roof and a round of drinks would duly arrive. Occasionally, when we remembered, we would send Jonathan 'mincing' to the back of the aircraft with a free drink for Steve. Any further back and he would have been sat on the loo.

Two at a time, we visited the flight-deck, only to find that the crew were far more interested in submarines than we were in looking out of the front window. I have always had a nerdy fascination with aircraft and perhaps if I had worked harder at school I might have become a pilot so, I spent quite a bit of time trying to absorb all of the information from myriad dials and screens, whilst trying to answer the flight-deck crew's questions about our submarine. There seemed to quite a lot of confusion between nuclear power and nuclear weapons but, I assured them that Sovereign was only powered by a nuclear reactor and all of our weapons were conventional whoosh-bangs. With the tour completed, I returned to my seat and pushed the magic button to order another round of drinks.

When Jonathan had not responded to my call, I wandered back to the galley area, where I found him sat down with his feet up reading a copy of 'The Sun'. I asked him if we could please get some more drinks, he replied, "Look, you know where they are, so why not help yourself?" so I did. In short, the nine of us in Club, and occasionally assisted by Steve in 'Scumbag Travel', managed to drink this Boeing 747 dry of Bacardi and vodka. I would just like to take this opportunity to thank the tax paying public.

About five hours after leaving Heathrow, we safely touched down in Boston, only to find that we had missed our connecting flight to St Croix by minutes. After whistling through immigration and collecting baggage, a quick council of war ensued to discuss the best plan of action. The Wrecker, Kev Mullord, suggested that we pooled our resources and book a couple of rooms for the night, until the next flight to the Virgin Islands in the morning.

A couple of hours later and we had rented three rooms, between ten of us, and after checking-in and deciding on the sleeping arrangements, we went off into Boston to spend the rest of our collective cash on food and drink. One of the mottos of the service is, "Improvise, Adapt and Overcome" and we had certainly done that. Out on the town, I wanted to go 'Cheers' and we actually drove past the bar, but I was dismayed to learn from a local cab driver that it looked nothing like the TV set on the inside. At the first bar we tried, the oldest looking member of our group was asked for ID before they would serve him. Chief Petty Officer 'Polly' Parrott was not at all amused. At the age of forty, you do not expect to have your ID requested by a spotty American youth, so we boycotted the place and found a much friendlier reception in another bar just around the corner.

Sensibly, we only had a couple of drinks before retiring for the night to share a bed with a '*friend*'. I was mightily relieved that sharing a bed with a bloke for the first time did not result in me losing my anal virginity.

Early the following morning, we were all up, repacked and back at the Airport for our seven hour flight to the sunshine. This was a standard domestic flight and apart from in-flight meals and drinks, it lacked the luxury of the BA flight. On a scheduled stop at Newark, we were told to disembark whilst the aircraft was refuelled. It was then, whilst grabbing some breakfast in the terminal building, that we caught some breaking news on CNN. An aircraft, experiencing turbulence, had landed following an in-flight incident. The fuselage had peeled back, cabriolet fashion, like a tin of sardines. As it was getting a bit bumpy, the Captain had ordered seatbelts to be fastened so the only casualty was a flight-attendant who whilst checking seatbelts took up flying lessons and was never seen again. The footage showed the clearly damaged aircraft safely on the ground. I dare say the passengers were mightily relieved having probably soiled themselves. Therefore, after seeing this disturbing episode, we now had to board the refuelled aircraft and spend most of the day in the air.

We needn't have worried, the flight south was without incident and after bouncing briefly at St Thomas, we made a short fifteen minute hop over to the neighbouring island of St Croix. Circling the island, in preparation for landing, we caught sight of a huge passenger liner alongside a finger jetty with a tiny black blob on the other side that assured us of HMS Sovereign's arrival.

Safely on the ground, we disembarked into a late-afternoon blast furnace and walked across the baked tarmac into 'Arrivals', that was basically a hut, constructed out of corrugated iron. Inside, there was a lot of hustle and bustle. Some local chap accosted me almost immediately and in a broad West Indian accent, said "Welcome to St Croix, mon," before handing me a small glass of the local hooch 'Cruzan' rum. Collecting our baggage, we looked around for a friendly face; somebody we recognised from the boat. A black chap in shorts, T-Shirt and a floppy hat, nudged me and again said "Welcome to St Croix, Plug." I thought this was quite surreal, as he knew my nickname, before I realised he was our Coxswain, 'Black Jonno', from the boat. It was lovely to see him, but he blended in so well.

With the formalities completed, it was not long before we were transferred by minibus to our hotels in Christiansted where we were reunited with the rest of our shipmates.

As the submarine's living accommodation was rather cramped, many people were forced to 'hot bunk'. As a practical perk, whilst visiting a foreign port, submariners were accommodated in hotels, which were usually of quite a decent standard. We were also paid subsistence on a daily rate to pay for food. Naturally, as a Junior Rate, we got the lowest standard of hotel, but the bar was set pretty high and the hotel was very nice. It was situated right on the boardwalk, with rooms overlooking the pool. This meant, fuelled with a moderate amount of alcohol and stupidity, one could jump, dive or bomb into the pool from the balcony; which caused much merriment until the management ordered us to stop. We were apparently upsetting the paying guests

For reasons known better to himself, an American Vietnam veteran, staying at the hotel, had decided to bring his war medals on holiday with him. In the drunken confusion, these somehow ended up on the bottom of the pool with various people diving down to retrieve them before chucking them in again. His wife joined, us wearing only a skimpy summer dress, before somebody decided that she should join in the fun. Without warning, he picked her up and unceremoniously chucked her in the pool. She shrieked as she, seemingly in slow motion, entered the water causing her dress to balloon up around her neck. It was then that we noticed she had neglected to wear anything else and was now completely naked, apart for her sodden dress that floated on the surface. As luck would have it, she had a tremendous body and was very entertaining. After removing the dress from around her neck, she spent the rest of the afternoon swimming naked in the pool.

We spent another seven days, enjoying the weather, drinking cocktails, eating the local food and mucking about in the water. A few of us, one fine day, chartered a boat to dive on a local coral reef called 'Buck Island', which is an underwater national park. A local character called Captain 'Big Beard', so named because he was sporting a mass of hair resembling a dead badger on his lower face, operated the boat tour. Included in the price of the charter was a buffet lunch and as many local cocktails as we could drink. In the burning midday sun, this was not such a great combination, but we had a lovely time in the crystal blue waters, swimming amongst the multi-coloured fish. For a modest fee, we could hire fins, a mask and a snorkel. When something of interest hove into view, I would take a deep breath through the snorkel and majestically dive down to investigate. Then forgetting I was on a limited air supply, breath out before sucking in a mouth full of saltwater. This caused the inevitable panic and emergency surface coughing and spluttering from a depth of about twelve feet. After a while, I did get the hang of it. There were proper cylinders we could hire, but as the water surrounding the reef was so shallow, I really didn't see the point.

With the government paid holiday coming to a close, I relieved 'Taff' Austin, so he could fly back home to his wife and kids. I was now in charge of removing the carbon dioxide from the submarine's enclosed atmosphere. There were three CO_2 scrubbers especially built for the task. They utilised a horrible, gloopy, greeny/yellow chemical called mono-ethanolamine or amine for short. The amine would readily absorb CO_2 from the boat's atmosphere when it was cold and then release it when it got hot. It was actually very effective, but as a strong alkaline, it had a tendency to burn the skin and also smelt of wee, when spills were not mopped up. A build-up of carbon dioxide in an enclosed area is lethal. If the CO_2 scrubbers were not working, a hundred and ten people all breathing-out would increase the CO_2 concentration to dangerous levels within a few hours. Initially, people would start to feel lethargic and tired. Many would get headaches as they slowly became poisoned by the gas. Left unchecked, the levels would continue to rise until people eventually, fell unconscious and died. For that reason and preferring not to get a carbon dioxide induced headache, I took my work very seriously. When they were working, the scrubbers worked very well, but they needed a lot of love and attention. On more than one occasion, I was caught, talking to the machines, willing them to work. Many of my fellow maintainers also swore by the loving bedside approach to CO_2 scrubber maintenance.

Back in Devonport, the submarine entered another period of maintenance to prepare for yet another patrol up north. There is often a lot of frantic activity prior to the boat sailing for patrol. After weeks of working twelve hour days and not seeing your house in the daylight for months on end, we were glad to get back to sea for a bit of a rest.

With all of the stores and supplies on-board, we again slipped quietly out of Devonport for another eight-week patrol. As we were operating on a war footing, we carried enough food and supplies to support the entire ship's company for a full three months. This usually involved laying false decks of tins of beans and cartons of long-life milk. The caterers had packed the fridges to form 'tunnels' of various food groups. As the walk-in fridge was stacked to capacity, without this undoubted skill, we may not have eaten chips or indeed sweetcorn until about week-six when they had been excavated. Goodies such as Cornettos or choc-ices would be kept squirrelled away in a safe place and duly handed out on a Saturday night, following the ritual steak-night and cheeseboard.

Mealtimes were sacred, whilst at sea. With no formal dining area, we were forced to transform the mess from a living area into a dining room and later in the evening, into a cinema. Smoking would cease in the mess fifteen minutes before food would be served to allow the ventilation system time to clear the air.

As I was on-watch, but usually stood down prior to the 7pm watch change, I would assist the chefs in the tiny galley, frying chips or scampi. It was either that or serve food in the mess. When the on-coming watch arrived, we tried to treat it like a small bistro. Someone would show the diner to an empty seat and take orders for fillet steak, scampi, or if they preferred, an omelette. These would typically be served with my freshly cooked chips, peas, a mixture of fried onions and mushrooms smothered in a black pepper sauce.

After everyone was seated and eating, someone would stand by the stainless steel sink in the mess and wash plates as they were finished with. Meanwhile, in the galley, I would be sweating buckets, constantly frying mountains of chips. This may seem an odd job to be doing for a stoker, but there was an ulterior motive. Helping the chefs allowed me to choose the biggest, baddest fillet steak for myself and then cook it exactly as I liked it.

After the watch change, it was our turn to sit down. This was my favourite meal of the week. A large white plate, covered in steak with a heap of freshly cooked chips, mushrooms and onions on top. If there was any scampi left, we might scam a few bits to make an improvised 'surf and turf'. This would be washed down with a bottle of red wine, shared between two. It was all very civilised.

After the main course had been cleared away, as we finished off the wine, it was time to start on the cheese. The chefs would cover some large trays with silver foil and then arrange a selection of cheeses, from the usual cheddar and stilton, to brie, camembert, boursin, smoked cheese and port salut. These would be garnished with celery and grapes and accompanied with a couple of boxes of Jacobs assorted crackers. With the cheese dished up, the lights would be dimmed and a Saturday evening film, such as 'Top Gun' would be shown.

Later in the evening, as a weekly treat, the caterer would come round and hand out ice creams such as choc-ices or Cornettos. Yes, Saturday evening was my favourite meal time.

Sailing to our usual patrol areas was relatively uneventful. We successfully managed to transit the 'Faslane Triangle' and continued north. Within a week, we were on station, remaining dived, but at periscope depth, listening and watching. Again, there was little activity from our Soviet friends, so we just sort of stooged around, drawing some comfort from the familiar routine but also getting bored rigid in the process.

A few weeks into the patrol, the tranquillity was broken when we received intelligence that the Soviet submarine 'Komsomolets' was on the surface in the Norwegian Sea with a fire raging on-board. Sovereign's Captain took the decision to gradually close the stricken vessel so, if ordered; we could surface and render assistance. Therefore, over a day or so, we left our position and *sped* towards the area at a near-silent five knots, whilst monitoring the communications traffic. The idea was to get quite close, whilst also remaining covert. We could then be on hand very quickly, if assistance was required. The Norwegian Air Force overflew the scene and offered to drop life rafts and render assistance, but were warned by the Soviet Navy to stay away from the crippled submarine, as this would be considered an act of war.

Tragically, the submarine, the only one of its class, sank and many of the Russian sailors perished in the freezing waters of the Norwegian Sea. This hit us hard, they were no different to us and the accident could easily have happened to Sovereign. Not much was said; as people brooded with their own thoughts. Servicemen are often renowned for their callous humour in response to a tragedy, but this is just a defence mechanism designed to hide true feelings. After the loss of 'Komsomolets' nobody much felt like joking; this was just too close to home.

Every Sunday at 10am, the submarine held an inter-denominational church service in the wardroom. The half-dozen religious types, that usually went along, sang a couple of hymns, said a few prayers and got a free glass of port. Not normally a churchgoer and without discussing it, the following Sunday, I went to the wardroom to remember the Russian sailors that had perished. Half of the ship's company also *needed* to do the same; the wardroom was packed to capacity and we ran out of port. I am not ashamed to say that a few tears were shed.

Safely back alongside in Devonport, having been away from home and essential maintenance for some time, the submarine was scheduled to go into dry dock for a mini-refit. This was due to last around six months, so I took the opportunity to study for my Petty Officer's exam. There was, of course, much to learn, but in every promotional written examination, there would be the same mandatory questions relating to leadership and discipline. This was a simple memory test as Queen's Regulations and the Articles of War were to be found plastered on the walls of the mess and as alternative reading literature on the back of toilet doors. I also needed to find cerebral storage space for all of the submarine's systems and be able to reproduce any diagram on request. There were masses of temperatures, pressures and parameters that I also needed to commit to memory. When I considered myself confident and ready for the examination, the 'Wrecker' quizzed me informally and uncovered vast holes in my knowledge, resulting in my confidence levels taking a nosedive. Eventually, one afternoon, when I was as ready as I could be, I sat my written examination in the health physics' lab invigilated by a series of very bored POs and chiefs. This was not a timed memory test, so in effect, I could spend as much time as I needed to answer the questions and draw all of the required diagrams.

My studying and revision, to my relief, was completely worthwhile and more importantly, relevant as I found that I could answer most of the questions and have an educated stab at the others. Even so, after six hours of constant writing and drawing, I was completely exhausted and bursting for the loo. A toilet break in the middle of the exam would have been seen as an excellent opportunity for some directed revision, so I just had to tie a knot in it. Granted it was a very small knot, but enough to stifle the urge and concentrate on the matter in hand.

It only took a few hours for the paper to be marked and I found, to my immense relief, that I had passed. There was now only two more hurdles to jump; first I had to sit a mock oral exam in front of the MEO and his deputy for an hour before they deemed me competent enough to sit the real thing in front of a Commander.

Whilst we were in dock, an opportunity arose for me to go on a training flight in an RAF Nimrod operating out of RAF St Mawgan near Newquay. Borrowing a car from the transport section, four of us made the journey down to RAF St Mawgan quite early in the morning. On arrival, we were kitted-out in flight suits and given the usual safety brief. As it transpired, our security clearance was more than sufficient for us to attend the classified pre-flight brief. On this occasion, the Nimrod would be taking-off and conducting an aerial reconnaissance training flight over the south-western approaches, looking for sneaky Russian AGIs. The AGIs are seemingly innocent looking Russian ships, bristling with sensors, that stooge around gathering intelligence. We had come across them many times before on our travels, but ironically, we gained loads of intelligence from them without the Soviet's ever knowing we were just a few feet beneath their keel.

The pre-flight brief covered navigation, training objectives and the anticipated weather for the sortie, which was expected to take about six hours. Immediately following the briefing, we were ushered towards a waiting bus; one of the things I noticed about the 'Brylcreem Boys', is that they never walk anywhere. Following the short bus ride to the aircraft, we were shown to four seats near the small galley and requested to stay seated whilst the crew readied the aircraft for departure. We were issued headsets allowing us to listen in to what was going on. It all seemed very ordinary and gentlemanly as the 'crab fats' went about their daily business. Over the net, we heard, presumably the pilot, say, "Good morning gentlemen, are you ready back there for engine start?" One by one, all of the stations reported that they were ready before the engines started to spool up. We heard the pilot getting clearance to taxi to the end of runway three zero before the doors were finally secured and the huge aircraft slowly commenced its taxi.

Finally in position, St Mawgan tower gave the pilot permission to depart before we heard the four Spey gas turbines slowly wind up to full power. The brakes were released and within thirty seconds, we were airborne over the north Cornish coast, climbing hard and banking left giving us a wonderful view of Newquay and the Cornish peninsular.

Wheels up and established in flight, a member of the flight crew invited us to unbuckle and look around the aircraft. Not really knowing where to begin, I decided to start at the tail and work my way forward to the main event on the flight deck. One thing that struck me immediately, was the similarities between a submarine and a 'nimbat'. We had a signal ejector to blast things to the surface, whilst they had a similar device for dropping sonobuoys into the water. Further forward, a line of screens, each with an operator, watched the results of the 'stick' of sonobuoys. There were two navigation tables further forward, one of which was operated by the Captain. This struck me as a bit odd, I had always assumed that the Captain was the bloke in the driving seat. It makes sense when you think about it; the Captain can tell the pilots what course to steer after receiving information from sonar, radar and communication. In short, it was quite a slick operation and I was very impressed, though it galls me to admit it.

Having always been a bit geeky when it comes to aircraft, my self-guided tour ended up on the flight deck where the two pilots looking out of the window, and a flight engineer facing his panel on the starboard side, greeted me warmly. First of all the flight engineer gave me a brief overview of how he controlled the fuel to the aircraft's engines and trimmed the aircraft by transferring fuel around to keep it nicely balanced. This was very similar to my job on-board Sovereign, though what he did with fuel; we did with vast quantities of seawater.

Finally, chatting to the pilot in the left hand seat, he gave me a brief tour of his myriad dials, levers and gauges before posing the question, "What is the most important gauge on the flight deck?" I went through the predictable answers of altitude, artificial horizon and indicated air speed before finally giving up. The pilot then pointed forward and said, in all seriousness, "Window." Frankly, I thought he was taking the piss out of a gullible matelot well out of his comfort zone, but he went on to explain that reliability on instruments is dangerous, especially if they fail. He pointed out the rivets along the side of the windows. Agreeing that we were flying straight and level, he said that as long as the horizon remained level with the third rivet from the bottom, we should be flying, more or less, straight and level. He then surprised me further, by asking if I would like to fly the aircraft. Now, he might have been joking, but as the co-pilot had left his seat and ventured aft for lunch, I was invited to jump into his seat. Not quite sure where to put my feet to step over the central console, the flight engineer assisted me. Quite aggressively, he pointed out a lever underneath my hovering foot "Tread on that, and I break your face." Not very friendly, but he went on to explain that this lever shut off fuel to the engines and as we were at five thousand feet, the inevitable crash would have caused a lot more damage than a broken face.

Safely seated and strapped in with my feet on the rudder pedals and hands lightly covering the control stick, the pilot said "Ok, you have control" before announcing over the net that LMEM Atkinson from Her Majesty's Submarine Sovereign was now flying the aircraft to much laughter and sarcastic comments from the flight crew.

Flying roughly west, the pilot first got clearance, amazingly from London Air Traffic Control, to climb to fifteen thousand feet before starting-up another engine. He explained that in level flight, to conserve fuel, three of the four engines were shut down. When he was happy that we had the power, I was instructed to slowly pull the stick back until the sea just disappeared out of the window. This would give us a climbing attitude of about fifteen degrees. Sure enough, he was right as, looking at the sky and altimeter, we climbed steadily towards our desired altitude. With about three hundred feet still to go, he advised that I start to level off so as not to overshoot the assigned altitude. Established in level flight again at fifteen thousand feet, the next evolution was a tight right-hand turn onto a new course of zero two zero degrees. My instruction, was to put the horizon across the diagonal corners of the centre windows whilst maintaining altitude with some backward pressure on the stick. This seemed quite a scary thing to do, as it was a very tight turn, but following some excellent tuition from the pilot, I started the turn before he instructed me to level out and using the visual reference, fly straight and level. I was starting to get the hang of this. Heading towards the Welsh coast, it looked gorgeous. I could see many tiny green islands, ringed by golden sand, that I never knew existed. It was at this point that the co-pilot returned and asked for his seat back.

Remaining on the flight deck, totally hooked with flying, we started to receive instruction from some girlie on the ground at RAF Brawdy in South Wales. This instruction vectored us onto final approach as she guided us in "Zero Romeo Romeo, you are two degrees left of centreline, on centreline, two degrees right of centreline, on centreline … etc." "Select sixty degrees of flap, throttle back to forty percent." Leaning on the back of the pilots' seats, a runway appeared dead ahead as the co-pilot, following instruction from the air traffic controller, now descended towards it. Lowering the undercarriage, he levelled out nicely, before touching down perfectly, right on the centreline. We started to decelerate slightly before the co-pilot pushed the throttles forward and the Nimrod increased in speed, before taking-off again. This seemed a little odd to me as the wheels and flaps were again retracted. As the aircraft climbed back towards our previous cruising altitude, the pilot explained that this was an exercise called a 'touch and go' and familiarised pilots with landing at strange airfields. That was possibly my shortest ever visit to Wales.

Returning across the Bristol Channel to Cornwall, the co-pilot was instructed by the Captain to conduct some 'touch and go's back on the familiar runway at RAF St Mawgan. Descending towards the airfield, I noticed that the runway appeared to be some way to the left of our heading, but not wishing to interfere, said nothing. The co-pilot corrected to the left and then quite late to the right to bring us on centreline. The starboard wheels touched down hard before he slammed the port wheels down. Quite hairy, but I thought this was normal for these guys. Not so, the pilot first screamed at full volume in his clipped 'Battle of Britain' accent, "That was fucking awful, Simon, now go around and do that again," before explaining, calmly, over the net, "Sorry about that, chaps, we are going around again."

Safely back on the ground after about six successful, touch and go's, we were sort of hoping for a debrief in the form of a few beers, in the sergeant's mess, but this was just the end of another day's work for them, they got changed and went home. Something of an anti-climax, we retrieved the car and drove back to Plymouth after a tiring but thoroughly enjoyable day.

After the excitement of the previous day had subsided, we still had a vast amount of work to do in order to get the submarine out of dry dock. Like any self-propelled vehicle, when it is disconnected from shore power, it requires its own generator to provide electrickery to make the engine run. We therefore needed fuel to run our diesel engine, as all of our tanks had been emptied for maintenance. Under the supervision of the chief stoker, I organised my team and connected the two ten-inch diameter fuelling hoses in preparation for the tanker turning up. As we had a nuclear reactor within a few feet of us, a senior rating was required to take charge of the fuelling process. My instructions from the CMEM was to get all of the hoses rigged with drip trays, rags and fire fighting equipment and then to call him prior to embarking fuel. This suited me fine, he was quite useless and we worked much better as a team without his interference.

Later that morning, I called him on his walkie-talkie, "Chief, we are all connected up and ready to embark fuel." He replied, "I'm finishing my pint and will be there in a bit." Brilliant, we were slogging out guts out and he was in the mess drinking, at 10am. After about twenty minutes, he had not arrived, so plucking up the courage, I called him again, "Chief, we are still waiting here to embark fuel." His reply, was a shouted, "Look, I will be there in a bit, don't call me again." I waited for another thirty minutes for him to arrive before I finally lost patience. Using the same channel, so he could hear what was going on, I called my side-kick, Simon Geary, who was on the casing, manning the fuelling point, "Casing-Jetty, standby to receive fuel." Simon replied by saying, "Roger fuel," and giving me the thumbs-up from the casing about twenty yards away.

As the diesel fuel glugged slowly into the tank, my boss turned up next to me on the jetty. "Morning, leader, how's it going? Where's the chief stoker?" Thinking fast and despite my feelings for the malingering chief I said, "It's all going fine, sir, the CMEM is on the end of this," waving my portable radio at him. Clearly a man of intelligence and not one of the 'bullshit baffles brains' officer cadre he replied in a tone that belied his seriousness, "Not what I asked; where *is* the chief stoker?" Hmm, I was in a quandary. Throughout my naval career, I had been taught that we look after our shipmates and do not grass them up to the wardroom. I replied, with a semi-truthful and non-committal, "I don't know, sir!" He then said, "I will talk to you later. When you are all finished and cleared away, report to me in my office," before he stormed off.

Towards the end of the day, all of the fuel had been successfully embarked, none had been spilled and all of the hoses had been disconnected and stowed away. It was then that I reported to the AMEO(S), proud of a job well done. Instead of receiving praise, he gave me the bollocking of my life, lasting for a clear ten minutes. At full volume, he shouted at me, "Who gave *you* permission to fuel the submarine? You never, ever fuel the boat without senior rate supervision..." Like most bollockings I had had in the past, you tend to switch off after a few moments and absorb the wrath. Finally, he concluded, "...with this attitude, you will never make petty officer, now get out." Completely deflated, after what I thought would be a chuck up, I was shutting the door to his office when he shouted, "Oh and Plug? ... Well Done!" Now I understood what had just happened. I had been reprimanded because protocol demanded that I was disciplined, but he was intelligent enough to realise that I had acted in the best interest of the submarine and the real culprit was the chief stoker. I never found out exactly what happened there, but he left the boat very shortly afterwards, with suspected angina.

About two weeks after that incident, I presented myself, with my buddy, Nige Thornber, one hot and sunny afternoon, to the office of Commander Tim Cannon for my formal oral examination for promotion to Petty Officer. Dressed in my best uniform with shoes bulled to a high gloss shine, I hoped my appearance alone would be sufficient to convince him of my suitability for advancement.

Also in his office, to assist on my examination, was my boss, Lt Bob Parsonage, who had previously balled me out over the fuelling incident. The board was only designed to last about thirty minutes and started with

Commander Cannon presenting the scenario, "The submarine is preparing to sail on patrol for up to ninety days, store for war." Properly prepared for the question, I went through a rehearsed checklist of all engineering stores that I would need to embark to sustain the submarine for three months away from base port. Having answered that question satisfactorily, Lt Parsonage then posed the question, "Take me through the procedure for embarking diesel fuel onto a nuclear submarine?" You beauty! I knew then that I had been forgiven and also that they wanted me to pass the board, so it was with relief, but no real surprise when I was informed I had passed my Petty Officer's exam after a very short discussion. Thirty minutes later, Nige also passed, heralding a few celebratory drinkies back in the mess.

I left HMS Sovereign shortly after that, having spent nearly five years on my first submarine and joined HMS Defiance for a well-deserved period of shore time. This presented me with quite a culture shock. Sure, I was glad to leave, but also saddened at the same time. As a crew, we had undergone many adventures, some of them downright scary and some extremely amusing. Due to the amount of time we had spent submerged in the same steel tube, isolated from our loved ones, we had become very close. This may sound like life in a Turkish prison, but trust me on this one, you had to be there.

We were highly trained and focused on our mission. Apart from the occasional run ashore when hair was allowed to be let down, we were completely in tune with the submarine's systems and routines. When I finally left Sovereign, Lieutenant Dave Thomas, one of the Auxiliary Marine Engineering Officers, commented that it would take about six months to slow down after the frantic activity of the previous five years. Actually, he was not too far out.

HMS DEFIANCE

20th November 1989 to 16th July 1991

I joined HMS Defiance again on Monday the 20th November 1989 and after the usual 'dockyard runaround', I was assigned to work in STALAG which, despite sounding like a German prisoner of war camp, actually stood for Special Tools And Lifting Associated Gear. I dare say some creative soul, in the past, had dreamed up the title to make it sound Gucci.

The section essentially consisted of a POMEM called 'Zac' King who was a legend in his own lunchbox and an LMEM called 'Smudge' Smith whom I had joined to relieve. Both of these chaps were completely unique characters and, as we have always said, the service needs characters.

I was drafted into the job to allow 'Smudge' to go into hospital for testicular cancer treatment. Cancer is one ailment that even the most heartless matelot cannot joke about, but 'Smudge' himself was endlessly taking the piss out of himself with the same three one-liners over and over again. He was told that one of his knackers had to be removed, so he further nicknamed himself 'Womble' or 'One-Ball', saying that as he would soon be unbalanced, he would not be able to ride a bicycle anymore and that the other one would have to work twice as hard to cope with the demand. Oh dear, those long winter nights must have simply flown by in the Smith household. What a pity he could not have had a personality transplant instead.

STALAG, it appeared, was just a glorified tea room for the fitters and slingers of the Nuclear Repair team. It was a windowless cubby-hole where they could sit in relative comfort, smoke and drink tea whilst telling tall-tales. The POMEM, 'Zac' apparently, if the stories are to be believed, single-handedly sank the Argentine cruiser General Belgrano using an 'over-the-shoulder shot' with Sub-Harpoon, whilst he was serving on the submarine HMS Courageous. Unfortunately for him, whilst his story might have stood up in a bar in Tahiti, in STALAG, it was instantly rubbished by people who actually *knew* that she was controversially sank by HMS Conqueror using a Mark 8 Tigerfish torpedo. We have a saying in the navy, "Don't spoil a good dit with the truth," and 'Zac' was no exception.

As the killick now running the Special Tools and Lifting Gear store, I was treated pretty much like a dogsbody, being the lowest ranking person in the section. The chief took an instant dislike to me for reasons of his own that I am, to this day, unsure about. He was a very short and loud Glaswegian fellow called Joe McCrannar who was something of a tyrant. He drank excessively and also suffered from small man syndrome. During the eighteen months I spent there, we managed to cultivate a healthy dislike for each other. Fortunately, his desk was in an office on the floor above, so I tried to keep my distance from him.

After consolidating my position in the organisation, which frankly did not take too long and to ease the boredom, I decided to reorganise the store, as it had been neglected for far too long, resulting in items of lifting-gear being returned broken and not fit for purpose. Each chain block had a unique number and was supposed to have an individual annual test certificate issued by Lloyds. As I discovered, many of the items were without certificates or their test date had expired. For this reason, I quarantined these items, which of course brought the wrath of Joe McCrannar crashing down on my head. From time to time, the slingers would require more kit than I had serviceable. I managed, somehow, to weather the storm as I had the law on my side and set about sending the defective and out of date items away for repair and test. I also ordered masses of new strops, shackles and chain blocks which of course came with their own test certificates and over a few weeks, I established a shop counter rather than the previous 'help yourself' regime. This, of course, caused me a lot more work, but I took a certain amount of pride in restoring the store back to its intended glory.

During the quiet times, Zac, despite his bullshitting nature, would do anything for his friends. In fact, he did not actually do a great deal himself, instead he got me to do it. We had a seemingly endless supply of orders for barbeques. These were quite simple to make and involved an empty 45-gallon oil drum and some lengths of angle iron to make the legs. This became a welcome distraction, as I happily made a mess out in the workshop, cutting the oil drum vertically through the centre to make two troughs. Four identical lengths of angle iron were then cut and drilled in the centre which were then bolted together form sturdy scissor-action legs. The grills were fabricated from galvanised mesh before the first prototype was ready to roll off the production line. Subsequent commissions evolved slightly to include wheels, carrying handles, warming trays and lids. Apart from the pride and eventual thanks from the grateful recipient, it was only 'Zac' who profited with the black market currency of the day, which happened to be beer. After making all of this mess, there was always the need to clean up for Captain's Rounds.

Captain's Rounds is a periodic, cleanliness inspection designed to boost morale, though in actual fact, it pisses more people off and arguably causes more nausea than it's worth, though it does give the place a good clean and an opportunity to get rid of all the accumulated dirt and rubbish. In the run-up to rounds, the workshop was absolutely gutted and, working from the top down, under Zac's direction, we scrubbed the place out completely, which, strangely, I actually enjoyed. After scrubbing, I managed to scam some signal red paint and gave some metal shelving a freshen up and with some metal polish shone up the bright work. The only job left to do before rounds, was the deck and this dubious honour fell to me. Therefore, one Friday afternoon, when it was quiet, I scrubbed the green painted concrete deck, dried it and then prepared to give it a fresh coat of paint in preparation for the Captain's inspection on the following Thursday. In my haste to get the job finished, I accidentally knocked over the twenty-five litre tin of green paint. Two litres would probably have been a suitable amount for the task but now, with the deck swimming in a gloopy green puddle, I set about distributing it until the whole deck was covered and looked immaculate and shiny. Pleased with my afternoon's work, I locked up and went home for the weekend, reasoning that the paint should have dried by Monday. When I arrived at work on Monday morning, the paint was still very wet indeed and took a full week to harden sufficiently enough for us to walk on which seemed to be hilarious to everyone but me. I was sure that Joe would surely beat me up when he found out. Fortunately for me, Captain's Rounds was postponed for a week, giving me a stay of execution as the chief was now baying for my blood. This was an unplanned cock-up on an unprecedented scale, but at least it lightened the mood with everyone, except Joe.

Captains Round's eventually went very well, receiving a special mention from the Captain for the deck, this resulted in a rare smile from Joe. I tried hard to get along with him but, it is a trait of human nature, if someone dislikes you, you tend to dislike them back. As a punishment, for embarrassing him with the green paint incident, he invoked a ruling which prevented me from doing anything without first consulting him. This included talking to my officers and going home at the end of the day. He also demanded, quite illegally, that I drive him to the pub at lunchtime and collect him in the morning from the dockyard gate, if he was running a bit late. As a senior leading hand, this was quite unacceptable to me, but as Joe was a chief petty officer and two ranks above me, I was powerless to disobey his direct order and he had expressly forbidden me talking to my divisional officer without first consulting him as my divisional senior rate.

I became increasingly unhappier in my work which was having a detrimental effect on my home life. On more than one occasion, I came home from work, ready to explode. There was a giant, golf ball-sized lump in my throat and I had a face like thunder. Talking was impossible, without breaking down, so in an attempt to calm myself, I got a beer and whacked on some very loud music through my headphones. My wife, Anita, becoming increasingly concerned and tried her hardest to relieve the tension, but I was too strung up and needed to wind down, slowly, in my own way. Unbeknown to me, Anita, in desperation, had called my mum and handed me the phone. Mum's voice was the catalyst required to release the tension and I dissolved into tears, putting the phone down. A couple of hours later and more composed, I called her back and explained the situation. I was at the end of my rope and could not see a way out of it.

The orders from Joe carried on for some time. I became increasing unhappy with his victimisation, for want of a better word, until one day he pushed me a bit too far and I snapped. During the resulting 'discussion' he finally realised that this mild mannered pussycat had teeth and claws so, from that moment on, he resolved to cut me a bit of slack and we managed to rub along ok. I have never forgiven him for his bullying, never trusted him and was always forever wary of the stormy little Jock.

A few weeks later, Joe came into the workshop carrying an ancient flintlock pistol that he was renovating. Apparently, it was made out of walnut and was really nice. He asked me to drill a small hole to re-secure the trigger guard that had become detached. Using a hand drill in the chippy's shop and applying no downward pressure, I slowly started to drill the pilot hole when without warning, the drill went straight through the seventeenth-century relic's body. I was absolutely mortified, Joe would surely murder me on the spot. I agonised on how I could explain away this latest cock-up when he came in to see how I was getting on. Reluctantly, I explained the problem before showing him the damage. His response was uncharacteristic in the extreme, He simply replied "Good job it wasn't a new one," and set about showing me how to repair the damage to the rotten wood.

One of the other fringe benefits of working in STALAG was that 'Zac' had managed to purloin some gunmetal submarines that had been cast in the foundry. These were very rough and only loosely resembled the shape of a nuclear submarine. What followed though, was weeks of filing and finally rubbing down with emery cloth before buffing out scratches until the result was a highly polished model submarine. In my spare time, I made a few of them. One of which, I presented to my brother, Simon, for his desk.

After a short, but very eventful eighteen months in the job, I was summoned to see my DO to sign a draft order to join the Swiftsure-class submarine, HMS Spartan which was newer, but almost identical to HMS Sovereign, so I was quite happy with the draft. The problem was, that the boat was based at the Clyde Submarine Base in Faslane on the banks of the Gareloch. This is slap bang in the middle of nowhere, about an hour north of Glasgow. That meant I had to put up with more gobby Jocks. Having just bought our first house in Plymouth, I was not happy with my sudden base port change to Faslane, so I went to see if I could get it changed. The answer was not the one I wanted, but as they say, every cloud has a silver lining.

As it was highly classified at the time, I was informed, very quietly, that all of the Swiftsure-class submarines were being recalled for repairs to an area of the steam generator known as the 'Trouser Legs'. Some cracking had been detected and as a result, HMS Spartan could well be required to go into dock in Plymouth.

Somewhat relieved, I eventually joined HMS Spartan in Faslane on a rainy day in July 1991.

Ian Atkinson

HMS SPARTAN

17th July 1991 to 6th July 1993

Relieved to be away from HMS Defiance and more importantly, Joe, I joined HMS Spartan, as a very experienced leading hand, full of expectation. I was not happy with the boat being based in Scotland, but figured I needed to make the best of it. Up until this point in my submarine career, all of my experience was working forward of the reactor compartment with ship's systems. Due to manning shortages, *the* Charge Chief, 'Jimmy' Green, had other ideas. He needed me to qualify as a 'Diesel Room Killick'. This, was not at all in my comfort zone, so I moaned and pleaded as much as I could for him to change his decision, and move me forward, to where I could be of more use. 'Jimmy' was having none of it, but did concede, once I had qualified in the lower level of the engine room, in the diesel room and finally as a shut down junior rate, he would grant my wish and send me forward. I thought that his decision was a bit odd, but I was powerless to do anything about it. After resigning myself to the inevitable, I set about studying the engine room lower-level systems that included learning how to operate the two evaporators that made the fresh water and also how to the transfer water to the reactor systems, adding chemicals as required. After mastering the steam, water and oil systems, I escorted 'Jimmy' on a walk-round to demonstrate my competency. He asked me many questions and pointed at some obscure valves that I had never seen, before proclaiming that I had passed the exam and could be considered as a qualified lower level watchkeeper. With no time to consolidate, I was moved immediately down to the diesel room and started again, making comprehensive notes and diagrams as I went. In the middle of the diesel room, as the name suggests, was a huge sixteen-cylinder Paxman Ventura diesel generator. As it was so difficult to get around, it needed two people to start it up; one each side signalling to each other across the banks of cylinders.

Prior to starting the diesel, there was always the requirement to 'blow-round' when I first witnessed this, it struck me as a very dangerous, but also spectacular evolution. As the engine was turned, fuel ignited in the cylinders whilst valves called 'explosion cocks' were opened. This resulted in orange flame spurting in firing sequence from the open valves. This procedure was simply to ensure that there were no explosive gases left in the cylinders and also to ensure that the fuel was reaching all of the injectors.

Once all of the checks had been completed, using hand signals, the diesel would then be started up and checked around, prior to being put on load.

Once running, the chief would generally make his excuses and disappear for a cup of tea, leaving me to watch over the thumping engine for about an hour. He would then return and allow me some brief respite. It was not permitted to leave the engine running unsupervised in case the submarine had to go deep in an emergency. On such occasions, the order would be given "Stop snorting, stop snorting, stop snorting," which would then prompt a flurry of activity, as we made sure that the fuel was no longer being pumped to the diesel and all of the big holes were shut before we finally opened up the explosion cocks. We did not need to run it often, thankfully, but it was a major part of the qualification for a diesel room watchkeeper.

Once fully qualified, I became far more comfortable back aft. I was in a watch rotational system that rostered four hour watches during the night and three hour watches during the day, allowing for meals and a decent amount of sleep in between watches.

There was a certain amount of pride in handing over the watch, having completed all the rounds and watchkeeping routines. The last thing to do, at the end of every watch, was to make your relief a cup of tea, because unless he was happy, he would not take the watch and then you could not go to bed.

One morning, having just fallen out of bed with a mouth like the bottom of a birdcage, I climbed into my overalls, slipped my feet into my boots and trundled aft, with a toothbrush in my top pocket, to take the watch at 3am. LMEM 'Sandy' Sanderson was the off-going killick and, as tradition dictated, he had my cup of tea ready and motioned me to sit in a spare spot on the bench seat in front of the lathe. He busied himself at the sink, tidying up, before he would explain what was going on in the diesel room. It was at that moment that I received a jet of cold water in the back of the neck. As a practical joke, 'Sandy' had rigged up a garden hose from the sink tap, and threaded it up, around the submarine's hull and through the lathe where it then waited for some poor unsuspecting soul to sit in the firing line. Getting drenched in the engine room was not as bad as it sounds as it was routinely quite warm, consequently, I dried out in a few minutes, vowing silently to wreak my revenge.

I didn't have to wait long. The following day, 'Sandy' was sitting in position in front of the lathe. The hose was still in place and all that was needed, was for me to reconnect it to the tap and give him a taste of his own medicine. However, with 'Sandy', things were never that simple and unbeknown to me, he had snipped the hose in the middle and doubled it back in a loop so it squirted whoever was at the sink. Therefore, twice in two days, I got a soaking, only this time, I got a jet of water into my starboard lug hole.

It took me a couple of months to finally exact my revenge. 'Sandy' was bent over in the lower level, working on one of the evaporators, when I came on watch. Seeing him, crouched down below me, was an opportunity too good to miss. Filling a bucket with icy seawater, from the depth gauge vent, I called his name before emptying the bucket over the top of him. As they say, revenge is a dish best served cold and this was very cold indeed. Fortunately, he saw the funny side and although his practical jokes continued, they were not directed at me.

After a short period of consolidation in the diesel room, I was sent forward to replace the two leading hands who were going on draft at the same time. This was a daunting task as these lads, 'Gorgeous George' Hyde and Bob Crossfield, were both extremely competent killicks. This was brought about by the navy reducing the level of manning. Strangely, now being fully qualified back aft, I was not too keen to return forward. As they say, be careful what you wish for.

About this time, some cracks had been discovered in the steam generator pipework in the reactor compartment known as 'Trouser Legs'. This was because they looked a bit like a fat blokes trousers. HMS Spartan sailed to Devonport to dock down for essential repairs.

As it happened, Spartan was due to go into dock around that time anyway for a mini-refit, so there was a tremendous amount of work to do as the ship's company moved off the boat and into the Submarine Refit Complex adjacent to fourteen and fifteen dock. It seemed to take all week to move our books and paperwork off the submarine and into the dockside offices. We also had to move messes into another junior rate's mess, high up on the seventh floor, overlooking the refit complex. The accommodation was not of a great standard, it was squalid and largely unloved. The mattresses, mostly had large dried wee stains and some smaller unidentified staining on them. The previous occupants obviously had weak nocturnal bladders. In hindsight, there was quite a drinking culture, during lunchtime and also by the duty watch in the evening, so it was little wonder that there was the occasional 'accident'.

The food was also pretty awful. Pre-cooked and chilled food was delivered in a truck and subsequently warmed-through by HMS Spartan's chefs who had also relocated. The food, known as 'meals on wheels' or, in naval terminology, 'scran in a van' or 'muck on a truck' arrived daily from the main galley in nearby HMS Drake.

Fortunately, as I was married and living locally, I went home at the end of most working days and was only required to live in the mess on days when I was duty. Being considerably younger and fitter in the early nineties, I used to cycle into work on a mountain bike, which was a doddle. Working close to the sea meant that everyone travelled downhill into work. Cycling into work was not too physically demanding, though it was sometimes hazardous, as my most direct route crossed a footbridge over the A38, before cycling down a very steep and slippery slope full of rotting leaves. I came a cropper on a couple of occasions whilst cycling in the dark, at speed. Unexpected obstacles such as dog walkers or occasionally, the rare treat of a recently stolen and burnt out vehicle would suddenly materialise, forcing me to eject or risk serious injury.

The journey home, following the reciprocal route, would be considerably slower. At the end of the day, I would be knackered even before struggling to cycle uphill, towards home. Occasionally, I would take the car if the weather was not too good. It was on one of these days that my wife, Anita, called me at work, asking if I had taken my bike to work because it wasn't in the garden where it had been chained up. As she had waved me off in the car, a couple of hours previously, I found this slightly amusing if not a little concerning that my bike had obviously been nicked.

The subsequent insurance claim was settled quickly and instead of a big fat cheque, a new bicycle arrived, in a cardboard box. Before I could ride my shiny new toy, I had to assemble it in the lounge, much to Anita's annoyance.

On the boat, after the initial flurry of activity to move stores, administration and accommodation into shore-side offices, things slowed considerably into a more relaxed, working environment. This allowed time for the ship's company to take some leave, attend courses or perhaps go on exped. On Spartan, one of the W.E Chief's had decided to organise a coastal walk from Land's End to Plymouth on the South West Coast Path in order to raise money for the Wessex Children's Heart Circle after they had helped save his daughter's life. One of the Wreckers, Charlie Portman, also wished to raise money for the Derriford Renal Unit as his wife was, at the time, receiving treatment. As both were worthy causes, the decision was taken to split all proceeds equally between the two. The plan was simple, eight of us would drive to Land's End in a minibus and over the course of seven days, walk back to Plymouth along the coastal path, stopping every evening in whatever free accommodation we could scrounge.

On the first evening, we were very fortunate and managed to scam a senior rate's cabin in RNAS Culdrose. This allowed us to shake a bucket in the pubs of Helston and relieve a few drunken sailors and locals of their hard-earned shrapnel.

Continuing east, on the undulating path, keeping the sea on our right-hand side, it was impossible to get lost. The support team were driving the minibus which carried our overnight bags and if necessary, sufficient tents to sleep us all.

Stopping at a convenient café, after a couple of hours hard slog, we simply ordered and paid for a pot of thirst quenching tea for eight. We quickly ran out of milk and being the only customers, this was soon replenished by the kindly waitress. Next we ran out of water so another pot of boiling water was requested. At the end of the second cup, we had also used all of the sugar sachets and with tea still in the pot, more sugar was asked for. So far, the staff had complied with all of our requests, but drew the line when Charlie, suggesting that the tea was now looking a bit wishy washy, asked for another tea bag.

Re-hydrated, we continued eastwards, stopping for a night, camping on a rugby field near Mevagissey. That evening, fund-raising in the pub, somehow we ended up standing on the tables in a singing competition with the locals. Our Chief Stoker, Hughie Porter, started us off with a rendition of 'Climb, Climb up Sunshine Mountain' before little by little we were all standing on the tables, very drunk singing our hearts out. We did raise quite a bit of cash though.

Every evening, the fund raising effort was different as we slowly made our way towards Plymouth, walking through Carlyon Bay, Fowey, Polperro and Looe. Any mention of our worthy charities had the locals reaching deep into their pockets and chucking any loose change into the bucket. Many methods of extortion were tried and in each case, people were found to be extremely generous.

At the end of the week, on schedule, we crossed the Torpoint Ferry on the last leg of the exped and trudged the last two miles through the dockyard to the welcoming committee of several young renal nurses from Derriford Hospital, looking extremely sexy in their uniforms. Unfortunately they were not as grateful as we would have liked, though we did get a letter of thanks.

Back on the boat, after a week of walking, there was still work to be done, but the section chief metered this out. Having already passed my examinations for petty officer, I generally worked for Hughie Porter, the chief stoker, who was an old mate from Sovereign.

Hughie's maintenance responsibilities, primarily involved firefighting, fuelling and not least, submarine escape. With about eight years of submarine experience, I was his right-hand man and essentially whatever Hughie wanted, Hughie tended to get. He was an instantly likable chap with a cheerful outlook on life, who was seemingly always smiling and joking, and always had an enthusiastic story to tell. However, one afternoon when he came to see me, he was deadly serious.

We had received a report that the Trafalgar-class submarine, HMS Turbulent, was on fire and requesting assistance from all neighbouring vessels. Hughie simply said "Plug, Turbs is on fire, get into a woolly bag," before disappearing to get dressed himself. A 'woolly bag' was the nickname for a fearnought suit, which was a fireproof suit made from compressed wool. Complete with an anti-flash hood and gloves and with breathing apparatus on my back I was ready to assist. Hughie reappeared wearing identical kit before we jumped on to the back of a naval truck called a 'FMW'. Nothing about these little trucks was luxurious. It had a top speed of about twenty mph, virtually no suspension, but it could carry a load of up to two-tons. They had been in service since the sixties and had generally been loyal but uncomfortable workhorses.

So, sitting side-by-side in the trailer, with the chief stoker, we were driven by 'Jacko' Jackson who managed to find every bump and divot in the road as we trundled towards the burning submarine. On arrival at the scene, with thanks, 'Jacko' was dispatched back to Spartan whilst Hughie reported to the person in charge, offering our assistance. The officer of the day was grateful for the offer, but requested that we sit on the jetty, in readiness, as the ship's company were currently coping with the blaze.

It is amazing how, in a crisis, everyone pulls together. The jetty was full of fire teams from other ships and submarines. Turbulent's chefs had knocked up some soup, rolls and cold drinks as sustenance. The fire, we were told, was on an electrical breaker in the switchboard room. Irritatingly, stores arrived on a forklift piled high with CO_2 extinguishers that, I had been previously told, were completely out of stock!

We sat on the jetty for a couple of hours, quite cold, watching lots of activity by the ship's company. The civilian fire brigade and ambulances added to the scene, whilst Television South West had a film crew on a commandeered pleasure boat, reporting the local news from the safety of the harbour. First black and then white smoke billowed from the engine room hatch, before eventually, reports filtered through that the fire had been extinguished and that there was no chance of re-ignition. Exhausted fire-fighters, blackened and soaked, gradually emerged from the submarine and were medically examined by the waiting ambulance crews. Fortunately, nobody was seriously hurt.

Feeling somewhat redundant, and as 'Jacko' had now buggered off home, myself and Hughie slowly trudged back to Spartan still wearing our fearnought suits and breathing sets, feeling exhausted. I am sure that onlookers thought we were the heroes of the hour, but in actual fact, I was stuffed full of soup and rolls and ready for a bit of a lie down.

The lead story on the local news, when I got home, centred on the Turbulent fire, making up details to fill in the gaps, thus making the report far more viewable. It sounded much more exciting on the telly, than I remembered, but in the time-honoured traditions of the service, you don't spoil a good dit with the truth.

In the aftermath of the Turbulent fire, Hughie was invited into the senior rate's mess for a few lunchtime drinks to thank us for assisting. Hughie *forgot* to mention it to me until he returned after lunch, quite pissed and with an inane grin on his face.

Having now taken over, as the only forward killick stoker, there was an awful lot to do but, unfortunately, only one me. Just like being on Sovereign, I was solely responsible for maintaining the CO_2 scrubbers. This was a bit of technical wizardry that did exactly what it said on the tin, it actually scrubbed the submarine's atmosphere and removed the carbon dioxide from it before reintroducing it back into the atmosphere.

Foolishly, trusting 'George' and Bob to have left the machines in a serviceable state, I concentrated my efforts on getting the submarine ready for sea. Under the guidance of Hughie Porter, we topped off the diesel tanks with eighteen-thousand gallons of fuel, replenished the hydraulic tanks, embarked loads of 'come-in-handy' stores and assisted with general maintenance as we routinely worked twelve-hour days, getting the submarine ready to finally leave Devonport, following the successful repair to the 'Trouser Legs'.

With the sailing date now published, after a bit of a prompt from my boss, I went to set the CO_2 scrubbers to work. They had not been run for about eighteen months, so I figured there would be a day or so of work, draining all of the stale chemicals out of the machines and topping up with fresh amine. Whilst doing this, I carried out the pre-start checks on the three scrubbers until I was ready for a test flash. The function of the CO_2 scrubbers, was to remove carbon dioxide from the atmosphere. Obviously, in an enclosed steel tube, this collected gas had to go somewhere therefore, it was channelled to a reservoir and then, when there was sufficient pressure, one of two CO_2 compressors would start automatically and dump it over the side.

Like the rest of the machinery in the space, the two compressors had been untouched for quite a long time, so it was important to ensure that they hadn't seized. Gripping hold of the drive belts, I tried unsuccessfully to move the two-cylinder compressor. Bringing out the big guns, I then tried a huge spanner, as a lever, but to no avail. There was nothing left to do but strip-down the compressors one at a time and try to identify the problem. After two hours of grunting, sweat, tears and a little blood, the answer was staring me in the face. The two pistons were rusted solid and, in insurance terms, a total write off. This presented HMS Spartan with a serious problem. The compressor's seizure represented a serious showstopper and, with the sailing date looming, this was rapidly becoming a very embarrassing defect with the ship's company looking at me, to make it better.

My boss was none too chipper. He had to report to the Marine Engineering Officer, who then had to report to the Captain. The directive from on high was short and to the point, "I don't care what you have to do, or where you get them from, but you fix this before you go home again. Do you understand?" There was nothing else to say except "Yes, sir!"

As luck would have it, in the next dock, HMS Courageous had been decommissioned and was gradually being raped of her serviceable kit. The system was well known in the navy, we called it 'Storerob' which, as its name implies, means to legally nick stores from another vessel that did not immediately need them. One thing was for certain, Her Majesty's Submarine Courageous would never need these bits again.

HMS Courageous was a 'dead boat', so, persuading a couple of lads to help, carrying a toolkit, some rope and torches we embarked on a mission inside the pitch-blackness of the deserted submarine to see what we could find. As the layout was quite different to HMS Spartan, it took a little time to locate the right compartment, whilst trying to memorise the way out. If all the torches failed, we were stuffed.

Eventually locating the CO_2 scrubber compartment, I was delighted to discover that Courageous was fitted with exactly the same machinery as Spartan. I had just entered an Aladdin's cave and despite it now being quite late in the evening, I loved it. With the two lads holding the torches, I set about unbolting and removing the two compressors whilst at the same time 'nicking' just about everything we could collectively carry. Although they were old, these parts would come in very handy as spares, should the need arise at sea. To order a spare part from Naval Stores generally required the old bit to be returned, to effectively balance the books. I could therefore now order new, serviceable parts and return the 'stolen' components, thus keeping a brand new spare part in the event of a breakdown.

It was well after 10pm before the two compressors were finally lowered into place on-board HMS Spartan. Taking a break, I bought beer for the two lads, before sending them home with my thanks. There was not enough room in the tiny compartment for any more people than the maintainer, and unfortunately, that dubious honour fell to me.

It took me until 2am before I finally tightened the last pipe connection. I had a last look around, to ensure that I had not missed a pipe off or something equally obvious, as I was now getting very tired. I decided that sleep was more important, as I was far more likely to make a mistake or miss something through sheer exhaustion. Trudging wearily off to the bunk space, I lay on top of my bunk in my smelly overalls, just to get a few hours' sleep before the day began again.

Four hours later, I felt like shit! There appeared to be a compost heap growing in my mouth and my hands and overalls stunk of a mixture of oil, dirt, blood and sweat. Following a brush of the teeth, washing the sleep from my eyes and a quick coffee, I was ready to roll again. Stealing a sausage from the breakfast counter, I was back at it, before the majority of the ship's company arrived for work.

Having checked all of the mechanical connections again, I now needed an electrician to connect the two compressors to the starter box and finally replace the fuses. Tidying up the space and removing all my tools, I prepared for the first run. I turned each compressor by hand to ensure that it would run under power. As they were usually activated by CO_2 pressure, I had to fool them into thinking there was ten pounds of pressure in the reservoir.

Bending double, with an air hose in my hand, I forced some pressure into the reservoir drain whilst watching the pressure rise on the gauge. At the desired pressure, with a 'Woooeee', the first compressor started up. Looking at the three gauges on the panel, something was not right. The oil pressure gauge had not moved. Everything else seemed good, but without oil, that would not be the case for very long.

Switching over the compressors brought the same result, it ran, but without oil pressure. Stopping both and disconnecting the oil gauge, I turned the compressors by hand revealing a small amount of oil through the gauge line. This proved that the oil pumps were working, but what could be the problem? Duff gauges? Not both of them at the same time, surely? After trying several things, without success, and rapidly running out of ideas, I went to seek a second pair of eyes. It was always possible that I had missed something.

Due to the high-profile importance of the defect, one of the charge chiefs, 'Buster' Brown, came to help me out. I briefly explained the situation before starting one compressor. He immediately saw the problem "It's running backwards," he announced. When it was spinning, it was impossible to see which direction the flywheel was turning, but as he saw it start, it was clear where the fault lay. To illustrate, we swapped places and sure enough, the electricians had wired them both back to front. So after about four hours and a lot of head scratching, it only took about twenty minutes to reverse the wiring before finally, I could report to a relieved Lieutenant, that, the CO_2 scrubbers were now ready, in all respects, for sea. Unfortunately, although none of this was my fault, it took quite a while for my boss to forgive me for potentially preventing us from sailing.

With the CO_2 scrubbers finally working as they should, HMS Spartan sailed from Devonport to conduct sea trials. After a couple of weeks at sea, we called into Liverpool for a welcome run ashore. Not knowing the area too well, I was expecting a few jolly nights out in Scouseland, but as is often the case, local politics got in the way. The submarine was allocated a berth in Seaforth Dock, which apparently came under the jurisdiction of Sefton District Council. It was considered, by the local councillors, that as they were hosting our submarine, they should also accommodate the crew in Southport, which is a short distance from Liverpool, but a separate town in its own right.

I arranged for Anita to come up by train as the navy was graciously paying for the hotel and we had a wonderful time. Southport is a seaside town which is a bit like God's waiting room; full of newlyweds and nearly-deads. That said, it was quite affluent. In short, it is Blackpool for the elderly. As I was thirty-one at the time, I considered myself to be somewhere in the middle with a foot in both camps. A lot of the younger lads decided to try out bungee jumping, which was the hot new craze of the day. This cost thirty pounds to effectively jump off the top of a crane with a big elastic band strapped to your ankles. For another thirty quid, you could buy a video of you jumping and for a further tenner, a crappy T-shirt, proving to the world how gullible you can be. Not for me, thank you. Death-defying leaps into the sea were not my idea of fun, though we did watch quite a few of the younger lads parting with their hard-earned cash.

Following a very enjoyable interlude in Southport, we sailed back to Faslane where I prepared to hand over my beloved CO_2 scrubbers, which were now running perfectly. A draft chit had arrived on-board offering me the opportunity of a shore job in Plymouth.

About a week prior to leaving HMS Spartan, I started the now familiar drafting routine. Some of the routine involved hassling people on the submarine and returning items of kit that had been loaned, but most involved traipsing around the naval base, HMS Neptune, and obtaining stamps from the medical and administration departments. Planning the most efficient route around the base, I first visited the sickbay. I did this for two reasons, firstly, it was at the bottom of the hill and secondly, they only accepted joiners and leavers between 10am and midday.

Introducing myself to the receptionist, I handed over my drafting routine, expecting her to make a few notes of where to send my medical records to, stamp the appropriate box and send me on my way. Unfortunately, the jobsworth behind the counter told me that I needed to visit the dentist first up two flights of stairs. Muttering something unmentionable under my breath; I climbed the stairs only to be met at the top by a jolly young chap. He simply said, "Through the double doors, mate, and into the office on the right." Thanking him for the directions, I entered the office to find a woman in a white medical uniform sitting behind a desk. Without looking up, she invited me to take a seat, before she started asking questions and making notes:

"Name?"	"Ian Atkinson."
"Rate?"	"LMEM."
"Obviously male!"	"Er yes!"
"How old are you?"	"Thirty-one."
"Right, have you ever given blood before?"	"What?"

It was then, that it dawned on me, I'd been had. It turned out that there was a massive recruiting campaign to enlist blood donors. I must say, I felt a little stupid, but not wishing to wimp out, I went ahead with it. After a bit of poking, prodding, and having my blood pressure taken, I was invited to have a bit of a lie down. Things were looking up, not only was I having a mid-morning rest, I was also being solely attended to by a very lovely young nurse, in uniform. Unfortunately, that is where reality and my fantasy parted company, but I did get a free drink and a biscuit … result!

After being fed, watered and patched up, I was finally directed to the dentist, where my drafting routine was duly stamped without any further fuss. Returning downstairs to the sickbay I finally collected my stamp from the jobsworth receptionist. I then spent the rest of the afternoon, pleasantly tootling around HMS Neptune, collecting stamps and eventually completing my drafting routine.

The usual leaving piss-up was not really my thing, but when someone mentioned food, my eyes lit up. The suggestion was to go for a meal at the 'Akash', an Indian restaurant in Helensburgh, followed by a few sociable drinks, as the lads, collectively, toasted my health.

The evening started well, but it was prone to failure quite early on. One of the stronger personalities suggested that we first get a drink in the 'Imps' which was quickly followed by another one in 'The Royal' as we slowly pub-crawled through the little town to the 'Akash', where 'Dennis', the manager, showed us to a table for ten. By this time, we were quite well-oiled and a bit of silliness ensued. Somehow, and I am not sure how, a mirror managed to get broken in the gents. All I can say, with any degree of certainty, is I did not do it. Dennis, however, was less than amused and demanded payment for the mirror. This resulted in a bit of alcohol-fuelled discussion before we were quite firmly asked to leave. Fortunately, I had already finished eating and had had enough to drink. With a long drive ahead of me the following day, I made a decision to head back to my cabin in HMS Neptune.

After some difficulties hailing a taxi, I eventually arrived back at the main gate of the Clyde Submarine Base, seven-quid lighter. As I entered the accommodation block, I was immediately jumped upon by 'Jacko' and a couple of the other lads, who carried me towards a bath full of cold water and, in a sort of reverse initiation ceremony, I was unceremoniously dunked, fully clothed, into the icy cold water. This had a number of effects on me; firstly, it took my breath away, secondly, it sobered me up and more importantly, it made me question my sexuality as my manhood rapidly withdrew into the relative warmth of my body.

Dunking over, a very pissed 'Jacko' went looking for another victim, whilst I disappeared back to the mess to get warm and dry. In a stupid act of revenge, I decided to 'apple pie' his bed before 'Jacko' got back into the mess that I shared with him and three others.

'Jacko' came storming into the mess some time later, waking everyone up. He undressed and leaving his clothes in a snotty heap on the floor, tried unsuccessfully, to jump into bed. With the bottom sheet folded in half, he simply could not get his legs in. This infuriated him as he started shouting in the mess, demanding to know who had trashed his bed. Furious, he was jumping around, telling everyone that he was a boxer and could have everyone in the mess. With that, he grabbed the cast iron frame of one bed and lifted it one-handed up to chest height forcing its occupant, a chap called Nick Jones, to slither back towards the headboard. 'Jacko' then dropped the bed, causing the frame to snap. Nick ended up with his head on the floor, his legs up in the air and the headboard on top of him. Having not been ashore and still perfectly sober, he rightfully got very annoyed. Still unable to get up, Nick shouted at 'Jacko', "You've broken my fucking bed!" 'Jacko' replied quite aggressively, "I'm a boxer I am and I'll break your fucking head in a minute." Before anybody could do anything, 'Jacko' had punched the still prone Nick twice in the face, causing his front teeth to pierce his bottom lip. There was blood everywhere. The joke had gone too far and now Nick needed some urgent medical attention.

From then on, things got very messy. One thing was certain; nobody would be getting any sleep that night. Hastily getting dressed, I escorted Nick down to the sickbay holding a loo roll to his lower face, whilst another Scottish killick, not surprisingly called 'Jock', escorted 'Jacko' down to the regulating office where he was subsequently assessed and chucked in the cells for the night. As luck would have it, 'Jacko' 'grand-slammed' in the cells. For the uninitiated, this means, he wet and messed himself as well as vomiting everywhere. As I was in the sickbay with Nick, I didn't get to witness this, but it made me chuckle nethertheless.

Well, what started out as a quiet leaving curry with mates, had ended up going very badly wrong. The mess, as the name suggests, looked like a crime scene with blood on the walls, light switch, doorframe and wardrobes. Nick's bed was beyond repair and covered in his blood. This was going to be difficult to explain.

Usually, in cases such as this, when drunken high jinks get out of hand, submariners tend to look after their own and sweep it under the carpet, but as there had been an assault, criminal damage and an arrest, this was not going to be possible, 'Jacko' was well in the poo.

Frankly, all I wanted to do was pick up my hire car, load it up and head south on leave, but the Coxswain had other ideas. He was not a nice chap at all. He was not interested in 'Jacko' as he was still locked up and clearly not going anywhere. That would take its natural course through the naval discipline system. No, he wanted more scalps to get his tally up. I was told, in no uncertain terms, that I would be interviewed shortly and was not to leave the submarine under any circumstances. I was eventually interviewed under the new PACE regulations in the radar-shack, with my boss present as a seemingly impartial witness; just to ensure things were done properly. It became clear, quite quickly, that he was trying to blame me for everything and if found guilty, could be demoted. This was not looking good at all. Every avenue of questioning he tried, was leading to same place; he wanted my head on a silver salver. Finding myself cornered, like a rat in a trap and with every possible answer incriminating, I turned in the narrow office and asked my boss, who had been silent up to now, for help. As I had sought advice, the Coxswain then suspended the interview, telling me to wait in the junior rates' mess whilst he decided on the next course of action.

Sitting in the mess, the lads wanted to know all the gossip, but I was in no mood for a chat; I had too much on my mind. I had a hire car waiting for me on the base, my bags were all but packed and the submarine was sailing on the afternoon tide and I had been expressly forbidden from leaving the boat.

In a blinding flash of inspiration and with nowhere left to turn, I climbed the ladder up into the control room and went to say goodbye to the Captain who was working in his cabin. Knocking on the doorframe, he drew the curtain aside and invited me to enter and sit down. I explained that this was my last day and, as he was a good bloke, I wanted to wish him all the best and to say goodbye. He thanked me for my service over the last couple of years but was curious about the happenings of the previous night. I briefly explained it to him, but added that the Coxswain was baying for my blood and added that he had prevented me from leaving the submarine. The short interview over, the Captain thanked me again, wished me luck for the future and shook my hand.

No sooner than I had returned to the mess, there was a pipe over the main broadcast "Coxswain, report to the Captain's cabin." Five minutes after that, the twat knocked on the mess door and announced that he had concluded his investigation and was not taking any further action against me. He added that I was now free to leave the boat. Thanking him, out of courtesy, he didn't get a handshake as he was a knob but I wished the lads in the mess all the best as I got the hell out of there, just before they piped 'Harbour Stations'. I was knackered and it had been a hell of a morning, but I still had an eight-hour journey to complete.

Up until the last day, I had enjoyed my draft on HMS Spartan. It was such a shame that it ended so badly. I later heard that 'Jacko' eventually got released from cells and after a brief investigation; he went on an unplanned holiday to the armed forces' prison in Colchester for twenty-eight days. I never saw him again.

Back in the mess, I showered and changed; finished packing and grabbed some lunch before picking-up my hire car, which was secreted in a car park at the far end of the base. I was quite impressed with the gold coloured

Rover 216 SLI as it went like hot-snot. Chucking my stuff in the boot, I finally left the base and headed south down the A814 towards Helensburgh catching my final glimpse of HMS Spartan as she cleared Rhu Narrows and headed out into the Firth of Clyde.

Ian Atkinson

HMS DEFIANCE & HMS NEPTUNE

6th July 1993 to 6th June 1994

Following an uneventful journey back from Scotland, I arrived home totally knackered. The day had been long and the events of the previous night were still very fresh in my mind, as I did not manage any sleep at all. I dumped my stuff in the house and returned my rental car to Camelshead car park, outside HMS Drake. Returning home again, I crawled into bed intending to sleep for at least a week. Well, it could only be a week, as that was all the leave I had. The following Tuesday, I was required to join a nuclear repair facility, on a barge called 'MAC1014' in Devonport Dockyard.

It did not take me the full week to recover from my epic journey, just one good night's sleep. The following day, Keith Roberts, a good friend, called and asked if I fancied going gliding. Well, I knew Keith was an experienced glider pilot and I loved flying, but something about flying without an engine bothered me slightly; you only get one chance at parking the thing. Deciding to at least try it out, I made a flask and packed my rucksack with the Devon equivalent of the European sandwich mountain before setting off for Brentor, near Tavistock.

Arriving at the Dartmoor Gliding Society, a senior instructor took me under his wing and briefed me on the various parts of the aircraft and what they did. I found this incredibly interesting, and as a new-born glider geek, I absorbed every word. As it was quite a slow day at the airfield, my turn in the flight schedule came around quickly. My instructor, a chap called Robin, worried me slightly as he handed me a parachute "You'd better wear this." Well, I knew enough already to know that if I had to part company with the glider, a thousand feet above Brentor, the chances of survival were almost zero. Reassuringly, Robin pointed out that the main purpose of the parachute was to act as a seat cushion. Putting the parachute on and then helping me to strap into the tiny cockpit of the K13 glider, Robin talked me through all of the controls and instrumentation again, before strapping himself into the rear seat. He then went through the pre-flight checklist, covering the controls, ballast, straps, instruments, flaps, trip, canopy and finally the brakes. The acronym 'CBSIFTCB', taped to the instrument panel, acted as a reminder. I must say, I felt a bit like Tom Cruise, sitting in his F14 Tomcat, nervously waiting for launch, in the final sequences of the film 'Top Gun'.

Eventually, after a signal from Robin, the port wing was lifted from its resting place on the ground and a chap started waving a table tennis bat underarm whilst he shouted, "Take up slack, K13." The snake of steel cable attached to the underside of the aircraft, slowly straightened, until I could feel a slight shudder of movement through the airframe. The man with the table tennis bat then swung it above his head, shouting, "All out, all out," and we were off.

Amazingly, with Robin at the controls, we were airborne almost immediately, climbing steeply. Everything seemed to be happening very quickly but Robin, in the comfort of routine, calmly explained what was happening. We were climbing past eight-hundred feet at sixty knots at an angle of about forty-five degrees. Eventually, when the pilot considered that we were as high as the winch could get us, He eased the nose down, and in a well-practiced movement, simultaneously released the cable, by pulling a big yellow ball on the left-hand side of the cockpit.

Levelling the glider at a respectable twelve-hundred feet, Robin adjusted the trim so the aircraft would fly straight and level at forty-five knots. Safely established in level flight, he instructed me to take control, as one-by-one, he had me move all of the controls independently, to witness their effect on the glider. I quickly learned, in order to fly effectively, the rudder pedals, and the ailerons on the wing, needed to be operated together to prevent the feeling of the glider skidding through the sky. It therefore didn't take too long for me to get to grips with the basic concept of flying the K13.

Just as I was beginning to get a feel for it, Robin started to prepare for landing. With no engine, and no lift evident, the glider had descended to an altitude of seven-hundred feet so, before we got dangerously low, Robin joined the left-hand circuit, flying parallel to the airfield, over the church at Brentor, before turning sharply to the left onto 'base leg' and almost immediately, he banked left again, to line up for final approach. Grabbing the vertical lever on the left of the cockpit, Robin released the airbrakes and slowed our airspeed as he descended towards the grassy airfield. A few feet off the ground, he pulled the stick back and levelled the glider. With a slight jolt, we were back on terra firma and rolling slowly to a stop. Looking at my watch, the entire experience had taken only about five minutes, but it was enough to know that I was hooked.

For the remaining days of my leave, flying every day, I packed in as much gliding as I could, until finally, I was trusted to launch and land the aircraft. Of course, the instructor was there in case I screwed it up, but as my technique and skill gradually improved, his vocal and physical prompts reduced significantly. I was really getting the hang of this flying lark.

After a week of gliding, it was time to go back to work. Early on the Tuesday morning after a thoroughly enjoyable week, I cycled into Devonport dockyard, locked up my bike and in the absence of any allocated changing rooms, I located the gents and changed out of my cycling gear into my 'No8's'. This consisted of, steaming boots, dark blue cotton trousers and a lighter blue shirt decorated with my branch badge, name tally and on the shoulders, the single fouled anchor, denoting my status as a leading hand. Suitably dressed and with my cycling gear packed away, I reported to the Unit Personnel Office to start the mandatory joining routine, a little before 8am. If the navy had taught me anything, it was always to arrive five minutes before any allocated time. It is a lesson I have never forgotten.

After being handed a sheaf of paperwork, I was off on the usual dockyard runaround, collecting stamps and introducing myself to the various departments. An hour later, I presented myself, to the 'MAC1014' nuclear barge that was tied up along the west wall of 5 Basin. As it was my first time on-board, I wasn't too sure where to go. The barge was quite wide in the traditional sense of the term and had a single gangway spanning the gap from the jetty to the green-painted metal deck. Following the white-painted bulkheads along the narrow external passageway, I eventually came to a weathered sliding wooden door displaying a 'Main Office' plaque.

Knocking and entering, I was reunited with one of my old bosses from HMS Sovereign, Warrant Officer Tony Worsfold. Tony was a good bloke and after the usual handshakes and introductions, he escorted me on a guided tour of the barge. In the mess, I was introduced to LMEM 'Deano' Astley who I was joining to relieve. 'Deano' was an athletic, confident bloke with a broad Lancastrian accent. Thinking he might be a fellow Burnley supporter, over a cup of tea, I asked him which team he supported. I recoiled in mock horror when he admitted to being a loyal Blackburn Rovers' fan. This was the start of much mutual piss-taking, as we got to know each other. 'Deano' had been on the barge for a couple of years and as his shore time was now coming to an end, he was off to join another sleek black messenger of death, that is a submarine to you. I had about three weeks to learn his job and effectively take over. The job, known as the 'Nuclear Barge Killick', generally involved looking after the cleanliness and preservation of all areas and ordering stores for the various workshops. In short, it was not a very taxing job, but after the hustle and bustle of Spartan, it was just what I needed.

At least I would have a couple of months to get some more gliding in. I was getting quite comfortable in the air now and confidence is half the battle. Overconfidence, however, is a bad thing, as I found out one glorious day in September 1993. I had launched in a K13, with Roger Matthews as my instructor in the back seat. There was quite a crosswind on the launch, but compensating for it, I managed to come off the winch at eleven-hundred feet and trimmed for level flight. I searched unsuccessfully for some lift but within four minutes, I had lost four-hundred feet and started to consider joining circuit to land. The instruction, due to the wind direction, was to line up and land on the shorter stub runway. I noticed that the windsock on the ground had changed and was indicating almost in-line with the main runway. Informing Roger of my intentions, I commenced a two-hundred and seventy degree left-hand turn to line-up with the main runway. This was when things started to go very badly wrong. I flew into an invisible patch of sinking air dropping three-hundred feet in about five seconds, causing my stomach to end up in my mouth and my lunch to nearly end up in my pants. Cool as you like, Roger simply said "Oh dear, we are not going to make it back … pick a field." "WHAT!" I replied; this was not in the script at all. "That one down to your right looks good," he continued. Noticing a strip of relatively flat green carpet, starting to panic, I replied, "It's full of sheep." "Don't worry about the sheep, they'll move." Regaining my composure, I lined up for my first emergency landing. As promised, the sheep, seeing their territory being invaded from above, scarpered, and after I had rounded out, I made a safe but very bumpy landing in the field.

Thankful to still be in one piece, I unbuckled my straps and climbed out of the cockpit. Immediately, my legs turned to jelly and I collapsed onto the field of sheep poo. Roger congratulated me on a successful outfield landing, promising to sign off the necessary task in my logbook. Asking how he knew that the sheep would move, he simply said, "Sheep move, cows don't." Safely on the ground, with an undamaged glider, I was feeling quite pleased with myself, but the Chief Flying Instructor was less impressed and awarded Roger the 'Wooden Spoon', for supervising an unscheduled outfield landing.

Back at work, it wasn't long before 'Deano' left the barge draft. Frankly, it is always better when the previous incumbent leaves, as there was barely enough work for one person to do, let alone two senior leading hands. Even so, I still found myself getting a bit bored and overdosing on caffeine in the rest room. After a week or two of watching daytime TV, I was so bored, I actually requested some more work. Needing some help, I was subsequently assigned to work for chief petty officer 'Dodger' Long in the steam drains workshop. This was far better, it involved using an air-powered grinder and a cutter to remove a welded valve on-board a submarine undergoing maintenance. The removed components would then be taken back to our workshop for refitting or replacement of the worn or damaged bits. The fully refitted valve would be greased and screwed back into its body before the welders would come along during the night shift and zip it up again, to prevent it being removed or tampered with. At sea, there would be hundreds of pounds of hot fog behind the valve and steam-drenching your shipmates is generally frowned upon. After a bit of practice, I got quite proficient at refitting the steam drains valves, whilst at the same time, not neglecting my other duties on the barge.

Unbeknown to me, following a round of compulsory redundancies and some voluntary redundancies, the Clyde Submarine Base in Faslane found itself with quite a few gapped billets. These were basically vacancies, where sailors had opted to take the cash and leave the navy, in the vain search of a better job. This left the grownups with a gargantuan problem, that resulted in myself and about a hundred and fifty young stokers being summoned by their respective bosses and told to get kit packed for a temporary draft back to Scotland. I was not happy about this arrangement at all, but was powerless to do anything about it. I could see a pattern emerging, that would see me perpetually bouncing backwards and forwards as the demands of the service were met. This thought snowballed into a bout of severe grumpiness, having just escaped Spartan in Faslane, I was now being sent back.

As I had recently persuaded the navy to pay for a gliding course at RAF Bicester, I convinced my boss that it would cheer me up immensely, if they still allowed me to go. I was getting close to my first solo flight and wanted to pass this milestone, whilst I still had the free time.

The week-long course was brilliant. For a start, the flying ratio was much better than at Brentor and more importantly, the navy was footing the bill. I was allocated to a syndicate of one instructor, five students and one shiny glass fibre K21 glider. Weather permitting, I would get to fly at least five flights a day, whilst the remaining four students would act as my ground crew. The launch was by aero-tow, which was something new to me, but it meant that I could be towed up to two-thousand feet before the tug aircraft got fed up and waggled his wings, signalling that he wanted me to release the cable. It took a day or so for me to master the techniques of aero-tow as I found I over compensated, but eventually, as my gliding continued to improve during the week I mastered it. Different instructors tried wacky manoeuvres with me until it was considered that I was ready to fly solo.

After a routine early morning flight with my instructor, he climbed out of the back seat and I went to do the same. He simply said, "Stay there," as he secured the rear harness. "Err…I'm not ready for this," I stuttered. He replied, that he had done nothing, apart from look out of the window for the last four flights and it was time to cut me loose. Draping the radio handset over my right shoulder, I went through the pre-flight checks as the tug aircraft landed to my left and taxied in front of me. My wings were brought level and the cable hooked on. I heard the instructor call the tug on the radio, "Two-thousand feet please – first solo," and I was on my own.

Looking to my left at the guy holding the wing, for no particular reason but probably because I saw it in 'Top Gun' I chopped him off a salute and then I was moving. Due to the reduced weight, I was off the ground and flying very quickly. Holding the stick firmly, I attempted to hold the glider level, to prevent it pulling the tug aircraft up by the tail. Slowly, the aircraft in front rotated and we cleared the hedges surrounding the field climbing steadily towards the drop off point. I could hear some chatter over the radio but, as none of it was directed towards me, I ignored it and concentrated on staying in position behind the tug. Eventually, at the pre-assigned altitude, he waggled his wings and I pulled the release cable twice and banked hard right, whilst he banked in the opposite direction to give us both airspace. Levelling off, I adjusted the trim and attitude of the aircraft before whistling off to soar gracefully above a small Oxfordshire village. As usual, there didn't appear to be any significant lift evident, so I just enjoyed the view as my altitude gradually decreased. The standard instruction, was not to try anything clever and to never leave sight of the airfield. This limited me somewhat, but on my first flight, I was happy just to pootle round in circles until my altitude dropped to around eight-hundred feet. Higher than normal, I declared my intentions over the radio and joined the circuit. I did not want anything nasty to happen, so I just played it safe, knowing full well that with the use of the brakes, I could lose any excess height quite quickly. Turning from base leg onto final approach, I noticed that there was a glider on the ground, preparing for launch, right where I wanted to land. I was now at three-hundred feet and inside the perimeter fence. There wasn't enough room to safely land behind him and to overfly and land ahead of him might cause him problems. Alternatively, I could turn right, and land further down the field, but this would be a crosswind landing and quite dangerous.

Fortunately, it only took a couple of seconds for the tug aircraft to land, taxi, be attached to the launching glider and take-off again. Subsequently, the glider was well airborne before I flared and touched down, in exactly the same spot he had just vacated. I rolled slowly to a stop, using the wheel brake and breathed a huge sigh of relief as the left wing came to a rest on the field. The ground crew joined me a few seconds afterwards, congratulating me on not bending *their* glider. Whilst gaining my gliding certificate and a set of 'wings', this later cost me a fortune in the bar, but it was worth it.

One thing that life in the navy and probably the armed forces in general teaches you, is to remain flexible and to adapt to changing circumstances. So, I eventually cheered up and looked forward to my latest Scottish adventure. In preparation, I joined the British Airways Executive Club and learned that each return flight from Plymouth to Scotland, contributed fourteen points. After six return journeys, I would have accumulated more than the seventy-five points required to be upgraded to Silver Membership, and granted access to the Executive Club lounge. This was most definitely an aim, as amongst benefitting from priority boarding, I would be allowed to sit in a comfortable quiet lounge, with a free bar, papers and nibbles. Therefore, it was with mixed feelings that I completed the customary drafting routine, left the barge and headed north. I had a tremendous amount of *essential* junk to transport, so the navy hired me a car for the initial journey.

Arriving at Faslane North Gate in the early evening, I was dismayed to learn, the security guards on the gate were not expecting me, so I was forced to spend another half an hour in the pass office, whilst the security guards made all of the necessary phone calls and confirmed that the nuclear repair team in Faslane were actually expecting me. In short, the Royal Navy identity card simply did not carry sufficient authorisation to allow free access to the base. Subsequently, colour-coded passes for certain areas had to be issued. The main gate is only the first line of defence, and inside the base there are numerous other gates, all requiring their own colour-coded pass and all guarded by armed MoD Plods. Eventually, I was issued with green and red area photographic passes, which allowed me to wander, unchallenged, almost anywhere within the base.

Having now got my passes, I still needed to find somewhere to sleep. This was far easier, after locating the accommodation office in HMS Neptune, I was directed to a very tired looking cabin in Cameron Block. After I had humped all of my stuff up a few flights of stone steps, I returned the hire car and spent the rest of the evening unpacking.

The site for the Clyde Submarine Base at Faslane was chosen for strategic reasons. It is located on the eastern shore of the Gareloch surrounded on three sides by hills and is shrouded underneath virtually constant cloud cover. Whilst the scenery is very beautiful, the television reception is utter crap. It was with great relief therefore, that I discovered my cabin faced south and visible in the far distance, was the TV transmitter at Greenock. Even so, it still took me a good couple of hours of balancing on a chair on one leg waving my TV aerial around, to find the best reception. Eventually, with a Heath Robinson contraption of coaxial cable, coat hangers, drawing pins and Blu-Tack, I managed to get a half-decent signal on three of the four, readily available, channels. Channel 4 still eluded me, but electing to quit whilst I was winning, I went off to find the dining room and more importantly, the bar.

I found, to my annoyance, that I had missed dinner, so, I had to settle for a bag of nuts and a pint or two of Tennents 70/-, otherwise known as 'heavy' until the camp chippy opened at 8pm. The chippy, known locally as 'Soapy's', was next to the bar and at closing time, they did a roaring trade of just about everything you could imagine – deep fried! Pies, pizza sausages, black pudding and burgers all went into the fryer. There was a standing joke around the camp that you could pop into 'Soapy's' and just ask for a pint of milk and twenty No6 cigarettes and be told "Aye, that'll be twenty minutes, sir." The menu terminology also took a bit of getting used to, everything was a supper. Fish supper, Scottish pie supper etc. This caused some confusion when I simply asked for fish and chips. "Fish supper is it for you then, sir?" "No," I replied, "just fish and chips please." Not a hard set of rules to follow, just a different culture to adopt.

The accommodation, was a concrete jungle of covered walkways with steam escaping through the gaps in the concrete slabs. The cabins, were all built on stilts into the side of a hill. Not a very nice place to live, but I had to make the best of it. Fed and watered, I retired for the night, really quite exhausted.

The following morning, feeling a bit more lively, I showered, dressed and sauntered off to the dining room for breakfast. Having spent some time previously in Scotland, it was very pleasant to see some familiar faces tucking in to their bacon and eggs. Silently electing a duty friend, I ate a hearty cooked breakfast and made polite conversation until the Queen woke up at 8am.

A 'dabber' piping the 'still' on his bosun's call, whilst another hoisted the White Ensign, heralded the daily ritual of Colours. This occurred, in the winter months, at 8am on the dot. During the ceremony, every naval base and ship alongside comes to a standstill until the 'Carry On' is piped. Choosing not to look like a prize prat, I continued to finish my breakfast until the flag had been raised. It was one less thing to be shouted at for getting wrong. Assigning nicknames, is all part of being in the forces, so 'Colours' is generally known as 'Waking the Queen' and conversely, 'Sunset' is generally regarded as 'Putting the Queen to bed'. I dare say Her Majesty would be slightly amused.

With the flag now fluttering from the main mast, I ditched my dirty breakfast plates and went in search of the UPO to start my joining routine. The familiar routine still involved filling-in several forms and trudging miles around the camp to the various locations listed on the form. It was like a treasure hunt, in slow motion, but with no real prize at the end of it.

As a general rule of thumb, most new employers would cut you a bit of slack on your first day to allow the necessary administration to be completed. For that reason, after asking several questions and receiving directions, I eventually ended up at the office of Warrant Officer 'Brum' Wasteney, who was to be my new boss. As first impressions are vitally important, we greeted each other with a firm cheery handshake before he made me, what was to become, the only cup of tea I ever saw him make.

Over tea, he briefly outlined his role as the liaison officer between Rolls Royce and Associates and the Royal Navy. Rolls Royce, apart from making posh motor cars, also make aircraft engines and nuclear reactors. It was the nuclear contract that 'we' were interested in. Apart from just manufacturing nuclear reactors, Roll Royce were contracted to maintain and repair any problems as they arose. 'Brum' acted as a sort of go-between to troubleshoot problems and make them go away. If he was so good at this, why did he need me to assist? Basically, he needed a dogsbody, to fetch and carry for him. In short, the job was reactionary and every day could be relied upon to be quite different.

After our introductory chat, he told me to finish off my joining routine and he would see me the following morning. This suited me just fine, as I was still a bit knackered from the previous day.

In the morning, I arrived for work before 8am and my first job was to wet the tea. This was to be done at least once an hour, or more frequently as visitors and contractors turned up. To allow 'Brum' to get on with his day job, without too much interference, I would call clients, arrange meetings, collect visitors from the gate and make more tea.

'Brum', however, was a really good guy, he recognised that I was six-hundred miles out of position, so he encouraged me to use up as much leave as I could, to legally extend a weekend into the occasional week at home. This, amongst other things, allowed me to get some more minutes in the air as I continued to improve my gliding.

There was a travel agents in Helensburgh who had an office in HMS Neptune called Murray and Biggar. They specialised in arranging flights for stranded sailors and generally offered a good deal. After consultation with 'Brum', he agreed to let me finish work at 4pm one Thursday evening, so I arranged a flight home, via Bristol, departing at around 6pm. This was still going to be tight as it took about an hour to drive from Faslane to Glasgow Airport. Due to the isolated location of Faslane, the Transport section ran a regular and more importantly, free bus service via Helensburgh into Glasgow Airport. Therefore, after checking the bus timetable, I paid for my ticket and started preparing for my weekend return to Plymouth.

This became a regular routine, as I had twelve travel warrants to use up, which equated to about one a month. The warrants originated as rail warrants and could be transferred to a return journey on a choo choo to a destination of your choice, though you were meant to go home. As more and more people acquired cars, they evolved into warrants that could be converted to mileage. These generally paid out handsomely, though on occasion, evidence was demanded to prove that the journey had actually taken place and you weren't just withdrawing cash from the pusser to top your personal beer fund. When it became cheaper, quicker and more convenient to travel by air, the travel warrant evolved to permit the holder to buy a plane flight and then, on return, submit the ticket for payment. Of course, the reimbursement was restricted to the equivalent return mileage by road, so depending on the deal at the travel agents, it was possible to whistle off home for the weekend, arrive in a couple of hours and still get paid more than the plane ticket cost. It was a winning scenario provided your boss played the game.

During the time that I was in the office, the work turned out to be quite varied and interesting. Despite being at the wrong end of the country, surrounded by bad-speaking haggis-munchers in drag, I adapted to my situation quite well. 'Brum', would occasionally entrust me with something a little more interesting than "Tea, white with one sugar please."

Unfortunately, or indeed fortunately, depending on your point of view, this job was only temporary and in February 1994, I was summoned back to the MACCO, where I learned that my presence, was again, requested back in Devonport. What I also learned, was not quite so jolly, I already had a draft in the system to re-join HMS Sovereign, undergoing a refit, in Rosyth on the Firth of Forth. This was not good! Having nearly escaped Scotland again, I had received another two-year sentence north of the border. This put me in a grumpy mood for the rest of the day as I trudged around a miserable Faslane in the rain.

After bidding 'Brum' a fond farewell, I packed my kit and personal belongings into another hire car and waved goodbye to Faslane again. I dare say it wouldn't be long before I would be back again. The journey home was largely uneventful, and after a weekend to recuperate and do a bit of gliding, I was back in the dockyard, this time to re-join the lagging section.

As health and safety was now starting to rear its ugly head, the job had changed subtly from when I was in lagging back in 1982. The dirty and the clean areas had been completely separated and a separate area just for making lagging pads had been created. Having said that, it was still a seriously mucky job. As a senior leading hand, I was given the prestigious position of Shift

Leading Hand, which was second-in-command to the petty officer. This meant that if we had a number of smaller jobs to do, I would take a couple of the lads down to tackle one job, whilst the PO would supervise the rest of the jobs.

Having already received my draft back to HMS Sovereign, I did not really settle into my new job. I enjoyed the shift-work, as it offered a lot of time off and a structured routine, but as I was only going to be there for about three months, I was only 'holding the fort' until a more permanent chap joined.

I subsequently loaded up my hire car in June 1994, left Devonport and made a decent attempt at the land speed record in my borrowed Rover 216 SLI. Let's face it, there is nothing faster than a rented vehicle. Despite not really knowing where I was going, I still made the northbound journey to HMS Caledonia, near Rosyth in a little under six hours.

HMS SOVEREIGN

7th June 1994 to 13th October 1996

Arriving at the main gate of HMS Caledonia, quite early on Sunday evening, I was quickly directed towards the junior rates accommodation in, what appeared to be, a run-down former naval base. The place was deserted, it was like walking around a ghost town, apart from the security bloke on the gate. Finding my accommodation, it appeared that I had a four-bed mess to myself. The mess was arranged in a line, with four beds, separated by partition walls to allow some privacy. One bed space clearly showed signs of occupation, with personal effects scattered around, whilst the others were deserted. Having the place to myself, for the time being, I spent some time ensuring that my chosen bed, in the far corner, had everything in good working order. I swapped the bed for another, with a full set of springs. The mattress, for one without suspicious staining and ensured that all the drawers had functioning locks. I then set about making my bed, unpacking and tuning in my travelling telly.

Feeling rather ravenous, after travelling all day, I drove into Rosyth in search of food and within the hour, I had returned with a pizza and a can of Coca-Cola, only to find that the other occupant of the mess had returned. He was a stoker called Dave 'Nick' Carter and despite being a Nottingham Forest fan, was actually a really nice bloke.

Whilst I devoured my pizza, 'Nick' explained that we would be working on the same section and exactly how Sovereign was progressing with her refit. The accommodation base was quite a trek from the offices adjacent to HMS Sovereign's dry dock, but with my newly found friend in tow, I was quite happy to offer him a lift into work, in the hire car, as it did not have to be returned until midday the following day.

Re-joining a submarine that I had previously served on, was always going to be a surreal experience. Five years on, I didn't really expect to see any familiar faces, so it was some surprise when I wandered into the propulsion offices to be greeted warmly by Johnny Ryan and 'Spit' Whitwell who were now both chief petty officers. I had trained both of them when they were killick tiffs, some six or seven years previously.

I was introduced to my new boss, John Strickland, who was the 'Primary Tiff'. This was not a section that I had experience of, so I was quite concerned with my lack of knowledge of the primary systems and around the reactor compartment. Everyone brings something different to the party and being something of a geek, I was able to use my computer prowess and my clanky experience as a stoker to quickly settle in to my new job.

Having worked aft, in my last sea-going job on-board HMS Spartan, I still had a decent set of notes, but there was seemingly no requirement to re-qualify as a submariner as every member of the ship's company would be required to sit a Watertight Integrity Board before the submarine's dock could again be flooded.

The WTI examination, was far more comprehensive than the usual BSQ and involved tracing every system and memorising every hull valve and hull opening. It was nothing short of a nightmare. As the examination was a level playing field, everyone had to study to the same exacting standard. I paired up with 'Nick', as a training buddy and we spent a good couple of weeks constantly firing questions at each other, trying to catch each other out. I was more experienced than 'Nick', but we pretty much held our own, until finally, with sweating palms, we sat awaiting the fleetboard, where I had to demonstrate to the MEO, and two warrant officers, that I could recall all of the information that I had tried to cram into my head.

The oral examination lasted about an hour and despite feeling terrified for much of it, I actually managed quite a good pass. This was due in no small part to the assisted revision from 'Nick' so, I was equally gratified when he emerged an hour later, triumphant.

Now qualified to watchkeep in the submarine again, I had begun to feel useful, but the downside to this was, I now had to keep duties and that meant conducting rounds on a freezing cold, deserted submarine, in the dead of night. My only comfort was an hourly check-in from one of several yellow emergency boxes, positioned around the boat. It was intolerably boring and lonely as there was nothing to do and nobody to talk to, frankly, it was quite spooky. I used to make a flask of coffee and some sandwiches and try to meter it out until around 4am. A book also helped to pass the time until I was relieved by the chap who had the morning watch. Only then could I try and snatch a couple of hours sleep.

Having spent half of the night trying to stay awake on watch, I would usually be granted the afternoon off to recover lost sleep. On one such occasion, 'Nick' was working, so I had the mess to myself. I had eaten some lunch, taken a lovely hot shower and then jumped into bed, for a wee siesta. I must have been tired as I fell straight off to sleep. In a surreal dream, a couple of German Shepherds were licking my face and sniffing my groin. As I thought it was a dream, I was quite happy for this to continue, but then, in a startling realisation, like dreaming of running water, *you know what I'm talking about*, I became wide awake and sure enough, in my mess, there were two ferocious looking guard dogs accompanied by two burly coppers carrying automatic weapons and searching my room. They did not seem in the least bit apologetic about disturbing my slumber, as they demanded to search my locker and bed. Finding nothing of interest, but a well-thumbed copy of Fiesta, they explained that some gunshots had been fired the previous evening from a nearby window and they were now searching for the gun. Scary stuff! They left a short while after that, empty-handed, leaving me tired, but now wide awake and unable to get back into the same, somewhat surreal, dream.

Being a leading hand, I was entitled to my own cabin and as the block where I was housed was scheduled for demolition, I enquired and was subsequently moved into quite a large private cabin on the corner of the first floor. This was ideal and enabled me to bring my computer up to Scotland for some evening geekiness, playing games and doing some stuff for work. Of course, the internet was still in its infancy, so I contented myself with playing the new 'must have' game called 'Command and Conquer'. This was a game, which involved collecting resources, by mining or harvesting, and then building huge armies of tanks and soldiers and kicking hell out of your opponent. This was a massive time accelerator and the evenings just seemed to fly by.

Often, in the summer evenings, the lads would get together and kick a ball about on a bobbly pitch, using jumpers for goalposts. This usually carried on until we were knackered, somebody got hurt or it became too dark to see the ball. There were other leisure pursuits such as swimming at lunchtimes, and for those with mechanical acumen, a car club where members could happily pull things to bits before reassembling them, in the hope that there was nothing left over.

As the summer of 1994 drew to a close, Johnny Ryan had designs on joining the wardroom and becoming an officer. In order to achieve this, he had many academic and organisational hoops to jump through to prove that he was worthy of the Captain's recommendation. One such hoop was to organise and manage a triathlon event, in and around HMS Caledonia. This was an ambitious project, and not one he could manage by himself. Being somewhat gullible, he enlisted my help. Not really being of an athletic build, I wondered how I could help him. He requested, that I produce about fifty certificates, to award to the contenders, with their times and overall position. I had some decent quality paper and a newly purchased 24-pin dot matrix colour printer in my cabin. With the promise of reimbursement, I set about creating a template of which I was quite proud. On the day of the event, it all seemed to go well and the following morning, after an evening of typing in times, all of the competitors received a certificate, hot off the printer, that recognised their achievements and left me considerably out of pocket, as I never was paid. I learned a valuable lesson that day.

With Christmas fast approaching, I organised the duties and shortly afterwards whistled off home, for Christmas leave. This was achieved by catching a naval bus, that shuttled from HMS Caledonia, across the Forth Road Bridge, to Edinburgh Airport. Having now racked up enough points in the British Airways Executive Club to achieve silver membership, not only did I get the chance of a better seat on the plane, I could also take advantage of the free hospitality in the club lounge. As I was allowed to take a guest with me, one of the charge chiefs, Terry Rickard, accompanied me into the lounge.

Hearing that our flight to Bristol had been delayed due to the late arrival of the inbound flight, we settled in for a wait of at least two hours. This gave us plenty of opportunity to help ourselves to free drinks and nibbles until we were pretty well lubricated. Time was knocking on and we still had not heard anything regarding the flight home. Around 10pm, some four hours after the departure time. An airport official came into the club Lounge, "Is there a Mr Atkinson and a Mr Rickard in here please?" We identified ourselves before being told, "Please follow me, gentlemen, your plane is boarded and awaiting departure." Apparently, they had been calling us, but we hadn't heard a thing.

Once boarded and getting disgusted looks from passengers and crew, the aircraft had its doors shut and we were finally on our way. The in-flight meal was accompanied by a large Bacardi and Coke and a small bottle of wine, which we easily consumed before the aircraft started its descent towards Bristol. Despite being horrendously late, the descent seemed to be taking forever. Terry, sitting next to the window, peering through the darkness for signs of civilisation, suddenly proclaimed, "Either, we are going round in circles, mate, or there are five moons out there." Sure enough, a couple of minutes later, the Captain made the announcement that as Bristol Airport was closed, due to fog, the plane would have to divert to Exeter.

This caused us some concern, as it would undoubtedly mean getting a bus back to Bristol for the onward journey to Plymouth. Fortunately, the aeroplane gods were smiling on us that day. As the aircraft was required in Plymouth for the following morning, after landing, the stewardess made the announcement, "Passengers for Bristol please disembark on to the waiting buses. Passengers for Plymouth please remain seated as we will be departing shortly." Therefore, with only five passengers including Terry, and myself, we departed Exeter and made the short fifteen minute hop over Dartmoor arriving shortly before midnight, to be received by a group of extremely grumpy ground staff and a seriously pissed off Anita, four hours late.

After a well-deserved and needed Christmas break, I had booked the return flight back for the 28th December. This would allow those who had been duty over Christmas, to get home for the New Year. Unfortunately, the weather forecast for Scotland was mega-cold with reported temperatures of minus twenty-one degrees centigrade. I made enquiries about the availability of the airport bus, to be told that the roads were virtually impassable and the buses were not running but the airport was still open.

Well, I still needed to get back, which was only fair. Therefore, with bags packed and my birthday cards and presents stuffed in the top, Anita dropped me off at Plymouth Airport for the short flight to Bristol. I changed planes and flew north, into the deep freezer known as Scotland. Flying past the Forth Bridge, on approach in to Edinburgh, I could see that Scotland seemed to be blanketed in thick white snow, but being the frigid north, they are fairly used to it. From the air, I could see some cars moving on the roads, so I was relatively confident of scrounging a lift or calling a mate to come and get me for a small financial consideration.

Sure enough, my mate, 'Spike' Hughes, one of the electrical killicks agreed to come and get me for five pounds. What a nice man. As the entrance to HMS Caledonia is very steep, he dropped me at the main gate and after thanking him for rescuing me, I trudged up the hill towards my cabin with my heavy bag slung over my shoulder.

Being the middle of the silly season, there was absolutely nobody about and as forecast, it was a bitterly cold minus eighteen degrees. I reached my cabin and only then did I realise, that the heating in the block was either broken or switched off for Christmas. There were even icicles hanging from the ceiling, the windows had thick ice on the inside and my curtains were stuck to them. Dropping my bag, I considered what to do first, as it was too cold to even take my coat off. I decided first to call Anita and let her know that I had arrived safely, albeit frozen stiff. Hearing of the frozen conditions in my cabin, she immediately ordered me to open the largest of my three birthday presents. I protested that my birthday was not for another week, but she was adamant, telling me to keep the extortionately expensive mobile phone line connected whilst I unwrapped it. Within a minute, and through gloved hands, I managed to rip the paper off revealing an electric fan heater. You beauty! Destroying the box in my haste to get the thing plugged in, I whacked it up to full power. Thanking Anita for her foresight, I left my cabin to defrost whilst I trudged off down the corridor and immersed myself in a steaming hot bath in a final attempt to prevent the onset of hypothermia.

Returning about twenty minutes later, with a lobster red body, wrapped in a towel, I entered something akin to a tropical rain forest, as my cabin was now in the throes of a full defrost. Water was now dripping off the icicles and the windows and curtains were steaming as the ice turned to water before evaporating into a cloud of mist.

It took a further hour on full power before my cabin was dry and warm enough to reduce the temperature to a more a comfortable setting and seeing as the navy was paying for the electricity, it remained on constantly until about April.

The cool Scottish weather did have its advantages. As I didn't have a fridge in my cabin, I still needed to keep my milk and a few tins of illegal beer cold, so, following the example of others, I stuffed them into a strong carrier bag and suspended them out of the window into the 'big fridge'.

The navy, at the time, had some rather archaic attitudes to 'dammed ratings', such as me, possessing alcohol in their cabin. I was now thirty-three years of age, a senior leading hand, but not trusted to have a beer or two in front of the TV after work in the evening. Frankly, I struggled with the logic, as there was nothing to prevent me visiting the bar or local pubs in the evening if I desired. Pretty much everyone ignored the rule and around the camp, carrier bags with milk and beer could be seen dangling out of windows.

Towards the end of the refit, most of the work had been completed on the hull and it was time for the submarine to undock. Before water could be flooded into the dock and the boat floated again, there was much to be done. One such task was ensuring that the shaft was in the correct position for undocking. One of the petty officer 'tiffs', Johnny Plum, was entrusted with this potentially dangerous job. Moving the shaft and propulsor whilst there were people working in and around it, was a recipe for disaster. Johnny, however, diligently checked around the whizzy bits at the back to ensure that there was nobody around and that there was no scaffolding likely to be caught up. He also detailed a young stoker to stand guard in the dry dock whilst he busied himself with lining up the required systems inside the engine room.

Following the checklist, Johnny started the oil pumps and water pumps as well as fusing up the turning gear motor, that would very gradually turn the gearbox and in turn, the shaft. Everything was seemingly ready, so, using a two-way radio, Johnny called the sentry and warned him to keep clear, before starting the turning gear motor. At first, nothing at all appeared to be happening until a huge bang shook the entire submarine on its blocks. In his haste to complete the job, Johnny had forgotten to remove the locking gear. The locking gear, was in fact, a crude lump of chunky metal positioned between two equally huge nuts on the shaft that should prevent it turning. Unfortunately, for Johnny, the torque on the motor had other ideas and two of the huge nuts, each the size of a cricket ball, had sheared off causing untold stresses on the gearbox.

Well, fair play to Johnny, who, like every naval engineer, was taught to own up to your own cock-ups, picked up the nuts and with one in each hand went to report to the MEO, Lt Cdr Mick Moreland. Knocking on his door, he simply said, "Sir, I've done a bad thing," before putting the nuts on his desk. The MEO replied, "I hope those are not what I think they are."

In short, Johnny was in the poo, but not nearly as deep as he would have been if he'd tried to have hidden it. What this eventually meant, for the rest of us, was lots of extra time, out of bed, acting as a sentry whilst the huge gearbox, which was about the size of a standard living room, was opened up and checked for damage.

Whilst Johnny eventually got a slap on the wrist for the honest cock-up, it resulted in the lads being very upset with him because after a boring three hour watch, they then had to spend a further three hours of total tedium sitting next to an exclusion area monitoring the open gearbox. A case of beer for the lads would have cheered them up considerably, but in a poor error of judgement, he did not even offer them an apology.

Around the same time, the mess had a break-in. Whilst the submarine was being ripped to bits, the accommodation on-board was uninhabitable, so a mess, dining room and some skanking beds were provided for those men who were duty, but not actually on watch. As a leading hand, I often ran the bar in the junior rates mess when I was duty. The mess was furnished with a decent sized telly, a pool table and a couple of fruit machines that each promised a jackpot of one-hundred pounds. Naturally, these were popular amongst the lads and it was quite common for some of the lads to come in to work with a fiver in their pockets, just to play the 'bandit'.

One morning, I arrived at work to find that the mess had been sealed off and the MoD Police were crawling all over it. Apparently the chief's office had been broken in to and money stolen from the safe. They first questioned the lads who had been in the mess overnight, including the duty leading hand. It appeared, on further investigation, that the culprit had climbed up into the roof space of the nearby weights room, clambered through the roof space, across a stairwell before dropping down in to the chief's office. The thief then helped himself to the petty cash from the safe, before letting himself out of the door.

What drama! It was all very exciting. Speculation was rife, as to who would have dared to carry out such an audacious heist, but it wasn't long before the perpetrator confessed. Under the glare of intense questioning, one of the other killick stokers cracked under pressure. So the story went, he had been playing the fruit machine, quite late the previous evening and was convinced the jackpot was about to drop, when he ran out of cash. He therefore *needed* to borrow some more money, with the intention of replacing it from his winnings. Well you can guess what happened, he had already emptied the till in the mess and then decided to 'borrow' some money from the petty cash box in the chief's safe. Still the machine refused to pay out, so he was snookered. He had used up all of the 'shrapnel' in the mess and now had no way of paying it back. The only winner here was the one-armed bandit.

Nobody likes a thief, and this chap had committed the cardinal sin, stealing from his messmates. To prevent the inevitable public lynching, he was spirited away by the police and we never saw him again.

Whilst still living in HMS Caledonia, I was required to be duty every other weekend, working alternate days with my buddy, Will Clements. Having completed the duty on Friday night, 'Clem' arrived for work just before 9am on Saturday morning to assume the duty. After the usual "Same old shit mate, you've got it," he kindly lent me his aging red Peugeot 205 GTI as transport for the day. The plan was, I would drive it back to HMS Caledonia and then back into the dockyard on Sunday, when I arrived, to reassume the duty.

As it was a weekend, most of the lads had gone home and my other mates were working, so I intended to spend a quiet evening of watching telly and doing some washing. Getting together with the previous night's duty watch for dinner, leading radio operator 'Foxy', Fox asked me if I fancied going out for a drink. After refusing twice, opting for the quiet option, I finally relented to his incessant pressure and agreed to transport the lads to the pub, but not drink myself, as I was driving somebody else's car.

We had decided to visit the nearby 'Ship Inn' at Limekilns, on the banks of the Firth of Forth, and to watch the sun go down over an alcohol-free beer or two. In the pub, over the course of a couple of hours, 'Foxy' and two other lads got steadily shit-faced. I didn't mind, the atmosphere was good and despite just drinking alcohol-free lager and Coca-Cola, I was starting to feel quite light-headed. We somehow managed to stay in the pub until closing time. Leaving the pub, I went to retrieve Clem's car from the other side of the road. I knew the door lock was a bit dodgy and in the darkness, I had quite a bit of trouble getting it unlocked, but the lights from an approaching police Transit van helped, as he drove past.

Pouring the lads into the car, I did a quick U-turn and headed back up the darkened country lane, towards the main A985. It was not long before a set of headlights appeared behind me. It was too dark to properly identify the vehicle, but as the headlights were quite high off the ground, I correctly guessed that it was the police van I had seen minutes earlier. Maintaining my speed below 30mph, I hoped he wasn't interested in me. I felt quite drunk, though I had not knowingly drunk any alcohol. Perhaps one of my 'mates' had slipped a vodka into my Coke, to liven me up a bit. Approaching the T-Junction with the A985, I indicated and turned right at about the same time as his blue flashing lights came on, inviting me to stop. Shitting myself, I pulled over onto the side of the deserted main road, before getting out of the Peugeot. I was greeted by the copper driving the patrol van, "I noticed that you were having trouble getting into your car, sir." "Yes, officer…" I replied, "...it's not mine." In hindsight, it was a silly thing to say, but he let that go. "Have you been drinking, sir?" "Only Kaliber and Coke, officer." "Then you won't mind blowing into this bag for me, will you, sir?" Following his instructions, I took a deep breath and inflated the bag, until he told me to stop. He examined the breathalyser carefully under torchlight, to see if any of the crystals had changed colour before passing it to his oppo who, in the meantime, had checked that the car had not been reported stolen. As neither of them could detect any colour change, the nice policeman apologised for detaining me and invited me to continue on my journey.

The lads, of course, thought this was a hoot and tried to persuade me to drive them into Dunfermline, for more drinks and food, but frankly, the encounter with the law, no matter how innocent, had shaken me up. I forcefully declined their request and drove back to HMS Caledonia. Now, all I had to work out was, how I was going to tell 'Clem' that I had been stopped by the police, for suspected drink-driving.

Not long afterwards, I was summoned to see the MEO. I was given no clue as to what I had done wrong and racked my brains to identify what misdemeanour had I been caught for. The common one, of course, was travel expenses fraud. As I was currently travelling home twice a month, by car or by plane, money was always short. The accepted method, was to first book your plane ticket, complete the journey and on return, claim for the expenses. This meant, it was sometimes difficult to keep track of what I had been paid and what was still to come. Therefore, it was with a sense of dread, that I finally knocked on the MEO's office door. "Come in, Plug," he called, as I entered the office. He was smiling, which was a good start. "I have some good news for you, your Long Service Medal has just been received on-board, so I need to get you up to see the Captain." Phew! Of all of the possible reasons I had permutated, this was not one of them. Finally, after serving something in the region of sixteen-years, I was actually being awarded with my first medal. The LS&GC medal rewards all servicemen who have completed fifteen-years' service from the age of eighteen without being caught for anything serious. It was generally known as the 'undetected crime medal'. Of course,

the downside to getting a medal was, I would now have something other than shoes to polish, when getting dressed up in my best uniform.

The following week, looking as smart as a guard's van, I presented myself outside the Captain's office for the monthly ceremony of 'Captain's Requestmen and Defaulters'. To prevent the Captain getting in a bad mood and to make the agony of waiting for punishment even longer, he always saw the good guys first and this was always in descending rank order, so I was positioned third in line, outside of his office and duly awarded with my first gong.

At the same time, the authorities had decided to close down HMS Cochrane and sell off the real estate to raise some more cash. This caused a bit of a logistical problem, as HMS Cochrane was the main accommodation base on the east coast of Scotland and HMS Caledonia, where I currently lived, did not have sufficient beds to accommodate all of the sailors. I am not too sure of the politics that led to the decision, but all of Sovereign's ship's company were told to find alternative, rented accommodation 'ashore' in Rosyth. The upside to this arrangement was, the navy would pay each individual, five-hundred pounds in lodging allowance to pay for rent and food. Initially, I was fairly reluctant and sceptical about this arrangement, as I was quite comfortable where I was.

My mate, Bill Collard, nagged me incessantly, until I finally agreed to share a flat with him. Bill was the eternal optimist and could see no disadvantages, as he correctly pointed out, we could have a fridge full of beer with no autocratic 'wee jocks' telling us that we couldn't have a beer after work. So, having signed up to the plan, we went house hunting and eventually found a first floor flat, about a mile away from work that was well within our combined budget.

It may sound a little gay, but Bill and myself opened a joint bank account and agreed to transfer four-hundred pounds each into our collective fund, which would be more than adequate to cover rent, bills, food and most importantly, beer. The tenancy agreement was signed and our moving in date was set. The improvement in our standard of living was instant, we suddenly had more money than we needed and routinely went out for dinner at the 'all you can eat' restaurant, 'The Taste of India', a short walk from the flat. In fact, it became a regular social gathering for most of Sovereign's marine engineers. This included the charge chief, Jeff Nesbitt, petty officers, 'Clem' Clements, Johnny Plum, 'Paddy' Kearney and 'Smudge' Smith. It wasn't an exclusive club, and anyone could join if they wished, provided they paid their own way. We usually met in the 'Gladyer' public house for a couple of quiet ones followed by a slow trog down the road to the curry house before retiring back to the 'Gladyer', stuffed, for a few more noisy ones.

As the 'Gladyer' was only a diagonal walk across a football pitch from the flat, it became our local watering hole. The pub was incredibly popular and it wasn't long before a few of the more confident lads had attracted attention from the fair sex. Two of these women informed us, in heavily accented English, that they were au pairs from Sweden. After some ultra-smooth patter, 'Smudge' Smith managed to 'trap' one of them, who we all nicknamed 'Svede'. Of course, 'Smudge' professed to be single. Technically, in Scotland, he was. As somebody helpfully pointed out, "It's not unfaithful if you're in a different postcode."

As an accomplished liar and full of the gift of the gab, it did not take 'Smudge' long before he had charmed 'Svede's' pants off. Of course, this was just a bit of weekday fun for 'Smudge', until he travelled back to the marital home in Manchester at the weekend.

The affair went on for quite a while. The ever inventive 'Smudge', had created quite a plausible double life and getting great sex from a fit Swedish bird into the bargain. Unfortunately, like most deceptions, he was to be found out in a tale that could easily have been an outtake from 'Fatal Attraction'. Things started to fall apart on 5th January 1996.

By coincidence, 'Smudge' and I shared the same birthday and 'Svede' had a birthday surprise for him. We all agreed to meet in the pub for a few birthday drinks at around 7pm. 'Svede' and her mate entered the pub, carrying a massive birthday cake, that she had baked for him, full of candles and singing 'Happy Birthday', to us both. 'Smudge' gave 'Svede' a hug and a kiss and invited her to sit next to him on the semi-circular seating in the corner. It was then that she noticed 'Smudge' was wearing a wedding ring. She asked him, quite suspiciously, why he was wearing it. Spontaneously, and in a brilliant piece of acting, he burst into real tears and had to go to the gents to compose himself.

Back at the table, we thought he might have escaped out of the back door and legged it, but some time later and still visibly upset, he returned. In another Oscar nominating performance, he lied to 'Svede', "I always wear my wedding ring, on this day every year, in memory of my wife, who died of cancer," as he dissolved in to floods of tears. 'Svede' swallowed his lies hook, line and sinker and decided to take him home as he was clearly too upset to enjoy his birthday party. After they had left, the lads were all dumbfounded; they could not believe the plausibility and despicability of the lie, but on the upside, he did get a 'sympathy' shag.

That is not the end of this particular tale though. It turned out that 'Svede' was not the gullible blonde bimbo that he took her for. He had recently bought a second-hand Skoda from a garage in Manchester. Playing detective, she took the number of the garage from the sticker in the rear window, called the dealership and explained that she had found the wallet of a Mr Andrew

Smith. She explained that there was a sum of money inside the wallet, some credit cards and a business card from the garage. She had called them to try and find his address, so she could return it. The garage were evidently very happy to oblige and gave away Smudge's home address. 'Svede' then turned up at his house in Manchester, confronted and confessed about their affair to his '*dead*' wife, who as I am sure you might have gathered by now, was alive and well though, I imagine, quite pissed off.

'Svede' now needed some answers from 'Smudge' who was being uncharacteristically elusive. A few days later, 'Smudge' told us how, one evening after a few beers, he had got out of bed, in HMS Caledonia, for a pee in the small hours, left his cabin, wearing only a towel, to make the short journey down the corridor to the heads. Opening his locked door, he was confronted by a drunken and enraged 'Svede' who had evidently snuck past the security guards on the main gate and somehow, perhaps we will never know how, managed to find out where he slept. 'Smudge' went on to embarrass himself with the story of how he never made it to the toilet. The total shock and his very full bladder combined to make him lose total control, in his doorway, as we roared with laughter, at his humiliation.

During a submarine's refit, after the initial flurry of activity, there was plenty of time to enjoy pleasurable activities. In fact, we were encouraged by the command to organise anything that might keep the lads occupied during long periods of relatively little work. As a qualified as a mountain leader, I suggested that I lead a minibus full of lads on a day walk through the Scottish hills.

After discussing it with Bill, who was always looking for excuses for a day off, I approached the MEO, who also seemed keen on the idea. Limiting the numbers to a manageable, but friendly group of six, I organised transport, rucksacks, boots, waterproofs, food and crucially a route plan.

To be on the safe side, I left my phone number and the route plan with the boss, but it was planned as a fun day out. Walk up the hill, eat your butties, drink your tea and trog down the hill to the pub for a well-deserved chip butty and a shandy. I tried to do it every Wednesday, but that was considered to be taking-the-piss, so every other week was considered a reasonable compromise. After a couple of weeks, word soon got around the ship's company that my day walks were not the generally perceived route marches and actually rather enjoyable, especially in the summer months. It wasn't long before I had quite a few of the lads eager to join us. As it was such a hit, my confidence soared and I started to consider a weeklong exped, to my old stomping ground in Snowdonia. Having trampled over most of it with my brother, Simon, and a few other mates, I knew the area quite well. Once again, Bill was up for it; hailing from Connah's Quay in North Wales, he also knew his way around quite well.

I requested meetings with the Captain and the MEO and subsequently received agreement to take eight people to Snowdonia for the week. With the first hurdle cleared, I visited the Adventurous Training store to earmark the use of a minibus and a rucksack full of additional kit, for those who did not possess their own. That done, I submitted traces of my route plans to HQ160 Brigade in Brecon for an army Major to authorise the trip. Apparently, the army train extensively in Snowdonia and as firearms were not permitted, they carried iron bars, to represent the weight of a rifle. This caused much merriment, as we imagined our fighting elite pointing lumps of metal at each other and shouting "BANG." The irony was, civilians could just turn up and climb whatever hills that got in the way. As we needed funding and accommodation, there were quite a few hoops to jump through. Therefore, the only way, was to tow the army line. The pongos tended to get a bit tetchy if ill-disciplined matelots trampled through their back yard without permission.

I planned three, longish day walks, that I had previously walked. The first was the well-trodden 'Snowdon Horseshoe', followed the next day by Tryfen and the Glyders and finally the Llyn Eigiau Horseshoe around Carnedd Llewellyn. On the first day, it appeared that I had vastly underestimated the confidence of my group. Within the first couple of hours, having followed the Pyg track and scrambled up to the knife-edge ridge known as Crib Goch, two of the lads were crying for their mummy and maintaining four points of contact, clinging to the ridge. This caused a bit of a rethink and with the safety rope unfurled and everyone tied together, we made better progress. Fortunately, the weather was kind and with improved confidence, all of the team made it past the pinnacles without incident. After climbing Crib Y Ddysgl, with the promise of a cup of tea and a bacon butty on the top of Snowdon, we easily made the railway track and followed it to the summit. Resting at the halfway point and with only one serious ascent left, we finished our lunch and made our way up Y Lliwedd. With all of the climbing done for the day, we jarred knees and scrambled down a rocky path to intersect the Miner's track at the edge of Llyn Llydaw. Having made the track without injury, the team relaxed and trogged slowly down, what is essentially, a five lane 'motorway', towards the start point at Pen-Y-Pass. Someway down the path, we passed a military looking Land Rover, containing a couple of serious looking fellows. Looking down into the valley, there was a group of very weary looking soldiers, wearing full battle kit, including full bergans and carrying the obligatory iron bars, running down to the stream, then up to the road again, before repeating the seemingly pointless exercise. We assumed they had pissed the instructors off and were now carrying out some form of summary punishment. This caused us to giggle inwardly to ourselves, as we most definitely did not want to incur the wrath of, what we assumed, were SAS recruits, undergoing their selection process.

Back in the car park, we ditched our rucksacks in the minibus and laid waste to another bacon butty and a huge mug of tea in the café at Pen-Y-Pass, before heading back to the cottage, knackered, for an early night.

The following morning, after the traditional sailor's fried breakfast, with cold stiff legs, we struggled into the minibus for the short drive to the base of Tryfen, on the shores of Llyn Ogwyn. I love Tryfen; as a mountain, as it is more of a scramble than a walk. We started with a heart-pounding slog up to Milestone Buttress and turned left to continue the uphill trudge until we gained the north ridge. From there on, it was a scramble. Short, easy climbs followed by safe, wide ledges allowing a bit of sightseeing, whilst we got our breath back.

Keeping the group together, we continued the scramble until finally, we made it to the top for lunch and a most welcome flask of tea. Two huge

standing stones, called 'Adam and Eve', mark the top of Tryfen and it is sort of traditional to climb up onto one of the stones and then take the leap of faith across to the other. I could just imagine the air-sea rescue helicopter airlifting me off the mountain, after breaking something crucial, so I abstained and contented myself, by watching others try and fail.

After lunch, with no broken bones, we scrambled down to the col before tackling the slightly more technical scramble up Bristly Ridge, on the northern side of Glyder Fach. Reaching the top, without too much difficulty, again we stopped to take in the views and before trudging across a rocky plateau to the Cantilever Stone. I overcame my fear of breaking something vital and wandered out gingerly onto it, but even with my fifteen stone bouncing up and down on it, it did not budge an inch.

A short walk later and we reached Glyder Fawr before scrambling down through Devil's Kitchen and the long walk out to Ogwyn Cottage. This marked the end of the day, for most of the lads. Unfortunately, the minibus was about half-a-mile down the road, parked in the lay-by. After the obligatory mug of tea and bacon butty, I left the weary walkers at the café with my rucksack and took a slow bimble along the lakeside to collect the vehicle.

On our final day, we awoke to torrential rain. The weather forecaster didn't inspire confidence either with his comment that it was "Welly-fillingly wet." We therefore prepared for a thorough soaking, on what was to be the last, but also the longest and most exposed trek. Full Gore-Tex kit and good boots kept most of the weather out, but by the end of the day, I was not the only one to complain of wet feet. The ground got steadily spongier as we struggled against the gradient, the wind and the rain. This was not what I signed up for at all; I really had to convince myself that I was having fun. With heads bowed, we trudged onwards and upwards. There was no talking as we conserved our ebbing strength. More than once, I slipped and fell, sliding a few feet on the slippery grass. I was soaked to the skin and not enjoying it at all. I had since discovered, basically three things piss me off, being cold, tired and hungry. Each one of these, on its own, is generally enough to make me grumpy, but combine all three together, like they were on that cold, wet and windy hillside and the net result, not a happy bunny.

Fortunately, as the day wore on, the wind eased and with it behind us, the going became slightly more pleasant as we neared the end of the ten-mile walk. The eight drowned rats finally headed down the track and back to the minibus. There was no café awaiting us here, but a few miles down the road, struggling to see through the misty windows, we were sitting in a café, by the fire, warming ourselves on huge pint mugs of tea. The general consensus was that we get back to the cottage, get showered, dry and into clean warm clothes before heading off for a morale-boosting curry to rejuvenate our spirits and reflect on a generally good week away from work. The next morning, it was all hands to the pump to clean the cottage and pack up the minibus for the long journey back to HMS Sovereign in Rosyth.

Back on-board, the refit was nearing completion. The boat was now in the water and had moved out of the dry dock, but there was still much to do before we could raise the rods and commence reactor start-up. As the plant had been shut down for a couple of years, every valve concerning the reactor had to be checked, cycled and then locked into the correct position. A lot of this responsibility fell to me as the killick working for John Strickland, the primary systems' chief. It was interesting work, crawling around the reactor compartment and tunnel and occasionally falling asleep in a quiet, barely accessible corner, underneath the port steam generator. Of course, this was particularly naughty, as the whole place was oozing background radiation. We were taught the principle of ALARP that basically means, do what you have to do and get out. However, everyone is given an annual radiation limit and if that dose is exceeded, then you are not allowed into the RC. This sounded like a viable plan, rack up as much dose as you can in a few weeks and then someone else will have to go down 'the pot'. Unfortunately, as the background radiation was so low, there was little chance, even working for primaries, that I would exceed the acceptable limit. Bugger!

In the spring of 1996, I was summoned to see the new MEO, Lt Cdr Jim Schmit, who, after sitting me down in his office, informed me that a promotion order, called a B13, had been received on-board, bearing my name. After seven years as a leading hand, I was finally being promoted to petty officer.

Naturally, there was a lot of celebrating to do and after buying the customary crate of beer for the lads, we followed it ashore, getting totally and utterly wasted in the 'Gladyer'. Somehow, and I am not altogether sure how, we ended up eating pizza in Dunfermline before heading off down the main drag in search of a pub that would serve us. This all became quite confusing. Bill turned right, for what we assumed was a comfort break in a doorway, but we never saw him again. It is well known that sailors have an inbuilt homing beacon, which automatically activates when you have had enough to drink. We assumed that Bill's beacon had activated and that he had staggered off back to the flat.

After the clubs had finished for the night, I got a taxi back to the flat and was alarmed, in a tired drunken sort of a way, to discover that Bill had not yet made it home. Well, he was a big lad, and I was far too drunk to care, so I went to bed.

Waking up around 7am, bursting for the loo, I stumbled off to the bathroom to relieve the situation before heading into the kitchen to make strong coffee to clear my banging head. Confusingly, I was faced with a pile of sodden muddy clothes, on the kitchen floor, near the washing machine. To my relief, Bill had made it back in one piece, but obviously, something very bad had happened for his clothes to end up in such a state. As he was still comatose in his room, the explanations would have to come later as I left him to sleep it off and I stumbled into work.

Later that day, Bill made it into work and I was able to find out exactly what had happened to him. Apparently, or so he remembers, he veered off down a side street with every good intention of walking home, until he could find a taxi. As it transpired, he was heading in the opposite direction and before he knew it, he was trudging through a ploughed field where he apparently stumbled and fell, losing his glasses in the process. Finally making it to the far side of the field, caked in mud, he negotiated a boundary hedge before discovering he was on the A823, a road out of town to the north. Being quite late, there was little traffic about, but he eventually managed to flag down a car and somehow persuaded the driver to bring him home. That explained the muddy clothes, but he had still lost his glasses.

Later that day, after piecing together his movements, we drove back to the road where Bill had emerged from the field. A hole in the hedge, that he had evidently made, marked the correct spot before he retraced his drunken steps, through the muddy field, until amazingly, he found his glasses, unbroken. Clearly, his homing beacon needed recalibrating.

About a week later, the Captain promoted me to Petty Officer. As I was the only one seeing the 'skipper', it was a relaxed affair. My boss, Lieutenant Des Rendle, had fudged some nice words together, in the form of a citation, which generally told the Captain that I kept good kit and worked well when cornered. He finished his spiel with the usual, "...and has my strongest recommendation for promotion to petty officer, sir." Anything less and the Captain could of decided to defer my promotion date for anything up to six months. In extreme circumstances, he could refuse it completely if he considered that I was unsuitable for promotion.

Fortunately, he didn't, and after a brief chat, he promoted me to Petty Officer Marine Engineering Mechanic. In a symbolic gesture, he handed me a pair of petty officer's epaulettes and a certificate, before shaking my hand. I thanked the Captain before saluting him and leaving his office as a senior rate.

Within five minutes, I heard the summoning broadcast "Petty officer Atkinson, control room." This was a traditional broadcast, designed to inform ship's company of my promotion and also to correctly, but perhaps unfairly, point out that I was out of the 'rig-of-the-day' as I still had my leading hand's uniform on. This was all a bit tongue-in-cheek and signified the start of the celebrations.

Being promoted meant, I needed to leave the junior rates mess and then join the senior rates mess. Moving messes heralded another excuse for beer. Getting 'rated-up' is generally an expensive business. After leaving the mess, by tradition, they had to invite me back to buy the beer, as I was not a leading hand anymore.

With the beer bought for the lads, the next course of action was to enter the senior rates mess for the first time, without knocking, head immediately for the bar, grab hold of the bell rope suspended above the bar, tug it once and emit a single loud clear 'DING'. This was a welcome sound, as it signified free beer. The celebrations continued for the rest of the day and long into the evening, until I was quite squiffy and had spent a fortune, buying beer for freeloaders. Fortunately, you do not get promoted every day.

A few days after the hangover had subsided, a draft order was received for me to join HMS Excellent for Petty Officers Leadership Course. This was essentially four weeks of running around, washing kit, ironing to a high standard, giving lectures and carrying out practical leadership tasks as directed by the instructors.

As it was a very physical course, attached to my joining instructions was a list of preparations that needed to be completed before my divisional officer could permit me to attend. I needed to have a thorough medical examination and to prove my fitness around a track by running a mile and a half in less than eleven and a half minutes. In addition, I needed to ensure that any scruffy or poorly-fitting items of kit were replaced. Finally, I had to prepare a fifteen-minute presentation on just about anything, provided it was not work related.

Being generally healthy, the medical was a simple formality. Obtaining replacement kit was not too much of a bother either, though I did need to borrow the ship's transport for the day and whizz over to the clothing store in Faslane, to be measured for my new uniform adorned with petty officer's badges. I took good advantage of the visit and scrounged as much kit as they would allow.

Running a mile and a half presented a challenge. I had not run anywhere, competitively, in quite a while and considered myself, whilst being healthy, to be extremely unfit. Fortunately, the lads were very supportive and encouraged me to run into work, from the flat and more importantly to run home again, which was about a mile each way. Getting into work in the cool summer mornings of 1996 was not too much of a problem, as it was downhill. The return journey at the end of a full working day, took some building up to. The problem was, I didn't have anybody pushing me; there was nobody running with me to encourage me to continue when my legs felt like lead and my heart was threatening to explode.

Help was at hand in the shape of Will Clements, who, whilst being very short, was a very good footballer and very quick on his feet. He offered to run around the track with me every evening, carrying a stopwatch. Every lap, he would call out the time and tell me if I was doing ok or needed to speed up a bit. It was hard work, but eventually, after much encouragement, I managed to get my time down to eleven-minutes exactly. This was considered, by some, to be thirty-seconds of wasted effort, but at least it was within the allotted time. There is no doubt in my mind, I could not have achieved that, without the help of my friend 'Clem'. It is a worthy trait of service life, most people will help those who try to help themselves. Do nothing and people will generally sit back and watch you fail.

With my fitness now at an acceptable level, I now had to complete an assessment run, supervised by the physical training staff. A few of my mates came along to watch and everyone, including the PT staff, shouted words of encouragement as I finally sprinted the last hundred meters, using up my last ounces of energy to cross the line, about ten-seconds faster than my best ever time.

With all of the remedial preparations complete, I was now ready; so my boss sent off the form, confirming my attendance on the course and certifying my fitness level.

After having spent two years on-board HMS Sovereign in refit, I had made some firm friends and living in the flat with Bill, despite my initial reluctance, was brilliant. He tended to do the cooking, whilst I did the cleaning and looked after the money. Financially, when we closed down our joint bank account, we each walked away with about five-hundred pounds, having never been overdrawn. It was also nice to have somewhere to relax, off the base, but it wasn't the same as being at home.

It was with mixed feelings, therefore, that I loaded my stuff into a hire car and finally drove south. I loved the area; Edinburgh, just across the water, is a wonderful city and the scenery is gorgeous. What a pity it is inhabited by bad-speaking, skirt-wearing, jocks. Only kidding! If I knew I was going to be based there forever, I would happily have moved Anita north of the border and bought a house. Anita, however, had a much different opinion. Due to the amount of rainfall and the temperature difference between Edinburgh and Plymouth, she had long decided that she was never moving to Scotland.

After the usual leaving run and the hangover had subsided, I finally waved goodbye to HMS Sovereign and commenced the long drive back to Plymouth.

HMS EXCELLENT and HMS SULTAN

14th October 1996 to 9th May 1997

Arriving home after an exhausting drive, I had a couple of weeks leave before I was due to report for Petty Officers Leadership Course. I had worked hard on my fitness, in readiness for the physical aspects of the four-week course and had managed to achieve the required standard before leaving HMS Sovereign in Rosyth. A couple of weeks spent vegetating at home, if I allowed, my fitness levels would slip again. Consulting a local road map, I devised a two-mile circular route, starting and finishing at my front door. I planned to run each day and time the circuit on a stopwatch, keeping track of any improvement. Initially, it took around twenty minutes to complete my route, but I rationalised that the route was moderately hilly, longer than it needed to be and I was held up crossing roads. Over the couple of weeks, it did not feel any easier, but my time improved. Eventually, I was finishing in under fifteen-minutes, which by my standards, was a huge achievement.

One of the other modules of the course was to give a fifteen-minute presentation, although I had a plan of what I was going to talk about, there was a lot of preparation to do before I was even ready to practice it. Unless you have ever spoken in public, you probably don't realise just how long fifteen minutes actually is. Even speaking to an audience for two minutes can seem a daunting task, unless the speaker is totally knowledgeable about the subject matter. For that reason, I had already nicked and plagiarised a presentation from someone else that had previously completed POLC. We have a saying in the navy called the 'Six P's standing for 'prior preparation prevents piss-poor performance', so it was as well to be prepared. Another saying goes something like this, 'Fail to prepare and you prepare to fail.' Therefore, my two-weeks leave was not actually that restful, as I ensured that my kit was spotlessly clean, my shoes were polished to a high gloss finish and that I had everything on the required list. I was confident that I was fit enough for the course and finally, my presentation was as good as I could make it.

Never had I been so worried about flunking any course as I had about screwing this one up. Failure on POLC could mean reversion back to leading hand. It had took me long enough to get promoted in the first place, so I was not going to give it up without a fight.

The day before the course started, I collected a hire car from HMS Drake and loaded it with a surprising amount of kit, consisting of everything I would need to survive for four weeks away from home. I had been told that the leadership course was like an advanced form of basic training, so I didn't pack my usual telly, video recorder and ghetto blaster into the car, but instead, took a decent book and hoped that I might have enough spare time to read it.

Whale Island is situated within the city limits of Portsmouth, at the end of the M275 and is joined to the mainland by a substantial road bridge. I had always regarded HMS Excellent as a rather strict place as the naval regulators trained there. Arriving at the main gate early on the Sunday evening, I was directed towards one of five, ancient 1920s accommodation blocks. These were long, two-floor, brick-built, accommodation blocks, each housing about fifty people. The beds and messes had been pre-allocated so, quite early in the evening, I found myself unpacking in a mess of five beds. The bed spaces were subdivided by old wooden wardrobes, allowing a small amount of privacy. As a petty officer, I would normally have been granted the privilege of a single cabin, but as the course was designed around teamwork, we all had to share. The only exception to this rule, was Tracey. Being the only girlie on the course, for obvious reasons, she was given her own room, though I would have been more than happy for her to bunk up in our mess, if the authorities had permitted it.

After unpacking and preparing for the following day, I met some of the new arrivals. After the initial introductions, we retired to the bar for a couple of 'getting to know you' pints, before an early night.

It was probably first day nerves, but I was up, showered and dressed in a crisp, starched uniform by 7am. A couple of us then decided to go for breakfast. Not eating breakfast was actually an offence under Naval Law, but those who would rather have a bit longer in bed, generally ignored it. Not me though, I didn't get my manly physique by not eating breakfast. It was a long time before lunch and I needed the energy, as I knew the mile and a half run was almost the first task of the day.

Similar to basic training, an instructor came into the accommodation block shortly before 8am, and told us what we would need in our bags for the first day. This included running gear, wash gear, a towel, a notepad and pen. He then instructed us to muster on the roadway, as a squad, for an introductory tour of the camp.

The course was well organised and everything was done strictly by the book. During the initial march around the camp, the Royal Marine, who introduced himself as Colour Sergeant Huggan, pointed out places of interest such as the sickbay, dentist, kit-issue store and adventurous-training store before we finally arrived at the leadership school.

Sat in class, the Commander of the school popped in to pay us a welcoming visit before our course officer, Lieutenant Sugden, made his introductions and we completed the joining paperwork.

With the formalities complete, the dreaded mile and a half run was the next item on the agenda. It seemed as if everything was done at the rush, we were given only two minutes to get changed into our running kit and out onto the road. C/Sgt 'Huggy' Huggan then formed us into a squad and, positioning himself at the front, he took us on a gentle run around the camp, just to warm us up before the real test of our fitness.

Huffing and puffing, after a mile or so, we were nicely warmed up and positioned for the start of the mile and a half run. This would be invigilated by the PT staff, who first checked all our names, before taking us through a routine of limb stretching. I was knackered and really needed a bit of a lie down. As the course members were all different ages, we were allocated different times in which to complete the run. Women were, for reasons that escape me, given about two minutes longer to complete the same distance, so much for sexual equality. A chap next to me, of approximately the same size and age, asked me what time I did my qualifying run in "Ten-minutes fifty, mate," I replied. "Right, I'll stick with you then." I remember thinking, you can do what you like, mate; I'm not hanging around for you. I needed to run as if my life depended upon it.

After the 'club-swinger' set us off, we initially ran as a group, until fitness and age determined the batting order. A young racing snake, called Kris Westerman, established himself as the leader of the pack. Personally, I was never going to catch this whippet, so contented myself with trying to catch the bloke in front whilst trying, at the same time, not to be overtaken. It was hard work, but I realised I had more energy than I thought. Rounding the final bend, after five complete circuits, I managed to sprint the last two hundred yards, passing the finish line in a respectable ten minutes forty seconds, almost a minute inside my allocated time and beating my personal best by ten seconds.

Tracey, the only girlie, was having trouble; she had another couple of minutes left, but still had one lap to go. I am not sure who started it, but all of the lads, who had finished, including myself, ran alongside her, shouting support. Whether she wanted it or not, it worked. She increased her pace and lengthened her stride. Maybe she was just trying to get away from the chasing pack. Either way, in a tremendous display of teamwork, she crossed the line inside her time. Granted she was never going to win any awards or indeed run a marathon, but at least she did it.

The chap who had elected to run with me, was not quite so fortunate and finished the course in over twelve minutes thus failing his fitness test. Absolutely gutted, he was a classic example of somebody who had failed to prepare. Later that day, he failed in a second attempt and was removed from the course. We never saw him again.

Showered, changed and back into class, it was now time to get to know each other. This was achieved by our first nerve-racking attempt at public speaking. As usual, I was first, but fortunately, there was a board at the back of the class. We were instructed to try to talk for two minutes on a subject that we probably knew quite well, ourselves. This was quite awkward, but with the support of the class, I stood up, introduced myself and using the bullet points on the board, I started telling the assembled group who I was, what my last job was and when I had joined the navy. They learned that I was also married with no known children, I lived in Plymouth with my wife, Anita, and a couple of cats called 'Biscuit' and 'Wellybugs'. As I started to dry up, Lt Sugden asked me what sort of car I drove and what hobbies I had before I realised I was speaking comfortably and had over run my two minutes. It was now time to sit down, get my breath back and enjoy the next victim's life story.

After everyone had spoken, we stopped for a quick brew before the next exercise. On the lectern, at the front of the class, was a pile of cards face down. Each had a word or phrase written on it. We then had to take the top card, look at it and then speak on that topic for a further two minutes. Fortunately, I had been given a helpful hint from a chap on Sovereign. Describe the object before likening it to other things and whizzing off on a tangent. The exercise was not about the subject matter, just the ability to talk bollocks in front of an audience. This is not something that I usually have trouble with. Picking up the card, it just said 'ping pong ball' Fuck! I started slowly, by describing a table tennis ball as a small white plastic sphere about an inch and a half in diameter that is used to play table tennis otherwise known as ping pong. As a sphere, with a bit of imagination, it could be likened to a small planet. There was, at last count, thousands of planets in the universe. I then went on to talk about the planets in our solar system until, after two minutes had elapsed, I was told to shut up and sit down. Job done! After everyone had had at least two opportunities at speaking in front of the assembled group, we found that we were starting to gel.

As it was a leadership course, the next task was to devise a name for our class. We were told that we could choose the name of any great leader in history. 'Suggy' issued a word of caution, before we selected the final name. In week three, we would be required to stage a play, recounting the exploits of the character in history and everyone would be required to act. This clearly ruled out Margaret Thatcher, Genghis Khan and Adolf Hitler as the play would be either boring and political, or just too difficult to stage whilst involving the entire class. Someone suggested doing King Arthur and the Knights of the Round Table. This caused some discussion. A round table could be nicked from the dining room; we had a woman on course to play Guinevere and several blokes to play the knights. Yes, it was agreed that the course name would be 'King Arthur'.

After lunch, with this decided, we were shown into the back row of the theatre to watch the play being directed by the course currently in their third week. This was so we could appreciate the acceptable format and the tone of the script. Somewhat unexpectedly, the Captain and Commodore of the camp made an appearance and sat in the centre of the first row.

It all seemed very professional, there were ushers to see us to our seats, someone handing out programmes and at the side of the stage, a man stood quietly behind a lectern, as the narrator. When everyone was seated, the narrator welcomed everyone and explained the storyline before the curtains were opened to reveal a scripted scene. It was clear that the class had written the play around the course buzzwords, so a lot of it just swept over our heads. Even so, it was light-hearted and funny and only lasted for half an hour. These were clearly big boots to fill and we had much to think about.

By the end of the first day, we had learnt a lot about the course and more importantly about ourselves. We now had a course timetable that told us where to be and what uniform to be wearing for any given activity. There was also a roster designating a duty class leader which changed daily. It was the class leader's job to ensure that everyone was wearing the correct uniform, had the right books with them and to march the class around the camp. It was so easy to forget that you were constantly under observation and being continually assessed.

As I have previously mentioned, improving fitness levels was a huge part of the course. Quite what fitness has to do with the ability to lead a group of men, I have no idea. In the field of battle, I suppose a platoon leader might choose to lead by example and lead from the front, but on a ship or more relevantly, a submarine, running is frowned upon and walking from one end of the boat to the other is generally not considered too arduous. As the course was generic, there was little to be gained by complaining, though the few submariners did have a bit of a moan to start with.

Every evening, between 4pm and 6pm, in a period traditionally known as the Dog Watches, we would don our sports kit, to compete in a competition between the other courses. This would include volleyball, dribbling a football around cones or anything that involved running around as a team. It was good, competitive fun, though it did result in the occasional bloody knee or twisted ankle.

Weekend leave was a bonus that had to be earned by jumping through all of the hoops that the course presented us with. The first of which was a two-mile squad run around the camp. As this was conducted at the pace of the slowest chap and not a timed run, it was not too bad. I was positioned in the middle of the squad, shepherded by the much younger and fitter blokes who had the breath to shout words of encouragement. Consequently everyone was permitted to leave the camp at midday on Friday and travel home for a weekend of rest and recuperation. As I had arrived in a hire car, I scrounged a lift from a grumpy Yorkshireman, on the course, called Phil Hilton.

I had known Phil for quite a few years and we had learned to pretty much tolerate each other. It was a classic love-hate relationship. I think we sort of liked each other, though neither of us would ever dare to admit it.

Phil was a creature of habit and although he probably didn't realise it, he did the same things repeatedly. One example of this was when we had been driving for about an hour, he would pull into a layby on the A303 for a comfort break, a bacon sarnie and a cup of tea. During this break, Phil would, as regular as clockwork, stretch, yawn and then ask if I fancied driving for a bit. Personally, I prefer to be the master of my own destiny and never made a good passenger so I always agreed. This was never discussed but it became a regular routine and quite comical, though Phil always remained deadpan.

During the second week, the emphasis on fitness increased with a US Marine Corp fitness test. This was followed by a two-day trip to Erlestoke, on Salisbury Plain. Erlestoke, was a disaster exercise. The scenario was simple, a plane had crashed somewhere in the 'jungle', the pilot had ejected and needed to be 'rescued' as well as locating two pods of stores from the 'downed' aircraft. My role for the exercise was Damage Control Officer and I had to take charge of the entire exercise and relocate into an abandoned 'village', which in fact, was a collection of shipping containers. Once established, my priority was to organise food and water, detail search parties to comb the area for the pilot and stores pods as well as trying to cope with 'unfriendly natives'. Fortunately, with everyone working as a team, the search parties located the 'pilot'. The pods were eventually located and little by little, the chef managed to rustle up a stew whilst a couple of 'tiffs' improvised an evaporator, managing to produce half a cup full of fresh water.

The exercise was going ok. Occasionally, I would receive a prompt from the staff about something that I had forgotten to do, or not checked recently. This was all designed at keeping me on my toes, as it was quite a busy day. At about 8pm that evening, when it was fully dark, I received a signal which heralded the start of a night navigational exercise. The course was split up into four groups and dispatched in different directions, with the brief to collect as many of the high value markers as possible, with a cut-off time of 6am. There were numerous checkpoints dotted around the area, the further afield they were, the more points could be gained, so we plotted a course on the map to a high value marker and then joined the dots between them, collecting as many as we could. The army, in their tracked vehicles, had used the ground recently, so the going was quite tough, especially in the dark. Fortunately, it was a cold clear night, so the moon assisted our navigation. By 5am, we were doing quite well so we considered making a beeline back towards camp. It was then, with about a mile or so to go, one of the lads, a Scouse git nicknamed 'Sully', started to develop knee problems. I do not entirely blame him for that, but he was incessantly whinging about everything. Despite his four years in the job, he seemed very knowledgeable and had an opinion on just about any topic. As an upshot of his knee problem, we divided his rucksack contents between us and using a couple of the fitter lads as crutches, we walked and he hobbled back to camp. Tracey, the only girly, coined an imaginary ailment that we were all apparently suffering from called 'Sicosully' or sick of 'Sully'. Nethertheless, we made it back to camp with about fifteen minutes remaining on the clock. We were absolute knackered and too tired to even eat, though I did try, before we got on the coach for the drive back to Whale Island.

The end of week two culminated in a three-mile run along Southsea sea front. This was preceded by a warm-up on the stony beach near Eastleigh Barracks, that was bloody hard work. The run along the wide concrete promenade however, with a cool breeze blowing in off the sea, was actually quite nice. By the end of the week, I felt a lot fitter. That's not to say I wasn't knackered, but my recovery time was getting quicker and I no longer sported a head that looked like a beetroot.

In week three, things started to get busy. We were off to Wales to trog over the Black Mountains. Being into hill-walking, I was looking forward to stretching my legs in the hills for a bit. As it turned out, the night navex at Erlestoke had been a practice for the Black Mountains.

My map-reading and compass work has always been quite good, but back in class, we were given a dicky lesson. As I probably knew more about it than the instructor, I didn't pay much attention. Evidently, I wasn't the only one, as we ended up lost in a very short period of time. It was foggy, raining and apart from the ground, there was very little to see. A confident Scottish chap, with a chip on his shoulder and a point to prove, seemed to know better, but unfortunately, the only point that he proved was, he couldn't take information off a map and walk on a compass bearing. On that day, we lost an awful lot of time looking for checkpoints that, in clear visibility, would have been obvious. You might argue that perhaps I should have stepped in and corrected him, but this was *his* leadership task and the staff were, of course, observing him. Later in the day, a chap took over who was a Fleet Air Arm Aircrewman. In contrast, his navigation was superb. He processed the information from the map quickly, took a sighting and off we went. We would maybe stop every 100-200 metres to take another bearing and sighting, making up lost ground in the process.

As this was a two-day trek, we were carrying three-man tents, split down between five people, which would be a bit snug, but less weight to carry. When we finally reached our allocated campsite, someone set about cooking the food whilst Phil and I erected the tent. As it was pitch black outside, Phil had snapped a Cylume light stick and when the tent was fit for habitation, he had put the light source in a pocket at the apex. When the five of us had eaten and were squashed into our sleeping bags, with Tracey in the centre, Phil piped up "Tracey, be a love and turn the light out will you?" The ever compliant Tracey reached up, got hold of the Cylume light stick and after fiddling with it for a while asked, "How do you turn the bloody thing off?" Much to the amusement of the lads, including myself.

The following day, the weather was bright and clear, so navigation did not present a real problem. Without too much trouble, we detoured off the path into the woods and found a previously elusive checkpoint, nailed to a tree. After that, it was pretty much a direct route march back to the camp, where the instructors were staying. Fortunately, there was a carrot waiting for us in the shape of a hearty cooked breakfast, whilst the results were collected in and points awarded. A couple of hours later, after breakfast and a hot shower, we were on the bus heading back towards Whale Island with rucksacks full of wet muddy clothes.

The next major obstacle, was the previously feared play, on the subject of King Arthur and the Knights of the Round Table. One evening we had a course meeting, chaired by Tracey, who was the reluctant producer of the play. Everybody was allocated a task to research and some of the major parts were cast. Tracey, we thought, would play the only female role in folklore, but chose instead to be the narrator. Out of character, Phil Hilton, usually a grumpy bugger, volunteered to dress up in drag as Guinevere and Kris Westerman, the smallest guy on the course, volunteered to be King Arthur. To inject a small amount of comedy into the proceedings, the knights were given silly names such as, Sports Knight, who was dressed in sports gear and Green Knight, who was dressed as a Royal Marine in honour of 'Huggy', our Royal Marine instructor. Not feeling particularly theatrical, I offered to produce the programme and manage backstage. Tracey wrote the script before we had a couple of dress rehearsals to iron out any kinks.

By Thursday afternoon, everything was ready. Costumes had been improvised and with some make-up, Phil's appearance had been drastically improved. Tracey had also lent him some of her underwear. This was not actually needed, but I think, secretly, he liked it. Kris was looking vaguely regal, with a crown fashioned from cardboard covered in gold coloured foil perched on his head and a cloak wrapped around his shoulders.

Surprisingly, it actually went off very well. It was written as a comedy whilst incorporating most of the leadership terms. The measure of a comedy is managing to get a laugh from the audience and we certainly did that.

In the final week, there were a couple of tasks still to complete, one was the dreaded five-mile run and also there was another mile and a half run. The former was a squad run to HMS Dryad, high up on Portsdown Hill and the latter, another fitness test, to prove that all the running around had been beneficial.

Early one morning, after a light breakfast, carrying bottles of water and wearing shorts, training shoes and orange course shirts, we climbed onto the bus for the short ride to Boarhunt, just off Junction 11 of the M27, where the driver pulled into a car park and chucked us off. The physical training staff lined us up for the ritual of stretching and running on the spot until we were all knackered and gasping for breath. Forming into our usual squad positions, with a member of the PT staff wearing a high viz jacket out front and another at the back, Lt Sugden shouted "POLC 2280, by the left, double march," and we were off. To the uninitiated, a double march is similar to jogging and is not too arduous, though we did have quite a few hills still to climb. After a while, when I thought that my chest might explode, I got the fabled second wind. The pain subsided as I realised that I had fought my way through the pain barrier.

As we approached the gates of HMS Dryad, sensing the finish line, the front-runners, opened the pace and the gaps between us started to widen. Surprising myself, I found that I still had running left as I quickened my own pace to keep up. The guys out front just kept getting faster, as we broke ranks and sprinted for the last couple of hundred yards to the finish line totally and utterly exhausted. There was water in abundance, allowing us to re-hydrate before stumbling onto the waiting coach for the journey back to Whale Island for a shower and to get changed.

The next day, as the course was ending, we again lined up for the final mile and a half run. After all of the running I had done over the previous four weeks, I was not worried about this in the slightest. It had all become fairly routine. Following the usual warm up of stretching, we were off. After the first lap, the PT staff called out the time as I passed and to my relief, it had been completed in a respectable time. With a long way to go, I plodded on, closing the gap on the chap in front. Having caught him, I switched targets towards the next fella and slowly gained ground on him as I ran as hard as I have ever run. This had to be a good time. The whole point of the course was to demonstrate an improvement, so anything more than ten-minutes forty-seconds would be totally unacceptable. With about two hundred yards still to run, the guy I was chasing started quickening the pace. I dare say he was chasing someone else and now he was getting away; we couldn't have that. Digging deep, I lengthened my stride and increased the pace, planning to expend my last reserves of energy as I sprinted after him towards the finish line. Crossing the line at a dead run and taking about twenty yards to stop. Sweating profusely and taking deep breaths, I wandered back to the 'club-swinger' with the clipboard to find out my time. I had crossed the line at nine-minutes forty-seconds. Ok, that is not going to win any records, but it was a whole minute off my previous run and I was rightly chuffed to little mint balls.

The final module of the course was 'Divisions'. This is a parade, to show the world, just how bad the navy are at marching. It was also an excuse for me to get my dress uniform out, dust it off and polish up my only medal. The ceremony would also be an opportunity for the girlie swots in the class to be presented with trophies, marking their achievements on the course. As a class, we were all being presented with a certificate and a trophy called the 'Richardson Trophy' this was awarded to any course that collectively visited every checkpoint in the Black Mountains. Divisions culminated with a formal march past, whilst the Captain took the salute. With the course over, all I had to do now was to pack my stuff, conduct a leaving interview with Lt Sugden and bid farewell to the many friends that I had made on the course.

My interview was quite an informal affair as we chatted about my progress and fitness on the course. It was generally considered by 'Suggy' that I had done well on the course. Apparently, in his opinion, I would make good petty officer and also a chief petty officer in due course which was nice of him.

Out of the class, five of us were transferring, a few miles across the water, to HMS Sultan, for the second part of our Petty Officers Qualifying Course; this was what we termed the navy's D.I.Y course. Myself, Phil Hilton, Paul Whitaker, Billy Nichol and Jim Bryson were all petty officer stokers so we all needed to complete this course to become confirmed as PO's in our own branch.

Putting all of our stuff into a couple of cars, we made our farewells and headed out of Portsmouth on the M275. Exiting onto the westbound M27 for one junction, before heading down the A32, on the other side of the estuary, towards Gosport and the spiritual home of the Marine Engineers.

On arrival, we were each allocated a small single cabin in Exmouth Block, about as far away from the mess as it was possible to get, but at least they were single cabins, which was a marked increase in our standard of living. It certainly made a pleasant change to sharing a mess with five other snoring and farting blokes.

The following morning after breakfast, I made my introductions and completed the customary joining routine before climbing the bridge over Military Road to commence the course.

PO stokers are regarded by some to be more academically challenged than the PO 'tiffs', but what they may lack in academic achievement, is more than made up for in mechanical experience, and, there is no substitute for experience. This course was designed to concentrate more on practical engineering and less on cerebral learning, which was absolutely fine with me.

There were two variants of the course, one concentrating on lathe work whilst the other concentrated on welding. The five of us had been assigned to the latter but just so we didn't dip out, we would start with two weeks of instruction on the lathe as the other course would have two weeks tinkering about with welding rods. This was actually quite good fun as we were each given lumps of metal and a technical drawing, showing the measurements of the shape that we were required to produce. Annoyingly, Phil had a natural aptitude for this sort of work and was seemingly always ahead of the rest of us. Paul 'Wingnut' Whitaker, in contrast, was spectacularly bad at everything he did, not that he actually saw it that way. He had a natural, infectious enthusiasm and confidence in everything he did. This often manifested itself as over-confidence, resulting in him cocking-up. As for me, the whole thing was a learning curve, so I took it slowly and generally did quite well. Phil was constantly giving me abuse in an attempt to make me speed up on the lathe and in doing so screw up my work, but I wasn't having any of it. Like wood, it is so easy to remove the material, but impossible to put it back if you shave off too much. Fortunately, with the exception of 'Wingnut', everyone produced a test piece that was subsequently marked above the eighty percent. 'Wingnut' had to start again, which, with more care, he managed a pass mark.

After two weeks of swarf generation, turning a steel bar into scrap metal and becoming quite competent at it, we transferred to the 'Allied Trades' workshops to learn how to weld with an oxy-acetylene welding torch. This was a new skill to learn and, if I am honest, it took a little while to get to grips with the technique. This was not helped when, Phil, for a joke, occasionally knocked off my oxygen tap, causing my welding torch to issue a huge orange smoky flame, instead of the neat sharp blue flame that we learned was characteristic of an efficient welding flame. Wearing a dark green welding mask, I was eventually able to identify the crescent shaped weld pool and through practice, I successfully learned to 'chase it' across the joint, topping it up with the welding rod as I went. After a couple of weeks' of practice, we were required to produce a complex test piece which would demonstrate our ability to create all of the joints we had learned. This was completed successfully without any huge dramas.

The next topic to be covered was oxy-acetylene cutting and again, after a bit of practice, this was quite easy for us all to master.

Changing workshops and instructors, it was time to get to grips with arc welding, otherwise known as MMA. We were each allocated individual booths, complete with a welding machine, a selection of welding rods, a metal bench, some tools and a metal stool. The goggles we were issued were far more tinted and we were also required to wear a heavy leather apron, gloves and spats to prevent burns from the hot metal.

After some communal instruction and learning the settings for the welding machine, we disappeared to our respective booths and proceeded to cause random sparks, flashes and occasionally stick the welding rod to the practice metal. This would result in swinging the welding rod backwards and forwards until it snapped off with yet another blinding, crackling flash. Tweaking the settings on the welding machine, produced varying results, until finally, I was able to stick the two blobs of metal together. It did not look pretty, but you cannot teach experience. The only way to improve was practice and we had a couple of weeks to get it right.

Phil, being the girlie swot that he was, told us how good he was getting. Personally, I wasn't doing too badly. I quickly learnt what to look for and the best angles to adopt. Striking the arc like a match and then holding the tip of the electrode a couple of millimetres off the metal I would allow the welding rod to transfer itself to the joint and gradually draw the weld to the left. At the end of the run, with the electrode spent and discarded, I would lift my mask up to see how it looked. The joint would be covered in a brittle black shale that, if I'd done it right, should just fall off. A tickle with a chipping hammer and a wire brush finally exposed the joint.

We would practice continuously, until we were all fairly proficient. On one occasion, Phil was late back from lunch, so the ever-practical joking 'Wingnut' decided to *weld* Phil's metal stool to his workbench, amid much snickering. On his return, Phil grabbed hold of his stool and pulled it away from the bench with little resistance. It turned out, unsurprisingly, that 'Wingnut' needed a bit more practice than the rest of us.

The following day, when 'Wingnut' had a medical appointment, Phil and I seized upon the opportunity to exact revenge on him. Inside his booth, we welded everything he owned to the desk. His hammer and all of his spanners were *properly* welded to the bench. His stool was welded in three places under his bench and all of his welding rods were left sticking out of the bench like a porcupine. Finally, we changed all of the settings of his welding machine before sneaking off to our respective booths, to await the fallout.

On his return, 'Wingnut' was forced to borrow a hammer and an angle grinder, just to remove his tools and stool, much to the amusement of everybody else. This revenge was long overdue.

Eventually, I was handed a drawing of the test piece that I needed to manufacture. This would demonstrate all the different welds in one blob of metal. It took me several hours of welding before I was finally ready to present my test-piece for marking, where it gained a very respectable pass mark.

With that module now complete, the next type of welding to learn was MIG. Similar to arc welding, this was somewhat more sophisticated and looked more like an electrical blow torch, with a wire being fed through the centre, shielded by argon gas. After a bit of practice, we all found this a doddle, even 'Wingnut'. The trick, we found, was to select the right electrical settings, the wire feeding at the right speed and also the gas setting. Once all of these were working together, it was easy to zip two pieces of steel together.

The final welding discipline was TIG. The technique was similar to gas welding and like MIG, used argon to shield a tungsten electrode. It was all starting to make sense, and I was getting quite good at it. Before long, everyone had created a passable aluminium box as a test piece. I found that I liked TIG welding, there was no need for heavy leather gloves, and the metal was always clean and shiny afterwards.

With all of the welding now complete, it was time to get messy and learn how to fabricate shapes, using Glass Reinforced Plastic. This is like papier-*mâché* for grownups, using fibreglass instead of paper and resin instead of paste. With a bit of preparation, it was relatively simple to build up a structure, that when hardened and removed from the mould, was rock solid. As the course was now starting to draw to a close, this module was only three days long, but that was more than sufficient to learn the principles of layering GRP into a mould of a small model boat. The following day after my fabrication had properly hardened; it was prised from the mould to reveal a perfectly smooth hull.

The final module and the bit I was really looking forward to was woodwork. I have always enjoyed tinkering with bits of wood, but since leaving school, I have never had any formal tuition. To start with, the instructor demonstrated how to sharpen a handful of chisels before, under supervision, we crafted some dovetail joints. This was achieved by firstly marking up and using a tenon saw to carefully cut to the waste side of the line. With the cuts made, I went to work with the chisel, gently shaving away the waste before starting on the other bit. I was actually quite impressed with my first effort. The class had varying results and most had done well, though predictably, 'Wingnut' had not listened properly, resulting in quite a sloppy joint.

With the practice complete and time running short, the next task was to construct a carpenter's toolbox from a supplied drawing. The method was to measure and fabricate an enclosed box that resembled a very large ice cream wafer. This was then planed and sanded, leaving a smooth six-sided box. Using a tenon saw, I very carefully cut the door flap. Predictably, 'Wingnut' screwed his up and ended up veering off to one side, which was totally unrecoverable. I am chuffed to admit, mine went perfectly, after the instructor had showed me how to correctly balance the saw in my right hand.

With the door finally cut and hinged, the next task was to make a smaller tray to fit inside the toolbox, before finally sanding and varnishing. The box now has a few battle scars but still houses my wood-working tools in the garage.

Finally, after about fifteen weeks, the course was over. I had enjoyed it immensely and gained a load of new skills, most of which were useless within the confines of a submarine.

After a bit of Easter Leave and glad to be finally back in Devonport, I joined the Fleet Maintenance Base to complete my shore time before being drafted to join another submarine.

Ian Atkinson

HMS DEFIANCE

10th May 1997 to 11th September 1998

Having spent the last few years working away from home, it was quite a novelty to be actually kissing the wife goodbye on a Monday morning and saying, "See you later, darling."

Cycling into the dockyard, I parked the bike and headed off to the gents toilet to change into something resembling a naval uniform. A few minutes before 8am, I wandered off to the UPO to make my introductions. After most of the formalities had been completed, I was introduced to my new boss, Warrant Officer 'Burt' Reynolds, who was in charge of the nuclear repair facility. Since I last worked for nuclear repair, the nuclear barge, MAC1014, had been decommissioned and the staff and workshops relocated to a brand new building on the north-western corner of the fleet maintenance base, adjacent to the submarine jetties on eight and nine wharf.

'Burt' Reynolds informed me that I was to be employed, with a team of other POMEM's, as a slinger. This would involve lifting and transporting awkward and heavy pieces of equipment throughout the submarine, using a combination of strops and chain blocks. When they were ready to hoist off the boat, hand signals would be used to direct an overhead crane, the crane operator would then lift the kit skywards and drop it on the jetty.

Up to this point, I had limited experience using lifting gear, so it was essential that I attend a course in the dockyard that would provide the necessary qualification. Until then, I was to work under the direction of the lead slinger, a petty officer stoker, called Kevin 'Panzy' Potter, who, whilst being a Londoner and an all-round good bloke, was also a fanatical West Ham United fan, but we should not hold that against him.

There were a couple of teams within the nuclear repair department. The fitters, concentrated on repairing and replacing equipment, but if the need arose, then a slinger or two would be required to assist and lift out the pump, valve or motor, after the fitters had finished unbuttoning it. Fortunately, 'Panzy' had been doing the job for a while and had a good idea how heavy everything was and what slinging route to take out of the submarine. This was not always obvious and when you are lifting a pump, weighing around two tons, there is little room for error.

I enjoyed the work, as it relied on the team working together. Every job was also a situational puzzle that needed solving in the mind before rigging up the various strops, shackles and chain blocks. At this point, I was doing exactly as I was told, until I received my qualification. Typically I would be in charge of one chain block and under Panzy's direction, I would hoist or lower as the weight was transferred from one chain block to another, moving the load through the submarine. It was hard, physical and noisy work but there was a huge amount of pride to be taken from removing a pump from its position and not damaging anything in the process.

The slinging course was held in a disused workshop in the 'Factory' that was situated in Devonport dockyard. There was a fair bit of theory to learn, which was necessary but also very dull. After the classroom work, it was then time to get down to the interesting, practical stuff. In the workshop, dressed in overalls and hard hats, we were introduced to a mock-up of a ship, made out of scaffolding and planks. Placed somewhere inside the rig, would be a motor or a pump. One by one, we would be instructed to move the item from its resting place to wherever the instructor directed using any equipment from the small mound of supplied lifting gear.

Having had quite a bit of on-job experience, I actually found this quite easy. The trick, was to visualise what was going to happen to the load and the planned route before even commencing the first lift. The route I had to take using chain blocks, strops and shackles was essentially a maze of passages over three 'decks' and all without allowing the load to hit anything or touch the deck. Not everyone could instantly see the solution, but as slinging is a team effort, advice was sought and the agreed plan signed up to by everyone.

Having passed the physical slinging module, we decamped down the road and into the 'Frigate Refit Complex'. This is actually a huge building, known affectionately as 'The Frigate Sheds'. The FRC houses three large dry docks adjacent to 2 basin. Inside the building and on the dockside were several cranes, positioned to lift heavy items on or off the ships. The beauty of working inside was, it was out of the weather, but more importantly, it was out of the wind. Quite a few of the cranes on the dockside could not operate if the wind was gusting in excess of sixteen-knots. The purpose of this module was to communicate with the crane driver using only hand signals and to lift, move and reposition a load precisely. Fortunately, the crane driver knew his onions and was quite used to numpty crane signallers like us and our crazy adaptations of the standard hand signals. Therefore, despite us waving our arms frantically at him, he calmly did what was required and subsequently, we all graduated from the slinging course.

Now qualified and back on the section, I was able to assist the fitters doing a bit of spanner work, under their direction, whilst they then assisted me, slinging the various bits of kit out of the boat. Due to the nature of the job, the work had the tendency to be sporadic, so a lot of time was spent in a rather smoky, windowless, restroom, reading papers, drinking tea and eating sandwiches out of sheer boredom. Usually by 10am, we were awash with tea and losing the will to live. By midday, if there was no work in the pipeline, I would generally take the initiative and get off home for a make and mend.

On the 1st September 1997 my wife, Anita, was admitted to hospital with a mysterious illness, which was causing her a great deal of pain and myself an equal amount of concern. On the Saturday night, when Princess Diana tragically died, unbeknown to me, Anita had been downstairs all night, in agony, watching the story unfold on the TV before waking me up quite early complaining of tummy pains. With my limited medical knowledge exhausted, I called an ambulance and it wasn't long before she was whisked off to hospital.

I followed the ambulance to Derriford Hospital in the car, but when she was settled in a room, sedated and tucked up in bed, there was little else I could do, so I popped off home to figure out how to work the cooker, washing machine and more importantly, how to feed the cat.

After an eventful weekend, there was nothing useful I could do to help Anita and with no children to look after, I went into work. The news of Princess Di's death was all over the papers and it hit us hard. Diana had visited the dockyard only recently with Prince Charles and we still held her in the highest regard. That did not however, prevent the service brand of humour creeping in. Servicemen are often renowned for their seemingly callous humour which is designed as a coping mechanism. The theory goes something like, if you can laugh about something, then it doesn't make it seem too bad. On this particular occasion early in September 1997, drinking tea in the restroom, I was reading the paper whilst 'Panzy' Potter was reading a recent Auto Trader, looking for a new car. Without looking up, and in a broad London accent he announced, "Hey, this one looks good; a 1994 Black Mercedes S280 with light frontal damage for only £500. The trouble is, it's in Paris," which resulted in a few groans and a bit of reluctant laughter.

My boss, 'Burt' Reynolds, was sympathetic to Anita's hospitalisation and told me to take all the time off I needed, but apart from visiting her every evening, there was little else I could do, so I opted to work, if only to take my mind off things.

The following weekend, with Anita still in hospital, a chap calling himself 'Commander Walker' woke me up at around 7am. "Hello is that Ian Atkinson?" After I had replied, he said, "Could you come to the hospital please? Your wife is very distressed." My response was a bleary, "Well, she was ok last night, what have you done to her?" he replied "I will explain everything when you get here, but please hurry." This set alarm bells ringing and even before I was properly dressed, I was out of the house and driving, quite fast, towards Derriford Hospital.

On arrival, Commander Walker, who turned out to be a naval surgeon and looked for all the world like 'Captain Birdseye' from the fish finger adverts, explained that Anita had been taken down to X-ray earlier that morning and that there was an urgent need to operate and frankly he didn't have time to discuss it. The look in his eyes and the tone of his voice told the rest of the story. Realising the gravity of the situation, I told him to get on with it and frankly, save her life. It was that serious!

It turned out that she had developed an infected colon and a condition called ulcerative colitis. This was slowly poisoning her and left untreated, would kill her. Simply put, it needed to come out. Anita was unable to grasp the enormity of the situation, therefore, it came down to me to give consent for her lifesaving operation.

Anita was confused and scared as she was prepared for the operation. It was coincidental, that at the same time, gathering in London, the crowds were forming to pay their respects to the people's princess whilst Anita was being wheeled down to theatre. So I wasn't mistaken for a surgeon, I was given a very tight orange coat, so I could hold her hand until the anaesthetic took effect. I was then advised to go home, not to worry and await a call.

Not sure what to do, I somehow ended up in Plymouth town centre just wandering around in a daze. My mind was all over the place, but I kept it together. Any public outpouring of emotion might have seemed a bit soft, considering the televised funeral of Princess Diana so I just wondered around waiting for the telephone call, that would hopefully give me my wife back.

Sitting in McDonalds with a 'Big Mac' meal in front of me, uncharacteristically, I could not eat it. I just kept checking my mobile phone still had a signal. Starting to feel a little more positive, I visited a card shop and spent a fortune on a huge 'Get Well' card, a teddy bear and a balloon. She always liked her balloons.

With the car park ticket about to expire, I returned home and called the hospital for news. Still there was none, so I made a drink and put on a video to try to relax, but it was no use, I could not concentrate on anything. Equally, anxious relatives started calling for news, but I needed the phone to be kept clear so I am afraid I was rather short with them. I am sure they understood.

Finally, in the early evening, the phone rang and the caller announced that the operation had been a success and that Anita, although still dopey from the anaesthetic, was in recovery. Armed with the card and prezzies, I made my way back to Derriford Hospital just as Anita was being wheeled back onto the ward, where the nurses told me everything had gone according to plan. Anita, although drowsy, was awake and in some discomfort, though it would be several weeks before she would be strong enough to go home.

Over the next few weeks, I continued to work during the day and visit Anita in the evening. I was exhausted! Getting home at around 8pm, I would typically spend a couple of hours on the phone, repeating myself to various friends and relatives on her recovery progress.

Slowly regaining her strength, Anita surprised the nurses with her speed of recovery. Once her pain levels were under control, she was allowed home towards the end of September where she continued to recover in her own bed, supported by the cat, who I had just managed to keep alive.

Despite this upheaval in my domestic life, I was getting my teeth into working as a slinger and enjoyed the day-to-day problems that every lift presented. It was very physical work, and quite mentally challenging, but there was nothing that the team could not collectively handle.

One morning, the boss, 'Burt' Reynolds, asked me to conduct a simple lift for him on the new Weston Mill Jetty. He gave me a hint that I would need four of the red five-ton nylon 'Spansets' and a few large shackles. It turned out, he wanted me to hoist a thirty-three foot yacht, called 'Storm Dragon', out of the water and place her in a cradle so she could have her bottom scraped and painted. This was quite scary as the yacht could have easily slipped out of the grip of the strops and to make matters worse, we did not have the right lifting beam, so a couple of improvised wooden spreaders needed to be used. A mobile crane subsequently turned up on the jetty and after a detailed brief of what was actually required, the kit was rigged.

With the strops in place around the hull, the crane started to take the strain. With one eye on the crane driver, I slowly inched 'Storm Dragon' clear of the water before I halted proceedings and checked all was as it should be. If she fell now, it might have caused some damage, but no more than falling off a wave. With the team satisfied that she was secure, I ordered the crane to winch 'Storm Dragon' well clear of the water and then slewed slowly towards the waiting cradle.

With somebody holding the painter and another at the stern, 'Storm Dragon' was manoeuvred into position and lowered slowly into the cradle. The whole operation, went like a dream.

It appeared, 'Storm Dragon' was being prepared for a month long expedition, starting from Plymouth, that was to be split into four legs. As luck would have it, they were short of crew members for a couple of the Spanish legs. Successfully managing to persuade 'Burt' to let me go, I attended a couple of meetings in April 1998 to meet the crew and to discuss the logistics of who was to perform which role on the voyage. It was finally arranged that the team would meet at the continental ferry port in Plymouth at 11am on Wednesday 6th May 1998.

After a bit of last minute money-changing, we boarded the Brittany Ferries ship, 'Val de Loire', for the twenty-four hour crossing through the Bay of Biscay to Santander.

Leaving Plymouth, covered in mist and fine rain, we promptly adjourned to the bar for a team brief that was to last for several hours. After a film, a good meal and cabaret in the bar, we retired for the night slightly squiffy. We awoke the following morning to a bright sunny day and after a mammoth breakfast, prepared to disembark.

Arriving on schedule, the welcoming party from the off-going crew were already waiting on the jetty waiting to board. A hurried handover took place before we loaded our luggage into the two waiting taxis for the twenty-minute journey to where 'Storm Dragon' was berthed. At the marina, Skipper, 'Tug' Tugwell, suggested that the boaty types sort out the yacht and the non-sailing types, pop off to the shops for supplies. That was to prove the under-estimation of the trip as it took myself, Ray and Alison over an hour to reach the shopping complex. Armed with only a phrase book and a wad of pesetas, we made a two-hour assault on the aisles filling one trolley completely. Ray was dispatched to find a taxi, whilst Angela and I returned, with a second trolley, to stock up on liquid refreshment.

Ray returned a short time later, with the news that we had to phone for a taxi, so, bristling with confidence, as the others waited at the checkout, I went off to call a taxi from the free phone in the supermarket and was surprised when, a few minutes later, one arrived.

Back at 'Storm Dragon', Steve had been *very busy* sunning himself whilst the First Mate, 'Sandy', and the Skipper, 'Tug' had gone to investigate the gas situation. After a cool beer, I volunteered to prepare dinner and an hour later, a very acceptable chicken in pepper sauce with rice was dished up before we all retired for the night.

'Storm Dragon' slipped quite early the following morning from Santander and turning eastwards, we followed the coast under sail into a lumpy sea, which severely tested the stowage for sea. The wind rose to a gusty twenty-eight knots, which required a reef in the main, but as Ray could testify, the ride was not at all comfortable. Angela and I struggled, in the pitching cabin, to knock up some sandwiches for lunch, which duly arrived and were much appreciated by those on deck. It was becoming increasingly difficult to stay below deck, but matters eased considerably a few hours later, when we turned in towards shore, nearing the coastal town of Castro Urdiales, near Bilbao.

Motoring into the harbour, about five or six lanes of yachts were sighted moored forward to aft in a maritime version of a car park. Steve and Ray were dispatched in the dingy to recover the mooring rope from a buoy. Shortly afterwards, we discovered that some fishing line had become entangled around the propeller shaft. Two young Spanish boys were trying in vain to retrieve it, obviously feeling quite guilty about using the mooring as a fishing mark. In a blinding flash of light, Steve emerged from the cabin looking like an American comic book hero, in his speedos, and jumped into the water, instantly regretting it, as it was freezing. He made two dives under the boat before surfacing with a loose end. 'Sandy' turned the shaft by hand, as I reeled in the line and reported the progress. Frozen stiff, Steve had had enough so I reluctantly volunteered to swim underneath and cut it loose. Armed with a knife, secured by a lanyard around my wrist, I made two dives under the boat before announcing that the shaft was clear.

After a couple of sociable beers ashore, it was decided to slip from Castro Urdiales on the ebb tide, after a final Spanish breakfast, some last minute shopping and a touch of sightseeing.

'Storm Dragon' slipped on time and motored out of harbour before setting a course of 030 degrees towards the French former submarine base at La Rochelle. The wind started to get up quite nicely, so the sails were set and the engine shut down. This was an opportunity for all of the trainees, including myself, to take turns at the helm before the wind dropped later in the afternoon. The foresail was then dropped and we motored, for most of the night, under a perfect moonlit sky. During the morning watch, a storm front passed over giving us a good soaking. With thunderstorms forming ahead and astern, the sails were raised as the wind increased to seven-knots. This lasted for approximately four hours before it again died and we were forced to continue under power.

The passage across the Bay of Biscay continued on Sunday without incident and coincidently without wind. The watches were split into six-hour shifts during the day and four hours at night with 'Tug', Ray and myself in one watch whilst 'Sandy', Steve and Angela formed the other.

Later in the day, numerous reports of land were made but these turned out to be nothing more than sea mist, before I eventually spotted a hard looking splodge of land at around 8pm as we slowly approached the entrance to La Rochelle.

It was estimated that it would still take a few hours to close the land and it wasn't until about 11pm that we finally rounded the cardinal, that warned of shallow water. As there were loads of white shore lights masking the 'intense' leading lights, which were supposed to guide our approach, it was then that the confusion started to set in,

With 'Sandy' and 'Tug' examining the chart and myself at the helm, we motored very gingerly through the harbour approaches, with the rest of the crew keeping a sharp lookout for obstructions. It was only after careful examination of the charts, almanac and tide tables did we eventually manage to identify the cardinal lights and leading lights by their respective flash configurations. With the tide only just on the flood, extreme care was taken to stay in the channel. I must say, I was crapping myself; it was pitch-black and I was steering blind, accepting orders only from the Skipper who was below, poring over the chart and GPS. It still took us two hours to negotiate the channel, narrowly missing a huge stone structure with a cardinal light perched on top of it. As it was so high, we assumed it must be some distance away. By 2 am, we had finally entered the inner harbour and with a great deal of relief, berthed on the visitor's jetty. The debrief continued until about 4 am when the beer finally ran out.

After a predictably lazy start, the morning was spent sorting the yacht out. Steve and I went shopping for food and gas whilst Angela, Ray, 'Sandy' and 'Tug' dealt with the business of packing sails away and swabbing the decks, generally making 'Storm Dragon' ship-shape again. When all of the chores had been completed and 'Storm Dragon' was cleaned, stowed and replenished, the crew headed into La Rochelle for a bit of sightseeing, a superb meal and a couple of glasses of wine at a typical French restaurant.

The following morning, we motored slowly out of La Rochelle. The channel was now so clear to see in the daylight that it was hard to imagine the difficulties we had encountered during the approach. We turned to the north, and in the absence of wind, chugged, on a hot and sunny day, towards the island of Ile d'Yeu. With the tiny island now in sight, the wind got up, so we spent a little time practising tacking and racing tacks before heading into Port-Joinville and berthing on a very short and seemingly unstable finger jetty.

After a pasta bolognaise that I had prepared at sea, leave was granted and we proceeded ashore into Joinville in search of some liquid refreshment and a bit of local life. Unfortunately, the town appeared to be asleep, a bit like a one horse town after the horse had been shot. We managed, however, to avail ourselves of what local hospitality we could find, before arriving back at the yacht, quite late, disturbing the local populous with a rousing drunken chorus of 'Alouette'.

The master-plan in the morning was for the Skipper, 'Sandy' and Ray to slip from Ile d'Yeu early, whilst the rest of us had a slow start. However, despite the best-laid plans of mice and men, the Skipper did not wake up until much later. With everyone suffering from the excesses of the previous evening, we slipped and motored slowly out of the harbour into a very lumpy sea for the passage to Pornichet. Lobster pots and a good deal of driftwood hampered our progress as we meandered around the floating obstacles.

Approaching the harbour, with the visibility down to less than a mile, the on-board GPS was employed to confirm our position on the chart, when disaster struck! The keel hit and bounced over an underwater obstacle. We immediately stopped in the water, shut bulkhead doors and carried out phase-one damage control checks. After confirming that we were not taking in water and that the keel was still firmly bolted to the hull we continued very gingerly into Pornichet harbour, berthing alongside at around 3pm.

Safely alongside and *needing* to play with a new gadget, I backtracked to the point where the boat had hit the rock using 'Sandy's new hand-held GPS that had been left switched on, on the cabin table. Using the bearing and range it gave, the Skipper managed to pinpoint the rock on the chart. We assumed that the on-board GPS, due to an inbuilt American error, effectively put us out of position so it was no wonder we hit the rock. To add insult to injury, we later discovered we were using an out of date chart, which showed *our* channel shut to shipping. Presumably due to the rock that we managed to find.

As an experienced engineer, 'Sandy' inspected the boat thoroughly whilst the rest of the team started to fold the sails. After the yacht was clean and stowed away, the skipper, 'Sandy', Steve and Ray went off to investigate the town and returned proclaiming it to be a bit like a French version of Blackpool.

That evening, we all went ashore, with the sole intention of eating at one of the marina restaurants. The first one we sat down at had a very good menu, but we seemed to be getting the royal ignoring treatment. Madame, eventually, pointing at a large table of diners, informed us that they had eaten everything on the menu. Still hungry, we quickly re-located to the next restaurant on the boardwalk and enjoyed a very acceptable meal to round off the week.

On the final day, after awaking at about 9am, the team set about cleaning the boat ready for the handover, which we expected to be early in the afternoon. Earlier than expected, at around 11am the relief crew arrived, having made good time driving from Roscoff. Whilst they went shopping, we loaded our bags into their rental vehicle and after lunch and a detailed hand over, we wished them luck before heading northwards across Brittany to Morlaix, to drop the vehicle at the local Hertz dealership. After looking around the town and doing a bit of shopping, we were then forced to hire two taxis for the short drive to Roscoff.

On arrival at the ferry port, it appeared to be closed. Ray pottered off on his own into Roscoff to see how far it was and returned sometime later with news of restaurants and bars. After yet another very good 'final' meal, we arrived back at the terminal in good time and boarded the Plymouth-bound ferry. After a few drinks and a visit to the duty-free shop, we retired early for the night arriving back in Plymouth at around sunrise with a bag full of smelly clothes and a small prezzie for the still convalescing, 'magic washing fairy'.

Back at work again, 'Burt' informed me that a draft chit had arrived for me to join the Trafalgar-class submarine, HMS Talent, in Devonport, on Monday 14th September 1998. I was quite chuffed about this as it was a Devonport based submarine and I could quite easily have been drafted back to Faslane, where all of the Swiftsure boats had now been moved.

With a couple of months before I was to report for duty, I had a couple of courses to complete to ensure that I was up to date for fire-fighting training and also to requalify in the Submarine Escape Training Tank. Another course I was required to complete was the Nuclear Propulsion Intermediate Course. It had been discovered, by trial and error, that PO stokers were not exactly gifted at the academic stuff and there was a real need to qualify all of the engineering senior rates to watch the nuclear reactor when it was shut down. Despite it being shut down, it still generated a lot of heat, that needed to be controlled. NPIC, was designed to teach the *thicky* POMEMs some of the electrical wizardry that made it all work.

I must say, I found the electrical theory very challenging and spent every evening on the course, studying, trying to make sense of it all and striving to stay ahead of the game. At 10pm every evening, we had an unofficial course rule, which was to put down the books and go to the bar for a couple of relaxing beers before bed.

The course was only a week long and culminated with an exam, but fortunately my extracurricular study paid off and I managed to pass the exam without too much trouble.

Back in Devonport, I took my time completing the customary drafting routine and ensuring that I had all of the kit I needed, before I left Nuclear Repair and HMS Defiance on Friday 11th September 1998 to join HMS Talent on the following Monday.

Ian Atkinson

HMS TALENT

14th September 1998 to April 2001

I joined HMS Talent at nine wharf in Devonport, where she was undergoing routine maintenance. Having satisfied the initial security questions and listened to a safety brief delivered by the duty PO, I was shown to the bunk space on 3 deck where all of the 'back afties' slept. I dumped my bag onto an unoccupied bed and changed into overalls and boots, ready to start work.

HMS Talent, a Trafalgar-class submarine, was quite different to any class of submarine that I had previously served on. From the outside, to the casual observer, a Trafalgar-class submarine looks pretty much like a Swiftsure-class submarine, but, the more you look, the more differences there are to see. For example, compared to the older Swiftsure-class, the rudder on a T-boat is higher out of the water and the diesel exhaust mast is funnelled upwards, whereas the S-boat has a horizontal open-ended box at the end of the mast.

The layout inside is also quite different. It appeared to me, the designers had taken the lessons learned from the Swiftsure-class and tried to implement them into a newer class of submarine. There were many similarities of course, the Swiftsure submarines were essentially a good design, but the more I wandered around, the more differences I found. The wardroom, for example, was directly opposite the senior rates mess on 2 deck, which did not initially strike me as a good idea. There was also a senior rates bunk space located on 1 deck, adjacent to the sonar room. Some of the differences were obvious; other, more subtle differences, were not so easy to spot. The hatch to the switchboard room and the weapons stowage compartment were essentially in the same place, but now they were on the starboard side of the boat rather than the port side on a Swiftsure-class boat.

Continuing my exploration aft, thorough the tunnel and into manoeuvring room I was accosted by a cheerful, bloke, who introduced himself as 'Sharky' Ward. He clearly had the advantage on me as he knew all about me, but this was the first time we had met. His opening words were, "You must be 'Plug' Atkinson, welcome to Talent, mate. You are flying down to the Falklands on Thursday to get qualified on Triumph." This was clearly not a joke and quite a shock, I wasn't expecting to go to sea for a few months, as Talent was still covered in scaffolding and clearly not going anywhere for a while.

He explained, there was an urgent need to get myself and another new joiner, POMEA Mike 'Woody' Woods qualified as engine room upper-level watchkeepers as soon as possible. As such, we were to fly south to join an identical submarine, HMS Triumph, that was patrolling the South Atlantic.

Armed with this depressing news, I set about completing my joining routine, before making my excuses and getting off home, firstly to give Anita the news that I would be leaving her again for a couple of months and also to donate blood at the hospital, later in the afternoon.

Being a regular donor, this was a routine visit and after the usual checks had been carried out, I was led to a bed, opposite a very attractive woman who was plugged into another blood-sucking syphon. With nothing else to do but admire the scenery, I chatted to the woman. Coincidentally, she was a stewardess on an RAF Tristar operating out of Brize Norton. As a joke, I said she could look after me on Thursday, as I was flying down to the Falklands. Getting quite excited, she said she was slated to crew that flight and that we should have a sociable drink, once airborne. After the session, we parted with a formal handshake as she said, "See you on Thursday, Ian, you won't forget my name, it's Kim Wilde."

With my sea-going kit packed for a two-month patrol, I met up with three other Talent trainees, for our journey to RAF Brize Norton in Oxfordshire. In the car with me were Petty Officers Sean Frow, Mike Woods and CPO Gordon Campbell. Gordon was to train as a Nuclear Chief of the Watch. 'Woody' and I were to train as engine room upper level watchkeepers, whilst Sean, when qualified, would be an electrical panel operator. The journey to Brize Norton was uneventful and on arrival at the security gate, we were shown where to dump the hire car before being directed to 'Gateway House' where a hot meal had been prepared for us, which was all rather civilised. After dinner, we boarded a bus, which transported all of the assembled passengers the short distance to the passenger terminal.

After checking in, by coincidence, I bumped into Phil Hilton, who was also flying south to join HMS Triumph, the difference was, this was actually his boat and he wasn't just utilising it as training platform. The woman I had met on Monday afternoon, tapped me on the shoulder smiling, "Hiya Ian, remember me?" As expected, Kim was on the same flight, but not actually working. She had been given a couple of days leave on Ascension Island before she was due to crew the Ascension to Falkland's leg of the journey from Monday. She said as soon as the aircraft was settled in flight, we would have that drink.

Departing from Brize Norton shortly before midnight, most passengers got themselves comfortable and dozed off, as the cabin lights had been dimmed. About half an hour into the flight, Kim tapped me on the shoulder again and motioned me to follow her into the galley area of the Tristar aircraft. Along with a few of her colleagues, we enjoyed a sociable drink for a few hours, paying for the drinks by means of an honesty box, until I was tired enough to sleep.

After the drinks, I sat at the back of the aircraft with Kim for the remainder of the flight. Kim's colleagues looked after her and her friends much better than they would have looked after me, sat on my own. We were served all kinds of sandwiches and coffee and even managed to watch a movie on a portable DVD player as sleep eluded me. After being in flight for about eight hours, there was a distinct lightening of the sky, the aircraft started to descend towards Ascension Island, for a planned refuelling stop.

On the ground, I kissed Kim farewell and thanked her for looking after me. Being aircrew and familiar with the fuelling stop, she disappeared quickly onto some transport and was whisked away, presumably for a sleep. As for the rest of the passengers, we were instructed to disembark at the aptly named Wideawake Airfield and herded into, what could only be described as a sheep pen, with picnic tables and a kiosk, where coffee and beer could be bought whilst the Tristar was refuelled.

Back in the air, a couple of hours later on the final leg of the journey, I tried my best to sleep, though sleeping in planes, trains and automobiles has never been my strong suit. I think I must have dozed off for a bit as the eight hours seemed to whiz by and before long, the Captain made an announcement that we were commencing our descent into Mount Pleasant Airport and had been joined by a couple of RAF Tornado fighters. Looking out of my window on the starboard side of the aircraft, sure enough, a Tornado had appeared from nowhere and the chap in the back was waving at us. With our escort in place, the pilot lined up with the runway in preparation to land. A chap in front of me, looking out of the window, commented to his mate that the islands looked very much like Dartmoor. His friend agreed with the noticeable difference that you could drive off Dartmoor.

With a slight jolt, we were finally on the ground and to my amazement, lining the runway, were people waving silly foam rubber 'Gladiator' hands and holding up banners saying, amongst other things, 'Welcome Back Smudge'. It occurred to me that the islands were a bit like an open prison and the arrival of the aircraft not only meant that reliefs had turned up, it also meant that the return 'taxi' back to the UK had also arrived.

Disembarking, we crowded into a very small arrivals hall and waited by a baggage carousel that did not appear to be working. Standing in the centre of the carousel, was a chap in army fatigues, looking rather serious. "Good afternoon ladies and gentlemen…" he began, "my name is Staff Sergeant Jones from the Royal Ordnance Corp, may I have your attention for a few minutes please?" Holding up a green painted lump of metal, he continued, "If you find one of these, please do not touch it, it will kill you." Replacing it, he then held up another of the collection of six similar looking blobs, "If you find one of these, please do not touch it, it will kill you." He continued in a similar vein, showing us all of his collection of munitions with the same warning before finally adding, "…and may I wish you a very pleasant stay." After the sobering warning from the resident 'pongo', we retrieved our bags and after getting passports stamped, were ushered into the back of a three-ton truck, for the short drive down to Mare Harbour, where we learned to our dismay, that HMS Triumph had already sailed. A small boat was waiting, however, to ferry us through some extremely choppy water on the final part of our journey to join the submarine.

The craft pitched and rolled heavily as the Skipper struggled to make way in the heavy seas. The submarine's Captain, noticing his difficulties, manoeuvered Triumph to provide a small degree of shelter as the Skipper finally managed to come alongside Triumph. Bags were first thrown up to the waiting lads on the casing, before one by one, we made a leap of faith onto the rope ladder that had been lowered down the casing of the submarine.

Finally, on-board and at the end of our journey, I was shattered. I had been travelling since lunchtime the previous day and had been awake for nearly forty hours, not withstanding dozing on the plane. After the mandatory safety brief, we were allocated visitors' bunks in the WSC. I was forced to hot bunk with Sean Frow, one of my new mates from Talent. Now I knew I had plummeted to new depths. I was eight-thousand miles away from home, freezing cold, absolutely knackered and forced to share a bed cuddled up to a Sub-Harpoon missile; could life get any worse?

'Woody', a confident chap, who would be my training buddy, got straight into his overalls and said, "Mate, lets make a good first impression and get straight to work." So, reluctantly, we headed through the tunnel and made our intoductions to the Engineer Officer of the Watch in the manoeuvring room. It was a safety requirement that he knew exactly who was in the machinery spaces, in the unlikely event that we had an emergency.

As Sean had gone to bed for a couple of hours, I was committed to stay awake and work, until the 1am watch change. In the meantime, HMS Triumph headed out of the comparative shelter of the Falkland Islands and east, towards South Georgia. A couple of hours later, when there was sufficient water under the keel, the submarine slipped quietly beneath the South Atlantic. Discovering a second wind and managing to scrounge a notebook, I went to work tracing the systems. I already knew the theory of how water was turned into steam by the heat from the reactor. The steam then turned two steam turbines that combined in the gearbox to turn a single shaft and propulsor. The same steam simultaneously drove two turbo generators that made all of the electricity. What I now needed to do, was *simply* find every single valve and where every pipe went and what to do when it all went wrong. When I had done that, I then needed to prove my competence, walking around the compartment with one of the charge chiefs before taking a written exam and finally sitting an oral board. Who said this was going to be easy?

On top of all that, as I was new to the Trafalgar-class of submarine, I was required to re-qualify as a submariner. This examination was called a BSQ and similar to the Part 3. It required me to learn all of the ship's systems including all of the routines and weapon systems. In short, I didn't have much time to sleep anyway. By 1am, I was dead on my feet.

Sleeping in the 'bomb shop' was not ideal; the lights, although dimmed, stayed on all the time. At hourly intervals, the fore-endies, would visit the compartment, take readings and dip tanks which was always a noisy evolution. Although they tried to be quiet, they had a job to do and inevitably, we got disturbed. I must have slept though, because in no time at all, Sean was shaking me at 6am for a wash and breakfast before I went back to work and he jumped into my recently vacated bunk.

It took a couple of days for me to establish a routine and recover my lost sleep. Keeping busy tracing the systems, eating and sleeping made the time fly by and before we knew it, four days had passed and HMS Triumph was on the surface and proceeding to anchor in Grytviken harbour, South Georgia.

Having never visited the island before, myself, 'Woody' and Sean took the opportunity to don just about everything we owned and go ashore for a couple of hours. The British Army still maintained a small garrison on this lonely island in the Antarctic and in the true sense of inter-service camaraderie, they ferried us ashore in inflatable ribs. These guys were fully kitted out for the sub-zero temperatures with ski goggles, facemasks and huge mittens whilst we were dressed in anything we could scrounge, to keep out the cold. Skimming across the inner harbour, riding the rigid boat like a bucking bronco, I was shot blasted with tiny, invisible particles of ice that stung my face like a thousand needles. The obliging Army 'taxi driver' dropped us off at a dilapidated, frozen, wooden jetty. Many of the planks had long since rotted, the resulting holes disguised by fresh snow and ice. So, actually getting onto the island was extremely precarious. Struggling ashore, the boat driver returned to the submarine to collect more naval sightseers.

Freezing cold and not really knowing what to do, we headed towards the nearest inhabited building, in an attempt to get out of the cold. Opening the door and being hit by a blast furnace of warmth, we quickly entered and shut the door behind us. For perhaps the first time, on a naval run-ashore, I had stumbled into a museum. The greeting from the two curators, was surreal in the extreme. Eight-thousand miles from home and in a broad Lancastrian accent, the woman pointed at me, "You're not coming in 'ere wearing that."

Thinking she was referring to my snowy boots, I offered to take them off, but found that it was my Burnley Football Club woolly hat and scarf that was causing offence, as she jokingly added, "We're all Blackburn Rovers fans here." What are the chances of that? Thousands of miles from home on a frozen, forgotten, barely inhabited corner of the world, I manage to stumble upon two Rovers' fans. As it happened, they were nice people and glad of the company.

We took the opportunity to thaw out whilst we talked to them and toured their whaling museum, displaying exhibits from a former thriving industry. Warmed up and armed with a bit of local information, we thanked them and, back in the cold, we trudged around the harbour, past their ice-bound boat and eventually, reached a snow and ice covered standing stone, denoting the final resting place of the intrepid explorer, Sir Ernest Shackleton.

After paying our respects, we turned around with the intention of exploring some buildings on the far side of the harbour. As a motley bunch of frozen submariners we approached what turned out to be a collection of workshops, when a stern looking woman dressed in boots and combat fatigues passed us. We issued a cheery wave and a pleasant, "Good morning," as she was only the third person we had seen on this frozen wasteland. Her reply as we passed, was a shouted, "So, don't you salute officers then?" We turned to find her looking quite pissed off and only then, did we notice the tiny green crown of a Major on the epaulette camouflaged on her chest. "Ooops, sorry ma'am," I uttered as, in unison, we saluted this exiled megalomaniac.

Once we had recognised her rank and shown the proper respect, she invited us for a cup of tea at the nearby 'Shackleton House' that turned out to be an army base. The soldiers inside clearly didn't relish the idea of having their peace shattered by this ill-disciplined and scruffy bunch of matelots, but nevertheless, they made us a brew before ignoring us completely.

We had been informed at the museum, that it was possible to get our passports stamped at the Post Office. Rightly assuming that we would never be in this neighbourhood again, we asked one of the lads for directions. He pointed to a seemingly uninhabited building a couple of hundred metres away, that looked anything but a Post Office.

Passing a few sleeping elephant seals, that we had been warned to give a wide berth to, we approached the building that seemed derelict. Knocking on the door had no effect, but trying the handle, it opened and we were again engulfed in warm air. Calling out, a woman opened another door and cheerfully invited us into her comfortable living room, where she quickly produced coffee and cakes.

As we sat with this friendly woman and her husband, drinking coffee and eating their cakes, I explained that we were looking for the Post Office. “You’ve found it dear, more cake?” Well, this was not like any Post Office I had ever visited. They went on to explain that they were on a six-month detachment from a sub-Post Office in Newton Abbot and would soon be returning to, the relative warmth of the English Riviera. We enjoyed a very hospitable half hour with them. Buying some postcards, we wrote them quickly and gave them back to her to mail. We also then requested the sought after stamp in our passports before realising that we were out of time and had better get back to the jetty for the short painful ride back to HMS Triumph, still swinging at anchor in the harbour.

The following day we were back to work. HMS Triumph had left South Georgia, submerged and was now heading back towards the Falkland Islands. ‘Woody’ and I were starting to make progress as we worked together and constantly quizzed each other about the various systems.

Four days later, we berthed alongside RFA Diligence, that was being used as a depot ship, within hailing distance of Mare Harbour. The crew on ‘Dil’ were not too chuffed about having their space invaded by a group of stinky submariners who occupied their spare bunks, used their hot water and ate their food. Scrounging a couple of days off, a few of us managed to get ashore, booking rooms in the military accommodation at Mount Pleasant Airport.

MPA, was a rabbit warren of interconnecting huts and corridors, that was fortunately well heated. For the soldiers, sailors and airmen who were based on this god-forsaken lump of moorland, there appeared only to be two viable activities, get fit or get pissed. We unanimously chose the latter, but as drinking on an empty stomach is not too clever, eight of us wandered into the senior NCO’s dining room and, finding an empty table, sat down. We noticed that all of the tables had been set with eight place settings, including the usual salt, pepper and a jug of water. In the centre of each table was a decoration that epitomised the military presence on the Falklands. In the centre of our table was a model of a GR7 Tornado in flight with its wings swept back. Other tables had different models of armoured vehicles or ships, using the models as table identifiers rather than numbers.

A waitress delivered our food choices from the simple menu before we settled down to eat a surprisingly good meal, whilst chucking some cheerful banter across the table. As we were finishing off, a chap came and stood quietly behind one of the chairs. He didn’t say anything, he simply stood there. A few others joined him until eventually, every seat had a bloke stood behind it. This was rather disconcerting and a little bit intimidating until one of my mates finally asked if we could help. The reply was a polite, “No, it’s ok, sir, please finish your meal.” When the last of our group had finally finished, we excused ourselves and as we left the dining room to venture into the adjacent bar, noticed that the table was now being hurriedly cleaned and the waiting chaps had taken their seats. The men, as we later found out, were Tornado aircrew and as such, this was *their* table. We must have appeared very rude, but it was a simple mistake that wasn't made again.

The RAF Warrant Officer who ran the bar explained that he would be closing up shortly and, as we didn't have any work to do, then he was quite happy for us to stay in the bar and play cards. Taking the hint, we clubbed together and bought three bottles of Captain Morgan Spiced Rum, a slab of Coca-Cola and a bucket of ice before settling down to play cards, getting slowly ratted.

Early that evening, one of the lads bumped into a woman that he knew in the army. As they chatted about old times, she invited us to an impromptu party that was being held on the camp. As nobody has walked anywhere on the Falklands since 1982, she whistled up a Land Rover and ferried us, in two trips, around the corner to where the party was starting.

Inside, the army had really gone to town to make us feel welcome. There was music playing, we could smell a curry being prepared and the bar was open. One of our lads went to the bar and was awarded with a round of free drinks. How very hospitable. Occasionally, a bell in the centre of the room would 'ding' amidst cheers from the rest of the room. This was slightly confusing and got explained when I later tried to pay for my round of drinks. "Are you on the submarine, mate?" asked the barman. "Yes," I replied. "Well, your money's no good here!"

I noticed the long bell rope had a safety pin attached to the end. As a practical joke, someone would attach it to an unsuspecting victim and as he moved away, he would 'ring' the bell. This signalled that it was his round. There was no argument, no fuss, just acceptance that he had been caught. The final bar bills must have been enormous as we drank all evening and never spent a brazz razoo.

I do not remember much about the evening, as it all became rather confused. I do recall, however, eating a rather splendid curry, though the fact that I was drunk might have dulled my taste buds. We also had a sort of Army v Navy group singing competition where we would sing sea shanties and the Pongos would sing their regimental songs. Overall, it was a fantastic evening that came from nowhere. Thanks lads.

The next morning, with banging heads, it was time to get back to the boat where I was asked to assist in the changing of one of the hydraulic pumps in the engine room. Having changed this particular pump on a number of occasions, I was very familiar with the procedure and despite my hangover, took charge of the evolution, finally getting the new one lifted into place by the end of the day.

With the AC hydraulic pump replaced, HMS Triumph finally left the Falkland Islands and headed north at max-chat towards the Caribbean. With the shaft turning at 104 rpm, the boat was being pushed pretty much to the limit. During this high speed transit, myself and 'Woody', both qualified as engine room upper level watchkeepers, this meant life became considerably more comfortable. Moving bunks from the WSC into the 3 deck bunkspace, we rotated four bunks between six of us. Meaning that at any one time, one chap would be on watch, one would be watching a movie or studying and the remaining four would be asleep. It sounds complicated, but it worked well and was far more comfortable than sleeping in the 'bomb shop'.

As we were steaming north, towards Port Canaveral, the ambient temperature in the engine room grew steadily hotter as we got ever closer to the equator.

Crossing the equator is referred to in naval circles as 'Crossing the Line' and is generally a cause for celebration. HMS Triumph finally 'Crossed the Line' at 35 degrees, 39 minutes west, somewhere off the coast of Brazil on the 12th October 1998. Usually, the Royal Navy would celebrate in style, paying homage to King Neptune and his 'bride' Amphitrite, but being dived on a nuclear submarine meant the celebrations would have to be somewhat subdued. That didn't stop me being force fed some blisteringly hot chilli, having a mock haircut and a shave with some comedy scissors and a razor before being forcibly led, fully clothed, into an icy shower. That was the second time I had 'Crossed the Line' in my career and both times I had got wet. The argument was that on the surface did not count. Crossing the line submerged meant that I was still a sub-surface crossing-the-line virgin. There was no point in arguing and after my dived initiation; I was presented with a certificate.

Approaching the coast of Florida, still transiting fast and deep, the Captain had an overwhelming urge to do something exciting. Normally, when a submarine approaches the surface from deep, it is usual for the Officer of the Watch to reduce speed and alter course to allow the bow sonar a chance to 'see' behind us before returning to periscope depth. Once at PD, with the periscope raised, the Captain would have an all-round look at the surface picture, before giving the order 'SURFACE'.

However, on this occasion, the Captain decided, unusually, to put the boat on the 'roof' from deep, using the order, 'PANEL, EMERGENCY SURFACE'. Immediately, following the order, the SCC operator opened all of the main ballast tank blows, whilst the helmsman pulled back on the wheel to achieve a 20 degree bow up angle. Simultaneously, the engineers in manoeuvring room adopted Full Ahead, driving the submarine to the surface.

HMS Triumph broke the surface in seconds. The Captain immediately ordered the search periscope to be raised and following a quick all round look, nearly filled his pants. Bearing down on us from astern was a huge super tanker. Immediately ordering a course alteration, he steered the submarine out of danger but unfortunately, the super tanker clipped our towed array sonar, snaking behind us like a huge worm, causing considerable damage. This would have resulted, I dare say, in a few awkward questions for the Captain and an unplanned 'holiday' for the towed array party in Devonport, as they flew out to repair the damage. I have no idea if the Captain was reprimanded for his error of judgement, but I presume he got his arse kicked around the corridors of Whitehall.

Alongside, Cocoa Beach was unrecognisable from the last time I had visited in 1979. One of the benefits of living on a submarine, apart from the extra cash, is being put up in hotels, usually some distance from the boat. 'Woody' and I elected to share a room whilst Sean shared a room with Gordon Campbell, another of the trainees from Talent.

Having checked into the hotel, I did what all submariners do after a few weeks at sea, and enjoyed a lengthy Hollywood shower. 'Woody' chose to have a siesta whilst I spent the better part of an hour in the shower, using the hotel's free soap and shampoo to wash off the unmistakable musty smell of the submarine.

With us both washed and changed and with a fist full of dollars, we set off to find some food in the warm Floridian evening sunshine. Spoilt for choice, we eventually decided upon a seafood and steakhouse restaurant that produced monster portions of surf and turf that included, would you believe, a whole lobster. Thankfully, the taxpayer was footing the bill as the navy had given every man the equivalent of twenty-five pounds per day subsistence, just for food. As I said, it was one of the benefits of being a submariner.

Following an excellent and very substantial meal, washed down with a few second-grade American beers, we stumbled back to the hotel, knackered and vowing to try a different nationality of cuisine every night.

The following morning, we discovered a restaurant for breakfast, called 'Ponderosa'. The deal was this; on entry, you were shown to a table where you subsequently bought a plate, a bowl, a glass and a coffee cup for the princely sum of seven dollars. After that, it was the original 'All you can eat' restaurant that was popular in the States long before the Brits adopted it. You could just keep going round and round the 'buoy' as we called it. 'Woody' devised a strategy allowing us to lie in until around 10ish, get washed and dressed, group-up with Sean and then wander down the sidewalk with an aim to eat at around 11am. The plan was devious in the extreme. Having eaten our own body weight in bacon, eggs, pastries, fruit, juice and coffee, the counters would then be cleared and lunch would be served. This meant that we could cram in two meals in one sitting. Is it any wonder that many Americans are the size of a house?

After brunch on the first full day, we decided to hire a car for a few days with the intention of seeing Mickey and his friends as well as the nearby Kennedy Space Center. Our flights home had already been booked, so we used the remaining seven days wisely. 'Woody', Sean and I had a day trip to Orlando where, like big kids, we queued for all of the fast rides in the Magic Kingdom. On another day, Sean and I toured the Space Center and actually climbed aboard the Space Shuttle 'Explorer' that was absolutely amazing but smaller than I imagined.

Unfortunately, after a week of eating, drinking and sightseeing, it was time to go home. All three of us had qualified in our respective watchkeeping positions and I had also re-qualified as a submariner and made a decent start on qualifying as a shut down senior rate which was, arguably, the most difficult qualification that I would ever study for.

To celebrate our last night in Florida, and in keeping with the different nationality theme, we visited a steakhouse restaurant, called 'Durango'. This was a typically American restaurant; friendly waitresses in skimpy costumes whizzing around on their roller skates whilst holding a loaded tray in one raised hand. We were shown to a booth with simple bench seats and a solid wooden table adorned with a few battle scars.

The waitress spun to a halt at our table with a cheery greeting before taking orders for starters and main courses. 'Woody' opted for an often seen, but never tried 'Wild Onion' that looked like a deep-fried dahlia with a salsa dipping sauce. Sean opted for 'Buffalo Wings' and I finally decided on the old Mexican favourite of 'Nachos', served with beans, diced chicken, steak, melted cheeses, pico de gallo, jalapenos and seasoned sour cream. For the main course that was ordered at the same time, I quickly chose the familiar steak and chicken fajita whilst 'Woody' and Sean both went for huge steaks with fries, onion rings and mushrooms.

It sounds a lot, because it was. In a nutshell, the starters wiped us out. The three dishes with a drink each totally filled the table. As we were all very hungry, we had a good go at it, making a serious mess in the process and just about cleared our plates. The trouble was, we were now absolutely stuffed and that was only the appetiser. We asked for a few minutes before the next culinary onslaught, to allow the food a fighting chance of going down before another absolute mountain of culinary delights was delivered. There was absolutely no way we could eat all of this. There was enough food on the table to feed the entire mess, so, after doing our level best we reluctantly admitted defeat. 'Woody', looking at the virtually untouched food, made the remark, "You could just tart it up a bit and send it round again." Fortunately, the waitresses at 'Durango' were used to English lightweights and produced boxes for us to take it away for the lads that had drunk all of their money and could not afford to eat.

After a leisurely morning, the submarine's minibus turned up at the hotel to transport us to Orlando International Airport for our overnight Virgin Atlantic flight back to England. The flight was uneventful and unusually, I managed to get a bit of sleep before we landed at Gatwick Airport early the following morning.

After collecting our bags, following the ever-confident 'Woody', through the red channel, we queued up to declare our duty free booze. "Anything to declare lads?" the man asked. 'Woody', produced his ID card, "We are all in the Royal Navy and have just returned from active service overseas." "What have you got to declare?" the man persisted. "Three bottles of rum," 'Woody' replied. "Any cigarettes or perfume?" "No sir," we replied in unison. Then to our surprise, he said, "No problem lads, on you go." We didn't need telling twice as we walked away without paying the duty on the two litres we were each over our allowance. What a nice man. I suppose we all worked for the same company, in a roundabout sort of a way.

Hiring a car, we made good time driving back to Plymouth where I just collapsed into bed totally exhausted.

Fully rested, I re-joined HMS Talent on the following Monday morning. I was presented, almost immediately, with a watchbill that had me slated to keep a duty once every three or four days. Some reward! Well, at least they were pleased to have another couple of qualified watchkeepers to help out.

Talent was now out of the maintenance period and everybody was clearly working hard to get the submarine back to sea. Looking around the submarine and seeing all of the special fit communications kit that had been installed, it was clear that we were heading north to patrol our old stomping ground in the Barents Sea, north of Russia. Deep Joy! These patrols were typically eight weeks long, during which time, there would be no outward communication with home. The details of the patrol were, and probably still are, highly classified, but having been to the same part of the world on many previous occasions, I knew to expect long periods of boredom with very little excitement. From a stoker's point of view, it really didn't matter where we were going. All we were required to do was keep the engines turning and push the boat wherever the Captain told the helmsman to steer.

Before such a patrol, there was much to do, storing the submarine for ninety days of unassisted endurance away from home. Fuel was not a problem as we probably wouldn't be using either of the two diesel generators and the reactor had sufficient U235 to boil water into steam for several years to come. No, we needed food, loads of it. Fresh food only lasts for a few days and the milk for a week, two at most, so all available storage space was taken up with cans of food and cartons of long-life milk. False decks of tinned food were laid in most of the clean compartments. The fridges and deep freeze were completely topped up with meat, fish, frozen vegetables, chips and gateaux.

All carefully stacked so the chefs could find menu ingredients without having to excavate too deeply.

In the engine room, I was responsible for ordering the engineering stores, ensuring that each department had sufficient spare gear. All of the tanks were filled with a variety of lubricating oil, hydraulic oil, diesel fuel and demineralised water.

As we would be operating in a potentially hostile environment, we had to consider escape. The submarine was fitted with a one-man escape tower in the forward escape compartment and another in the engine room, on the after escape platform. This allowed an escapee to leave the submarine in a controlled manner and zoom to the surface wearing his life-saving Day-Glo orange escape suit. If it ever came down to us needing to escape from the submarine, something must have gone very badly wrong and I dare say we would be trapped on the sea bed without propulsion and most probably without power.

Without electricity, life on-board a submarine becomes quite tricky, not least because we need it to see and also because the electrolysers that produce the air we breathe would cease to function. Therefore, for that reason, we were fitted with six oxygen generators, three at each end. These worked by the controlled burning of oxygen candles that each lasted for one hour. Consequently, as the stores bloke, I would need to find storage for about fifteen hundred of the bloody things in addition to the three hundred that are normally carried. In short, they were everywhere; in the submarines framework, in the void spaces, in fact anywhere I could find some spare room.

Finally, after weeks of storing the submarine and ensuring that we had everything that we needed, it was time to get the reactor flashed-up and the engines tested. It is well known in submarine circles that the engineers go to sea about a week earlier than the rest of the crew and return a few days afterwards. This was not in the physical sense, but with the reactor hot and pressurised, there was a need for a full steaming watch as all of the machinery was running and there was 'hot-fog' flowing through the pipes.

With all of the crew on-board, everything stowed away and the engines tested, HMS Talent quietly slipped out of Devonport on the morning tide. Stopping briefly inside the breakwater to pick up the towed array, we headed south into the English Channel and turned right to follow the Cornish coast towards Lands' End. After a few hours of surface transit, clear of fishing trawlers and with some deep water under the keel, it was time to get the back wet, which is submariner speak for diving the boat. The submarine was therefore brought to Diving Stations and that required everyone to be out of bed, dressed and closed-up at their respective diving station.

Content that the submarine was ready to submerge, the bridge was cleared and the Captain ordered the Officer of the Watch to dive the submarine. There was no fanfare or klaxons reminiscent of the old black and white wartime films, just the simple understated announcement over the main broadcast "Diving Now, Diving Now." In the control room, Ship Control ordered the panel watchkeeper "Open 3 and 4 Main Vents." Complying with the order, the SCC watchkeeper opened the main ballast tank vents and as the air was now escaping in huge plumes of mist, the Officer of the Watch monitored the progress through the periscope as the after casing became awash and started to submerge.

Happy that the propulsor was well under water, he ordered "Ship Control, Open 1 and 2 Main Vents," as the rest of the main ballast tanks were vented to atmosphere. Seawater flooded into the tanks, displacing the air, making the submarine negatively buoyant. With the forward casing now awash, he ordered, "Revolutions two four, six down, sixty meters and then back to eighteen metres," as the submarine was driven beneath the sea. Ship Control then made the pipe, "Submarine passing eighteen metres, check all hatches from forward." In a well-practiced drill, in sequence, the reports came in that all of the hatches were dry and that no seawater was flooding in.

With the submarine now checked clear of leaks, there were a number of evolutions that still needed to be carried out to expel trapped air and to ensure that the depth gauges around the submarine were reading correctly. With all of these routines now complete, the submarine was taken down to a safe depth before the ship's company were eventually fallen out from diving stations.

The journey north would take about a week, which was sufficient time for the ship's company to adopt a good patrol routine. Noisy evolutions were frowned upon as we endeavoured to be as sneaky and as stealthy as possible. Many people adopted to wear soft-soled training shoes instead of clunky boots, in a personal effort not to be the one that let the side down. There was a list of patrol inhibits that were systematically put in place. This would prevent the running of noisy, unnecessary machinery and equipment. Active sonar was switched off and amongst other things, the electrolysers that made the air were shut down. Once we were in our allocated patrol area, the watertight airlock doors either side of the reactor compartment were opened because the 'thud' when they shut could apparently be heard by 'enemy' ears in the form of a noise transient. The medical types monitored the oxygen levels until it was deemed by the MEO that we should start burning candles to maintain the oxygen levels at around 21%.

The responsibility of burning the candles fell to me and the other two upper levels making the watch simply fly by. In addition to monitoring the running machinery, we also had to burn a candle every hour. After six hours, the Oxygen Generators needed to be stripped down, cleaned and the filters changed which was actually rather therapeutic, in a sad sort of way. It certainly made the time go by quickly. In addition to this, there were other watchkeeping routines to attend to, one of the most important tasks was baking potatoes on the main engine throttles. Another, was the somewhat naughty fermentation of lemon powder. This would be mixed with water, sugar and some yeast and left to ferment, with an improvised airlock, in the stifling heat above the main engines. A week or so later it was retrieved and filtered into another clean, plastic, ten-litre carbuoy and stowed in the starboard void space, surrounded by freezing cold pipework for another week or so, when it would transform into a sort of citrus-flavoured rocket fuel, deemed fit enough to drink.

Despite being extremely busy on watch, I still needed to study for my shutdown senior rates qualification. This was made more difficult by the fact that every time I ventured into the nice, clean air-conditioned environment of manoeuvring room, where I could study the books, I was soon shooed back to *my* side of the bulkhead by the Engineering Officer of the Watch. There was a golden rule that there needed to be at least one senior rate aft of 76 watertight bulkhead and as the chief, Tony Russell, preferred to be forward, that meant I was stuck in the engine room with the rest of the lads on my watch.

On station, in our patrol area, life continued very quietly and largely uneventfully. It appeared as if our friends, the Russians, had gone home on leave, so there was nothing particularly exciting going on outside of our submerged steel tube. I dare say, if they were permitted to, the control room watchkeepers would tell you different, but as back-afties, we were likened to a mushroom patch, kept in the dark and fed on shit.

Every evening, the intelligence coordinator, titled 'INTCO', would visit us in manoeuvring with a huge chart and attempt to keep us informed with a précis of the intelligence that Talent had managed to glean.

As a former control room watchkeeper, I was quite interested and without really trying, I managed to irritate my colleagues with questions relating to soviet submarines, ships and aircraft. So much so, that I earned the nickname 'Jane's Fighting Stoker' after the reference book of a similar name.

We did have a bit of excitement though. We received intelligence that a ship of significant interest was at sea some distance from us. This gave us the opportunity to detour on the way home to take a look at her. INTCO came aft again to brief us why this Russian AGI was of interest to us, when normally we would steer well clear of them. She was rumoured to have lots of 'exciting' bits stuck to her hull below the waterline so we were to approach her stealthily and then pop underneath and have a bit of a look.

As you may appreciate, this was a very risky evolution. If we were not absolutely on top of our game or perhaps the helmsman sneezed, then we could easily have bumped into her causing our pants to involuntarily fill themselves and her crew to wonder what had caused their black sugary tea to spill into their laps.

So, in an effort to prevent damage to the submarine and keep the laundry usage down to a minimum, the submarine was brought to Action Stations, so that everybody was out of bed and prepared for anything.

All of the exciting stuff was happening in the control room, so back aft in the engine room, at best it was crowded and boring. With no main broadcast pipes, and under strict orders not to make any noise, we sat quietly whilst the Captain conned the submarine directly underneath the target vessel with the periscopes up, photographing and recording our approach, whilst speaking quietly into a cassette recorder, narrating what he was seeing.

In the engine room, oblivious to the mounting tension forward, we became aware of propeller noises probably only a few feet above our heads. It was then that the scariness of the situation became *real* to me. Matching course and speed, we inched ever closer over a couple of hours, until finally, with the mission a success, the Captain took us deep as we snuck away from the Russian AGI. I doubt that they ever knew we were there. We were several miles away from the target vessel when we finally fell out from Action Stations with a collective pat on the back from the Captain for a job well done. We were happy for the simple fact that we had safely carried out the underwater-look and were now on our way home after nearly eight-weeks away, having gained some useful intelligence. As we transited home from patrol, this gave me the opportunity to sit and pass my shut down senior rates written examination and oral board.

Back in Plymouth again, HMS Talent prepared to go into dock for an extended period of pre-planned maintenance. This was an opportunity for the ship's company to take leave, courses or just to plan recreational activities away from the submarine.

After passing my shut down senior rates board, there was still the not inconsiderable task of qualifying in the simulator. This was basically a huge computer game, where the people driving it could simulate all sorts of naughtiness whilst the lone trainee had to deal with fires, floods, electrical failures and just about anything else that they could think of. The session usually started easily enough with a high bilge alarm, just to build confidence and gradually worked up into a full-blown primary coolant leak. This was the clincher. There was only three possible leak sites and it was essential to identify the right one, carry out the correct drills and then make the report. Get this wrong and you have failed, so we practiced, mercilessly, most lunchtimes, until it was almost second nature. I was more confident in the simulator than Woody and fully expected to pass, but fate has a funny way of biting you in the bottom when you least expect it. Woody managed to pass in a faultless round whilst I had a brain fart and screwed up monumentally, incorrectly identifying the leak site.

After beating myself up about it and spending another three training sessions in the simulator, I eventually passed a week later to become a fully qualified senior rate. What a relief, It had been a long hard slog, but now I could help my mates and watchkeep on the shutdown reactor looking, for all the world, like a British version of Homer Simpson.

Now fully qualified and with some spare time on my hands, I investigated putting together some adventurous training to take advantage of my mountain leaders qualification. This started with regular day walks over Dartmoor followed by a few sociable beers and lunch at the Plume of Feathers in Princetown.

The walks generaly took place on a Wednesday and were very popular amongst the crew. Lets face it, what would you rather do, work on-board the submarine day in and day out or go for a bimble on the moors, putting the world to rights over a few miles and a few more beers afterwards? I thought so.

One such walk involved the group being dropped off at Cadover Bridge in the pouring rain and following the River Plym eastwards over boggy ground. Charge Chief Steve Phillips had elected to bring his faithful hound, a German Shepherd called Blaze and the PO Caterer had also brought along his Staffordshire Bull Terrier for a walk in the park. Blaze was loving the freedom, chasing about and worrying the odd sheep and generally having a great time, but the Staffy was kept on a lead as he just couldn't be trusted to behave.

After about an hour of walking in the rain, we stopped for coffee, a bite to eat and a bit of shelter in the garden of the derelict Ditsworthy Warren House. Being walled, this gave the dogs a bit time off the leash to have a play as the rest of us enjoyed a soggy sarnie and a flask of coffee whilst deciding on the next waypoint. Ultimately, we were heading for Princetown, but how we got there was pretty much up to me, as the Unit Expedition Leader.

Steve started to get concerned when the Staffy started to become aggressive towards Blaze. Both of the owners fought with their respective growling and snarling dogs, trying to bring them under control as the two dogs were attempting to do real harm to each other.

In an attempt to defuse Blaze, Steve made a fist and forced it into the German Shepherds open mouth, considering, wrongly, that his dog would not bite him. Unfortunately, Blaze was so angry that he just tore at Steve's hand and before the rest of us really knew what was going on, Steve's hand was a bloody mess requiring hospital treatment.

As the leader of the trip, I always carried a first aid kit and, assisted by the other lads, we did what we could to patch him up. One thing was certain, I needed to get Steve, who was suffering from shock, off the moor to receive medical attention and a bit of needlework.

Consulting the 1:25000 OS map of Dartmoor, I quickly located where we were and then plotted a course across Ringmoor Down to the nearest road junction, noting the grid reference as 559,669. Steve then called his wife, Christine, and after appraising her of the situation, she agreed to head out to the road junction as that would be much easier to find, without satnav, than a footpath or track would be.

Packing up and with both dogs now calm and on their respective leads, we detoured about a mile to casevac Steve off the moor. When we arrived, Steve was feeling a bit shaky and his hand hurt like hell. I knew then that we had made the right decision to get him off the moor and Christine could get him straight to A&E.

With Steve now off to hospital, the rest of the team trekked due east to the trig point at Gutter Tor before regaining our original track up to Eylesbarrow Mine and following the five lane motorway past Nun's Cross Farm and into the back door of the Plume of Feathers for a well-earned pint.

The following day, the Captain, Commander Simon Shield, after hearing about the incident, congratulated me on a job well done. After that day, Ditsworthy Warren House was renamed by my walking group as simply 'Two Dogs Fighting'

Sometime after that, after canvassing opinion from my regular walkers, I decided to approach Commander Shield, for permission to mount another weeklong expedition to Snowdonia. As he had participated on a few of my walks before, I thought he would be cool with the idea. I broached the subject during a formal mess dinner in November 1999. The conversation ended with the Captain saying words to the effect of, "Don't talk about it SPO, do it." So I did!

The majority of the training was in the form of day walks over Dartmoor and the occasional coastal walk on the South West Coast Path. The plan was to build fitness and to get a feel for the undulating terrain and mountain weather conditions that are notorious for change. An overnight stay on Dartmoor added to the preparation and proved that two longish walks with a social evening in between could be accomplished without too much pain.

One of the biggest problems during the early stages of the planning was finding a suitable gap in a busy maintenance period. One of the only available weeks was 15th to 19th May 2000. The next snag was where were we going to stay? After a few phone calls, I managed to secure provisional bookings at three locations in the Snowdonia area, none of which involved the use of a tent. I eventually settled for Capel Curig Training Camp for three very good reasons, it was right in the heart of Snowdonia, contract caterers cooked the food and most importantly, it was absolutely free!

The staff at the Adventurous Training store in HMS Drake, promised to provide the transport and a fuel card. I wrote to HQ160 Brigade with traces of my route plans and also requested permission to train in Wales from the Defence Land Agency. We were forced to declare that we would not be taking any firearms into the National Park. We found this quite amusing as we were only planning a walk in the hills and not a major military exercise, as they seemed to think.

The next thing needed was a team, so I devised a poster and advertised on the submarine. Initially there was quite a lot of interest from people looking for a free holiday, but for one reason or another, some people had to withdraw. The final team of six was myself as the Expedition Leader accompanied by Clive Buckenham, 'Stumpy' Yardley, 'Paddy' Conway, Sean Frow and 'Woody' Woods.

After a few months of planning and several practice walks over Dartmoor, briefings were given detailing the routes and kit lists were issued. We were as ready as we would ever be.

With the weekend to conduct final preparations, I went home to pack my kit and to make sure that I had all of the maps and route plans that we needed. We finally loaded up the minibus with kit and essentials outside the office in Devonport dockyard on Monday 15th May 2000 and hit the road at about 9am stopping to pick Woody up at Ivybridge before heading off to Wales in bright sunshine and with high spirits. Paddy suggested that we spend the entire five days in the 'Plume of Feathers' in Princetown, propping up the bar and watching Arsenal in the UEFA cup final, which sounded an inviting proposition, but we trundled on regardless.

Stopping for lunch north of Birmingham, we headed off towards North Wales on the M54, meeting up with Sean near Telford. Woody remarked jovially that never in the history of naval expeditions had a plan come together so well, something almost certainly had to go wrong. It was at this point, following a bit of rustling in the back of the van, Stumpy shouted, "Shit! I've only gone and left my fucking rucksack in the office." After the laughter had subsided, we started to think what to do about it. Some team members had brought extra bits of kit with them and were more than willing to lend it, but Stumpy decided that as he needed his own, this would be a perfect opportunity to acquire it at 'Cotswold Camping' in Betws-Y-Coed. Therefore, after dropping him off in town, armed with his credit card, we continued on to Capel Curig arriving at the camp sometime in the late afternoon.

After settling in, there were some formalities to complete and also to meet the camp's Sergeant Major who cheerfully welcomed us to the camp and informed us that we would be duty on Wednesday night. Paddy was not a happy bunny, fearing that the duty would mean he might miss the opportunity of watching the UEFA Cup final. After unpacking and investigating the camp, we returned into town in search of Stumpy who we found, drowning his sorrows, basking in the sunshine, outside the Royal Oak, two hundred pounds lighter.

After surgically removing the chief from the pub, we returned to camp for probably the worst meal in the entire world. Contract caterers provided the food and ensured that portion control was strictly enforced. Still in need of refreshment and nourishment, the team went in search of the local nightlife. Knowing the area quite well, I directed Woody, as the duty driver, past some of the hills that we would be climbing over the next few days. We continued for about ten miles to the Vaynal Arms, that I used to frequent, and found to our dismay that it had been closed down. I was promptly sacked as the entertainments manager. We high-tailed it back to Betws-Y-Coed in search of a good pub and the run ashore began in earnest. After a couple of beers, we returned to camp and turned in, slightly squiffy.

After being rudely awakened at 6am by Paddy singing in the shower, the team reluctantly descended upon the kitchen for breakfast, flask filling and bag meals. The weather forecast was not promising but despite that, we arrived at Pen-Y-Pass for around 7:45. After posing for a brief photo call, we started the Snowdon 'Horseshoe', following the Pyg Track for about forty-minutes. On reaching the marker, a quick council of war ensued as to whether we could safely negotiate the notorious knife-edge ridge, known as 'Crib Goch', as a strong crosswind was whipping the clouds across the ridge. At the marker post, even standing still became a challenge, but on the ridge, it would be almost suicidal. Deciding unanimously on the less glamorous, wimpy option, we trudged along the easier Pyg Track and gradually the view disappeared as we entered the cloud base at around the five hundred metre contour line. The going started to get rocky as the path intermittently disappeared only to reappear after a hundred or so metres marked with a cairn. As the weather started to deteriorate, we stopped to don waterproofs and continued upwards. My inspirational promises of cups of tea, chip butties, phone calls to loved ones, postcards and lap dancing at the café on top urged the lads on. At the base of the zigzags, Woody pleaded for us to stop for a rest and a brew. As we were making good time, we found some shelter for a warming coffee and sandwich.

Whilst enjoying the moment and reassuring the team that I did actually know where we were, a young couple approached us through the mist. After a brief exchange, it turned out they were called Jimmy and Jenny and were Australian doctors from Sydney. As they went ahead of us Woody's pace increased saying, "There's nothing like following a girl's ass to help you up the hill." Sean replied in jest, "Women are alright, but you can't beat the real thing."

We struggled up the zigzags and eventually made it to the standing stone marking the top of the Pyg Track. Stopping for a brief respite against the wind, a train's whistle could be heard in the distance. As we laboured up the last twenty minutes to the summit of Snowdon, the whistles grew louder and eventually out of the mist, the train appeared. Jimmy and Jenny declared that the train was their ticket off this wet and windy mountain, only for their hopes to be dashed when the train turned out to be a diesel engine pushing a carriage full of workers to the summit. To make matters worse the café was not due to open for another week. Gloom and despondency set in and the team blamed me for not researching properly.

After lunch, sheltering behind the café, our party now numbered eight as Jimmy and Jenny had asked if they could tag along. They were not too confident about finding their way down in the limited visibility. We were only too glad to have two doctors along for the ride.

We left the summit, on a south-westerly bearing for a couple of hundred metres before joining the steep zigzag path that marks the end of the Watkin path. Watching our footing, we carefully made our way to Bwlch y Saethau and in heavy rain, started the last ascent of the day, up Y Lliwedd. Walking soon gave way to scrambling and for the first time hands were required. Clive, became increasingly concerned about the route, as did Sean but this was mainly due to the sheer drop into Llyn Llydaw slightly to the left of our route. With heads bowed against the wind and in heavy rain we climbed steadily upwards, skirting the summit of Y Lliwedd's peaks before slowly making our way down, out of the cloud base and following a steep path to the Miner's Track. With the wind and the rain now easing slightly, the eight drowned rats made good time following the track back to Pen-y-Pass, thoroughly soaked.

Thankfully, this time, the café was open and did a roaring trade in tea and pasties.

Warm and nourished, we said farewell to Jimmy and Jenny and piled into the van, only to be headed off at the pass by a car park attendant, in a Skoda, demanding four pounds for the use of *his* car park for the day. We had parked and disappeared into the mist long before he had arrived for work, so we paid the jobsworth and left.

Back at camp, after a good hot shower, attempts were made by Woody to turn our bungalow's redundant kitchen into an improvised drying room. It was working very well indeed until a bleeping noise was pin-pointed to a smoke detector in the ceiling. Unfortunately, the fire alarm had been sounded in the camp, resulting in all of the residents, including some of our country's fighting elite, to evacuate the camp into the car park. This caused much amusement as it was still pissing down and although we quickly informed the MoD guard that there was no fire, he seemed unconcerned, assuming that it was the main kitchen, as it was always going off. Knowing that it was *our* kitchen, we didn't press the point and got away with it.

Later that evening, looking for a change of scenery, the delights of Llanwrst were sampled. Myself and Woody then demonstrated to the locals how to play pool, by stuffing the town's youngest solicitor by three games to one before finally heading back to camp really tired.

The local weather forecast sounded quite gloomy, wet and getting wetter. Clive and Sean after the previous day, had serious reservations about climbing Tryfen, so, against my better judgment, the team was split. Clive, Sean and Stumpy would walk up the mountain from Llyn Ogwen to Bwlch Tryfen, whilst Woody, Paddy and I would climb Tryfen by the north ridge and descend to meet them some time later. With this agreed Sean dropped us off at the base of Milestone Buttress and drove the minibus to our finish point at Ogwen Cottage.

Starting the climb, with stiff legs from the previous day, we slowly warmed up and gradually made the north ridge. Once on the ridge the climb became a, hands-on, Grade 1 scramble. Tryfen is a mountain of a thousand routes and having climbed it many times before, I have never taken exactly the same route. About a third of the way up, we reached a distinctive rock known as 'The Cannon' that points upwards at forty-five degrees. Taking the opportunity, Paddy dropped his pack and shimmied up for a photo call.

I tried, unsuccessfully, to contact the other team with a progress report, but the phone signal was practically non-existent. This was probably due to having a bloody great mountain between us and the transmitter.

Scrambling above 'The Cannon', the climb became more difficult in places causing both Woody and Paddy to experience some bum-clenching moments, but to turn back would have presented more problems than it solved.

Climbing ever higher, aircraft could be heard approaching as two RAF Hawk trainers came screaming through the valley below us.

Eventually, after a few false summits and a lot of swearing, we made it to the summit, about ninety-minutes overdue. Stopping for a brief lunch and another photo opportunity next to 'Adam & Eve', we tried again to contact the other party before starting the comparatively easy descent down the south ridge where the going became considerably easier with a path winding its way round huge boulders. Within a few minutes, we saw the meeting point but were still a long way above it. Before long, we sighted Sean walking up the path towards us. Paddy recognised Sean instantly and was off down the path, scrambling over the rocks, towards him. On reaching him, he simply said, "Give me a cuddle." Tryfen has that effect on people.

Sean led us back to where Clive and Stumpy were waiting and after a coffee and a bit of a rest we discussed the way ahead. By this time, we were two hours adrift. Clive wanted to press on, but Woody declared that his knees were playing up and clearly, Paddy had had enough fun for one day. Therefore, I made the decision to call it a day and go down via a slightly different route that arrived directly at Ogwen cottage.

A tea and bacon butty stop at 'Snowdonia Café' restored spirits somewhat though Paddy was getting some pre-match nerves as Arsenal were playing Galatasaray in the UEFA cup final that evening, but we were duty.

One of the down-sides to staying at Capel Curig Training Camp was that the occupants were expected to keep a duty in the form of a fire piquet and long before we had arrived, my team had been slated for duty on Wednesday night. Paddy, of course, thought that this was a wind-up. How could anybody expect the most loyal of Arsenal fans to keep a duty on the day of the UEFA Cup Final? Unfortunately, it wasn't a wind-up. At the allocated hour of 5:30pm, we mustered at the guardhouse only to be told that they operated 'paper patrols' and that the MoD Guard would call us if we were required. Therefore, with two radios, we retired back to our bungalow to watch the match where, unfortunately, Arsenal lost 4-1 on penalties resulting in Paddy being the quietest that he had been all week.

We awoke the next day to torrential rain and stiff limbs, and again the weather forecast was not good, though it did promise to clear from the west in the afternoon. A likely story.

After breakfast, it was decided to at least start the walk and see how the weather held up. Stumpy drove the minibus via Betws-Y-Coed to the dam at Llyn Eigau and all the time the rain just got heavier.

Dressed in full foul weather gear and gaiters, we started walking towards the dam with heads bowed against the wind. Following the waterlogged path, we skirted the reservoir to a deserted farmhouse called 'Cedryn' where we, unsuccessfully, tried to find shelter for a coffee break. By this time, everyone had wet feet, but we trudged on, slogging uphill to Gledrfford. Following the Plateau, we slowly started to descend, following a wall, to a track that would complete the circuit. We arrived back at the van several hours later, completely drenched but with a strange sense of achievement.

After a shower and hanging everything we owned up to dry, we decided to go for a few beers in Llanwrst followed by a rather splendid curry, which rounded off the soggy week quite nicely.

Following the predictable late start, I went for breakfast alone and collected packed lunches for the journey home. Gradually, the rest of the team surfaced and the task of cleaning the bungalow began in earnest. With a Hoover borrowed and all hands in, the task was completed to the satisfaction of the camp Sergeant Major within an hour. The minibus was loaded and after fuelling up in Betws-Y-Coed, we started the long drive home, arriving in Plymouth late in the afternoon. It was universally agreed on the journey home that it had been an enjoyable break from the submarine and we were all glad that we had done it and lived to tell the tale and it had not cost us a bean.

Back on-board the submarine, the maintenance period was starting to draw to a close. Everyone was busy as we strived to get the submarine clean and stored again in readiness for another patrol *up north*. As the PO Stoker, much of the organisation in the engineering spaces fell to me. Getting everyone together, I delegated responsibility to a few killicks who in turn took charge of smaller teams of lads. They then started to clean all of the machinery spaces from top to bottom whilst the slimmer members of the department concentrated on crawling around the bilges to skirmish for rusty tools, lagging, nuts and bolts and anything else that had been previously dropped.

After the cleaning had been completed, the painting effort could begin. All of my lads had been allocated a section of the machinery spaces so it would be easy for me to see who was cleaning and who was not. This became readily apparent when the port side of the engine room gradually started to look whiter and shinier than the starboard side. After much nagging by me, the slower members of the department were shamed into doing their bit until finally we were ready to store the submarine.

On the 8th June 2000, I was summoned by the Captain to inform me that my name had appeared on the Second Open Engagement signal or 2OE as it was known. This was brilliant news and at a time when I was starting to consider resettling into civilian life, I had been granted a stay of execution and provided I accepted the offer, I had been awarded another five years of service, subject to me passing a medical. That evening after buying beer for the lads to celebrate, Anita and I went out to a restaurant in Brixham near Plymouth called 'Just Williams' to celebrate our fifteenth wedding anniversary and coincidentally, my 2OE award over a rather splendid steak.

Before Talent sailed, a couple of months later, I had a very strange premonition. Having been duty one Thursday in September 2000, spending much of the night working, I disappeared home early on Friday morning and fell into bed knackered. I woke up a couple of hours later, soaked to the skin with sweat, absolutely convinced that I had been selected for promotion to Chief Petty Officer. In my waking state, I totally believed it, but as I regained full consciousness, over the course of the next twenty minutes, I managed to convince myself that it was just a wishful dream and not to be so silly.

The following day, being Saturday, Anita and I went to visit some friends who lived near Exeter. They had kindly offered us a bed for the night so we could have a couple of drinks and generally make a night of it. The following morning, not too early, we drove back home to Plymouth still feeling the effects of one too many glasses of wine.

We had not long been home, when the phone rang. It was my Charge Chief and very good friend, Steve Phillips. "Good Morning Chief," he said. Thinking he had the wrong number, I replied "Pardon?" Again, he repeated, "Good Morning Chief... the signal came in on Friday afternoon, mate and you're on it. Congratulations!"

Well you could have knocked me down with a feather, I had only been a Petty Officer for about four years and now I had been selected again for promotion. My emotions were all over the place, but then I remembered my dream on Friday afternoon. How bloody strange is that? I had no idea when the signal was due out. My report from the MEO, Lieutenant Commander Neil Moffatt, was good, but I didn't consider it would be good enough to get me promoted. I was on cloud nine, but being somewhat pessimistic, I still needed to see it in black and white before I would allow myself the luxury of celebrating. Steve might just have been trying to cruelly wind me up so I would buy the customary barrel of beer for the lads.

Fortunately, he wasn't and on Monday morning, the MEO informed me officially of the news. Anticipating my thoughts, he presented me with a copy of the signal bearing my name and stating a promotion date of 6th April 2001. Now it was real and I had no excuse not to buy beer for the lads.

With the celebrations over, I was on cloud nine for quite a while. There was a time when, after spending more than half of my career in rosters awaiting promotion, I thought that I would never make it to the dizzy heights of Chief Stoker.

I was still a very happy bunny, when I decided to see if I could wind up a young and impressionable MEM(L) called James 'Dicky' Dickaty who was my Shut Down Junior Rate during a very quiet morning watch. We were alone in Manoeuvring Room when I struck up the conversation "So, where are you from Dicky?" "Southampton" was the singular response reply. "God, I haven't been to Southampton in years. Back in the early eighties, we used to go there quite frequently for a run-ashore." "Oh yeah", was the bored response. He couldn't really be bothered with tales of a time before he was born.

I persevered, "Yeah, we used to drink in a brilliant place called the 'Frog & Frigate' near the docks that brewed its own beer. It had bare floorboards covered in sawdust. I haven't been there for years." This sparked his interest, "My mum used to drink in there around the time I was born" he replied. "Well, I haven't been back there since I shagged a gorgeous bird called Louisette that got herself pregnant. That must have been around 1980."

He nearly choked on his coffee. "My mum's name is Louisette and I was born in 1980." His face fell as the shocking reality of the wind-up started to sink in. Of course, I knew his mum's name and his date of birth from his Divisional Documents. I learned a few months previously that he never knew his real father, as his mum really did fall pregnant to a visiting sailor.

With the scene now set and his brain working overtime, I sent him out into the engine room to do a full set of rounds, knowing full well that he had more questions formulating in his mind.

I kept the practical joke going for about an hour until some of the other lads started to arrive in Manoeuvring Room at the start of the working day. By now, as the lads were mercilessly taking the piss, he was starting to believe that I might actually be his father.

As he was starting to get a bit upset, I decided to put him out of his misery. "Dicky, go and look in the mirror, what do you see?" Looking in the small mirror by the door to Manoeuvring Room, he didn't know what I was getting at. "I can only see myself," he answered. "Look harder", I persisted, "tell me what you can see." He thought that I was referring to something behind him and turned around to look over his shoulder. Confused, he couldn't understand what I was referring to. "You're Chinese, for fucks sake," I shouted at him, as everyone dissolved into hysterics. His father was evidently an oriental gentleman from a merchant ship visiting Southampton.

The realisation of the wind-up finally dawned on him and eventually, even he managed to see the funny side to it. Even funnier though was the fact that I really did drink in the 'Frog and Frigate' around the same time, so there was a real chance that I may have been in the pub at the same time as his mum, but fortunately, I don't think I knew her.

Back at sea again, I started to think about going on draft and what Chief Petty Officer's jobs there were going as I knew that I would leave the submarine when I was promoted. However, until then, there were many trials to conduct to prove that all of the new kit, as well as the recently maintained equipment, was functioning correctly. After a couple of weeks of sea trials, HMS Talent called into Gibraltar for what would turn out to be my last foreign run ashore on the boat. It had been a great draft, I had made some good friends, and obviously, a good impression or I would not have been selected for promotion.

Gibraltar was a familiar stomping ground, though it had changed quite a lot in the twenty-one years since my first visit in 1979. That did not prevent me visiting a few of my old haunts and getting a bit squiffy. Staying at the Caleta Palace on the other side of the 'Rock' made the stopover feel much more like a holiday that a submarine visit. In company with a few good mates, we agreed a no drinking policy during the day as it was too hot and that it would give us the opportunity to walk around the rock and explore the many tunnels inside the rock. When the sun went down, however, that was a different matter. We would typically visit a bistro at the marina near the airport called 'Bianca's', have a clam chowder followed by a good steak meal, washed down with a carafe of their house wine. After dinner, there would be a few drinks with the rest of the lads in the 'Horseshoe'. There were many bars to choose from, before we inevitably ended up at the newly renovated Casements Square. This became a regular itinerary as we strove to spend the subsistence that allowed us to buy two meals a day. I must say, we did very well indeed, thank you.

Arriving back in Devonport it was time for me to leave. My relief had been nominated and I had received a Draft Order to join the Royal Naval Submarine School as an Instructor. The day before I left, the Captain, for three reasons, summoned me. Firstly, he wanted to give me an answer to a representation I had submitted about pay conditions. Secondly, with a handshake, he presented me with two Chief Petty Officers epaulettes and a certificate dated for the following day. Finally, with another handshake, he thanked me for my service and formally said goodbye. The following day, on the 6th April 2001, I turned up for work wearing the badges and epaulettes of a CMEM(M). It took the lads until mid-morning to notice. That was my last day on-board HMS Talent. I spent the day shaking hands, saying goodbyes and removing the last of my kit. I was now leaving the submarine to Join HMS Raleigh for the first time in twenty-two years.

HMS RALEIGH

9th April 2001 to 9th February 2005

Returning to where it all began, after twenty-two years, was a surreal experience. As I reminisced back to basic training, a time when I had absolutely no responsibilities, my memory filtered out the bad, and only pleasant recollections remained. It seemed as if there was always someone to point a frightened seventeen-year old in the right direction.

Things were different now, I had slowly progressed to almost the top rung of the promotional ladder and now, instead of being taught, I was the teacher. I was to be employed as an instructor in the newly-constructed submarine school, teaching little ducks fresh out of basic training the rudiments of what makes a submarine submerge and more importantly surface again.

The submarine training syllabus had evolved considerably since my Swiftsure-class course, back in 1984. This was in order to weed out any academically or medically unsuitable volunteers before the navy invested too much cash in their training.

Initially, as part of a small team of four instructors, I would present a five day course called the Submarine Introduction Course or 'SMIC' to three categories of trainee, including the aforementioned little ducks, artificer apprentices and also baby officers.

The course was basic in the extreme, but it gave the students a flavour of how the submarine does what it does, without blinding them with science. Although the course content was quite similar, the real difference came in the form of class participation. Whereas the ducks would sit there like frightened rabbits in a catatonic state, the 'tiffs' would occasionally ask questions but in contrast, the officers were embarrassingly inquisitive. On occasions, a bright spark might ask a question that I didn't know the answer to, heralding a cup of tea or a fag break, whilst I sought the answer and maintained my credibility as an all-knowing submarine guru.

After a couple of weeks in the job, I was summoned by my boss, Lt Steve Lovett, and informed that he needed me to train as a Divisional Officer, to lighten the load on the departing Warrant Officer. I was well chuffed about this, I had discovered that training and mentoring were my strong suits. Steve went on to say that he had booked me onto a course at the Weapons Engineering establishment, HMS Collingwood, in Gosport on the following Monday. All of a sudden, I had a lot of preparation to do. My kit was generally in good shape, but I needed to arrange a hire car and somewhere to sleep. HMS Collingwood is seriously massive and I had only made a couple of day-trips previously. Every shore establishment tends to run along the same lines, but has subtly different rules. Therefore, it is very easy for the infrequent visitor to get it wrong, or get lost.

That Sunday, with bags packed, I loaded up my hire car and kissing Anita goodbye, made the three-hour journey along the well-trodden path to HMS Collingwood without incident.

Unsurprisingly, the gate staff were not expecting me, so I had to wait whilst they verified my identity and decided that I was not a terrorist. After checking, they ascertained that the only items for concern were some slightly dodgy looking civilian clothes. With the initial forms completed and a car-pass issued, I was eventually directed to a senior rates transit cabin. This was basically a prison cell, without bars on the window. The furniture consisted of the bare essentials, a bed, a chair, a bedside table, a sink and a writing desk with fitted wardrobes half way along one wall. One wardrobe, as I discovered, contained blankets, some sheets and a pillow. Well, at least it was warm.

The following morning, by 7am, I was up, showered and dressed in a clean uniform, ready for the start of the course. In the time-honoured traditions of naval service, I then followed cup-carrying sailors in my quest for breakfast.

As I did not know a soul in Collingwood, it had the potential to be a very lonely place, so with my plate of bacon and eggs, I selected somebody sat alone as my 'duty friend' and asked if I could join him at his table. This was an excellent way to meet new people and to find out where the course might be held, my meagre joining instructions just told me the building name. My new, 'friend' said he thought that it might be down the 'Rubber Road', so, thanking him, I set off in search of a road sign. Everybody I asked, knew where 'Rubber Road' was, but could I find it? Every road junction within the camp had standard road signs, but none of them displayed the road name I was looking for. Getting desperate and fearing being adrift on the first day, using my rank, I grabbed hold of someone junior, who purported to know where it was and ordered him to take me there. Looking as if he had been kidnapped, he walked me all of twenty metres to the end of a long building and opened a door saying, "Here you are, chief, the rubber road." What stretched before me was a straight, wide corridor that you could easily have driven a vehicle down. It must have been at least half a mile long and the floor was covered in a thick, brown, bobbly, rubber sheeting. Now I understood where the training block had derived its name. As I later learned, most of the training courses were in rooms and workshops adjacent to the 'Rubber Road' but not mine. My breakfast buddy had given me a bum steer. Fortunately, the Royal Naval School of Leadership and Management was not too far away, therefore, it was still a little before 8am when I finally found the classroom on my first day of instruction.

What did come as something of a surprise though, after being in the navy for twenty-two years, I was the junior of the course. Everyone, without exception, was senior to me in terms of rank. One grumpy warrant officer, who was older than dust, was doing the course again as a refresher. Many things had changed since the days of Lord Nelson, but he came with an old school 'know-it-all' attitude, which was about ten years out of date, and much of his knowledge, in this ever-changing world, was now obsolete.

The course was actually very interesting. Issued with a load of reference books containing Naval Law and advice we were given some situational questions that might be posed by our division, and invited to look up the answer. Common sense is one thing, but it needed to be backed up with a proper reference, to add credibility to any advice, we might subsequently give.

One such question was, "A rating in your division has asked if his wife can run a business from his married quarter. What do you tell him?" Well, without looking at the books, I instantly thought no! Married quarters are owned by the Ministry of Defence and I know how stuffy they can be about a bit of private enterprise, but I was wrong! Delving deep into the books, apparently a naval wife *is* allowed to run a business from home, provided it is not something like car maintenance or prostitution that may bring the service into disrepute. Hairdressing or some other stereotypical business like selling Tupperware or cosmetics was apparently ok provided the chap requested permission from his Captain.

The course was not so much about learning all of the rules and regs but more about knowing where to find the answers. There was also quite a bit of situational acting which was filmed and critiqued by the rest of the class. There was also plenty of homework to be done in the evening. We would be given a profile of a typical sailor in our division and told to write a positive annual report, based upon his character. This was often quite challenging, if the chap sounded like a bit of a scroat. This all culminated in an exam at the end of the two weeks which everybody managed to pass without too much difficulty, even the grumpy warrant officer.

As a newly qualified DO, I drove back to HMS Raleigh to continue my day job as an instructor of submarine systems. Due to staffing shortages across the water at SMQ, I was asked by my boss, Lieutenant Lovett, to assist, which suited me just fine, as the travelling time from home to HMS Drake would be a fraction of that taken to reach HMS Raleigh via the Torpoint Ferry.

SMQ, which stands for Submarine Qualifying, was the next phase of submarine training after SMIC and tackled each system in much greater detail. The students would be first taught the function of the system before learning how it worked, with the aid of a diagram, showing the various valves and components. Finally, under escort, the submarine trainees would then crawl around a submarine, physically finding everything that had been discussed. This practical element would hopefully cement the system in their minds, in preparation for the weekly progress test. Failure of the progress test resulted in extra revision and resitting the exam, with the threat of being returned to General Service for repeated failure. There were other, less career threatening penalties that could be invoked for the under achievers, especially if it was obvious that they simply were not trying. Stoppage of leave was a favourite inspirational tactic. As we all appreciated, coming to work on Monday was only five days away from the weekend. After the progress test on Friday morning the students generally mooched around in the rest room waiting for the clock to strike midday when they would bomb-burst in the blinking of an eye, whilst myself and the other instructors, set about marking the papers.

At the start of each week, after twenty minutes of questions and answers to blow away the weekend cobwebs, the course manager would read out the marks from the Friday progress test. Nobody ever got full marks, but each course had a small group of high achievers who competed amongst themselves and were always up in the high nineties. At the opposite end of the academic scale, it was not uncommon to see percentages as low as forty for some of the non-technical students. They just found the technical content difficult and beyond their comprehension.

It was not in my nature to issue bollockings to guys that had honestly tried, but could not do it. Heaven knows, I had had my own difficulties as a trainee, so I adopted more of a mentoring role. The use of analogy helped a lot. For example, I would liken the trim system to a set of scales with the exception that instead of transferring weights from one side to another to achieve a balance, the submarine pumped seawater from big tanks at the heavy end of the boat to the lighter end, until the submarine was nicely balanced. At some stage in the past, some bright spark had created a working set of scales in the shape of a submarine with hooks, representing the tanks to attach small weights. This and a simpler instructional technique usually provoked some understanding.

Some of the other chaps really couldn't be arsed and just did not want to be there. The navy isn't a democracy, so the course warrant officer would invite them, one by one, into his office for a little, one way discussion, that would generally be heard along the corridor in the classroom. The re-briefed and usually red-faced student would then be invited to spend extra evenings studying and playing catch-up whilst his course mates were off duty. In extreme cases, he would be required to continue revision at the weekend as he strived to catch up and achieve the required standard.

At the end of the eight-week course, the students would sit a final examination that was a culmination of seven weeks of progress tests and a sack full of revision and Q&A. It was most satisfying to see the majority of pupils achieve the require standard, but that was only one third of the exam. For the next part, they had to accompany an instructor around the submarine pointing out valves and components and answering, "What is this …?" and "How does this work ….?" type of questions, as the student would only willingly talk about equipment and systems that were within his comfort zone.

The final part of the SMQ (Dry) qualification was a formal oral examination where the candidate, sat in front of the Course Manager and two other instructors would be asked questions on routines and stations, where various people would be stationed for certain evolutions such as Diving Stations, Emergency Stations and Action Stations. This would typically last for about an hour and culminated with the student being asked to leave the room whilst his fate was decided.

In testament to the standard of the teaching and the devotion of all of the instructors, most of the students eventually made the grade and graduated from the course. They would next be drafted to a Trafalgar-class submarine and have to do it all again, this time, at sea, as an SMQ (Wet) trainee. The simple fact was, if they had paid attention and retained all of the information during the 'Dry' phase, then the 'Wet' phase should be nothing more than a formality. At least that was the theory.

After about six months of helping out at SMQ, I was recalled back to HMS Raleigh to replace the Course Manager, Warrant Officer Charlie Matthews, who had been appointed to another boat. This was a big step for me, I was still junior in my rank, but clearly, the boss, Lt Cdr Chris Warn and his sidekick, Lt Steve Lovett thought I was capable of assuming the duties of the warrant officer's job. My new glorified title was, SMICOA, that stood for Submarine Induction Course Officers Assistant, which in a nutshell, was Steve's whipping boy.

After a brief handover from Charlie, I moved into my new desk in the corner of a huge office on the first floor of the Submarine School and spent the next week or so figuring out exactly what I was responsible for. The office was in a prime spot affording gorgeous views of HMS Raleigh and across the water towards the Cornish village of Millbrook. My job, as I learned, involved planning all of the courses, assigning the right instructor to teach it and administering bollockings for consistent under achievers. Of course, I still had my fair share of teaching to do, but as the senior instructor, as well as teaching the little ducks and the 'tiffs', it was my perk to also teach the officers. I didn't mind doing this at all, because they were an inquisitive bunch and were genuinely interested in what I had to say.

At the start of every day, irrespective of the course, I would quiz my students on what we had covered so far, in preparation for the exam at the end of the week. I do not so much call it cheating, as preparation. During the daily Q&A, I would make sure that I asked every question from the question bank at least once. I genuinely had no idea which of the four papers would be set, but covering every question, gave the chaps the best opportunity of passing the exam.

I am not saying the young lads were anyway less intelligent than the officers or 'tiffs'; actually, yes I am, they were generally as thick as mince, so the potential for failure was quite real. To give *them* the best possible chance of passing, the exam that the little ducks had to complete was a multiple guess questionnaire, requiring them only to write their name at the top. There were four possible answers to each question, two were completely bizarre and the other two were somewhat ambiguous, with only one correct answer. The lads had a marking sheet that simply required a tick in one of the four boxes. The beauty of this arrangement was I had a clear acetate-marking sheet that when placed over the answer grid instantly showed the correct answers. This meant that I could give silent thumbs up to a less than confident candidate after I had marked his paper.

With the officers, things were a little different. It was a given that they could all read and write, so they got a properly formatted exam paper that required properly formatted answers. In addition to that, it generally then took me about a week to decipher their handwriting and to conjure marks from the answers. There were times when a bit of creative marking was required if the student was just short of the pass mark, if only to alleviate the need to mark another paper. This was rare though and generally speaking the officers were very good students. What would continue to piss me off though, and I could see it in their eyes, was that in a couple of years' time, these fledgling submariners could be my Officer of the Day on a submarine. They so easy forget who taught them and then try to 'teach' *you* the systems; even then, they would fuck it up. What they tended to forget was, submarine systems were my bread and butter and as I operated them on a daily basis, I would always know them better than they did. I would never presume to tell them how to work out a firing solution on a submerged enemy contact because that was not my job. I had a reasonable idea and could probably fudge a solution, but its accuracy would be questionable at best.

Another part of my job was acting as the Divisional Officer to the MEMs and MAs. This was new to me as I had only recently completed my DO's course, but I liked a challenge. One such challenge came right out of left field as I was preparing to leave for the day, at a little after 4pm, one sunny afternoon. My new boss, Lieutenant Commander Colvin Osborn rang my office and ordered me to go and see him, as there was an urgent issue concerning a Glaswegian member of my division called Campbell. Tam Campbell was a 'grey' man; by that, I mean he passed all of his exams with average marks and did not get himself into too much trouble, therefore, I did not get to see him very often.

Colvin was unusually serious when I entered his office. The door was shut and I was asked to sit; both of which were distinctly out of character. I was sworn to absolute secrecy and handed a letter that confirmed, following a recent visit by the Compulsory Drugs Testing team, Campbell was the only rating, out of the whole camp, that had tested positive for illegal substances. I instantly knew where this was leading. The Royal Navy has a zero-tolerance policy towards drugs, so this fella, although he did not know it yet, was about to be binned by the navy.

After I had been appraised of the situation, I was ordered to find him, and then escort him to the regulating office, where the head honcho, Commodore David Pond, would be waiting to deliver the career ending news.

After locating him in the mess and ensuring that he was in the correct uniform, I escorted a very confused Campbell to the reg office where he was eventually marched before the Commodore who handed him the same letter that I had previously read in Colvin's office.

I am not sure how I would have reacted in the same situation, but to his credit, Campbell did not seem to be at all fazed. Following the laid down procedure, the Commodore invited Campbell, if he wished, he could have his second urine sample independently tested, at his own expense and, if he wished, he could have a few minutes to discuss this privately with me as his DO.

He saluted and exited stage left through the opening door. Commodore Pond said to me, "You'd better go after him, chief." I hastily saluted and followed Campbell out of the little room. Fortunately, both Steve and Colvin were there to 'catch' him and to give me moral support as I counselled the guilty bastard.

Making our job considerably easier, Campbell did not argue and accepted his fate like a man. He conceded that there was no point in paying good money to get the second sample tested, when he already knew what the result would be. There was nothing more to be said, by his own admission he had taken the drugs, so nothing I could say was going to change that.

Like a rehearsed play, when we marched back into the charge room, everyone was in their proper places. It was almost as if there were footprints on the carpet showing everyone where to stand. Commodore Pond knew his lines by heart and after asking about the second sample, he informed Campbell that he was going to request Admiral Sir James Burnell-Nugent, in his capacity as 2SL and Commander in Chief, Naval Home Command to chuck the fella on the scrap heap. This was duly granted a couple of weeks later, which gave the soon to be unemployed Campbell ample opportunity to figure out what he was going to say to his mummy and daddy.

Whilst we were awaiting the official discharge notification, there was little point in Campbell continuing on the course. In an attempt to keep him close at hand, he worked for me, doing menial paperwork and running errands. This gave me an opportunity to get to know the chap who, despite his penchant for smoking illegal substances, was actually a nice bloke. I was therefore quite sad, when a few days later, I escorted him to the main gate, shook his hand and wished him all the best. I have often wondered what became of him. I dare say his CV paints him as a submarine engineer though he never actually made the grade. I also suspect his nocturnal hobbies may have been omitted as well.

After consolidating my position in the charge chief's job, I asked Colvin about promotion. My idea, although naïve, was that as I was doing the job, I should also hold the acting rank for the time that I was in the post. Colvin, however, had other ideas. There were a few problems with my suggestion, firstly, there was no precedent for a chief stoker to assume the rank of acting charge chief, therefore, the only logical step was promotion to warrant officer. To be considered for promotion, I needed to bolster my educational qualifications with an English GCSE, something that I failed to achieve at school. This was only half of the battle though; I needed to pass the exam before the next reporting period, if Colvin was going to recommend me for promotion.

A visit to the camp education centre gave me all the information I needed. The boss there was a very nice woman, called Karen Truscott, who taught an English class for an hour every Monday lunchtime, before sending her students home with a goodly amount of self-study homework. Clearly, they had to condense four years of secondary education into about ten lunchtimes and a few evenings of essay writing. Karen was an excellent teacher though, and armed with a wad of past papers, she had a very good idea of the sort of questions that would be posed in the forthcoming exam.

Strangely, I actually enjoyed studying and found myself doing quite well, during the study periods. I religiously sat down every Monday evening to do my homework, largely because it got me out of the washing up.

I would then hand my homework into Karen the following day for marking. She would give me some guidance and sometimes another exercise to be getting on with. I became her best student, but it was still a massive surprise when after sitting the exam, I was eventually awarded with an 'A' grade and in the fight for promotion, I was now qualified educationally for warrant officer.

On Valentine's Day in 2002, Anita accompanied me, in my mess undress, to a Ladies' Night at HMS Drake senior rates mess. This was a splendid evening, which resulted in me getting very drunk indeed. I vaguely remember having a friendly conversation with an equally squiffy Scottish chap called Andy MacDonald. Andy was extremely loud, but also very passionate about something, that I couldn't quite understand. He seemed to be offering me a free holiday to the south of France, which, in my inebriated state, sounded like a great idea. He gave me his business card that I tucked away in my uniform pocket and promptly forgot all about.

The following morning, with my head banging, I surveyed the wreckage of my port-stained uniform, crumpled on the bedroom floor. Discovering the card, I remembered snippets of the conversation and vowed to give the chap a call when I had a clear head and could string a coherent sentence together without feeling the need to vomit. As it happened, this was the following day. Andy remembered our conversation well and promptly invited me to his house for a coffee and a proper chat so he could explain his earlier proposition.

With over twenty years in the navy, I was well aware of two things; there is no such thing as a free lunch and you never spoil a good dit with the truth. Both of these gems of wisdom were true of Andy Mac's proposition. There was indeed a 'holiday' in the south of France, but in the cold light of day, he preferred to call it a pilgrimage, which instantly set the alarm bells ringing in my head.

Andy explained, over a couple of cups of coffee and a wee dram, that many years previously, he had founded the Joint Services Hosanna House

Group. Every year, he took a group of up to fifty serving and ex-service 'pilgrims', many of them with mental or physical disabilities, to Lourdes for a bit of a holiday. The hope was that some sort of divine miracle might cure all ills.

Well, I was very sceptical to say the least, but Andy was very passionate and persuasive. I have never been particularly religious and had no wish to be brainwashed by a load of bible-bashing left-footers. I explained that I was quite happy to push a wheelchair but if I had to go to mass and preach allegiance to somebody else's god, then he had the wrong bloke. Andy assured me, that if I wanted it, there was religion by the bucket full, but equally I would not be pressurised to participate in anything I was not comfortable with.

Duly persuaded and reluctantly signed up, I was assigned to assist a veteran from the Second World War, called Eddie Commander.

Eddie was a fantastic bloke and we got along just great. Of course he was quite senior in years and had a few breathing difficulties, but with his bottle of oxygen and nebuliser packed, as a group, we set off on the journey to Lourdes.

Arriving at Hosanna House, later in the day, Eddie and I were shown to a traditionally basic room on the first floor of the house, affording fantastic views across the valley to the snow-topped Pyrenean Mountains in the distance.

Group Leader, Gary Wright, allowed everybody a couple of hours to settle in and to have a bit of a rejuvenating snooze before getting us all together for a drink to outline the programme for the week. After hearing the itinerary, we took our seats in the dining room for a traditional French, three course set meal, accompanied by wine and of course a basket of French bread.

Every evening there was to be a mass in the chapel at the house. Eddie, who was not in the least bit religious, welcomed the opportunity for a snooze whilst I went down to join in and have a bit of a sing-song and to see what all the fuss was about. Each service lasted for an hour, so it was not too arduous a task and was generally quite upbeat. Therefore, at the end of the mass, when the priest invited us to "Go in peace," I did, and strangely generally felt better for the experience.

By the end of the week, after pushing Eddie around in his wheelchair, I was knackered. I seemed to be constantly apologising to our nurses as Eddie sexually assaulted them by poking them up the bottom with his walking stick. Gary had guided us around the Rosary Basilica, the Grotto, Saint Bernadette's house and the Cache. We had taken part in a Torchlight Procession and had been unceremoniously 'sheep-dipped' in the baths. Dressed in uniform, we also took part in the annual International Military Pilgrimage. On another day, we also enjoyed a day trip to Gavarnie high up in the Pyrenees in the shadow of a mountain called Vignemale, which was superbly picturesque.

Every evening, after dinner had been cleared away, there would always be some form of entertainment. After the IMP Closing Ceremony on the Sunday evening, the British contingent of the IMP would be invited to join us at Hosanna House for a barbeque and a drink. This was the group throwing a party for about hundred or so uniformed guests. The Army supplied a marching band to play for us and to celebrate 'Sunset' at the appointed hour, following a fine military tradition. Getting all of these people together was not just an opportunity to feed and water them, it was also a sales pitch. When they were suitably stuffed and socially confused, one of our senior people would stand and explain what the group was all about. He would then invite those interested to leave their contact details. Caught up in the moment, many did sign up, but were 'too busy' to take a week off work when I contacted them several months later.

Flying back to Birmingham Airport at the end of the week, I reflected on what had been, beyond all doubt, a marvellous experience. My religious views had not changed, but now I had an understanding and a respect for Catholicism and frankly I think I did enough to gain the respect of the group.

At HMS Raleigh on the following Monday, it was back to work as usual but I had been having a bit of trouble sleeping. This was not a new thing, but it had been gradually getting worse for months, and as a typical bloke, I had put off seeing a doctor. As an engineer, oil or water leaking out of a pipe constitutes a problem that needs fixing but electrics still largely confused me. Similarly, with my problem, there was no blood or outward signs of anything wrong so it simply *could not* be fixed.

For a couple of years, I had been experiencing a slight numbness and achiness in my left arm. There was no loss of function, but gradually, it started to affect my sleep and it was only a matter of time before it started to affect my work. Prompted by consistent nagging from the longhaired admiral at home, I visited the sickbay where the naval doctor sent me for an MRI scan. Like many amateur physicians, I had already typed my symptoms into Google, which *told* me that I had 'Carpal Tunnel Syndrome,' a common and very treatable condition in the wrist. I was confused, therefore, when the MRI scan centred on my head and neck. I was later invited back to the hospital for a chat with the consultant who, with the aid of a model, explained that I was getting old. I didn't need a model to show me that. Apparently, the cushiony bit between my C5 and C6 vertebrae was wearing away, causing my bones to trap the nerves that ran down my arm. The consultant went on to explain that an operation was possible to modify the bones, thus freeing up the nerves and alleviating the suffering. There was a chance however, that it could all go horribly wrong and I could end up in a wheelchair. This was a potentially life changing operation, so I needed a little time to think about it.

Finally opting for the operation, I fronted up at Derriford Hospital in Plymouth on a Sunday afternoon in 2002 for my admission onto Moorgate Ward where my mate, 'Cuddly' Claire Lewis, worked as a naval nurse.

Claire seemed very excited to be checking in a friend onto *her* ward and I was more than happy to have a friendly face around which was actually very pretty, and ever so slightly sexy in her light blue QARRNS uniform. Unfortunately, Claire was very professional and went through her admissions questionnaire, quickly and efficiently, until we got around to her question, "Do you normally have a bedtime drink?" I replied honestly, that I sometimes have a whisky as a nightcap. Claire, instantly reverted to the bubbly nurse from Lourdes and excitedly told me, "We can do that, we have medicinal whisky on the ward, so I will put you down for one." Things were looking up. Claire then left me to get into my newly purchased pyjamas and into bed.

That evening, after Anita had gone home and Claire had finished her shift, I was left in a private room to brood about the forthcoming operation. I had a book to read, but I couldn't concentrate on it. Deciding to listen to a compiled CD of my favourite music, only made matters worse. I have no idea why, but the compilation disc, that I had put together for myself, was full of depressing 'dead and dying' music, such as the excellent 'Brothers in Arms' and Brian May's 'No One But You'. On the eve of a potentially life changing operation, the music reduced me to a bit of lonely weepiness.

At around 10pm, a very nice Egyptian doctor popped in to see me. He worked for my surgeon and wanted to try to persuade me out of the operation. He reiterated that there was a chance it could go badly wrong and I could lose the use of my legs, but equally, he told me how brilliant the surgeon was.

During this bedside visit, the tea trolley came around and I was asked if I would like a bedtime drink. Remembering Claire's promise, I said, "I'll have a whisky please." The doctor didn't bat an eyelid, and without hesitation added, "…and I'll have a gin and tonic please." Of course, this was something of a wind-up and I had to make do with hot chocolate.

After a reasonable sleep, I was collected very early in the morning and wheeled down to the operating theatre, where I was 'parked' ready to be put to sleep. The Egyptian doctor appeared again, scrubbed up, in his theatre gowns. Once again, he advised me that it was not too late to change my mind and go home, but by this time, I was psyched up and ready. To go home now would still leave me with the same problem. With the consent form duly signed, I was wheeled through to the anteroom where they would put me to sleep. I can remember staring up at a ceiling painted with cartoon characters, as people tinkered with me and then the next thing I remember was waking up in bed, on the ward, in a lot of pain.

This time, I was in a male section of six beds. As my senses gradually returned, I became aware of needing to pee very badly. I was also very thirsty and hungry, but scared to move my neck as it hurt like hell. Seeing I was awake, Claire came over to see how I was feeling. I told her that I needed the loo badly but didn't think I could make it to the toilet. The ever-professional Claire, disappeared and returned a moment later, with a couple of cardboard bottles. She put one on the side for later and with the other, she reached between my legs and positioned the bottle before telling me to pee away. Reminiscent of a scene from an Austin Powers' movie, I could not stop, and filled one and a half of the litre bottles. Very soon, I needed to go again, as a day's worth of urine decided to signal its departure. As I had not eaten in a while, I was thankfully still ok at the other end.

Gradually, I was helped into a sitting position, whilst the nurses bustled around and changed my blood-soaked bedding and cleaned me up a bit. Feeling a little more human, I was given a sandwich and water to drink, but it felt as if my head was being held in a vice; I could not move it at all. The following day, a physiotherapist arrived to get me out of bed. Apparently, before I could be allowed home to recuperate, I had to be able to walk unaided and I had to be able to climb and descend stairs without assistance. Moving gingerly, I accomplished these tasks to her satisfaction and the next day, I was loaded up with masses of painkillers and discharged. As the swelling subsided, more movement returned and I felt as if I could do more, but the instruction from the hospital was to rest, not to drive and most importantly, not to lift anything at all.

What followed, was an extremely boring few weeks, watching daytime TV, before I was finally deemed fit enough to go back to work. A few things had changed in my absence. There had been a bit of a manpower shuffle and a new warrant officer now occupied my old desk. I was also being moved to Phase 1 training to take over as the divisional chief of Drake division. When I arrived, however, there was already a newly installed chief called Andy Bryant occupying the desk. As Andy was new in post and had already 'moved in', there was little point in me muscling him out, so, reluctantly, I deferred back to an instructor's position, but without a portfolio. I didn't have a desk that I could call my own and didn't even have a class to instruct. Therefore, I just helped as best as I could. The instructors were all POs so, as a higher rank, I could be used for instilling discipline, as I carried more authority. Essentially, where I was working at that point, was a complete waste of my talents. Although we got along just fine, Andy didn't like having another chief in his domain. As a divisional chief, you are master of all you survey and to have another chief on the plot rather questions your authority. The PO instructors didn't much like having a chief in *their* office either so, for a few weeks, like a spare part, I made the best of it until, I was asked to assist Warrant Officer Bob Potts as the Training WO. This was more like it and I viewed it as a sort of upward step. In this new attachment, I was not assigned to any particular division but more oversaw the entire eight-weeks of basic training. Whilst Bob was my immediate boss, we both worked directly for the officer commanding the recruit school, Lieutenant Commander Mike Helliwell.

For a WAFU, Mike was a good bloke. We got along very well and he often asked for my advice and tasked me to troubleshoot individual problems. This was far more like it, I had a moderate amount of influence and a desk to call my own. I am a simple soul, I don't require much, just my own desk, a chair and a place to lay my hat. This job promised to satisfy all of my needs.

Back into a working routine again and with some spare capacity, I started a maths class that Karen was also teaching. Maths was always a subject that I had perversely enjoyed at school. Whilst some people were good at sport, I had always been relatively good with figures but only managed to achieve an adequate CSE Grade 2, due to my limited attention span.

At the age of forty-one, I was ready to learn. An old adage says 'Education is wasted on the young'. To her credit, Karen gave me all the time I needed to understand some of the more challenging mathematical topics. Adopting my revision routine, after tea every evening, I revised and worked my way through past papers and the exercises in the textbook that Karen had given me. When the examination date was published, to my horror, it coincided with my next visit to Lourdes. Karen quite calmly explained that as long as there was a uniformed officer who could invigilate, then the sealed paper could be entrusted into their custody on the understanding that the paper was set on the same day.

That evening, I called a friend from my first Lourdes pilgrimage and pleaded for her help. RAF Group Captain Jane Nottingham was very happy to assist, so, the following day, Karen liaised with Jane allowing me to sit the exam in Lourdes.

Due to my revision strategy, the exam, when it came, was a doddle. Jane, to her credit, was the consummate professional and followed the guidance notes to the letter before laying back and snoozing on a bed behind me. This allowed me, between snores, to work in silence. I knew that due to the absence of coursework, the best I could achieve was a Grade 'C', but that was enough. When I had completed the final question, I still had plenty of time to check through my work, but was confident that I had done enough to gain my pass. Jane also scanned through my paper, noticing only a few silly errors but announced, in her opinion, she was holding a paper worthy of the grade, which was subsequently awarded a month or so later.

Sometime later, I was called in to see my boss Lt Cdr Mike Helliwell. He had been tasked by Commodore Pond to review the outdated Phase 1 training. As the boss rightly pointed out nothing much had changed in the last thirty years or more, whilst the navy had changed beyond recognition. The Commodore had a vision to make the training more vocational and less academic. In short, he considered, rightly in my opinion, that people learn better by doing rather than reading. His brief therefore, was to introduce more physical aspects to the course and to reduce the amount of formal classroom training. Kit was another aspect of the review. Since time had begun, naval trainees had always been taught to wash and iron their own kit and fold it in such a way that it all fitted into a ship's locker, roughly two feet high and eighteen inches square. This archaic discipline, whilst instilling core values, was not required anymore, as most ships carried a Chinese laundry and lockers that were much bigger, allowing many items of clothing to be hung on hangers. Therefore, the new regime of kit maintenance was more about ironing shirts and trousers and shining shoes. Standards had not fallen, but there was now no value in teaching the young boys and girls to fold everything to 'book size', as I did back in 1979.

I was allocated another office and ably assisted by Chief Petty Officer Laura Tindall, who had masses of experience working with trainees, we started to pull apart the building blocks of basic training. Laura and I, working together over many months, liaised with the various departments around the camp and proposed suggestions for introducing new modules and ditching some of the now pointless stuff. Each day was broken down into nine periods with breaks and lunch in-between. After much discussion with the boss, we introduced incentives in the form of time off, for those who were up to speed with their exams and kit. This started as a couple of hours on Saturday afternoon in Week 3, which allowed the trainees the freedom to go into Torpoint for a beer and a bit of shopping. This gradually increased to a whole afternoon in Week 5. Obviously, those who hadn't made the grade were invited to stay on the camp to revise and prepare to re-sit flunked exams.

Eventually, when we thought that we had a workable plan, the boss, Lt Cdr Mike Helliwell, presented it to Commodore David Pond who made a few tweaks here and there. He wanted more time mucking about in boats. He also suggested culminating the eight weeks of training with a 'Final Military Exercise'. This exercise would be a whole day of running around the camp, putting out fires, stopping floods, doing battle on the assault course and generally proving that the young boys and girls were as fit as we could make them to join the fleet.

Finally, we stayed with the traditional Passing-Out parade. The senior class, dressed in their best uniform, with white belt and gaiters, carrying a ceremonial SA80 assault rifle, would march onto the parade ground to the tune of 'Hearts of Oak', followed by every class of trainees. This was not just a naval tradition but also a military one, so there was no way that we wanted to ditch divisions.

Shortly after the implementation of our new project, I received a visit from Lt 'Paddy' Beegan who had taken over from Steve Lovett in the submarine school. He had been in post for a number of months and realising that I was still on his books, he wanted me back, working for him. He went on to explain that he was championing a new initiative to give trainee submariners an identity whilst still under training in HMS Raleigh. It was therefore decided to turn part of their accommodation block into a submarine museum with artefacts and submarine memorabilia, thus giving the trainees a sense of belonging. He tasked me to help with setting up the accommodation in Nelson Block and preparing it for occupation.

The submarine school warrant officer, Jim Slater, had a lock-up garage full of submarine memorabilia, that he simply did not have room to display. After a bit of cajoling from Colvin Osborn, 'Paddy' and myself, we managed to *borrow* a Mark 8 torpedo, a set of wall-mounted 'Dolphins', a huge freestanding set of 'Dolphins' and a couple of submarine escape suits, as well as a few pictures and wall charts. The problem now, was where to put everything. I also had a lot of work to do, fixing all of the beds, wardrobes, curtains and doors, because many things had been broken or misused over the years.

With the aid of a couple of lads, I concentrated on one mess at a time, moving decent furniture to get at least one fully serviceable. I ended up bringing my toolbox in from home and turning the place into a virtual workshop, as we drilled holes, screwed, and glued things together. After several months of purely mundane office work, this was quite a refreshing change. Eventually, I took delivery of thirty new mattresses and a load of new bedding before I was ready to accept the first batch of baby submariners into the newly formed 'Mackenzie Squadron'.

As we slowly managed to get the other messes habitable, more lads moved in until we were full to capacity. Initially, this was my accommodation block to run. As the squadron evolved, we quickly realised that we needed more management on site to mentor, offer advice and if necessary discipline the lads. My office, which was just inside the main entrance, was scarcely large enough to swing a medium sized cat and had only room for two desks. Another large room, full of ironing boards was, for the most part, unused.

The master plan was to install a petty officer into my office as the Block Manager and after it had been refitted, with desks, computers and filing cabinets, move into the brand new DO's office, along with three other divisional officers.

Warrant Officer Martin Hoad came in as the DO for all of the artificers and as the senior man, he also took on the role of Office Manager. Myself, Mark 'Fanny' Craddock and Barry 'Baz' Craker, divided the rest of the wannabe submariners between ourselves, taking two branches each. The Petty Officer, who came in to assume the role of Block Manager, was Phil 'Nick' Carter and he assumed my former responsibilities for looking after the

accommodation, whilst we concentrated on the welfare of the lads. It worked well, we were constantly busy, with an endless stream of paperwork and frequent visits to see *the* Commander with naughty boys who had broken the rules, in a variety of imaginative ways from being adrift to alcohol, drug abuse and doing naughty things with the girls on camp.

I had a real issue with the kids taking drugs. The drinking, I could handle, just so long as the lads looked after their oppos. I had no real issue with the lads getting drunk; it's all part of the great learning curve of life and an essential part of growing up. Nobody likes to wake up with a banging head, but so long as his mates had brought him home and looked after him, then I was happy to turn a blind eye. One incident I couldn't ignore was when one of my lads was found, paralytic and face down in a grassy ditch, by a guard dog. Fortunately, the ditch was dry or he may well have drowned. The security guard managed to wake him and escorted him to cells where he slept and was frequently checked to ensure that he was still breathing. This did not prevent him from grand-slamming though. During the course of the night, he vomited, pissed and shit himself. Under normal circumstances, this would warrant a round of applause, but the chap was suffering quite badly. To add insult to injury, he was woken at 7am and made to clean up his mess before being allowed to wash himself.

A couple of weeks later, I escorted him to see the Commander, who after hearing all of the evidence, proceeded to bawl at him, at full volume, for ten minutes, spitting real venom and anger. The Commander was a good bloke, but he realised that if it wasn't for a bit of good fortune, he would be explaining to his mother that the Royal Navy hadn't looked after little Johnny well enough and as a result he was now dead. Consequently, the Commander awarded the lad fourteen days 'nines'.

All punishments in the navy are 'awarded' for some strange reason and each has an identifying number. No 9 punishment was widely used and often accompanied by a fine. 'Nines' as they were known, stopped a man's leave for a number of days and also required that he muster at predetermined times of the day and night, wearing the correct uniform, before he was required to carry out some menial work for an hour. The upshot of this 'award', for our drunken friend, was that he was not going home for three weeks and would be seriously inconvenienced. Sometimes this worked as a deterrent but that was not always the case. Just about every week I escorted naughty lads to see the Commander, but some of these were quite comical.

I was duty one night, which required me to be available all night, in a sort of parental role, making sure that the lads got to bed at 10:30pm with the lights out and no chattering.

Sometime after 11pm, when I was ready, I would take a silent stroll through the messes, to ensure that everybody was in bed and that each bed only had one lump in it. There was a fair amount of illegal sexual activity going on around the camp and the girls were just as bad as the boys as they sought dark corners of the camp to get 'friendly' with each other.

On one occasion, I came across an empty bed. I had already checked the heads and bathrooms, so I wondered where the lad was. Scanning the mess in the darkness, I noticed a faint shadow stood on the low windowsill behind the curtains. Following a suicide a year or so previously, all of the windows had been fitted with security locks, so there was no danger of him being a 'jumper'. I peeked through another curtain to see what he was looking at.

Stood on the second floor windowsill of an adjacent block, was a pretty young girl, of about sixteen, in a night shirt. Without noticing me, she raised her nightie to shoulder height revealing that she was totally naked underneath; proudly displaying her young breasts and lady garden to her male admirer. As I later discovered, he had also dropped his pyjama pants to his knees in a quid pro quo sort of display. Observing for a minute, I wanted to see if this was just a nightly ritual of flashing to each other, but it turned out, that was just the beginning as the girl started to explore herself downstairs. At the same time, the movement of the curtain suggested that the lad was also masturbating. I needed to put a stop to this, before I was discovered watching.

Creeping up behind the lad, I quickly pulled the curtain back revealing him about to explode with his erect penis still in his hand. The girl with a look of total shock on her face, quickly disappeared from view, but I knew who she was. I shouted loudly at the lad, waking up the whole mess. I told him to get dressed and report to my office where, after getting the facts of the incident, I sent him to bed in another block and posted a sentry on him.

After reporting the sexual activity in my incident log, the following morning, I went for a quiet cup of tea with Jane, *the* Chief Wren on camp and explained in detail the incident. The chief sent for the girl who blushed furiously when she recognised me. I finished my tea and then left, so Jane could interview her properly.

About a week later, I escorted my naughty boy up to see the Commander. Awaiting punishment outside the charge room, was Jane, the Chief Wren and her naughty young girl, dressed in her best uniform, still looking quite ashamed of herself. I went in first and after saluting, I outlined the facts to a smirking Commander, before the lad was marched in. We all tried desperately to keep a straight face as the Commander bawled at the lad. In a superb piece of acting, he managed to appear very angry indeed, but as soon as the lad had been awarded a fine and marched out, the spell was broken and he burst into laughter. I later heard from the Chief Wren that her girlie was also awarded a similar fine and bollocking.

With the accommodation now up and running, life became very comfortable. Four of us shared a massive office, so I had a quarter of it and two desks arranged at right angles with a computer on one, leaving the other one free for paperwork. There were lockers at one end, positioned to provide a bit of privacy whist getting changed at the beginning of the day. Life was good and not for the first time, I wished that I could stay in this job with the same bunch of guys forever.

However, this was not to be and in the next couple of months, I was summoned to see the commander of the submarine school twice. On the first occasion, Commander Ian Stallion presented me with the 2OE signal. I had known it was due, but hadn't even looked for it, as I had been awarded a five-year extension whilst serving on HMS Talent. Astonishingly, the powers that be had elected to award me an additional ten years' service meaning that my terminal date had now been extended to 4th January 2017. Well, if I wasn't already sitting, you could have knocked me down with a feather. There were two possible reasons for this, either I was terribly good at my job and this was being recognised or realistically, following a recent phase of redundancies, the navy was running short of experienced submariners. Personally, I couldn't care less; this would take me close enough to retirement and seriously top up my pension fund. Everybody is required to leave the armed forces at the age of fifty-five, so this was as good as it got. I could still submit twelve months' notice to leave if my circumstances changed, but at the time, it seemed very unlikely.

A couple of weeks later though and the inevitable happened. A draft order arrived for me to leave the relative comfort of HMS Raleigh and go back to sea on HMS Turbulent as *the* Chief Stoker. The chap I was due to relieve was an old mate of mine, called Craig 'Stan' Stannard. Following a phone call to him, I arranged a pre-joining visit and set about putting my affairs in order for the chap, or chapess, who would replace me in due course.

Due to my neck operation, I had managed to scam about four years' inboard time before, it was time to go back to sea again. It was a culture shock, I can tell you, but following some fond farewells, I left HMS Raleigh and packed my kit ready to join the nuclear submarine HMS Turbulent in the February of 2005.

HMS TURBULENT

10th February 2005 to 15th May 2006

Following some leave, carrying a rucksack containing my sea-going working clothes, I walked over the gangway of HMS Turbulent for the first time since I had attended a fire in her switchboard room whilst serving on HMS Spartan.

I was now getting quite used to joining submarines and knew precisely what to do. Even so, after twenty years in the submarine service, I was still being confronted with the usual bollocks of safety briefs and joining routines. Appreciating that everybody had a job to do, I was a good boy and pretended to listen before ditching my kit on a spare bunk, getting changed into my No8's and exploring my new home.

After about four years in HMS Raleigh, wearing nothing but a uniform white shirt and trousers, my steaming boots and the more casual working uniform felt quite strange. I was pleasantly surprised that they still fitted, to be perfectly honest.

Locating Craig 'Stan' Stannard, the outgoing chief stoker, in the laundry, we formally shook hands and trundled aft along 2 deck to the mess, for a coffee and an informal chat, before getting down to the serious business of transferring the responsibility for all of the firefighting, fuel and escape systems, on-board the submarine, to me.

In the mess, sipping the only coffee Stan would ever make me, he informed me that 'Turbs' was not programmed to go to sea for a number of weeks but, there was a real need to get me re-qualified before he could be permitted to leave the boat. For that reason, he said, I was to join HMS Trafalgar very shortly, for a week or so, as she sailed to Bermuda.

After finishing my coffee, I realised that I only had about two working days to complete my joining routine and get my steaming kit and tropical shorts together before I was off on my travels again. Therefore, I got weaving and went to find the Coxswain to confirm my travel arrangements.

Visiting the wardroom, I met the engineers; the MEO, Lt Cdr Martin Hanks, DMEO, Lt 'Paddy' Brennan and my immediate boss AMEO(S) Lt Rob Goodenough, nicknamed 'Ships', as he was responsible for the ship's systems. I must say he looked very young, or was it that I was getting old? It turned out in conversation that he was only twenty-five and not even born when I joined the navy and he was supposed to be my mentor and the chap I went to for guidance. I made a mental note to be gentle with him.

With the introductions complete, I went for the usual dockyard bimble, collecting joining stamps and informing the sickbay and dentist in HMS Drake that I had joined the boat. This allowed them to request my medical and dental records from HMS Raleigh. I also visited 'Slops', the clothing store, and scrounged as much kit as they would let me have, before calling it a day and slinking off home. I needed to tell Anita that I was off to sea in a few days and would not be home for a few weeks.

Well, I didn't really slink off, it is a sort of unwritten rule that chiefs can manage their own time and at that point in time I had managed to do about as much as I could for one day.

Completing my joining routine the following day, I scammed an extended weekend and took Monday off as well to pack. Anita dropped me into the dockyard early on Tuesday morning, in plenty of time to meet the 0730 boat from 13 Wharf.

It had been a while since I had boat-transferred anywhere, so it was quite a surprise when a wide-hulled, luxury, red and white Serco boat was waiting for me. Armed with a coffee from their on-board coffee machine, I had quite a nice chat with the crew on the hour-long trip down river and out into Plymouth Sound. HMS Trafalgar was secured to 'Charlie buoy' awaiting my arrival.

With the boat-transfer successfully completed, Trafalgar slipped the buoy and steadily manoeuvred through the western breakwater, steering a southerly course, towards Eddystone lighthouse before turning westwards and following the Cornish coast through the relatively shallow confines of the English Channel. A dived transit can be achieved, but the chances of 'catching' a fishing boat in the busy fishing grounds of the Channel were quite high. The Captain, therefore, preferred the safer, less embarrassing option of transiting on the surface until clear of the continental shelf when there would be sufficient sea room under the hull.

Safely underwater, some hours later, Trafalgar increased speed for the week-long, dived transit to Bermuda, which would be my first opportunity of getting home again. Back into a sea-going routine once more, I concentrated on familiarising myself with the ship, propulsion and weapons systems as, over the previous four-years, I had become quite rusty. It never ceases to amaze me though, just how quickly it all comes back. Concentrating initially aft of 56 watertight-bulkhead, in the machinery spaces, I was quite relieved to find that most of the valves, pieces of machinery and compartments were pretty much where I had left them. Of course, I still had some questions to ask, but the systems were almost identical to those on HMS Talent, with only a few subtle differences. By the end of the first full day of crawling around in the engine room, diesel room, switchboard room and the tunnel, putting my hand on valves, it was as if I had never been away. I therefore requested a walkround from one of the qualified engineers. As I knew the chap and he had seen me rummaging around in the depths of the boat, the resulting examination was something of a formality.

With my re-qualification of half of the submarine now complete, I rewarded myself some sleep. As a visitor to the submarine and with no free beds in the bunk spaces, I was allocated a berth in the weapons stowage compartment, cuddled up to a white torpedo-like container housing a Royal Navy Sub-Harpoon missile, but I was getting quite used to the way of things by now. In contrast to my time as a trainee on Sovereign, Spartan and Triumph, when I had to share a bunk, I was now a Chief Petty Officer and as rank has its privileges; I was allocated my own bunk. This enabled me to rig up a curtain of sorts and darken my bed space from the permanent glow of the bomb shop's fluorescent lights.

Following a good night's sleep, I ate a hearty fat-boy's cooked breakfast, before climbing into my now smelly overalls to start tracing the forward systems. I visited just about every compartment, asking loads of questions and generally getting myself noticed as I made a nuisance of myself in the control room. Many valves were hidden away in lockers and cupboards. Unlike the engine room, systems were not as visible, but fortunately, Trafalgar's systems were laid out in almost the same way as HMS Talent's.

Therefore, after another full day of system tracing, punctuated with the occasional coffee and a bite to eat, I was ready for the remaining walkround. Similar to my examination aft, the chief who was conducting the walkround knew me by reputation and had seen me working during the day. He adopted the rationale that if I didn't know something, then I would make it my professional business to find out. Consequently, at the end of a very short tour of the forward part of the boat, I was awarded with another signature, thus completing this phase. All I had to do now was sit a BSQ oral board the following day, where I would be asked all manner of questions to ensure that I held the standard of expertise required of a Royal Navy submariner.

After spending most of the evening with my head in the books, I was ready to be examined. If it all went pear-shaped, I still had about five days before reaching Bermuda to retake the exam. I needn't have worried, the following morning, cramped on bench seats in the tiny SINS room, with the XO, 'Ships' and the Wrecker, I was grilled for about half an hour before we all got bored and spent the rest of the time spinning dits and generally having a laugh. I finally left the small navigational compartment re-qualified as a submariner and a valuable member of the submarine community again. All I needed to do now was to qualify on the Systems Control Console that is often referred to as the SCC or simply the Panel.

In previous jobs, I had been qualified on the Panel as a junior rate, but that was only when the submarine was on the surface. Diving and surfacing the submarine was not particularly difficult, in fact a trained monkey could do it. It is as easy as flicking switches when somebody tells you to. The mere fact that this five-thousand ton blob of steel was underwater required somebody with something to lose, to instinctively flick the switches for the main vents and main ballast tank blows, in an emergency, in case it all went horribly wrong, but there was a lot of theory behind flicking those switches.

The Panel watchkeeper was also relied upon by the Captain to be a fount of all knowledge when it came to hydraulics, HP air, trim, bilge and ballast as well as raising and lowering all of the masts and periscopes, so there was much to learn. Fortunately, I knew a lot of it already and as there are only so many questions that can be asked on a written paper, all I had to do was learn the syllabus and be able to answer every question. What could be simpler?

Studying some past papers, it seemed that a few questions came up all of the time, so these were considered easy marks. Nothing seemed too difficult and so it proved when I was presented with a sealed envelope and told to sit in the computer room on 1 deck with as much time as I needed, to download my memory onto paper.

Due to the amount of trainees at sea on Trafalgar, they did not have sufficient time to mark my completed paper but instead, suggested I take it back to HMS Turbulent who would mark it, before sitting me down for a SCC oral board.

Therefore, after three days of frenetic activity, I had fully requalified BSQ and sat a written SCC paper but then everything came to a grinding halt. Trafalgar, quite rightly, needed to concentrate on her own trainees so getting some hands-on practice on the Panel was simply not going to happen.

Left with nothing to do for the remainder of the week, I watched a lot of movies in the mess, drank a lot of coffee, read my book and slept quite a bit. As a guest on-board, I volunteered to serve and clean up at meal times to try and earn my keep as I looked for ways to make the time go quickly.

Fortunately, it did go quickly and before long, we were surfacing on the approaches into the Royal Naval Dockyard in Bermuda. On arrival into this historic naval port, there was much to do by the crew whilst I was badgering the Coxswain, Tony 'Scouse' Rowan, for a plane ticket to get me home. Tony was in a difficult position. He needed my bed for other people joining, but did not own the budget to fly me home. As an old mate from Sovereign, he promised that he would personally beat up the Supply Officer if he hadn't bought me a ticket home within the week. Furthermore, he confirmed that I would not be sailing from Bermuda with HMS Trafalgar and to enjoy the 'jolly' whilst he got persuasive with the chap that held the purse strings.

Therefore, about an hour later, with bags packed, I walked off the gangway of HMS Trafalgar, into the searing heat of Bermuda and onto a waiting bus, which would shuttle the ship's company to three hotels at the other side of the island that had been pre-booked, according to rank. Naturally, the officers got the best and the most luxurious hotel, but frankly, compared to the cramped, musty, confines of a nuclear submarine, any hotel situated on a beach in the glorious Bermudian sunshine, with views over an aqua blue sea, paid for by the tax payer, was luxury.

It took about an hour, trundling down dusty roads, littered with palm fronds and ramshackle houses before we reached the hotel on the other side of the island. My room was pre-allocated, so it did not take long before I was showering off the unmistakeable smell of the submarine. Smelling sweetly again and dressed in shorts, baggy T-Shirt and flip-flops, I found the rest of my new shipmates in the hotel bar, sinking a rum punch, or two, and generally enjoying the jolly. This went on for several hours as we got steadily pissed. As the evening wore on, the bar got evermore noisier. This was the lads kicking back from the endless routine of keeping a submarine safe at sea. Life was good again.

The following morning, after discovering where the dining room was and refuelling for the day, myself and 'Dicky' Dickaty, an old mate from Talent, decided to hire scooters and explore the island. He had a hankering to visit 'Horseshoe Bay' arguably one of the best beaches in the world, whilst I wanted to look around the capital city of Hamilton and buy a souvenir rugby jersey for the world rugby tournament called the Bermuda Classic.

After walking next door to the bike rental shop, 'Dicky' and I found that we were not alone, as most of the junior rates mess had also decided to hire one of the few visible scooters. I considered that I had a distinct advantage over most of the lads for a few very good reasons; I was old enough, I had road sense whereas some of the lads could not even drive. I had sufficient credit on my Visa card, and more importantly, a full UK motorcycle licence. If that failed, I could have always pulled rank.

I needn't have worried though as the owner had a garage, full to the rafters, of 50cc twist and go machines. Having paid the money and a collision damage waiver, we were all given instructions on how to start, indicate, brake and turn off the machine as well as advice on how to lock it when leaving it unattended.

My difficulty was learning how to ride such a small machine again, as the centre of gravity was so much higher than on my 600cc machine at home. Therefore, for the first few hundred yards, I was teetering and wobbling about until I relearned my skills. With everybody more or less happy, off we went in the direction of Hamilton.

It is difficult, but not impossible, to get lost in Bermuda, so after a few false starts we managed to navigate noisily into the capital city. Parking up, 'Dicky' and I went shopping. After asking a few shop assistants, I found my rugby shirt and bought a small road map of the island to assist in our navigation, whilst 'Dicky' found a present for Rosie, his lovely young wife.

Having wandered around the shops for a little while and topped up on fluids, we decided to further explore the island. I managed to find 'Horseshoe Bay' on the map and also a colonial looking Gibbs Hill Lighthouse that I rather fancied going to look at. Therefore, memorising waypoints from the map, I led us around the bay and out of Hamilton towards the lighthouse with the plan of using that as our furthest point of the day, before winding our way back on the other coast, stopping at the idyllic looking beach.

We reached the lighthouse easily enough. Let's face it, they are designed to be seen and as this one was plonked on top of a great big hill, it was visible for miles. Parking the bikes, we bought entrance tickets and struggled up the iron spiral staircase, stopping briefly at a mid-way point to allow other tourists to descend. Finally, climbing to the top, we were not disappointed, as the views were outstanding. After a bit of orientation, we were able to locate HMS Trafalgar, alongside at the Royal Dockyard, across the sound, basking in the early afternoon heat. We were also able to see how the aqua waters changed colour into a dark inky blue, as just offshore, the waters deepened into an abyss. It seemed quite surreal that the whole island appeared to me to be at the top of a great big submarine mountain. Spending quite a while photographing the views, it was time to descend the long and winding road to the cafeteria at the bottom, for a well-earned Coke and a sandwich.

Suitably refreshed, 'Dicky' and I donned crash helmets and with a little guidance from the restaurant staff, made our way down from the lighthouse and steered course for 'Horseshoe Bay', a little way north on the same coast. Fortunately, it was well signposted and in seemingly no time at all, we were parked up and trudging down the sandy trail towards the beach.

Strangely, the beach was almost deserted. I rather expected it to be full of deck chairs, parasols and screaming kids but apart from a couple of swimmers and a few people strolling around, we had the perfect pinkish sandy beach to ourselves. The sea had combed the sand into a perfect billiard table finish that was actually quite hard to walk on. Without our speedos we simply opted to take a few photos whilst walking barefoot to the far side of the bay.

Approaching a Bermudian couple, we passed the time of day with the usual innocuous comments about the weather. They correctly assumed from our red sunburn that we were new to the island. The chap warned us to be careful of sand trails that could be concealing Portuguese Man O Wars, that were a sort of nasty stinging jellyfish. He cautioned that the sting was very unpleasant and whilst it was generally not fatal, it *would* ruin our day. Thanking them for the warning, we went looking for the little blighters and it wasn't long before we noticed a purplish blob of jelly half-buried in the sand, dragging behind it a long set of matching purple streamers. Giving it a wide berth and watching out for his oppos buried in the sand, we completed our perambulation and as it was getting quite late in the afternoon, decided to meander back to the hotel, via a different route. Having now got our bearings, getting lost on Bermuda was quite a challenge, as the island was long and thin, so, figuring that if we kept the sea on our right we should be heading northwards away from the dockyard and back towards the hotel. What we hadn't factored into our route was riding through a golf course and essentially ducking flying balls. I had the distinct impression that we had taken a wrong turning and had inadvertently trespassed onto the golf course, but no. This was the road and after successfully avoiding serious injury, it wasn't long before we were back at the hotel, showered, changed and in the pub eating a rather murky looking brown fish soup that strangely came with a double shot of Gosling's Black Seal Rum that could be added to taste. Some people opted to use the 140% firewater as a chaser, but being something of a traditionalist and wishing to savour the Bermudian experience to the full, I unceremoniously dumped the whole glass into the soup and gave it a swish. I was proved right a few seconds later as my first sip of soup gloriously set my mouth on fishy fire.

Following the delicious meal and a few glasses of the local beer, I was ready for bed, so I trudged back to the hotel for a cooling shower before flopping into bed exhausted from the day's activities. The rest of the week followed in a similar vein. I had no actual work to do so I was only killing time in this tropical island paradise before 'Scouse' could arrange me a flight home. Every evening, I would interrogate him in the hotel bar for a flight update. He was becoming increasingly frustrated as he currently had more sailors on the island than the submarine could safely accommodate. Of course, as an old mate, he appreciated that none of this was my fault, so promised to threaten physical violence to the Supply Officer if he did not release some cash to buy my plane ticket home.

Towards the end of the week, a smiling 'Scouse' was triumphant and presented me with an itinerary. I would be picked up from the hotel later that afternoon and deposited at the airport for the first leg of my journey home, via Miami. I would then transfer onto a Virgin Atlantic overnight flight to Gatwick, where a hire car would be awaiting collection.

Unusually, the flight and all of the travel arrangements went according to plan and by 9am the following morning, I was wearily doing battle with the M23 morning traffic as I exited Gatwick for the predicted five-hour drive home to Plymouth. It may be fair to say I did not exactly abide by the speed limits as I blasted the hire car westwards. Let's face it; it was not often that I got the opportunity to beast someone else's brand new car and play with all of the on-board gadgets at the same time. As we all know, there is nothing on earth faster than a hire car.

The reality was, I was running on an adrenalin-fuelled autopilot for most of the time, having been awake for much of the night and all of the previous day. Fortunately, I did not attract any attention from the boys in blue and by mid-afternoon, I was pulling up outside my house in Plymouth, knackered.

After sleeping the sleep of the dead for the rest of the afternoon and all of the night, I was feeling much more refreshed. I was back in the mess on HMS Turbulent by 8am being interrogated by 'Stan' Stannard on my progress concerning my requalification. I must say, he was delighted that I had qualified BSQ and at least got some way towards my Panel board. I had brought my written paper on-board for marking and subsequently handed this to the Wrecker, Ian 'Wal' Walton, for marking.

Stan wasted no time at all and was off to the wardroom to ask 'Hank', the MEO, if he could get off the boat now that I was 75% qualified. Unfortunately, Hank was having none of it and all efforts were now to be directed at getting my paper marked and an oral board sat. Wal marked my paper quite quickly and gave me some friendly pointers for the oral board that would be convened in a day or so.

As everybody had a vested interest in me passing the oral board, it was never going to be a real issue. It still had to be done properly though, and after about an hour of being quizzed in the wardroom on my system knowledge by the AMEO(S), Lt Rob Goodenough, and Wrecker 'Wal', I managed to increase my qualification status from 75% to 90%. Now, all I was required to do to finalise my qualification, was to pass a practical exam, but that could only be conducted at sea, dived and on the Panel, to make it as realistic as possible.

With my professional knowledge assessed, the boss permitted Stan to formally hand over the responsibility of Chief Stoker to me and leave the submarine on draft.

I must say, with the greatest of respect, that I was glad to see the back of Stan. Sure, he was a good bloke, but whilst he was still on-board, I could not do things my way. After he had left, I was free to explore my section and actually grow into the job. Everybody I spoke to told me that I had some big boots to fill, which frankly, did not inspire confidence. I was assured by Wal and the rest of the lads that Stan would be hugely missed and that he had left the section in a good state.

As the submarine had been alongside for quite a while, two important inspections quickly fell well within my remit. Firstly a fire-fighting inspection and then close on its heels an escape inspection, failure of either one would mean that the boat would not be sailing.

When the chief stoker from the Flag Officer Sea Training staff turned up on the jetty a couple of weeks later to conduct the fire-fighting inspection, I was all smiles and confidently showed him around my newly inherited domain. CMEM Joe Absalom observed that there was a few niggly things to sort out. As I hastily scribbled a list, the plan was, if the small things like labels and securing chains could be fixed whilst he was on-board, then they would not make it into the report.

Over coffee, Joe then asked to see all of the documentation for my extinguishers and air bottles that were fitted to the breathing apparatus sets. This was when it all fell apart. My predecessor, whilst being a good egg and all round snappy dresser, was not great at paperwork. The trouble was, he had already declared to the hierarchy that he was on top of the game, so having been on-board for only a couple of weeks, I incurred the wrath of the MEO and his deputy dog, 'Paddy' Brennan.

This mightily pissed me off, so, after being told in no uncertain words to make it better, I spent a few weeks with my lad, MEM 'Linda' Nolan, going through a voluminous check list with a fine tooth comb, righting all of the wrongs. Where I did not have a test certificate, I ordered a new extinguisher or an air bottle and meticulously catalogued all of the certificates. I was not going to be caught with my pants down like that again, but there was still much to achieve and I still had an escape inspection to pass.

Fortunately, my electrical sidekick, CMEM(L) 'Jakey' Foran, was lightly-loaded, so he gave me a hand with certain aspects of the defect list, allowing me to eventually switch target to the escape side of things. With the return fire-fighting inspection booked, I was confident that all of the points had been addressed so I popped over to the Escape Workshop, to chat with an old mate, called CMEM(M) 'Plug' Preston. He would be coming on-board with his box of tricks to test both of my escape towers. I confessed to 'Plug' that I was worried and had no idea of the material state of the towers. It is a bit like putting your car in for an MOT without checking it over first. Despite being physically huge, intimidating and well over six foot tall, 'Plug' was extremely helpful. He advised changing three major components on both towers as these were prone to failure and he would then set them up as part of the inspection. All I had to do in this respect, was the spanner work. The lumps of kit and associated pipework essentially took pressurised air from inside the boat and supplied it to the suit of an escaping submariner at a pressure slightly above the outside water pressure, thus giving the escapee air to breathe as he ascended. I got the distinct impression that 'Plug' Preston was there to help me get the boat ready for sea by telling me what I needed to do.

What followed was a couple of weeks of frenetic activity. As I concentrated on preparing for the escape inspection, I spent a day inside each tower changing the stole charging valve, HIS controller and G24 reducer and checking all of the points on the checklist by conducting my own dummy inspection.

My young lad, 'Linda' Nolan was doing some sterling work rectifying the fire-fighting defects and occasionally helping me out when I needed another pair of hands.

A week later and I was almost there. The escape towers were as good as I could get them. The bits had been changed, lights had all been proved to work, the security chains had all been replaced with new ones coated in rubber insulation and the upper hatch had been well greased and worked to give us confidence that if it was required, it would open under pressure. Added to that, both towers had been painted white and all the lettering had been repainted in red to make it easier to read in low light conditions.

The FOST chief made his return visit, so again, I had to switch targets back to fire-fighting, this time, I was properly prepared. All of the certificates were laid out in order on the mess table and all of the points in his original report had been addressed, consequently, Joe was all smiles and by lunchtime, I had passed the inspection. I only had the escape inspection to pass to spare my blushes, as failure of this inspection was a cast iron 'boat stopper' and would be mega-embarrassing for me, as I would inevitably face some difficult questions from the Skipper.

Fortunately, 'Plug' Preston, the Escape Coxswain had given me all of the advice I needed, so, a few days later, when I formally met him on the casing, I was quietly confident. 'Plug' spent all day tinkering around with the air on both towers, setting up the reducers and the controllers to ensure that an escapee would get the right amount of air to his suit in the tower.

With both towers passed, I was on cloud nine. The rest of the checklist was niff naff and trivia. Sure, it was important, but there would be nothing that I could not sort out very quickly.

By the end of the afternoon, HMS Turbulent had passed her escape inspection and as far as my section was concerned, we were ready for sea; not that I got any thanks of course. I am sure that the wardroom thought I had deliberately screwed up Stan's *good* work, as he was Mr Golden Bollocks. I clearly had a lot of work to do to gain credibility in the eyes of the grown-ups.

A week or so later, with many new members of crew, including me, HMS Turbulent let go of her ropes and with a couple of tugs in attendance, silently made her way down river. Turning the corner on her way into Plymouth Sound, she rounded Drake's Island and finally left Plymouth behind as the Captain navigated the submarine through the western breakwater and out into the English Channel.

The intention was for the submarine to exercise the crew and generally wash off the cobwebs and get everybody back into a sea-going frame of mind. Over the next few hours, Turbulent dodged the many fishing vessels and headed out to deep water, before in the early evening, with a decent amount of water under the keel, we went to Diving Stations.

Still needing to qualify on the Panel, I was tucked into a little corner in the darkened, quiet, control room, observing the Wrecker, Ian Walton, preparing to dive the submarine. The Captain was carrying out a final sweep on the search periscope ensuring that nothing was close before picking up the microphone and calling up to the bridge.

"Officer of the Watch, Captain."

"Officer of the Watch, sir."

"Clear the bridge, come below, shut the upper lid… I have the submarine."

Repeating the order, the Officer of the Watch and Look Out unplugged their communications and secured the upper conning position before the Look Out was heard in the conning tower followed by the OOW. With a whump, the conning tower upper lid was shut as the Officer of the Watch shouted out the progress.

"Upper Lid shut, two clips."

"Upper Lid shut, two clips, one pin,"

"Upper Lid shut, two clips, two pins."

The Look Out emerged from the tower swathed in a soggy wet red Gore-Tex suit before announcing, "Ship Control … Look Out below," as he simultaneously isolated the bridge comms.

The Officer of the Watch emerged moments later similarly attired and after reporting that he was also below, made a lengthy report to the Captain on the state of the bridge, conning tower and the nearest surface contacts.

Happy that the submarine was safe and that all of the hatches were shut and clipped, the Captain ordered Ship Control to dive the submarine.

Working from his check procedure, the Coxswain on Ship Control made a main broadcast pipe, "Diving Now, Diving Now." Then turning towards Wal, he ordered, "Panel… Open 3 and 4 main vents."

On the SCC, Wal repeated the order before reaching up to the three switches that would open the after main vents and expel the air keeping the submarine afloat from number three and four main ballast tanks.

Keeping an all-round look, the Captain satisfied himself that the after casing was awash before ordering 1 and 2 main vents open. Ship Control relayed the order to Wal on the Panel who immediately opened the remaining main vents confirming, "All main vents indicate open."

The Captain, wishing to drive the submarine underwater, gave the order, "Revolutions three zero, six down, thirty metres and back to eighteen metres," as he endeavoured to 'rock the bubble' and empty the ballast tanks of any remaining air. Ship Control again repeated the order and after ringing on the shaft revolutions, ordered the helmsman to his left, "Six down," whilst he ordered Wal to flood some water into the compensating tanks to initially make the submarine heavier than the water she displaced.

Slowly, the depth gauge above the helmsman started to move as Turbulent wallowed like a whale on the surface before slipping silently below the waves. Realising that all of the submarines hatches were now under water, the Coxswain made a main broadcast pipe, "Submarine passing twenty metres, report all hatches from forward." Immediately, the reports came in over main broadcast… "Weapons embarkation hatch, dry." "Forward escape tower upper lid, dry." "Conning tower upper lid, dry." "Main access hatch, dry." "After escape tower upper lid. Dry." "Engine room hatch dry." Content that the submarine was not leaking water through the hatches, the Coxswain issued the order, "Ship lower lids."

From the back of the control room, a shouted voice called, "Induction system flooding," as the forward stokers flooded the snort induction mast to prevent it being crushed by the water pressure. Safely under water, there were still some lengthy housekeeping procedures to conduct as the whole crew carried out long post-diving checks to ensure that the sea was staying on the other side of the hull. This was completed before the Captain ordered Ship Control to fall the submarine out from diving stations.

"D'yer hear there, fallout from diving stations, second watch, watch dived, patrol quiet state, damage control state three, weapon readiness state three." This essentially meant that half of the crew could now go to bed only to be awoken in a couple of hours' time for a mug of soup and a bread roll, in preparation for a six hour watch beginning at 1am.

Time on-board a dived submarine is a strange concept because at six-hourly intervals, everybody would be out of bed and either washing and eating before going on watch or just eating before going to bed. Timed right, there is the ability to sleep for very close to twelve hours a day, but personally I could never manage much more than about seven or eight in a couple of three or four hour stints. Working the 1 – 7 shift, my best sleep would usually be after breakfast. If my relief was feeling charitable, he would take over as soon as he was washed and fed allowing me to have a quick breakfast before diving into my bunk in the upper bunk space on 1 deck.

One of the lads from the other watch would generally wake me up just before lunch, allowing me sufficient time to have a quick wash and scran before resuming my watch at 1pm. Coming off watch at 7pm, I would eat before trying to get back to sleep. It was not uncommon for me to sleep for a couple of hours and then to awaken naturally at 10pm, sweating buckets and pondering life. Clearly, having had enough sleep, I would take the opportunity to have a good shower and shave before catching up on some personal admin such as changing my bed and getting my laundry together for washing whilst on watch. I would still have a couple of hours to take in a movie in the mess before it was time to go back on watch at 1am.

After having dived, in routine and in sufficiently deep water, the Captain decided to conduct a few exercises, to get everybody thinking and working as a team. None of this comes naturally and does need regular practice, especially as there was a large percentage of the crew on their first voyage. Whilst I was snoozing the following morning, I was awoken by the broadcast, "D'yer hear there, the Safeguard Rule is now in force."

The Safeguard Rule was conceived, many moons ago, to inject a bit of realism into exercises. Usually an exercise would be preceded by, "For exercise, for exercise, for exercise…" but the Safeguard Rule dispensed with all that. Should a real incident occur whilst the rule was in force, it would be preceded by, "Safeguard, safeguard, safeguard..." Which, when it happened, generally made you poo your pants.

With the Safeguard Rule now in force, there was little point in trying to sleep, so most of us dressed and lay on our bunks awaiting for the inevitable 'fire' or 'smell of burning' that would generally kick off the day's evolutions.

My job was fairly simple, if I was not unlucky enough to 'discover' it. If I was off-watch, I would go to my Emergency Station on 3 deck and assist as directed, conversely if I was on-watch, it was a simple matter of flicking a few switches on the Panel and starting a trim pump, when ordered, to supply water to the fire hoses.

After a few evolutions to shake the crew up, we stopped for lunch and the watch change before doing it all again in the afternoon to even up the sleep deprivation. This would continue until we were pretty much getting it right. All of these exercises were gearing up to a forthcoming period of work-up with the nice people from the Flag Officer's Sea Training Staff who were due to come on-board shortly.

All naval vessels, following an extended period of maintenance, were required to undergo training to test all aspects of the submarine's readiness for operational deployment. This not only trained us to fight fires, floods and famines, the FOST staff also looked at our administration in depth. Everything was picked over with a fine toothcomb, paying particular attention to the cleanliness and stowage for sea. It was quite common for a member of the staff to pose a testing question to any member of the ship's company. Failure to answer correctly, may well earn the unfortunate lad another BSQ.

Over a few weeks, the exercises gradually intensified, from small gash bag fire to multiple simultaneous incidents occurring all over the submarine. This tested the damage control organisation to the full as they aimed to control all of the incidents from the wardroom, allowing the Captain the comparative freedom to 'fight' the submarine and concentrate on the developing tactical picture from the control room.

Reports would be published at the end of each day so, we were able to critique our own strengths and weaknesses with the overall aim of getting it right. Everyone was pulling in the right direction, doing their level best to succeed, but inevitably making mistakes. Mistakes were expected and allowed provided that the chap making a mistake learned from it and did not make the same error again.

As I still had to qualify on the SCC, the Captain, to my dismay, decided that the visiting FOST Coxswain should assess me during a whole ship exercise. To this point, I had been closely supervised during all of my training sessions but now, my babysitter was nowhere to be seen as the Coxswain, 'Snowy' Sleet, kept a watchful eye on me during my assessment. As the exercise progressed, I reacted to reports of incidents around the boat. A fire, bizarrely, was the least of my worries, as that only required me to flick three switches and start a pump whereas a hydraulic burst and an electrical failure meant that my Panel was nearly useless. All of the remotely operated valves needed hydraulics and all of the illumination, control and indication required 24 volts, just to do their job. Without both, the SCC was basically a complicated looking chunk of black metal.

Gradually, DCHQ in the wardroom sorted out where the problems lay and directed teams of engineers and electricians to rectify the defects before my panel gradually came back to life and I could start the hydraulic pumps and restore control to the submarine.

After a frantic hour, all of the fires and emergencies had been made safe enough to fall the submarine out from Emergency Stations and for me to breathe a sigh of relief. I was eventually relieved on the SCC, allowing Snowy to debrief my performance during the exercise. I thought I had done ok, there was a lot going on, so keeping track of all of the reports coming in was a considerable challenge. In a quiet corner of the mess, over a cup of coffee, Snowy opened his notebook and started to reel off a list of minor errors, most of which were not operating errors, but more about the way *he* liked to do things. At the end of our chat, he drained his cup and put me out of my misery. He told me that I had exceeded the required standard and could now consider myself qualified, in all respects, to watchkeep on the SCC.

The lads in the mess were very happy. This was not because I was a useful member of society again, but because my qualification meant free beer. This was sort of a tradition and who am I to shy away from tradition?

The beer, however, would have to wait as we were still at sea, underwater and I was officially still on watch. Returning to the control room, I relieved Ian Walton on the Panel for my first watch 'flying-solo' on HMS

Turbulent. Fortunately, there were no more exercises planned so I could settle down and concentrate on my job, without any unwelcome interruptions.

Four weeks into the training, at the end of June 2005, Work Up was suspended so Turbulent could sail eastwards toward Portsmouth to take part in the International Fleet Review, as part of Trafalgar 200 celebrations. This was a welcome relief for us after four weeks of purgatory and we were all looking forward to a run ashore in Pompey, but it was not to be.

Anchored in the Solent surrounded by vessels from around the world, it was truly a splendid sight. Turbulent was positioned in formation with HMS Trafalgar and Trenchant and in the shadow of the French Aircraft Carrier Charles de Gaulle and the Spanish Carrier Principe de Asturias. Unfortunately, all shore leave was cancelled for us as there weren't sufficient boats available to ferry the crew ashore, so we had to amuse ourselves with watching the Son et Luminaire firework celebrations from the after casing whilst the sailors of the nearby ships assaulted the bars, and I dare say the ladies of Portsmouth in a night of drunken revelry.

The following day, after a couple of dress rehearsals, was the highlight of the visit as dressed in best uniforms, we filed onto the casing and lined up to cheer Her Majesty Queen Elizabeth as she sailed past on-board HMS Endurance in company with the Type 22 frigate, HMS Cumberland.

It's not often we get to dress up whilst at sea so after we had been fallen out and the Queen was long over the horizon, many of us took the opportunity for a photo call.

My boss, Rob Goodenough, was fortunate enough to get a visit on-board from his wife. She was a Lieutenant on-board HMS Ocean and as Ocean had a multitude of small craft, she was ferried across for I dare say, a very pleasant afternoon, though I can neither confirm or deny that.

That evening as we remained swinging at anchor in the Solent preparing to slip the following morning, the wind increased in strength.

HMS Trafalgar was not so patient and as the wind increased, she was having difficulty remaining in the same relative position and started to drag her anchor. Her Captain took the difficult decision to break up the party early and steered her out to sea as a collision between nuclear submarines in those confined waters would not make the best of headlines, especially as the Queen was still in the general area.

The next day, it was back to business again as the anchor was retrieved and under full rudder, the Captain conned HMS Turbulent clockwise around the Isle of Wight and headed south into the west bound sea lanes before ringing on the revs and making a good time back to Plymouth to continue with our Basic Operational Sea Training.

There was only a week to go as the exercises ramped up and we scrubbed the boat out for the Final Inspection, when all of the training culminated into a 'Thursday War' as a dozen or so ships, submarines and aircraft took sides and waged a mock war on each other. We, of course, were the good guys defending the fictional country of Brownia against the evil forces of the Ginger navy. We could expect to take considerable 'damage' but after licking our wounds dish out our fair share of mayhem on the bad guys before heading home for tea and medals after winning the 'war'. That was the tried and tested scenario when all of the weeks of training ended and the submarine's crew were assessed to see if we had learned to work as a team and win the war.

HMS Turbulent passed her Basic Operational Sea Training with a 'Satisfactory' pass, that any self-respecting matelot will tell you, is quite good enough. The crew of Turbulent was now operational and permitted to sail for deployment, and if called upon, do it all for real.

As a bit of a reward, we visited Rotterdam for a few days, to let off some steam and relax after a busy few weeks of sea training. It was a difficult surface transit through the English Channel and into the congested traffic separation scheme through the Dover Straits. Up on the bridge for a breath of fresh air and a sneaky phone call, I was truly astounded by the amount of huge shipping passing through this narrow channel between Dover and Calais. Whilst cross-channel ferries played chicken with super tankers, a small, seemingly insignificant black blob was stuck in the middle slowly making her way towards the entrance of the Hook of Holland. That presented its own challenges. I had previously no idea just how large, the Port of Rotterdam was, but with the help of a river pilot to give precise navigational direction, it still took several hours before we were safely secured alongside.

With all of the usual services that included shore power, telephone lines and fresh water attached, the Coxswain granted leave. People quickly emerged from messes and bunk spaces in their creased up civilian clothes carrying a holdall, making their way to the main access hatch at the back of the control room. Forming a human chain, we passed bags up through the hatch and onto the casing where a number of Dutch buses were waiting to ferry us to the hotels in downtown Rotterdam.

The journey to didn't take long and within the hour, I was checked into my hotel room, showered, changed and back into the hotel bar for the traditional first drink in a foreign port. A plan of action was then formulated that involved getting some food before getting mightily drunk. It had been a hard slog to get this far and everyone needed to let off a bit of steam. The submarine was alongside for a week and during that time, I only had two obligations; one was a duty, the day before sailing and the other, was a 'Dolphins' presentation to a handful of newly-qualified submariners in the officers hotel. This had been designated a three-line-whip, meaning everyone had been ordered to attend. Personally, I was quite happy to go, as it was usually quite a cheery occasion, followed by a bit of a party as the ship's company gladly welcomed new submariners into the brotherhood.

I had no issues with the duty either. It was always better, in my mind, to be duty on either the first night or the last night, so as not to spoil the 'holiday'. The last night meant that I had time to stow my kit, make my bed up with clean linen, and ensure that all of my stuff was washed and put away before the remainder of the crew returned, the following morning. The other advantage was that I would not have a hangover when we sailed.

However, on this first night, with food very much on the agenda, we traipsed from bar to bar looking for somewhere to eat. This turned out to be a false errand as during the course of the evening I learned the two phrases of a 'successful' foreign visit; 'Eating is cheating' and 'No sleeping on tour'. This was bad, at the age of forty-three and generous in my proportions, I had learned that I *needed* both, so, as the evening was starting to get a bit messy, I got my round in and surreptitiously left the bar on the pretence that I was off to the loo. Passing a Burger King, I decided that I needed to satisfy my basic human need for sustenance and in my inebriated state, ordered enough food for the entire mess and then proceeded to devour it. Now stuffed full of burgers, nuggets and fries and carrying a huge bucket of Coke, I staggered back to the hotel and flopped into bed exhausted.

The following morning at breakfast, my decision to retire from the battle early proved to be a good one, as I was now ready to fight again whereas some of the younger lads still hadn't surfaced. Stories started to emerge of a brawl that had broken out in a nightclub between some young local lads and our lot. One of our chaps had been arrested and had been locked up for the night, so not a great start.

After the predictably slow morning, a small gang of us made our way into town to a conference room in the officer's hotel. The Coxswain ticked off names as we arrived and invited us to get a glass of sparking white wine from a few silver trays at the back of the room.

Chairs were arranged in rows facing a single table at the front. This was covered with a white ensign and decorated with six half pint glasses full of

Pussers Rum. Each of these glasses had a small gold badge immersed at the bottom of the fiery brown spirit. The six chaps who were to be awarded their 'Dolphins' stood nervously in a line facing us, whilst the rest of the ship's company slowly filed into the room and took their seats.

Eventually, the Captain stood and made the traditional, stirring speech about welcoming new submariners into the brotherhood of the Submarine Service. He reminded everyone of the hard work and dedication that each of the graduates had accomplished to gain the coveted submarine badge before individually shaking the hand of each one in turn and handing him the glass of dark rum. The tradition was to down the drink in one go, catching your reward in your teeth, whilst at the same time trying to suppress the instinctive gag reflex. The Coxswain stood ready with a bucket and was very nearly called upon as a couple of the younger lads seemed to turn green. To their credit, and our disappointment, they all managed to keep their drink down.

On the third day, Wal, Scotty, the chef and a few of the other on-board Arsenal fans had decided to board a train to Amsterdam to watch the footie. The Gunners were playing in a pre-season tournament at the Amsterdam Arena. As there seemed to be a crowd of football fans belonging to a variety of different teams also going, I invited myself along. Wal had a spare Arsenal shirt I could borrow, but as any self-respecting football fan might tell you, watching another team is one thing, but to wear their shirt is nothing short of being unfaithful. An England shirt, though, was perfectly acceptable. Heading into Amsterdam early, by train, we decided to bomb-burst into smaller groups for a bit of sight-seeing before meeting up at a rather entertaining bar called 'Teasers', for a bit of lunch, a couple of drinks and a bit of table dancing by some rather lovely ladies. One of the lads, a young Aston Villa fan, by the name of 'Bazz' Rose, paid rather a lot of money for a shot of tequila that somehow he managed to lick off one of the waitresses breasts, complete with salt and lime, lucky git!

After a couple of hours of silliness, we made our way back to the railway station, for the short journey to the stadium which was the most imposing football stadium I had ever visited. From ground level, it appeared monstrous and even boasted a car park under the pitch, how mad is that? This consequently meant that we had an absolute mountain of steps to climb, just to get to the pitch side. Unfortunately, our seats were somewhere near the back of the stand, so, completely knackered, we trudged upwards until we found our seats in something like Row ZZ. I half expected to see oxygen masks dropping from the roof, that we could almost touch. After a while, I started to recover enough to appreciate the view. We were sighted high up on the corner of the pitch with a beautiful uninterrupted view of the entire stadium.

As the tournament was spread out over two days, apart from Arsenal and Ajax, FC Porto and the Boca Juniors were also participating, so, over the course of the afternoon we were treated to two ninety-minute friendly games of international footie.

After an entertaining afternoon, my bladder was just about fit to burst. A trip to the toilet would have meant missing half of a game, descending, and re-climbing all of those steps again and I still hadn't fully recovered from the first time. Concentrating on the footie helped to take my mind off it. With my bladder finally emptied, we made our way back to the station and after a short wait, headed back to Rotterdam for an early night as I was duty the following day and needed to pack my bag and check out of the hotel early in the morning.

On the day of sailing, after a busy but uneventful duty getting the submarine ready for sea, I had a bit of time to relax in the mess whilst the rest of the lads struggled to stow their kit, empty their pockets and get themselves back into sea-going mode again.

Alongside in Plymouth a week later, after an uneventful surface passage through the English Channel, all thoughts of work-up were put behind us as we concentrated our efforts on re-storing the submarine in readiness for another Arctic patrol.

Pallet after pallet of food and spare gear arrived on the jetty during the next couple of weeks. Even after more than twenty years in the submarine service, it never ceased to amaze me where everything got stowed. I had responsibility for the loading and storing of literally hundreds of oxygen candles and CO_2 absorption canisters, not to mention embarking more than eighty-two-thousand litres of diesel fuel for the diesel generators. Everybody was busy and everyone's work seemed, to them, much more important than everyone else's as people vied and bargained for extra manpower to get their stores into the boat and stowed.

It was a logistical nightmare; every spare corner had boxes of spare equipment piled up whilst false decks of tinned food and CO_2 canisters appeared in some of the lesser used compartments. In the escape compartments, there were dedicated stowages for many of the oxygen candles, but we needed to find temporary homes for at least another eight-hundred. There was talk at the stowage committee meetings of putting one underneath the head of each mattress, but thankfully, it didn't come to that.

Whilst manually rigging the ten-inch diameter rubber hoses to embark diesel fuel, I felt something bad happen in my groin area. These were seriously heavy lumps of armoured rubber hose with big brass connections at either end. Using my small group of lads and the lifting capacity of a crane, we slung them onto the casing but then had to manually handle them through the hatch to the connection point at the bottom. I knew I had strained something, as it hurt when I coughed, but I persevered, as we needed to get the boat ready for sea.

With a fuelling barge alongside, we filled the tanks to capacity with thousands of litres of diesel fuel. What a shame the barge didn't give 'Green Shield Stamps' as I would probably have had enough to buy a small car.

In other departments, spare pumps and motors were being brought on-board and lashed behind ladders. A party of sailors, detailed by the Coxswain, formed a chain gang and passed fresh and frozen food into the submarine until the freezers were packed to capacity and we had sufficient food on-board to sustain the whole crew for three months underwater.

Simultaneously, I had another boat-stopper. A routine sample of escape breathing air called 'BIBS' I had submitted to the lab, failed miserably with a high content of potentially lethal carbon dioxide. This meant that I now had a race against the clock to drain down the system, rig up some charging hoses and then send another sample to the dockyard laboratory. This was not technically demanding, but a very noisy and time-consuming evolution. Draining four-thousand pounds of high-pressure air is so loud it makes your teeth rattle and conscious thought, virtually impossible.

Despite the urgency, there was only so much that could realistically be achieved in one day. 'BIBS', once drained had to be charged extremely slowly, which allowed me, after working all night, to skive off for the afternoon and pick up my brand new motorbike.

My boss, Lt Rob Goodenough, wasn't happy, but what was he going to do, shave my head and send me to sea? Fuck him! There was a sort of urban myth that, as a Chief Petty Officer, you could manage your own time and I was doing just that. I spent a good twenty minutes showing my lad, MEM 'Linda' Nolan, exactly what I was doing and precisely what I wanted him to do and like an excited child, I skipped off to pick up my new toy.

My new motorbike was a brand spanking new Suzuki Bandit 1200 in dark metallic blue. After completing the formalities, I gingerly took it for a ride to get the feel of it. It went like hot snot. I was cautious not to beast it straight away, but out on the A38 Parkway, heading east, I gently eased the throttle open and felt the 1200cc machine smoothly accelerate as the bike took charge and propelled me effortlessly towards the ton. At that point, common sense kicked in as I approached Marsh Mills roundabout. Taking the fourth exit, I reversed course and headed home at a more sedate speed, making progress but not exactly slouching either. Safely back at home, I did what every new biker does with a new toy and filled a bucket. Using a new sponge, I gave my new baby its first bath.

The following morning, I was back at work again. 'Linda' had worked well topping up the 'BIBS' bottles allowing me to take a sample and get it off to the lab. It was now Tuesday and the boat was planning to sail on Thursday, it was going to be tight.

My groin injury appeared to be getting worse. I had largely forgotten about it as I was too busy trying to get the boat ready for sea. Calling into the sickbay in HMS Drake in mid-October, I invited a naval doctor to stick his hands down my pants. I am sure he didn't want to feel my bits any more than I wanted him to, but he knew exactly what he was doing. Instructing me to cough, he nodded knowingly and withdrew his hands, ripped off his surgical gloves and told me to get dressed. Once properly attired and sat next to his desk, the doctor explained that I had ripped a muscle in the right side of my groin causing an inguinal hernia. I had never heard of it. The doc explained that every time I coughed, my intestine was trying to push itself through a hole in the ripped bit of my muscle. This was going to need a minor operation to basically whack a bit of gauze in there to patch up the hole. After much tinkering around with his computer, he provisionally gave me a date for the procedure in February 2006, about five months away.

Back on-board, the news was not well received. My mate, Ian Walton, was due to leave the boat shortly and this was meant to be his last trip. Unfortunately, for Wal, the trip came at a really poor time as unbeknown to me; he had some significant domestic troubles at home. Despite my impending operation, Wal pleaded with me to go to sea in his place. This was a huge request as the boat was due to sail a couple of days later, and would not see daylight until a week before Christmas. Obviously, I couldn't answer him immediately as I needed to talk with Anita, who had not been too clever herself and had been prescribed medication for depression.

As it turned out, she seemed quite happy to have a bit of peace and quiet, but was confusingly a little tearful as I hastily started getting the kit together that I would need for the next couple of months.

As a bit of an afterthought, and requiring a project to help pass the time, I approached the education centre and in the hope of adding a science to my maths and English qualifications, enquired about taking a physics GCSE whilst we were away on patrol. As usual, the education staff were very helpful and after lending me some self-study books, I was assured that the sealed examination paper would be delivered to the submarine before we sailed.

On a last-minute dash into Plymouth for 'essentials' like decent coffee and sweeties, I also bought another couple of physics books as I wouldn't have a teacher on patrol. Of course, what I forgot to appreciate was, there were loads of suitably qualified engineers on-board who, unlike me, had taken the trouble at school to buckle down and learn.

With the submarine now fully stored with food and in all respects, ready for sea, HMS Turbulent finally left Plymouth and slowly made her way out into the English Channel, rounding Land's End early in the evening. Taking advantage of the sunset, I managed to scam a visit to the radar mast well for a breath of fresh air and a sneaky last phone call, as I knew we would be out of range of a mobile cell until just before Christmas. Phone calls were sort of forbidden whilst we were at sea, as it gave the opportunity for the crew to divulge the boat's position. We were not hidden of course, there was a fair bit of shipping on the horizon and I dare say the satellites and various radars were also keeping a watchful eye over us. So, after a final farewell to the missus, I made my way back through the maze of ladders and holes in the fin before reporting, "Chief Stoker below," to ship control and disappearing down the ladder in search of a warming cup of coffee and a bite to eat. Everyone was quite relaxed and starting to settle into a sea-going routine as we gradually made steady progress towards our allocated diving position.

Later in the evening and with a good bit of water under the keel, the submarine went to Diving Stations. After all of the necessary checks, Turbulent, once again, slipped quietly beneath the Irish Sea and continued her submerged transit north. Gradually over the next few days, we progressed further and further north as the crew adopted an operational mode of quietness. As was the norm, many people walked around the boat in training shoes, as they were far more comfortable and infinitely quieter than our clumpy uniform issue steaming boots.

As the water temperature dropped, condensation started to form on the cold surfaces of the hull, which caused it to 'rain' making the deck slippery. This was quite an inconvenience but tents of plastic sheeting were rigged to catch the drips and channel the condensate into plastic buckets.

Successfully clearing the 'Faslane Triangle' without a defect significant enough to warrant us going alongside, we crept further and further north towards the permanent ice pack. This was a familiar hunting ground for me, having now spent more than half of my life quietly sneaking around the Arctic Circle, Norwegian Sea and Barents Sea. Everyone was on top of their game and conditioned to keep the noise down. Rubber sheeting was placed on the backs of ladders; doors were tied open to prevent them slamming and the massive watertight hydraulic doors either side of the reactor compartment were left open as when they shut, the thud could be potentially heard by an enemy submarine. This made movement around the submarine considerably easier. Everyone spoke in hushed tones, whilst in the sound room, the sonar operators kept a listening ear to the outside world. If our sonar could 'hear' what was occurring inside the boat, then there was a high degree of likelihood that we would be detected and that would never do.

That said, we all made our own entertainment where we could. There was always a continuous, quiet chattering amongst the operators. Quizzes were set between departments and there was always a movie playing in the mess, before everything was cleared away and the tables set for mealtimes. Routine made the tedium go quicker and food was often the highlight of the day. Mealtimes also heralded the watch change and an opportunity to chat to your mates in the opposite watch about any on-going work that needed to be progressed whilst you were sleeping.

My daily routine would typically see me going on watch at 1am for the six-hour night shift. As we had the luxury of four qualified senior rates, there was only a requirement for me to spend an hour and a half on the SCC. I always tried to bag the first stint, which served firstly to wake me up and allow the mess to clear of all of the off-going watchkeepers. At 2:30am, after I'd been relieved, I would then descend from the darkened control room, allow my eyes to accustom to light again, get a coffee and set myself up at the far end of the mess with my physics books. This usually gave me about three hours of uninterrupted study, following the GCSE syllabus.

At around 6am, I would clear away my books, do a quick set of rounds of my machinery spaces before helping the other lads to set up the mess for breakfast, scamming a sneaky bacon roll from the galley in the process. Little by little, the bleary-eyed on-coming watch would emerge from the bunk space and sit down for breakfast. I had a vested interest in looking after my opposite number, CMEM(L) 'Jakey' Foran, so I always had a cup of tea waiting for him and stood hovering to serve his breakfast. Keeping him happy, allowed me to conduct my handover over the breakfast table whilst he tucked into his bacon and eggs. This meant that as soon as he had eaten, I could 'go deep' and get to bed.

Even after acclimatising myself to working nights, my best sleep of the day was always in the forenoon, after typically watching a recorded episode of 'Lost' in my bunk. Bedtime on a submarine is absolutely sacred. It is just about the only private time the crew has, apart from sitting on the loo. The golden rule was always, if the curtain was drawn and the bunk light was off, disturb only on pain of death or in the event of a dire submarine emergency. If a bunk light was on, it was considered acceptable to speak through the curtain in hushed tones. Under no circumstances would anybody ever pull the curtain back, as they could never be sure what might confront them. Everybody had their own bedtime ritual which might have been listening to music, watching a movie, looking at photographs of loved ones, or flicking through a girlie mag and subsequently dealing with the resultant stiffy. So, if the curtain was drawn, leave well alone.

I would generally be awoken by one of the lads, prodding me through the curtain at around midday. This would give me ample time to wash and grab a light lunch of soup and rolls before resuming the watch.

The afternoon watch from 1pm to 7pm, still required me to do another hour and a half on the panel, but I was not too fussed about the batting order as the work I had lined up could be done at any time during the watch. During the afternoon, I liked to keep up with my paperwork and planned maintenance. I always conducted an in-depth set of rounds, making notes before detailing the lads to sort out my little niggles. As we were all in the same boat, I didn't make a song and dance about stowage, maintenance routines and cleanliness, just so long as when I told someone to do something, it was done before my next set of rounds. I always adopted a cuddly and laid-back attitude to life on-board, but occasionally, I did get very ratty when the lads took the piss and mugged me off. This would invariably result in a private one-way discussion with the offender in the air purification space, explaining the error of his ways.

Coming off watch at 7pm, I was usually not too tired, so I would enjoy a leisurely meal before climbing into my rack. This sleep, generally only lasted about two or three hours and by 10pm, I was usually wide awake. At this time of the day, I attempted to catch up with my personal admin. As the showers were usually quiet at that time of night, I indulged in a very naughty, 'Hollywood' shower, shave and deal with anything else that needed brushing, cutting or trimming. This was generally discouraged, but getting properly washed on a submarine and dressed in clean clothing, was one of life's little pleasures. I would then gather up my dirty clothes and occasionally my bedding and stuff everything into a pillowcase or a net bag for washing. Freshly showered and shaved in clean clothes was always a good feeling. Due to restrictions with the controlled atmosphere, deodorant was banned, so smelling of slightly scented soap or shower gel, I would generally watch the end of a movie in the mess and drink coffee before 'one o'clockers' was served. This was usually a bowl of lumpy soup or anything that was left from the evening meal. This would provide enough sustenance for those working through the night to survive until breakfast.

With the routine firmly established, the time appeared to whizz by. I was making steady progress with my studying and had started practicing some old physics GCSE papers and getting 'Ships', my boss, to mark them. The exam was scheduled for the week before we arrived home, in December 2005, therefore, I had plenty of time to brush up on any perceived weak areas.

Quite a few of the lads were studying GCSE English and maths classes in readiness for their exam, but I was the only one stupid enough to be studying on his own and without formal instruction. That said, my confidence was growing daily. What I hadn't realised was, as an engineer, I had been practicing the subject all of my working life, so I had the better part of twenty-seven years of experience, therefore, when the exam date was set, I wasn't in the least bit nervous. Perversely, I was actually doing this for fun. If I completely flunked it, the only thing hurt, would be my pride.

To give the officers credit, the exam, when it came, was done as properly as it was possible to, in a steel tube, six-hundred feet below the surface. All of the candidates gathered in the senior rates mess with their pens, pencils, rulers and rubbers. I was sat alone in the alcove next to the TV, not that it made any difference, there was nobody's shoulder I could look over to gain a few vital marks, I was on my own.

As it turned out, the exam was a doddle. My studying had been worth the effort as I could answer all of the questions. Therefore, after two hours of writing and drawing diagrams, without the usual coursework, I was content that I had done sufficient to earn the maximum permitted Grade C, but it would be a while before I would find out, as the submarine was still at sea. 'Ships' did have a look through my paper and proclaimed that he considered I had done enough. There was one stupid schoolboy 'RTFQ' error where I had failed to 'read the fucking question' properly resulting in me dropping a few marks. Bugger!

About seven weeks since leaving Devonport, HMS Turbulent quietly left her secret patrol areas, and slowly made her way south. This time, the Captain opted to skirt to the west of Ireland and clearing the datum, put his foot down, driving the boat home, as if he had stolen it.

All of the patrol records were collated, bagged, sealed and serialised. These would need to be disembarked before we could be allowed back alongside in Plymouth. Everyone was looking forward to getting home, Christmas was only a week away and all thoughts were now turned towards the festive season and seeing the family. I knew Anita was planning a 'Welcome Home' party for me, but we still needed to get the old girl safely home again.

Turning towards the east, we entered the busy waters of the English Channel and prepared to surface the submarine for the first time in eight weeks. This honour fell to me as I happened to be sat in front of the SCC when the Captain commanded, "Ship Control, standby to surface." This was followed by the Ship Controller, Mick Cudmore, piping over main broadcast, "Standby to surface, drain down and open one, two, three and four LP master blows, line up ventilation state yellow, prepare the blower for running." This signalled a flurry of excited activity throughout the submarine, as the lads lined up the ventilation system and the sailors and officer of the watch dressed in their full red Gore-Tex suits, preparing to con the submarine from the bridge, once the submarine was safely on the surface, and opened up.

With everything complete and all of the required reports made, Mick turned to the Captain and made his report. Making an all round sweep on the search periscope to ensure that there was nothing close, the Captain ordered "Surface." Mick turned to me and ordered, "Panel, using a five-second blow, surface." I leaned forward and flicked the four switches that opened valves to allow pressurised air into the ballast tanks. As I was doing this, Mick made a pipe, "Surfacing now, surfacing now." The boat shuddered slightly as two-hundred and seventy-six bar of high-pressure air displaced the water in the ballast tanks. The submarine took on a bow up angle as the helmsman pulled the wheel towards him and 'flew' the boat towards the surface.

On seeing the forward casing and the after casing through the periscope, the Captain ordered, "Officer of the Watch; on the surface, open up." This command gave the young Lieutenant in the conning tower, the authority to open the upper hatch and proceed onto the very cold and wet bridge for the first time in two months. Although I did not know it at the time, that would be my last ever time submerged in a submarine.

Safely on the surface, off the Cornish coast near Falmouth, the casing was opened to allow the crew to call wives, girlfriends and in some cases, boyfriends. Anita seemed very excited to hear from me, she told me that she'd done all of the Christmas shopping, erected no less than three Christmas trees in our modest three-bedroomed semi and was all set for the party in three days' time. She went on to say that she had spent an absolute fortune buying gifts for all of our guests and that she couldn't wait for me to come home. There was something in her voice however, that had me worried. I couldn't quantify it, but I knew something wasn't right.

After removing the towed array and disembarking the patrol records at 'Charlie' buoy, HMS Turbulent arrived back alongside in Devonport early in the evening. After the formalities and domestic routines had been taken care of, the XO granted leave and like excited children, we clambered out of the main access hatch and into the cold winter's night to meet our families. Anita was waiting on the jetty.

Anita was as excited as I was, but she had a surprise up her sleeve. She suggested that we first went to collect my motorbike, which had been stored in a friend's garage, a short distance from home. Thoughtfully, she had brought my bike keys, helmet, jacket and gloves and within ten-minutes of getting off the boat, she was pulling-up outside a garage in the Manadon area of Plymouth.

Positioning the car headlights onto the garage door, Anita gave me the key for the white metal up and over door. As I opened it, she shouted, "Happy Christmas, darling." All I could see in the glow of the headlights was my dark blue Suzuki Bandit facing me on its centre stand, pretty much where I'd left it. The only noticeable difference was that it now had two balloons tied to the handlebars. Surely, she couldn't have been presenting my own bike back to me for Christmas? Entering the garage to inspect my machine, I noticed a package sitting on the seat wrapped in Christmas paper and on a quick inspection of the bike, noticed immediately that my brand new '55' plate had been replaced with a personalised registration 'P9LUG' which was as close to my naval nickname of 'Plug' as she could find. It was brilliant! Anita then urged me to open the package which was clearly a picture frame protected with bubble wrap. After carefully unwrapping the parcel, I was presented with a wonderful painting of my bike that had been drawn by my mate, Ian Walton, as a 'thank you' for going to sea in his place. What a lovely surprise.

The bike started, after a little coaxing, and donning my helmet, jacket and gloves, I slowly followed Anita home, getting the beast properly warmed up, only zipping past her for the last few hundred yards to arrive onto the drive first.

Back home after a long absence, my possessions looked strangely unfamiliar. The house was immaculately clean and decorated for Christmas. There was a large Christmas tree in the hallway and another in the lounge, though this one had masses of presents underneath it. In the kitchen/diner, another smaller tree completed the artificial arboretum. We were due to be having a Christmas/Welcome Home party two days later and Anita was well ahead of the game.

As my body-clock was conditioned to working overnight, by 8pm, I was yawning my head off. I was duty the following day, but I still had a niggling feeling that something was not right. I couldn't put my finger on it exactly, but Anita was not herself at all. Physically she seemed fine, but I suspected the anti-depressants she had been taking for the last few months, were not working as well as they once had. She seemed to be experiencing periods of euphoria followed immediately by periods of deep depression. I assumed that coming home had upset her routine. It was strange for both of us.

The following day, I was duty but I was also required to oversee a full day of exercises, which were designed to get the ship's company out of sea-going mode and back into a harbour frame of mind. The crew had worked really hard during the previous couple of months, but now there was a predictable slow down towards the Christmas stand-off period. With a reduced amount of people on-board, we had to be certain that they all knew what to do in the event of an emergency.

In short, it was a busy day for me. As *the* Chief Stoker, I would typically grab a poor unsuspecting soul, take him to a remote part of the boat and inform him quietly that the electrical motor in front of him was sparking and spewing smoke. After presenting him with the exercise scenario, I would then stand back, start my stopwatch and take notes on his initial reactions and the speed in which the attack party would arrive. After each incident, I would then debrief the teams, offer praise when it was warranted, but as was more often the case, critique and detail the errors to all involved. This was not a time to protect those who had screwed up, but to show them the error of their ways. A few minutes later, in a different location, we did it all again and kept on doing it until I was confident that, should a real incident occur, the teams had all the skills to effectively deal with the incident. At 1pm, the teams changed over and we began again until 7pm by which time, all of the ship's company had dealt with a fire, flood or an intruder alert and were confident with their own responsibilities.

Whilst I was debriefing the MEO, in the wardroom, I received a distressing phone call from Anita, pleading with me to come home. I explained that I was required on-board and actually very busy, but assured her that I would be home early the following morning. 'Hank' asked me if I *needed* to go home, but that would have meant somebody else, who had also returned from sea, having to cover the duty. As far as I was aware, everyone could have been experiencing the same sort of emotional difficulties.

About an hour later, I was in the wardroom briefing the officer of the day when my friend, Anne-Marie, called. She was quite blunt, "I don't care what you have to do, get yourself off that submarine now; Anita has had an accident and has been taken to hospital."

Obviously, I was quite shocked. The navigating officer I had been briefing, made an instant decision and phoned for a taxi. He said, "There is no way you are staying on-board tonight, chief," and sat me down with a cup of tea to await the arrival of my taxi. About twenty seconds later, the upper deck trot sentry made a brief announcement over the main broadcast, "Chief stoker, casing; taxi waiting." Bloody hell, that was quick. About three minutes from Anne-Marie's call and my cab was already on the jetty. 'Navs' followed me up onto the casing only for me to find another friend, Gary Bools, who was a self-employed black cab driver. He and his girlfriend Lisa had been with Anita at the time of the accident and he had taken it upon himself to come and get me, whilst Lisa called Anne-Marie for advice. "Mate, Anita has had an accident and has been taken to hospital. Can you be quick? I'm shitting myself here; some twat's just given me a nuclear badge." Gary was a civilian and did not understand the nuclear stuff at all. He probably envisioned his balls shrivelling up but, in a time of immense worry, it caused a bit of light relief.

Gary didn't hang around getting me to the hospital, nor did he accept any payment, though I did promise to buy him a few beers later. I found a heavily bandaged Anita sitting in A&E with Gary's girlfriend, Lisa, as she waited to be seen by the medical professionals. Her injuries obviously weren't life-threatening or she would have been seen immediately.

We waited a couple of hours before we were finally ushered into a cubicle and Anita's wounds could be properly treated. As it transpired, Anita had been preparing a meal when she lost concentration whilst chatting to Lisa and sliced her hand quite badly. The nurse confirmed that her injuries were only superficial but she was more concerned about Anita's mental state, as she was very distressed. Properly bandaged, we were escorted to a secure ward where we were eventually seen by a duty psychiatrist. The shrink didn't actually appear to do anything. I rather expected him to wave a magic wand and make it all better, but he contented himself with a little chat before I was allowed to take her home. Anne-Marie, however, had other ideas and instructed me to collect night things, clean undies and wash gear for us both as we were *ordered* to stay with her for a night or two.

After a relaxing brandy back at Anne-Marie's house, we all went up to bed. Despite all of the excitement of the past few hours, I fell asleep instantly. The next morning, as I awoke, Anita was still sleeping but hearing movement downstairs, I threw on some clothes on and found Anne-Marie bustling around in the kitchen, not looking her best. Unbeknown to me, Anita had had a restless night and consequently whilst I slept the sleep of the dead, she had spent a couple of hours placating Anita until she was calm enough to sleep. Anne-Marie, by this time was knackered and undoubtedly regretting her charitable offer. She informed me that we needed to get Anita to see her doctor urgently. She also wanted me to see a naval doctor, as she was concerned about my current stress levels.

On the stroke of 8am, she called Stirling Road Health Centre in St Budeaux, and demanded firmly, but politely, that Anita be able to see her doctor, as a matter of urgency.

At the surgery, the lady doctor, who at this point knew nothing of the excitement from the previous evening, listened intently whilst constantly observing Anita. The doctor suggested that she pop up to Derriford Hospital again and have a chat with their specialist psychiatric team in the Glenbourne Unit. Anita was understandably very reluctant and probably a bit scared, but agreed, after a bit of persuasion from Anne-Marie and myself.

Arriving at the hospital a short time later, we were shown into a room with comfortable seats and soft furnishings where a nice woman started to ask Anita what had been troubling her recently. Anita was not herself and became increasingly agitated. Out of character, she got up to leave and tried the door, but finding it locked, tried the window, but again found it locked. Her mental state was visibly deteriorating but she could not possibly come to any physical harm in this 'padded cell'. That did not stop her though; she ripped the curtains off the wall in sheer frustrated anger. The psychiatric nurse had seen enough and pressed a silent alarm to summon assistance. The intention had been that Anita stay on the unit voluntarily for a night or so, away from the pressures of home. After displaying some naked aggression, all bets were off and she was subsequently sectioned under the Mental Health Act.

I was devastated. In the space of twenty-four hours, my absolute world had been turned upside down. Anne-Marie was becoming increasingly concerned about *my* state of health and using her unique persuasive skills, made me go and consult a naval doctor. I didn't consider there was anything wrong with me; I was just understandably concerned for my missus. The doctor agreed and considered that getting me back to work and into some semblance of normality was the best medicine. He was right, what I actually needed, was to be around a load of matelots taking the piss out of one another, just to take my mind off things.

Back at the hospital, Anita had been dosed up with some medication and was now a lot calmer. A psychiatrist who examined her again, diagnosed that she was suffering from a Bipolar disorder and that her symptoms were typical of the condition. After a few days, when the medication started to kick in, I was permitted to take her for a walk within the hospital grounds. This was successful and although very fragile, she continued to improve. The next reward was about eight hours leave on Christmas Day in 2005. My saintly friend, Anne-Marie, invited us back to her house and cooked a rather splendid Christmas dinner for seven of us, including her mum, dad and sister Claire. This must have been really difficult for them, but as a good catholic family, they opened their arms to us.

The following week, Anita was allowed home for the night and this was soon followed by a weekend at home. To start with, I found that I could not let her out of my sight and I would be following her and just monitoring her moods. We had a couple of blips, but generally speaking, she started to show signs of improvement. In the meantime, NPFS, the Naval Personnel and Family Services called, asking me what help I needed. I am afraid I was a bit brusque with them. I had been successfully married for twenty years without their interference and had always detested the malingerers who had pleaded on the sympathy of the, cardigan-wearing, hippy, social workers so that they didn't have to go to sea. As it turned out, they could provide a lot more than just a shoulder to cry on. They could offer many things from financial advice to marriage guidance and in Anita's case, they offered a befriending service. Essentially, once a week, a woman would visit for a cup of tea and suggest outings to the shops or perhaps lunch, which would take the pressure off me and give Anita something to look forward to.

In February 2006, the date eventually arrived for my hernia operation. The minor procedure was due to be carried out at the Nuffield Hospital next to the main Derriford Hospital in Plymouth. This was an outpatient's appointment and I was told that I needed to be prepped for surgery by 8am. Anita, who was much more back to her old self, dropped me off at the hospital and left me to it. As requested, I was wearing loose-fitting tracksuit pants and also a baggy rugby top. After introducing myself to the receptionist, I was asked to take a seat with some of the other pre-op hernia patients in a waiting room, whilst the surgeon and his team got ready for a busy morning of surgical butchery.

Eventually, a nurse called us forward and I was ushered towards a rather comfortable looking reclining chair and after drawing some curtains around my area, I was told to strip off and dress in a theatre gown that did little to protect my modesty. One by one the assembled patients were visited by the surgeon, and after signing the consent form, were injected by the nurse and sent off to noddy land before being wheeled away. It didn't take them long to get around to me and after I had signed the form, the nurse, prepping a syringe, said, "Small prick," which I thought was a bit rude, as she stuck me with the sleep inducing drug.

I thought she had injected me with a duff batch of the anaesthetic, as I was feeling a bit drowsy, but nothing else. The nurse came over to see me and only then did I begin to realise that I had missed the whole show and was now waking up in recovery. After a short time, a trolley came around laden with tea and sandwiches, which reminded me that I had not eaten since the previous evening and was starving. Therefore, when asked, I scrounged as much free food as I could get away with.

After lunch, I was invited to gingerly get dressed in my loose fitting clothes and remain in my reclining seat until Anita arrived a short time later to collect me. Back home, I now had several weeks of sick leave whilst my wound healed, which suited me just fine. Since returning from patrol, nothing at all had gone right and I needed some respite to get my head back in order.

After eventually being passed fit to return to work, I'd been so bored that I was really looking forward to getting back to the submarine. After a coffee and a bit of a catch up with the lads in the mess, I went to survey my domain. HMS Turbulent had been alongside since returning from patrol, and was now starting to ramp up to going back to sea again. Frankly, by this time, I *needed* to get back to sea again, 2006 had been a shit year so far and there was a sort of comfort in routine. This wasn't to be though and by 10am I was in the wardroom having a chat with 'Ships'. Lieutenant Goodenough explained, that in my absence, it had been decided, since Anita's breakdown, that my efficiency at sea would most likely be impaired by me constantly worrying about her and that she would also benefit from having me home.

I must say, I felt that the rug had been pulled from underneath me. To be removed from a submarine is never a very good career move, but the more I thought about it, the more I understood that it was the right decision. He went on to explain that I would leave the submarine at the end of the day and join HMS Raleigh Fire-fighting School the following morning, as a temporary measure, as they were short of a submarine fire-fighting instructor.

Following this life-changing disclosure, I now had about four hours to hand over my section to Petty Officer Andrew 'Den' Denley. That was four hours to cover what was normally achieved in a minimum of two-weeks. Talk about a shit handover; the best I could do was to take him for an extended lunch break in the canteen with all of my work books and talk him through it without distraction. Finally, I gave him my phone number and invited him to call me with any queries. This was good news for Den as he stood a good chance of being selected for Chief Petty Officer, if he did a good job in my wake.

At the end of the day, after saying goodbye to my shipmates, with great sadness, I left HMS Turbulent and struggled home with a bag full of kit.

HMS RALEIGH

16th May 2006 to 3rd October 2006

The following morning, I arrived at the main gate of HMS Raleigh on my motorbike, loaded to the gunwales with overalls, a white shirt, trousers, boots, shoes and my Gore-Tex uniform jacket. As I had received no joining instructions, I'd guessed what I might need, based on my earlier visits to the Fire School. The school itself was situated in Triumph Squadron, nicely out of the way, in a far-flung corner of HMS Raleigh.

As jobs went, this one had the potential to be brilliant. A chief stoker likes nothing better than setting fire to things and then standing back watching other people attack the blaze before ripping them up for arse paper when they got it all wrong.

I had already discovered that I had a natural flair for teaching, so after getting used to the manner in which I had left HMS Turbulent, and accepting that I was only filling in a gap, I vowed silently to enjoy this job, not knowing how long it might last for.

Finding the staff changing room, I transformed myself from a commuting motorcyclist into a naval rating again. Dressed in 'number 5's which consisted of black shoes, black uniform trousers, a white uniform shirt displaying my Dolphins an inch above my left breast pocket and the epaulettes of a Chief Petty Officer, I went to work.

My first point of contact was a sit-down meeting with my new boss Lieutenant Commander Byrne who was the Training Officer at the Fire School. At first appearances, he seemed like a nice bloke, fairly quiet, but comfortable with his position. This was a very pleasant 'getting to know you' sort of meeting, which involved coffee, smiles and handshakes as he tried to get the measure of this chief stoker who had unexpectedly landed in his lap. After chatting about personal stuff for a while, we were joined by Warrant Officer 'Taff' Jones and after the formal introductions, I followed him across the corridor to his smaller office where we had a more *no nonsense* chat.

Clearly, from the outset, the warrant officer gave me the impression that he did not suffer fools and was obviously very proud of his seemingly meteoric rise to the top non-commissioned rate in the armed forces. My first impression of him was not very good at all.

I am not a bad judge of character, as a rule and generally, my first impressions are not too far off the mark. I cannot abide arrogance and this fella was demonstrating it in spades. It was clear from our introductory chat that we were not destined to get along. Having successfully held the rate of chief petty officer for nearly six years, theoretically, I was only one promotion away from sitting behind his desk and he didn't like that one bit. All of the other instructors were POs, which left a bit of a promotional air gap between him and *his* lads. He was very proud of the lads and made it clear that he did not want me, as the token submariner chief, upsetting his precious apple cart. I was given a training regime and instructed to assume parity with the other instructors. This pissed me off enormously, I had worked long and hard during my twenty-seven years and had earned the right to be called "Chief." He explained, for matters of discipline, that he already had a 'Chief Stoker' and although he was significantly junior to me, *he* was the Training Chief and would effectively tell me where I would be working on a day-to-day basis. He actually turned out to be a nice bloke, who was trying hard to make a good impression. He sympathised with my position, but not enough that he wanted to swap places with me.

With the introductions completed, I wandered off to the main camp of HMS Raleigh to start my joining routine that would take the rest of the day, as there was a fair bit of real estate to cover. Places like the dentist and the sickbay only accepted joiners and leavers at certain times of the day, so I planned my route accordingly. There was a fair bit of paperwork to complete, but this was not helped by the fact that nobody was expecting me. On my tour of the camp, I bumped into a few familiar faces, which prompted a coffee and a catch up chat whilst I waited for my next appointment.

After lunch, at the allotted hour, I visited the dentist and sickbay before traipsing around the camp for the rest of the afternoon completing my joining routine.

The following day, the Fire School had a class full of submariners starting a two-day course, prior to joining a boat. 'Taff' was not about to let me loose straight away, so I was asked to sit at the back of the class and observe quietly whilst one of the Petty Officers, who had been teaching the course for a while, stood at the front of the class demonstrating to the assembled lads each of the portable fire-fighting appliances. This was all basic stuff but what irritated me straight away was the 'always right' arrogance of the instructor. He thought he knew his stuff and, by and large, he did. Occasionally he gave out a wrong fact such as the duration of a CO_2 extinguisher. One of the braver members of the audience would question this, but the instructor would stick to his guns and continue to feed the class the wrong information, rather than lose his credibility.

This really annoyed me, and after the class has been sent for a tea and fag break, I took the PO instructor to one side and asked him about the several errors that I had detected. Even in a private discussion with a senior colleague, he refused to admit that he was wrong. In fact, quite the opposite, he said that I was quite possibly out of touch and not reading the most up to date publications on naval fire-fighting techniques. Well, this was possible, but I was still very angry at his uncompromising attitude towards something that had been my bread and butter for such a long time, so I went to check. The reference book in question was also the submariner's fire-fighting and damage control bible called BR2170 Volume 4. Being very familiar with the book, I quickly located the chapter on portable extinguishers and bingo! After starting to doubt myself, the book proved that I was right. Challenging the Petty Officer, during the next break, he was still very reluctant to believe even the printed word, and checked the most recent amendment had been inserted into the edition. I may have won this particular battle and gained credibility in his eyes, but this did little to integrate me into the tightly knit group of general service petty officer instructors. To my mind, if you are going to stand in front of a class of lads and lasses, spouting facts and figures, they have to be right or we would be sending people off with wrong and potentially dangerous information. This was most definitely a high horse I was happy to climb onto.

The more I listened to his teaching, the more points I took issue with. I have no problem with people making mistakes, we are, after all, human and that is what we do, but if you are later found to be wrong, stand up and admit it. I would have had much more respect for the chap if he had corrected his earlier errors, rather than continue with his pre-rehearsed spiel, that he knew so well.

Later in the day, out on the demonstration ground, again I took a back seat whilst another instructor demonstrated how to correctly extinguish fires using a variety of different appliances. This was far better and although I didn't learn anything apart from the script, I did not detect any practical errors.

During the lunch break, I tried on my newly acquired PBI Gold fire-fighting suit, fire hood and wellington boots for size. I checked that my nominated extended duration breathing apparatus was ready to wear and was surprised to find that it had been charged to a massive 300 bar, which, if I didn't panic, would give me a whole hour of breathable air. On-board, we only had the capacity to charge the cylinders to 276 bar thus reducing the endurance. Finally, I did a radio check with the control room through my helmet communication system and I was ready to get hot and sweaty.

The first task after lunch was to show the trainees around the gas-fired units while all of the lights were on and the escape doors were open. As this was my first day on the fire ground as an instructor, I listened intently, as others showed the lads where all of the fires would be set. Special attention was given to the emergency shut-down buttons in each compartment, which, if something bad happened, pressing these red buttons would instantly extinguish the fires, put the lights on and ventilate the unit of smoke making it safe again in a very short time.

After the familiarisation tour, everyone descended off the units and back into the rest room to await the inevitable fire. With myself and the qualified instructors staffing the compartments on the unit, the control room set a small fire in the compartment referred to as the mess deck. Smoke was injected and the lights switched off. Very soon, it started to feel quite realistic. I stood out of the way in a darkened corner armed with an Argus 4 thermal imaging camera that allowed me, quite literally, to see in the dark.

After a short time, a properly briefed young lad conducting 'rounds' of the 'ship' would discover the fire and hopefully, raise the standard loud vocal alarm, "Fire, fire, fire, fire in the mess deck," before picking up an appropriate extinguisher and pressing forward with his continuous and aggressive attack. Unfortunately it didn't quite go like that and after discovering the fire, he turned tail and ran away, leaping up the ladder three steps at a time screaming, "Fire, fire, fire..." Of course, left unattended, the fire was allowed to escalate until there were now two fires in the mess deck and also another fire in the neighbouring compartment, designated as the galley.

By the time the first fire-fighters, called the 'Attack BA', appeared on the scene wearing breathing apparatus and carrying portable extinguishers, there was little they could do apart from shut the doors and try to contain the inferno. It then was several minutes before the fire-fighting team returned, this time dressed from head to toe in a compressed wool Fearnought suit, wellington boots, anti-flash hood and gloves and wearing an EDBA topped off with a Cromwell helmet, which as well as being a hard hat, also contained a communication system allowing, in theory, the fire-fighters to speak to each other. Unfortunately, this only generally worked well when it was used in dry, quiet conditions and you were stood quite close to the person you needed to talk to. So, in a darkened, burning compartment where there was a lot of confusion and shouting, the communications were largely useless.

As you might have gathered, the first exercise was a complete pot-mess. After all the fires had been 'extinguished' meaning, that in the eyes of the instructors, the trainees had done enough to get the gas turned off, myself and the rest of the instructors gathered to compare notes and it made grim reading. The lead instructor for the afternoon session became our singular voice for the de-brief and spared nobody's blushes, as he collectively ripped them all a new arse hole.

Bollockings over, it was time to do it all again, this time with a subtly different scenario. This exercise was better, though there were still some elementary schoolboy errors such as stepping off the ladder and assuming, rather than knowing, that the deck was still there and that it could still support your weight. Many students wrongly assumed, that just because they couldn't see in the dark smoke-filled compartment that they were invisible, but there was no hiding from my thermal imaging camera as I shouted in their ear and provided some gentle encouragement with my boot.

By the end of the third and final exercise, I was starting to believe in the team. Sure, mistakes were still being made, but the team leaders were taking charge and the fires were being 'extinguished' in a safe and largely efficient manner.

With the exercise complete and after all of the equipment had been cleaned, charged, replaced and where necessary, hung up to dry, it was time for the lead instructor to tell the team how well they had performed, before sending them back off to their submarine with a warm fuzzy feeling. The truth was, they would only improve with practice, lots and lots of lovely practice.

The following day, we didn't have a course, but there was still work to be done. All of the notes and memories from the previous day's exercise had to be compiled so that the lead instructor could write the report, which would subsequently be sent to the submarine's Captain. Whilst it was fairly easy to get the words on paper, it was quite difficult to form them into a flowing positive report with a few recommendations for improvement, without swearing. The navy has a proofreading procedure called 'staffing', which ensures that a few sets of eyes read the report, before the boss finally signs it and sends it to the submarine's Captain.

For some reason, which never became clear, the warrant officer, 'Taff' Jones, never liked me at all. I was often invited into his office for a closed-door one-way discussion, without coffee, which had the result of making me really dislike what should have been a dream job. It didn't take long to figure out that his petty officer lap dog was misinforming him. He loved to run and tell tales about the new chief. I am not sure if he was seeking promotion for himself or what his motivation was, but whatever it was, it didn't work.

I have always considered, that if a department is managed well, then morale will follow, which in turn generates a happy team. Unfortunately, this was not managed well, and as a result, the team was fragmented, resulting in some bitching and backstabbing behind the scenes. Not a happy environment at all. It was for this reason, after a few months, I made a decision to request a job change. The Fire School was only destined to be a temporary job, so, taking the initiative, I decided to give an old mate a ring, as he had the enviable job of drafting submarine engineers between all of the available jobs.

Warrant Officer Clive Buckenham seemed quite pleased to hear from me, and we spent a short time just catching up and swapping stories on mutual friends and where they were now working, before I got down to business and told him exactly what the situation was at the Fire School. Of course, he knew that I was there, as he had been instrumental in getting me off HMS Turbulent in the first place. Hearing that I was unhappy, this gave him the perfect opportunity to 'nick' me back into the engineering world.

Clive went on to say there was a job in Portsmouth he would like me to consider, working for MCTA. Never heard of them! Clive went on to explain that it was working for the Maritime Commissioning Trials and Assessment team that were based in Portsmouth Dockyard. He urgently needed a submarine engineer that was either a PO or a chief to fill a gap that was about to become vacant. As I had never heard of them, I asked Clive for some time to consider his offer and also to chat to Anita, before I leapt out of the frying pan and into a fire nearly two hundred miles away.

After putting down the phone, I went onto the intranet at work and dialled up MCTA, before becoming amazed that I had never heard of them before, as their website was huge. Looking through the list of sections, I eventually found a telephone number for Warrant Officer Martin Cottam, who seemingly headed up the Hull Signature Survey Reduction Unit, that Clive had mentioned.

Adopting a formal tone, I called WO Cottam, told him of 'drafty's offer, by means of introduction and asked him exactly what the team did, whilst I considered the job. Martin Cottam, painted a picture of a proactive team who would arrange noise reduction surveys on ships and submarines, before booking flights, hire cars and accommodation. The team of two or three surveyors would then travel to the vessel, conduct the survey and write a report for the CO. He went on to explain that the team carried a laptop around with a portable printer, allowing them to effectively work detached. I must say it all sounded very exciting. During my later years in the Royal Navy, I preferred to be my own master and this job seemed to promise just that, but it was still in Portsmouth, and that meant effectively living away from home during the week and becoming a weekend warrior again. Coupled with this, I was still not too keen to leave Anita, so soon after her breakdown. I needed to speak to her about it.

Uncharacteristically, I kept quiet at work. This sounded like a brilliant opportunity to try something new and I did not want 'Taff' Jones screwing it up, just because he could. Martin Cottam had done a great job in selling it to me so, I was pretty much decided that I would take it.

Anita was absolutely fine with my job offer. She didn't much like the thought of me working away during the week, but recognised that it was something that I wanted to do. Mentally, she was feeling much better now as the medication was continuing to work its magic and as she reasoned, she still had the nice people from NPFS to rely on if things went pear-shaped during the week. Therefore, with Anita's consent, I called Clive the following day and accepted his offer.

Clive was delighted; he was an old mate anyway and this would be an opportunity for him to get a submarine engineer back into the fold, for him to solve an emerging manning crisis and for us to catch up over a beer or two. He promised not to say anything to 'Taff' and just send the paperwork through. This suited me just fine. The guy had shown me no respect, so consequently, I had no loyalty towards him at all.

Not for the first time, I reasoned, in life, you could count your true friends on the fingers of your right hand and your sworn enemies on the fingers of your left hand. Warrant Officer 'Taff' Jones was most definitely a left-hander. All of my other mates sort of fell into the middle ground, where you have no strong desires of love or hate towards them.

Within the week, the boss, Lieutenant Commander Byrne, called me into his office to show me a draft chit that had just arrived stating that I would be leaving HMS Raleigh at the end of the week to join Captain MCTA in Portsmouth. He then handed me an envelope with some joining instructions. Lt Cdr Byrne went through the motions of saying that he was sorry to see me leave after such a short time, but countered this by adding, my assignment to the fire school was only ever meant to be a temporary job. He was not a bad bloke, I liked him and more to the point, he hadn't done anything, that I was aware of, to piss me off.

I now had much to do, a hire car to organise for Sunday and a leaving routine to complete, as well as ensuring (whilst I was still in HMS Raleigh as it had a well-stocked clothing store), that I had all of the right kit for my new job.

By Friday morning, I was done. My fire-fighting kit had been returned, my drafting routine had been completed and I had toured the camp shaking hands and saying a few selective 'goodbyes' to my mates. For the first time in my naval career, I left without a backward glance, without even saying goodbye to the warrant officer.

Ian Atkinson

MCTA PORTSMOUTH

4th October 2006 to 11th February 2008

Arriving home, shortly after leaving the Fire School for the last time, I allowed myself the evening to relax, knowing that I had a busy day ahead compiling enough kit to survive away from home during the working week. My new Warrant Officer, Martin Cottam assured me I would be allowed home every weekend, therefore, I just needed sufficient clothes, uniform and entertainment to keep me out of the bar during the evening.

Rummaging around in the loft, I found a 19-inch flat screen TV and a DVD player. My laptop was in need of updating and charging as it had been redundant for a few months and, I decided that I needed a fridge. Things had moved on significantly since the good old days of hanging a carrier bag of beer and milk out of the window. Apart from that, it was October and still warmer outside than inside.

As luck would have it, the local Lidl had a small glass-fronted beer fridge on offer, which was exactly what I was looking for, but during my shopping spree, I also came home with a DAB radio and a kettle as well as the makings of tea and coffee. I just hoped that it would all fit into the hire car that I was due to pick up the following day.

Mentally, I pictured each scenario of my daily life and checked off that I had everything. A digital photo frame was a last minute addition as was a 1-in-6 extension lead to power all of the gadgets that I was going to need. Anita remembered my old saviour from Sovereign in the winter of 1994/1995 and retrieved my fan heater from the loft. The days were starting to get shorter and the nights cooler. Knowing the navy as I did, I didn't expect the accommodation block heating to be switched on for at least another few weeks.

The following afternoon, with my luggage packed and stockpiled in the lounge, Anita dropped me off at Camelshead car park, just outside Devonport dockyard, to pick up my hire car for my journey to Portsmouth. I had been travelling the same route for most of my career, so getting lost was not an option and under my leadership, the car knew the way already.

Half an hour later and I was back home driving a shiny new Vauxhall Vectra Estate. I only really needed it for effectively four hours but potentially I had a full twenty-four hours before I had to give it back. I planned to leave in the afternoon, ensuring that I arrived in Portsmouth and was moved into my new cabin before the light failed.

After folding the back seats down to increase the payload, Anita and I lugged all of my accumulated kit outside and laid it all on the drive before working out the puzzle of how to load the car. The fridge was the largest item, so that went in first and it was wedged in with two holdalls containing uniform and clothing. The TV, radio and DVD player went in next, protected by their boxes. This was followed by a collapsible plastic crate, full of cables and leads and of course the kettle. The car had taken on Tardis proportions and easily swallowed up all of the assembled kit, leaving me to wonder if I had forgotten anything. Reasoning that I only had five nights to survive before I was home again, I decided to risk it and reluctantly, said my goodbyes to Anita and the cats.

The journey to Portsmouth was actually very pleasant. The car was extremely well behaved and furnished with loads of gadgets. With nobody in the passenger seat to tell me off for fiddling, I started to play with the on-board trip computer and climate control as well as tinkering with the radio and cruise control. Out on a clear bit of A38 near Marley Head, with Plymouth well behind me, I decided to stretch the car's legs for a few miles. As I accelerated, the speedometer rotated smoothly into three figures. There was still a fair bit of poke left, but as the fuel gauge seemed to be visibly moving, I opted to cruise at a modest, finable, but not banable, 80 mph.

After being on the road for less than an hour, I automatically joined the M5 and, passing Exeter Services to the left, pulled into the nearside lane and joined the A30, signposted Honiton. Passing to the right of Exeter Airport, I eventually turned off onto the much slower A35 before bypassing Axminster, Bridport and Dorchester on the well-trodden coast road to 'Pompey'.

Unusually, the roads were quiet, so within the standard three hours, I was pulling up at the main gate of HMS Nelson, identity card at the ready. Fortunately, the gate staff were expecting me, so it wasn't long before I was parked outside Nile Block to the left of the Warrant Officers and Senior Rates Mess, which looked like a huge block of flats from the 1970s. I had reserved a cabin so it was little surprise when the Hall Porter issued me a key to cabin 2-17. As there were about nine floors and I had loads of stuff to transport, I was grateful that I was only on the second floor. There were two lifts, but these were not matelot proof, although thankfully they were working on that Sunday night in October 2006.

Making several trips, I eventually got all of my stuff into the single living accommodation and piled it on the floor whilst I considered where I was going to put everything.

The room had originally been constructed as a twelve-foot square space, but had been revamped a few years previously and another wall had been built to form an en-suite shower room with a loo and a basin. A couple of wardrobes, a desk with some drawers had been fitted against another wall, and opposite these was a single bed with a small bedside table and a reading light above the headboard. A covered foam easy chair stood next to the large radiator which had been plumbed in under the double window, though, as predicted, it wasn't on. It was clear to me, that the design had been thought about carefully as there was a TV aerial point and a collection of power points scattered around the room.

I spent the rest of the evening unpacking, making my bed and ensuring that my uniform was pressed and ready for the morning. By about 10pm, I was just about finished and also knackered. Deciding that I had earned a pint, I went off to explore and find the bar. The mess was run along the lines of a large three-star hotel with a Hall Porter who managed the reception. I found a games room with several snooker tables, and a couple of rooms designated as TV rooms, for those without their own. The TV rooms, to prevent people changing the channels were designated as BBC1, BBC2, ITV, and Sky. Each had a couple of rows of comfortable chairs but were largely empty. I found the almost deserted bar in the basement. This was quite large and resembled a quiet English pub. It was run by some of the more long-standing mess members and on first impressions, it seemed quite clique. Buying a pint, I propped myself up against the bar, in the hope that some kindly soul would take pity on me and strike up a conversation. No such luck and after supping up, I decided to call it a night.

The following morning, I was awoken by Radio 2 at 6:30am and after lying there listening to the news for five minutes, rolled out of bed and stumbled into the shower to get washed. Twenty minutes later and I was clean and sparkly again, dressed in a clean uniform, white open necked short-sleeved shirt, black uniform trousers and shiny black shoes. Leaving my jacket and cap in the cabin, I tootled off to find some breakfast in the dining hall.

On your first day in a new job, you are always permitted a small degree of latitude and it does not do to turn up at the crack of sparrow fart before everyone has drunk at least one cup of coffee. So, after munching on a hearty cooked breakfast, I returned to my cabin, put on my uniform Gore-Tex jacket and cap. Picking up my joining documentation, I waited for the Queen to 'wake up', which is signalled every morning by the raising of the White Ensign in every naval base and ship around the country. Flag raised, I locked up and headed out into the dockyard with my ID card blowing in the breeze from a lanyard that was slung around my neck. I had received some basic instructions on where to go, but as it turned, out finding the Central Office Block, where MCTA had their offices was a doddle. My section had their desks on the 5th floor, but as I hadn't got an entry card, I had to ring the entry bell and wait for one of my new colleagues to let me in and escort me up to the Hull and Signature Survey Reduction Unit where I was eventually shown to an empty desk.

The first morning was taken up with meeting the team, before I headed back into the dockyard and HMS Nelson to complete the mandatory joining routine. Having completed most of it by lunchtime, I took the command decision to take the afternoon off and have a bit of a snooze, after all it had been a tiring morning.

The following day, I was chucked right in the deep end. I was relieving a chap called Paul Strettle who was being drafted back to sea. Paul was doing his best to get me settled and helped me set up all of the accounts that I would need to do the job. I was told that the following week, we would be flying up to Scotland to conduct a noise and shock survey on a HMS Chiddingfold, a sort of plastic mine-hunter, so there was much to do. Paul had already booked accommodation in HMS Caledonia, near to Rosyth, and a hire car from Edinburgh Airport. He was flying from Manchester and now he knew where I was spending the weekend, he showed me how to book an Air Southwest flight from Plymouth via Bristol to arrive in Edinburgh within an hour of his arrival. This meant that we could meet up at the airport, collect the hire car and drive to HMS Caledonia.

In preparation, Paul had printed off the last report, so that it would be easy to see what had been ignored from the previous survey, a couple of years earlier. He also ensured that the laptop and printer worked and had all of the information stored that we needed for the survey.

It doesn't sound like much, but this took all of Tuesday and most of Wednesday to get everything checked and ready. Paul had a huge bag of yellow labels and an equal amount of small black cable ties. He also carried a couple of black marker pens to write on the labels, two reference manuals and a pair of calipers, a ruler and a set of feeler gauges, to check the tolerances.

Finally, needing to adopt the corporate image, I went off to the stores to sign for a couple of pairs of white overalls and a white hard hat. Both of these items were usually reserved for officers, but MCTA, as a trials and assessment team, wore them on visits with a blue and gold embroidered badge sewn above the left breast.

With my joining routine and all of the preparations for the forthcoming survey now complete, I turned my attention to packing a bag for the weekend. As I had arrived in a hire car and had no transport of my own in Portsmouth, I caught a train home, shortly after midday on Thursday. It had been explained shortly after I had arrived, that Friday did not exist in the MCTA working calendar, providing that we were up to date with our surveys and reports.

Early on the following Monday, Anita dropped me off at Plymouth Airport for the 6am departure to Bristol. I only carried hand luggage as I only planned on spending three nights in the frozen wastes of Scotland, so a holdall with wash gear, sufficient pants, overalls and civilian clothes was pretty much all that was required.

On time, the de Havilland Dash 8-400 turboprop aircraft taxied out to the far end of Runway 31, spun around and applied the brakes. As Plymouth Airport had a relatively short runway, the pilot applied full power and allowed the engines to spool up. Releasing the brakes, we sped down the runway and in a matter of seconds we were airborne, climbing over the A386. Banking right over Dartmoor, I was able to identify most of the landmarks on our short hop to Bristol. This was just about enough time for the stewardess to serve coffee and a small breakfast roll before we started descending into Lulsgate Airport, south of Bristol. On the ground, disembarkation was a simple affair. It transpired that Bristol was a hub for similar aircraft from Plymouth, Dublin, Paris, Glasgow and Edinburgh. Consequently, with passengers swapping between aircraft, there was a short wait whilst the Paris flight landed before we were allowed to board the Edinburgh flight and we were on our way, flying up the west coast and over Glasgow before turning right towards Edinburgh. As we crossed the Firth of Forth, with the famous bridge visible to the left, the pilot banked left to line us up with Runway 24 before touching down smoothly at Edinburgh Airport. Inside the terminal building, Paul was waiting, having already acquired the hire car and carrying only hand luggage, we were driving out of the airport only a few minutes after wheels down.

Wishing to get a head start on the week, after we had found our cabins in HMS Caledonia, we dropped our bags and changed straight into overalls, intent on hitting the ground running. With pockets stuffed full of yellow tallies, cable ties and measuring tools, we headed back to the car for the two-mile journey to where HMS Chiddingfold was in dry dock and pretty well deserted. Of course, you cannot just wander willy-nilly onto a naval warship without first making your introductions to the Officer of the Day. After the welcoming introductions, Paul led the way onto the quarterdeck of the Hunt-class mine countermeasures vessel, HMS Chiddingfold. The first thing that hit me was the smell. This class of Mine Hunter, due to the nature of the work, was entirely constructed of glass reinforced plastic and smelt, to me, like a car repair body shop.

Paul had a systematic routine of conducting a survey and quite simply, we started at the highest point at the stem of the small ship. Working slowly together, we worked our way down and aft, ensuring that nothing was missed. I was writing the tallies, attaching them to the defect that Paul had identified and making a note on a clipboard for the report. There were two different types of defect, 'Noise' that is self-explanatory, anything that rattles and 'Shock'. This was more complicated, as everything was either bolted to the hull or resiliently mounted onto a bedplate or raft. There were many different types of mount, which were all classified by a letter, and each had their own tolerances to check. Some were absolutely obvious to the naked eye, without the need to apply calipers and a ruler to them. Others were not so obvious and required the books to be checked for the correct tolerances.

Working from top to bottom in a section and then moving one section aft, we systematically covered the whole ship until, by Tuesday evening, we had completed the whole survey. Surprisingly, we had listed over three hundred defects. That was not the end of it though, we then had to type everything into a report, which could take much of the following day. The process had been polished over many years, so, we would be in a position to present our findings, in a draft report, to the Commanding Officer or his delegated engineer before flying home for the weekend on Thursday afternoon.

My introduction to the world of signature survey had been an easy one. As I discovered, our team of four engineers would conduct surveys on anything that the navy owns, that floats. This covered every type of ship from aircraft carriers to the mine hunters, like HMS Chiddingfold, and three different classes of submarine. For that reason, the team consisted of two highly trained, highly skilled, professional submariners and two 'skimmers'.

As I settled into the job, I started to enjoy the routine. Sure, living away from home is not ideal, but every evening, after I had met with some of my new mates in the dining hall for scran, I would check in with Anita on the phone. As a bonus, many of the surveys were conducted in Devonport, meaning that I could bug out home on the Thursday evening and wouldn't have to meet the rest of the team until about lunchtime on the following Monday, after they'd travelled down from Portsmouth.

The surveys often seemed to come in a flurry, meaning that we would be conducting back-to-back surveys and then after a few months, the workload would appear to dry up. This respite allowed us time to catch our breath. Back in the office, we would catch up an any admin and finalise any reports, before posting them off to their respective COs.

It was following a survey on the Type 23 frigate HMS Sutherland, in March 2007 that I sent myself home for Easter leave. Although I had been working from home that week, it was still nice to have a couple of weeks of potential nothingness. The news had just broken on the BBC about an explosion on-board the nuclear submarine HMS Tireless, so, naturally I was quite worried about whether any of my mates had been hurt, as I knew a good number of the ship's company. The report stated that there had been two fatalities, but at the time, no names had been released. Calling around my buddies for information revealed nothing more than the various newsreaders had already broadcast. Apparently, Tireless had suffered an explosion in the forward escape compartment and was now on the surface heading back to Devonport.

A couple of days later, I received all of the information I needed and more besides, when my phone rang at home. It was my boss, Lt Nick Tate, asking me if I minded conducting a survey on the affected compartment, as soon as HMS Tireless arrived back alongside. The submarine, in a desperate attempt to win back the hearts and minds of the crew, following a tragic accident, had requested MCTA and a bunch of other guys to survey the scene and report all defects, in the hope of eventually removing all traces of the incident. Despite being on leave, I owed it to my mates on the boat to help in whatever way I could.

One of those mates, Warrant Officer Martin 'Stumpy' Yardley, after confirming with Nick, called me early in April 2007, only a week after the incident, and asked me personally for help. As I had just returned from a survey a few days previously, I had everything I needed at home so, within the hour, I was walking on-board HMS Tireless in my white overalls and boots, carrying my clipboard and a pocket full of yellow tallies.

I was greeted, personally by the Captain, who thanked me for giving up my leave and requested a full and comprehensive report. Stumpy, whom I hadn't seen since I left HMS Talent, escorted me along 2 deck, through 29 watertight bulkhead and up the ladder into what used to be the forward escape platform. I was extremely familiar with the layout of the compartment, having trained many young submariners in the past, but nothing prepared me for the scene of devastation that confronted me. Everything was black and broken. Light fittings were hanging off, the melamine bulkheads had been smashed and wooden lockers had been splintered.

Knowing that two young sailors, Paul McCann and Anthony Huntrod had tragically perished in this small space made it really hard. I was grateful, however, that I had been asked to do a very small thing to help the boat recover from this awful tragedy.

Taking the Captain at his word, I spent a day and a half crawling over every square inch of the compartment, listing over three hundred separate noise and shock defects, from pipe brackets that had broken, to the mounts on the CO2 absorption units that had split. It was obvious to me, that HMS Tireless was in a very sorry state and would not be going to sea again for many months.

Having completed my survey and presented the report, the Captain again shook my hand and thanked me for my assistance. At home, I called Nick to report my progress, but the Captain of HMS Tireless had beaten me to it, singing my praises. This resulted in big chuck ups for me and an extra couple of days leave.

After Easter and back in Portsmouth, there was a lull in the workload that allowed us time to indulge in some adventurous training. I mentioned to the team that I had a gliding qualification and asked if anybody wanted to come flying with me at the former Naval Air Station, HMS Daedalus, near Lee on Solent. No longer belonging to the navy, it was still an airfield with a couple of runways and a few hangars that were used by the Royal Navy Gliding Club, Air-sea rescue and the police, for various activities.

Chief Petty Officer Mark Southland, another member of the team, sounded interested, so, one Wednesday, we were permitted to take the day off to go gliding. Armed with a rucksack full of pork pies, sausage rolls and a flask of coffee, nicked from the dining hall, Mark picked me up in his aging Vauxhall Zafira. We headed out of Portsmouth on the M275 and then followed the M27 westbound for one junction before exiting onto the A27 and then A32 towards deepest darkest Gosport. Forking right up Newgate Lane, we passed HMS Collingwood to the right and, as directed, followed the road straight ahead at the next roundabout to skirt the airfield.

As you would imagine, there are rules when driving a car around a working airfield, but we did not have a clue until a very grumpy police pilot shouted at us for driving on the runway. It seemed obvious to get to the gliding hangar by the shortest possible route, but pilot plod was having none of it and directed us in the opposite direction, driving anti-clockwise around the perimeter track. We were instructed to look up and right before crossing the active runway at the far side, wary of landing aircraft.

First bollocking of the day laughed off by Mark and myself, he parked up the Zafira next to some other vehicles and we ventured into the hangar to make our introductions. I had brought along my log book and also my pilot's licence which was next to useless. They were simply not going to trust a strange bloke to fly off into the sunset with one of their expensive aircraft, without first having a couple of successful check flights. Mark, of course, had never seen a glider close up before, so he was starting from scratch. Using my experience, I tried to fit in and lend a hand, preparing the gliders for flight. As the club members did not know me, it was like being a trainee submariner again, not trusted to do anything.

Under supervision, I was allowed to take a wing and guide a glider out to the launch point following the car that was towing it at walking pace. This earned me three flights early in the day, which needed to be good flights to prove my worth as a pilot, if I was to be allowed to fly solo.

Strapped in for my first flight, I was told to lightly cover the rudder pedals and stick, as the instructor would conduct the launch, and no sooner had I verbally followed the abbreviated pre-flight checklist, 'CBSIFTCB', which was taped to the instrument panel, we were airborne, climbing steeply. The familiar sounds and sensations all came back to me as I followed through with the controls. At around eleven-hundred feet, I felt the power come off the climb as the instructor pushed the stick hard forward and released the cable. Dust and shit in the cockpit swirled around my head as we momentarily went into negative g. Off the cable and flying free, the instructor trimmed the glider for level flight and calmly said, "You have control," as my hand tightened slightly on the stick. I gave it a slight wiggle to prove to myself that I was in fact in control and then took stock of my situation. I was flying straight and level, heading south towards the Isle of Wight at a just over a thousand feet. The variometer was bouncing around the middle, showing a little lift, but not sufficient to keep me airborne for long. I knew enough to turn away from the sea, as there was no cliff and only a sandy beach. Explaining what I was about to do, I looked left and seeing nothing close, banked the glider into a tight left hand turn to get out of the way of gliders that would soon be launching behind me. It was actually too early in the morning for any lift to be apparent, and noticing that my altitude had quickly fallen to around seven-hundred feet, I continued my left turn and joined circuit on the downwind leg, whilst talking through what my intentions were. The instructor, knowing the area better than me, advised a two-part base leg, which would position me better for landing. This was a new technique, so he guided me through it. It was all about angles and positioning. At about four-hundred feet and level with the perimeter track, he had me make a forty-five degree left hand turn shortly followed by another ninety-degree turn as I descended to about three-hundred and fifty feet. This then only took another forty-five degree turn to come onto final approach at around three-hundred feet. Unlocking the brakes, in a fluid movement, I started to trade off altitude for airspeed, as I tried to maintain forty-five mph aiming for an imaginary point, just short of the landing zone. Well inside the perimeter track and at about the height of a car, I eased the stick back, bringing the nose up and flared gently allowing the glider's airspeed to bleed off as the glider quite literally, with a gentle bump, landed itself. I allowed myself to roll out a bit before gently touching the wheel brakes with my left hand and slowed the K21 glider to a halt. Apart from the launch, that I didn't do, it had been a very short but successful flight. Many feelings had returned and like riding a bike, you never forget. I just needed the instructor to allow me to launch but I dare say he would want me to do some spins or stalls to prove I could cope with an emergency, before he cut me loose on my own.

Later in the day, and after Mark had launched on his air experience flight, I got the chance to fly again. Taking on-board the lessons and advice from my earlier flight, I readied the glider for launch. With the instructor strapped into the back seat, I talked my way through the pre-flight checklist to prove that I was doing it correctly. As soon as I closed and locked the canopy, my wingman picked up my port wing to level the glider. The cable had been clipped on underneath and as soon as I gave the launch controller the thumbs up, he started waving his table tennis bat under arm as a signal to the winchman to take up the slack on the cable. I could not see the winch from where I was sitting but I did feel the gentle tug as the winch started to take the strain. The winch controller then raised his bat arm above his head and shouted, "All out, all out." Within about three seconds, I was climbing steeply. The altimeter was marking my skywards progress as I kept a watchful eye on my instruments before at about four-hundred and fifty feet and about halfway into my climb, the cable snapped. So there I was with a serious nose up attitude, speed falling off rapidly and about a second to make a decision before I fell out of the sky like a stone.

Instinct took over and before I really realised what was happening, I had pushed the stick away from me and forced the aircraft into a dive to regain airspeed. This bought me time, but not much. I still had a serious decision to make, land ahead or do a short circuit. I opted for the former seeing that there was still quite a bit of field in front of me, so I snatched at the airbrakes and with full brake applied and the nose down I managed to get myself back into a landing posture. It was not pretty and I landed hard but at least I was down and nothing was broken. If I had the luxury of time to consider the danger, I may well have shit my pants, but as it was, I was on the ground less than a minute after launching. It was then that the instructor told me that I had passed the exercise and that the cable had not broken at all, the winch had just powered down to simulate the emergency. If I could have reached him, I may well have punched him, as adrenalin was still pumping through me and my heart felt like it was about to explode. Climbing out of the glider, my legs instantly turned to jelly as the reality of what had just happened started to dawn on me.

By the end of the day, I had flown again, this time I managed a reasonable seven-minute flight and practiced a few stalls and manoeuvers before a much gentler landing. On the drive back to Portsmouth, Mark was buzzing with excitement, his right foot was heavy on the accelerator as he gave me a blow by blow account of his three flights all the way back. He was hooked.

The following day in the office, he was still blethering on about it and by the end of the day, he had been onto Amazon and bought a book on the subject by the very knowledgeable Derek Piggott. So, after a cracking day off, it was back to the grindstone, preparing for my next survey. As luck would have it, this was to be in Plymouth on-board the Type 22 frigate HMS Cumberland.

I was not familiar with the layout of a Type 22 but that was not important, as I would be partnered with somebody that was. The plan for this survey was to have all four of the team working in two pairs and if all went according to plan, one pair would start at the front end and the other at the back, meeting in the middle. As it was a big ship, we also stood a fighting chance of scrounging a free lunch.

I discovered, after a week of crawling around HMS Cumberland, that I liked the layout. For a frigate, she was huge and the accommodation was far more spacious and luxurious than I was used to on-board a submarine. I was also starting to have serious doubts about my future career in submarines. The job I was in was great, but I knew I couldn't expect to stay in it for the rest of my career and there was a ruling that, if I had already been assigned to a new submarine, then I would not be allowed to transfer to general service until that job had been completed. After much thought, and realising that I needed to keep in touch with Anita, I came to the reluctant decision that being underwater on a submarine and out of communication was not tenable. She was coping a lot better now and the medication was doing its job but there were still 'down' days. Out of regular contact, I knew my mind would work overtime and I would imagine the worst, so, after thinking long and hard and speaking to Anita, I made the momentous decision to transfer back to General Service.

My buddy, Warrant Officer Clive Buckenham, was in charge of submarine engineering drafting, so I popped over to see him to discuss my options. Clive knew the reasoning, so, after a very sociable chat and a coffee, he introduced me to his skimmer counterparts. They had loads of questions for me, which basically boiled down to what use an aging submarine chief stoker could be on-board a ship and whether they considered that I would fit in ok. After the short and informal interview, they discussed what sea-going jobs were coming up in the near future that might suit my skills. There was apparently two, one on the assault ship, HMS Ocean, and another on the Type 22 frigate, HMS Cornwall. I had heard many bad things about HMS Ocean. Basically the Royal Marines use it as their very own 'combat ferry' and the Royal Navy are their 'taxi drivers', paid to deliver them anywhere in the world whilst they popped off to do all of the fun stuff and slot a few bad guys before coming home for tea and medals. Nah, I didn't fancy that and as HMS Ocean was not a purpose built warship, nothing was standard, so ordering spares was going to be a real nightmare.

HMS Cornwall however, was a far better option. As I had recently surveyed her sister ship, HMS Cumberland and crawled all over it I knew the layout and just how spacious and comfortable it was for a warship. The accommodation for CPOs was up to four to a cabin whilst POs shared a cabin with six bunks. Yes, this would suit my purposes quite nicely. With my name now pencilled in for Cornwall, the two drafting chaps went onto explain that I would spend a year doing a menial job on-board, whilst I got used to the way of life. The routines and just about everything else was completely different to the life on-board a nuclear submarine. They went onto explain that in due course I would replace the Marine Engineering Departmental Coordinator, which was a key role aboard any ship. There was much to learn and if I decided that this was the way forward, then I would need to retrain for not one, but two new jobs.

The rationale was always about maintaining communication with Anita whilst I continued doing the job that I loved. I simply just could not do that underwater on a submarine. Decision made and with a definite way forward, I returned to the office and logged on to my JPA account, which was fast becoming a way of life in the navy. JPA was a new computerised system used by everyone to apply for leave, check pay and more importantly, the mechanism for requesting my return to general service. In the old days, this used to be called a drafting preference form where you could unrealistically apply for hot and sunny drafts to Naples or Diego Garcia whilst at the same time avoiding Scotland. Now, with JPA, the request was instant. The chaps I had just been chatting with were expecting it, nevertheless, I was very surprised that by lunchtime, I had received official notification to Join HMS Cornwall in February 2008. Before then, I was required to retrain by completing a whole raft of courses at HMS Sultan, the Marine Engineering School. These had all been booked for me and listed in order. One thing was for certain, they were not mucking about. As a sort of afterthought, I spoke to my boss and dropped the unexpected bombshell that I was leaving and that my first course was due to start in June 2007, barely a month away.

Determined to get their pound of flesh, and in a twist of irony, I was asked to assist another team, who were shorthanded and conduct a Dynamic Machinery Trial on-board HMS Ocean, at sea. The team was required to observe and test Ocean's manoeuvrability whilst I was to make a report on several of the component parts of the ship, such as the fire pumps and the aircraft lifts. Despite my concerns about not knowing much about skimmer maintenance, the warrant officer still wanted me on the team as a generic engineer. As he once said, "A trained monkey can see if something is leaking or not working," and that's what he wanted me to look at. Fine. I would do my best.

Actually, as it turned out, it was good fun and confirmed my earlier fears about serving on the 'combat ferry'. They were drastically under manned, under maintained and largely under trained. Larger than anything I had ever been to sea on, she displaced over 21500 tons and was a devilish 666 feet long. Very slow and sluggish, she could wind up to a maximum speed of eighteen knots in a few days and had a turning circle of roughly the size of the Isle of Wight.

After we had sailed, I was wandering around, lost on 6 deck, which runs a racetrack around the ship, and did not see a soul down the entire port side of the ship. I was just not used to the amount of free space she had. Eventually, I accosted a young female mechanic and asked for directions to the Chippy's shop. She elected to escort the lost submariner whilst answering my questions. She explained that the ship got a lot busier when the flight and the embarked forces were on-board, so she advised that I enjoyed the peace and quiet whilst it lasted.

Safely deposited at the Shipwright's workshop, the Chippy, another chief stoker called George was happy to see me. As he made tea in the workshop, he explained some of the horror stories that he had encountered whilst trying to maintain his fire pumps. As HMS Ocean was built from a commercial design, he had experienced considerable difficulty obtaining stores, resulting in only two out of the five fire pumps being serviceable. This was clearly unacceptable. George hoped that my report might rattle some logistical cages higher up the food chain, allowing him to get his stores.

I spent a good couple of hours being escorted by George as he highlighted his problem areas. In summary, HMS Ocean was in a dire material state and if I was to do my job right, my report had to be scathing. Mentally, I was pleased that I didn't choose her as my next ship. After chatting to George, I discovered that I would have inherited *his* mechanical nightmare.

I spent the rest of the week crawling around the huge ship, making notes as I went, before typing up the report for the warrant officer. We eventually left the ship on Thursday evening. HMS Ocean had made its way slowly to Portland before the Royal Marines put us ashore by means of a small landing craft called a 'LCVP', which was most uncomfortable. The 'Booties' incredibly, managed to drop us off inside a secure area inside Portland dockyard and after hunting around for a gate, we were forced, unchallenged, to climb up over a fence and into the main area of the dockyard. Two hire cars were waiting for us outside the gate and after loading up, we headed off in opposite directions. The warrant officer and the rest of my team drove off back to Portsmouth whilst I bummed a lift with Gerry Lipscombe, a mate from my Sovereign days and his vibration analysis team who, luckily, were heading back to Plymouth.

Back in the office on Monday morning, I got big chuck ups from the warrant officer. He likened me to their pet Rottweiler, chasing down their defects and asking difficult questions. Frankly, I enjoyed having a free hand to do my own thing and being at sea on HMS Ocean for the week had taught me enough about general service to confirm that I had made the right choice in HMS Cornwall.

In preparation for my PJT in HMS Sultan, I booked myself a cabin in HMS Sultan's Senior Rates Mess whilst, naughtily, retaining my cabin in HMS Nelson. If I had had a car available to me, I could have driven the ten or so miles every day around the motorway. Alternatively, I took the lazy option, and borrowed a car from work for the afternoon, to transport most, but not all, of my kit around to Sultan. I had to leave something in my cabin to prove that it was still occupied, or I might have lost it. In Sultan, I just needed the bare essentials to survive. Going to HMS Sultan as a marine engineer is like coming home. I have never once entered the dining hall or the bar without bumping into an old mate or two.

HMS Sultan had a very transient population, with some people being there for a week whilst others were there for a couple of years, depending on the nature of their course. I had nine courses to complete, ranging from the couple of days NVQ Assessor's Course to a five week Ship's Structure Course. It was very full-on training, with seemingly an exam every Friday morning before we were allowed to go home for the weekend. It was during a stand-easy one morning in November of 2007 when I met the larger than life figure of Chief Petty Officer Andrew 'Taff' Cadwallader. Taff, as the name suggests, was as Welsh as they come. Hailing from Cardiff, he had been in the Royal Navy for almost as long as I had, but had almost exclusively, spent his entire career on the Type 22 frigate, in various forms. He had recently been selected for promotion to WO2 and was now on the same Type 22 COGOG course as me. 'COGOG' described the engine configuration and stood for **CO**mbined **G**as **O**r **G**as, meaning that the ship had four gas turbines, which could feed into a single gearbox, via clutches and drive the two shafts and controllable pitch propellers. As it turned out, Taff knew this stuff inside out and as luck was having it, he was joining my ship, HMS Cornwall. Well, strictly speaking, as he was joining it first, I would be joining his ship. Over a few beers in the evening, Taff would try to explain some of the classroom stuff that had passed me by and put it into simple terms, that even a bum submariner could understand. The extracurricular tutoring was paid for by me in the form of Guinness and was generally interspersed with a story of his own, before somebody interrupted and started talking rugby with him.

As we completed the acquaintance course in HMS Sultan, just before Christmas 2007, I was glad that I had met 'Taff Cad'. Knowing he was going to be installed on-board HMS Cornwall before I arrived reassured me.

After Christmas, I started my final course and it would be fair to say that the navy had saved the best until last. This course, known to all as simply 35s. It was the general service advanced fire-fighting and damage control course and whilst teaching all of the techniques, it also strived to turn the students into Q's, or teachers to you and me. On successful completion of the course, we would be able to set an exercise on-board a ship and then critique it afterwards.

This wasn't particularly new to me, as I had been teaching fire-fighting for years. The difference being, the fire-fighting techniques on-board a ship were quite different and the course also covered flooding as well as chemical warfare. On-board a submarine, if we came under attack from nasty chemical stuff, the safest option would be to dive the boat and wash it off. Conversely, if we had a flood, the procedure was simple, the submarine would emergency surface. This would reduce the outside pressure, slow the leak rate as well as giving us a fighting chance of getting out. On a ship, preventing a flood was very different and involved bunging up the hole with just about anything that would fit and then cutting lengths of wooden shoring to hold the bung in place. This was practiced in the freezing cold water of the DRIU, which was actually a fantastic fairground ride. The DRIU was like a mock-up of a ship. It had an 'engine room', a 'mess deck' and a few other compartments spread over three decks. The beauty of the DRIU was that its hydraulic legs could tilt the unit to mimic the roll of the sea. Water could then be pumped in through some readymade holes whilst we went to work with bags of wedges, bungs and hammers trying to prevent the water flooding in. Although it was really cold, and everyone got soaked to the skin, it was tremendous fun. Presented with a worst-case scenario, our time in the DRIU was more about promoting teamwork and technique. If we were faced with the same amount of simultaneous damage on-board a real ship, we would surely sink.

The chemical module of the course only took a day, followed by a tour of the gas chamber wearing my newly acquired S10 respirator, which, reassuringly worked well at keeping the CS gas out of my lungs.

I loved the fire-fighting though. Having already had a short placement as an instructor, I knew the units pretty well and the techniques that were being taught, so it was a breeze. Our instructors soon came to realise this, so they tended to employ me in the exercise scenario as the Officer of the Day or the i/c FCP, the bloke in charge, at the scene of the fire. This was really useful as these would be two jobs that I would be responsible for when I joined HMS Cornwall.

I enjoyed the course immensely, but the navy does not teach you anything without testing you on it at the end of the course. When it came to the exam, we had learned from a previous course that it was a multiple-choice exam and that there were only four exam papers. As luck would have it, somebody on the course had managed to find the exam papers buried on the chief instructor's computer and e-mailed the files to his home account where he sneakily printed them off. This gave us a head start, so it should come as no surprise when I got 100% and all of the class either matched my score or achieved the high 90s, allowing the instructors to quietly congratulate themselves on being excellent teachers.

With my pre-joining courses now complete, it was back to my desk in MCTA, to essentially say my goodbyes and pack my stuff. I had enjoyed the job and could easily have stayed there for a couple of more years. However, all good things come to an end and I had a huge new chapter in my life about to begin. Therefore, it was with a hint of sadness and a large dose of nervous excitement that I said my farewells and prepared to go back to sea again on the Type 22 frigate, HMS Cornwall.

Ian Atkinson

HMS CORNWALL

12th February 2008 to 11th July 2010

Hire car loaded, I had a last check around the cabin that had been my weekday home for the last couple of years and handed my keys back to the Hall Porter. I had to get a bit of a wiggle on, as I needed to get back to Plymouth, unload, return the hire car and then unpack before repacking with my sea-going kit.

I did have a couple of day's grace, but considering that the ship was in Belfast, I had to be careful to pack only what I knew I was going to need. Lt Cdr Barrie Harvey, HMS Cornwall's MEO, had sent me a joining letter, explaining exactly what my job was going to be and the usual welcoming bollocks. He had, usefully, enclosed a Longcast, whilst classified at the time, it gave me an idea of the ship's movements, including dates and port visits. From this I learned that the date I was scheduled to join, was the day before the ship was due to sail northwards to take part in a NATO exercise off Norway called 'Armatura Borealis', visiting Tromso in the process.

Knowing that Tromso was likely to be seriously cold and in February, probably quite dark as well, I packed all of my warmest clothing, as well as overalls and working clothing.

Unlike joining a submarine, where qualification is achieved on-board, I had already completed my courses and qualifications, so, initially I only needed to settle in and to get used to ship-borne life again. I dug out my portable DVD player and compiled a wallet containing twenty of my favourite films. With a decent book, my wash gear and flip-flops, I thought I had just about got everything. A last minute addition was a cheque book as warships did not carry cashpoint machines and mess bills still needed to be paid, as well as having a wee bit of cash for sweeties from the NAAFI on-board.

Due to needing to carry the damn thing, I had decided against taking my No1 suit and cap when I joined, as my bag was heavy enough. I was sure the Captain would understand. I only needed to be able to survive for a couple of months until the ship got back to Devonport. Back in homeport, there would be plenty of opportunity to make life more comfortable with my own pillows and quilt, but as these were bulky items, I simply could not carry them.

Another hire car had been arranged for my relatively short journey to Exeter Airport and after ditching the car at the airport, I checked in for the early afternoon flight to Belfast.

As luck would have it, whilst wondering around the departure lounge, I bumped into an old mate from HMS Turbulent, who as it turned out, was also flying to Belfast to join HMS Cornwall. 'Brum' Parkes was one of the Communication Technicians, which is a posh way of saying 'Spook'. Wrapped up in my own little world, I didn't consider that there may be others joining as well, but as I now looked around, I noticed quite a few young people who were obviously naval officers or ratings. Sure they were dressed in civvies, but some carried naval issue baggage, some had tattoos on their forearms and others displayed passes that were hung around their necks. Overall, I detected about a dozen people waiting to board the same flight. Well, at least the ship should arrange someone to meet us. Failing that, I would just follow the crowd.

My assumption turned out to be correct and after collecting baggage at George Best Airport, a uniformed chap was holding a clipboard displaying HMS Cornwall's ship's badge. Once the chap had ticked everyone off, he led the way to a parked minibus. I didn't get much of an opportunity to see Belfast on the journey to the ship as it was dark, raining and claustrophobic in the tight confines of the minibus.

HMS Cornwall, when I first saw her, looked huge. She was sat alongside a wide concrete jetty, illuminated by her own floodlights. Displacing over five thousand tons, she was slightly heavier than a Trafalgar-class submarine and sitting quite high out of the water.

Most of my travelling companions were returning to the ship after leave and, knowing where to go, quickly disappeared through doors and hatches leaving myself and 'Brum' on the flight deck awaiting the Duty PO, who would deliver the mandatory safety brief.

Formalities complete, the Duty PO escorted myself and 'Brum' down to the chief's mess and introduced me to the chap I was relieving, CMEM(M) Kent 'Elsie' Tanner. 'Elsie' was obviously pleased to see me and introduced me quietly to the dozen or so guys that were watching a movie in the darkened mess. He thrust a welcoming can of beer into my hand, which I quickly drank. As he was watching the movie himself, he invited me to go and get my kit unpacked and bunk sorted out.

I had already been allocated a bunk and more locker space than I had clothes, so my unpacking was completed in record time. With my bed now ready to accept a weary traveller, I had a bit of a wander around the ship, bumping into 'Brum' again who had also finished unpacking. Both hungry, we agreed to go into Belfast City Centre, have a couple of beers and a bite to eat before retiring for an early night.

By 7am the following morning, I was up, showered and dressed in what the navy now called No 4s. Formerly known as No 8s. This consisted of dark blue cotton trousers, and a lighter blue working shirt with a name tally. My branch badge above my left breast pocket and chief's epaulettes on my shoulders displayed to all that I was the new Chief Stoker.

After introductions to another CMEM in the same cabin, Mike Eggins led me off to breakfast. Mike, it turned out, was the 'Chippy' and as I later discovered, would be my mentor whilst I became familiar with the general service way of life and the routines on-board a ship. Mike was a good guy, very friendly, articulate and quite intelligent. As the ship left Belfast and slowly made her way northwards out of Belfast Lough, Mike introduced me to his lads in the Chippy's shop in '01P' section, high up on the upper starboard waist, overlooking the flight deck.

It was a novelty, after so many years in submarines, to have the freedom to open a door and wander out onto the upper deck. Silly as it may sound, I was mesmerised by the sea. Once we were clear of land and heading north at quite a lick, the twin screws churned our wake into a gorgeous white and aqua trail. It was getting cold but I just loved being up top staring out into nothingness, glimpsing ships so far away, that they were just grey hazy shapes on the horizon. I hadn't done a stroke of work yet, but I was convinced that I had made the right choice.

For the next week, I assisted Mike in whatever repair jobs and maintenance tasks he had planned, as he endeavoured to teach me his world. In the evening, it was customary to relax in the mess after showering and changing into 'Red Sea rig', which consisted of a pair of black uniform trousers and a white open necked short-sleeved shirt. Generally, we would have a pre-dinner drink in the mess whilst the 'killicks with ties', that's petty officers to you, queued for their dinner. It soon became apparent that there was quite a big class divide between the messes. Whilst submarine senior rates shared one mess, the larger general service ships had separate messes for petty officers. The warrant officers and chief petty officers shared another mess and on 1 deck, the wardroom accommodated the Officers. It also became apparent that the chiefs ran the ship. Sure, the officers made policy and thought that they ran the ship, but with an average age of about twenty-five, they needed the mature experience of the warrant officers and chiefs to make stuff happen.

After an aperitif, we would troop up the passageway into the next section and enjoy a leisurely dinner before heading back to the mess for a few more drinks and maybe watch a movie or play a game. As the new boy on the block, when the mess was full after dinner, I gave the mess bell a loud clang, signalling that the beers were on me, in the time-honoured tradition of joiners and leavers. Frankly, it was a small price to pay for being accepted into the mess in a friendly manner.

A week later, HMS Cornwall was approaching Tromso, very far north in the Norwegian Sea. It took the ship several hours to safely negotiate a path through the fjords and waterways, before we finally berthed alongside in the frozen Norwegian port. After only being on-board for a little over a week, my unfamiliarity with the ship's routine was going to cost me dearly for the second time in a week. The mess operated a drinking game called 'The International Entering Harbour Club'. After the ship had safely come alongside in a foreign port, all participating mess members,had a total of ten-minutes to present themselves into the mess. The time started with a stopwatch when the Officer of the Watch made the pipe "Fall out from Harbour Stations, assume CBRNDC state 3, condition xray." On arrival in the mess, every mess member would be presented with a double shot of their choice. The people that did not arrive within the ten-minute deadline had to pay for the drinks; those are the rules and guess who was late on his first foreign visit? So, whilst enjoying a sizable measure of brandy, the bar manager presented me with a bill for £18. What can you do except pay up and learn not to make the same mistake again? I secretly vowed that there would not be a next time … and there never was.

The first order of business, when arriving alongside, was to get rid of the gash. Generally speaking, the younger lads would form a chain gang and pass bags of smelly and often slimy rubbish down the chain to skips that had been arranged on the jetty. Due to marine pollution regulations, the Royal Navy had long since banned chucking gash bags over the arse end at sea and then using them for target practice, though that was absolutely brilliant fun.

With the gash gone and the ship, well ship-shape, leave was piped. My new buddy, Mike Eggins, had a hankering to go skiing. I had never been skiing before, so I only decided to go if I could muck about on the baby slope, or hire an instructor for a lesson. Mike had never been skiing either, but he reasoned, if kids can do it, just how hard could it be? Well, I found out about an hour later when I was in the back of an ambulance, in a lot of pain, being tended to by a rather beautiful Norwegian paramedic. So how did it go so badly wrong, so quickly?

On arrival at the slope, it turned out that there were no lessons or indeed instructors. The Norwegian kids apparently learnt to ski before they learned how to ride a bike and this was evident as we watched them effortlessly whistling down the slope and with a flourish, skidding to a halt, before jumping on the lift to be towed back to the top.

We queued to hire skis, boots and a couple of poles and outside, struggled to figure out how to put them on. With some assistance, I was eventually clipped into my skis and managed to stand up. Now then, how did I make them go? Together, with Mike, we shuffled slowly along the flat compacted snow and emerged on the slope about half way up. The lift was on the other side and to join it, we first had to get to the bottom. Mike went first and fell over within the first ten feet. He wasn't hurt but began to realise just how difficult this was, not that he let on, of course. Shuffling towards Mike, I hit the slope and I was off. Slowly at first and then gathering speed. I should have known better. One of the first rules of engineering is, don't start it unless you know how to stop it, and I didn't have a clue as I hurtled downwards towards the queue at the bottom of the lift. Crouching down, I sort of figured that if I fell over to one side then I would stop. It was not pretty and I was covered in snow, but it worked.

Mike was still where he had fallen as I managed to struggle back onto my skis again. I gingerly shuffled forward through a sort of turnstile to the base of the ski lift. The lift was in the form of wires, with hard rubber bars at the bottom, that you sort of had to grab and shove between your legs before it dragged you off up the hill. It was more of a towrope than a lift actually, as my skis stayed on the snow pointing uphill. A little above the halfway point, somebody shouted to me and as I turned on my toggle, my skis got tangled and before I knew it, I was in a crumpled heap on the ground, trying to claw my way out of the path of the next skier on the lift, as he couldn't avoid me. Fortunately, I managed to get out of the way, but I was stranded a good way up the hill.

In a now practiced movement, I managed to get onto my skis again and with a pole in each hand, launched myself into the next available gap between skiers and snow boarders. Trying to mimic James Bond in the ski chase from the film 'The Spy Who Loved Me', I bent my knees and started to gather speed. This was great. Having built up a fair lick of speed, I thought I would try to do the 007 thing and kick my ankles out to skid to an impressive halt. It bloody worked, how fantastic was that? I was still congratulating myself when I realised that my skis were pointing slightly uphill and I was moving backwards. SHIT! This was not in the movie. I tried kicking my ankles in the opposite direction, which seemed to work, but off balance, I came down hard on my right shoulder, instantly knowing something was not right. Lying in my own personal snowdrift, I tried to take stock of where it hurt. I'm not sure anybody realised that I was injured, as my new shipmates continued to whizz by, hurling jovial banter as they went.

Eventually, I managed to get my skis unclipped and, dodging kamikaze snowboarders, I managed to trudge across the slope holding everything under my left arm. My right arm was useless and aching like hell. Back at the hut, I dumped my skis, which promptly got 'nicked' by another shipmate and tried to summon medical assistance. It shouldn't have surprised me, but it did, the Ski Centre had the hospital on speed dial and within a few minutes this stunning nurse called Astrid was checking me over. Survey complete, she assisted me into the back of the ambulance and off we whisked, with sirens wailing and Astrid holding my hand and being all sexy nurse-like.

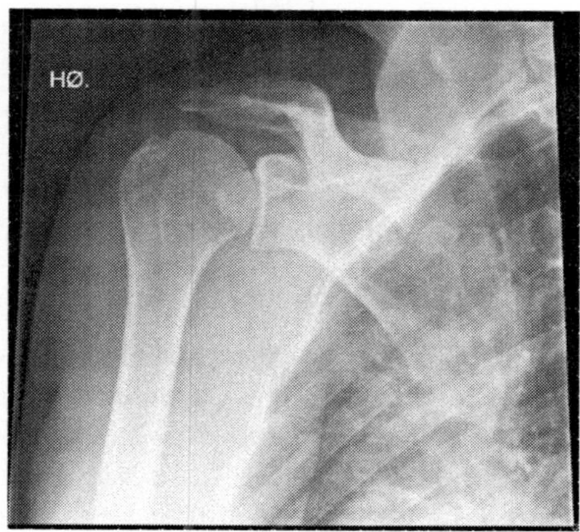

At the hospital, I was X-rayed, pulled around and examined by an English-speaking doctor, before he diagnosed a severe case of torn ligaments and chucked a bill at me. Fortunately, by this time our on-board medic, Petty Officer Katrina Camody, had turned up clutching my passport and more importantly my European Health Insurance Card, both of which had been liberated from my locker.

Back on-board, it had been quickly assessed that I couldn't sail with the ship, as my right arm was absolutely useless. It still cost me another case of beer though, for being a prat and having to be flown home after only being on-board for slightly more than a week.

The following day, I was taken off the ship and installed into a hotel in Tromso, near the airport, with another skiing casualty, to await a flight later in the week. In the meantime, we watched from the hotel bar as HMS Cornwall slowly made her way out of Tromso, to continue with the exercise.

Two days later, a taxi ferried us to the airport for the domestic flight to Oslo, on the first leg of our journey home. Lt Paul Conway was hobbling on crutches with dangerous looking spikes sticking out of the bottom. He had damaged his knee and I had my right arm strapped up in a shoulder sling so between us we had three legs and three arms. Getting on-board the small commuter aircraft was not too difficult, as we had some assistance from the flight attendants. Paul's spiky crutches were stowed away, as they really were potential weapons in the wrong hands.

Landing in Oslo, Paul's crutches were returned and in the arrivals lounge, we discovered a real problem. The airport was quite large and somehow, we needed to transit through passport control and into international departures, in a foreign country and not speaking a word of Norwegian. Carrying our own bags, it was bloody hard work. Paul needed to stop every few metres and rest. Fortunately, we had about four hours before our British Airways flight departed for Heathrow, but even so, it was hard going. In the distance, I spied an abandoned wheelchair next to a domestic departure gate and leaving Paul sat with the bags, dashed off to nick it. Reluctantly, Paul sat in the wheelchair as I arranged our collective luggage around him. Properly loaded and with Paul's bandaged leg sticking out, I tried to push the wheelchair with my good arm whilst he attempted to help with his two good hands on the wheels. It was very awkward and probably very comical to casual onlookers, but we were slowly making progress as I learned how to compensate.

Eventually, through passport control, we presented ourselves at the British Airways desk, still with two hours before departure. Checked-in, we made a base and I parked Paul with the bags whilst I went off in search of some lunch. Fortunately, the time flew by and aware that they had two disabled passengers, we were priority boarded and sat in Club Class with oodles of legroom.

Homeward bound and climbing out of Norway, the seatbelt signs were switched off and drinks were served. Presumably, because we were injured, the stewardesses fussed over us and plied us with food and wine, probably to dull the pain. Who cares, it was a great flight and I must confess that by the time we were wheels down at London Heathrow, I was pain free and more than a little squiffy.

Fortunately, Paul's mummy was there to collect him. After thanking me for looking after her 'little sailor', she asked politely if she could drop me somewhere. "Plymouth please," was my reply, as her face dropped. I was only kidding as it would have been at least two hundred miles out of her way, but it was too good an opportunity to miss.

I moved better on my own and before long I had transferred to Paddington and was finally on the last leg of my journey, courtesy of British Rail.

Back home about a month early should have been great, but I quickly got bored of daytime TV. A few weeks later, I asked if I could fly out to Amsterdam to re-join the ship that had now completed the exercise, but the Executive Warrant Officer on Cornwall was having none of it. Apart from that, my shoulder was still playing up and although my hand worked, I could not lift my arm under its own power.

It was shortly before Easter when the ship returned to Devonport. I was still having trouble convincing a doctor that I was fit enough to go back to sea. One of the things in my favour was that, in my absence, 'Elsie' Tanner had been selected for promotion to warrant officer. This was excellent news for him, but the ship would not release him until he had a relief in post; step forward Atkinson. This was the catalyst that persuaded the doctor to allow me back to work. I was supposed to have been shadowing the Chippy, Mike Eggins, for a year, but now the ship needed me in post as *the* Marine Engineering Departmental Coordinator or ME Depco for short, so I ended up being thrown into the deep end.

This was a huge leap into the unknown for me, I suddenly found myself in post and learning on my feet. Of course, 'Elsie' knew the job backwards and before he left he was always available to advise on certain aspects of how things were done. The position was, basically, the top job amongst the mechanics. I was able to grant leave to everyone in the department, apart from the officers, I was also empowered to punish minor offences, but the most difficult job was arranging the watchbill and getting the right mix of qualified people together into the same watch. There was also quite a few people under training, so it was a constant juggling act of qualifications and personalities.

I was also responsible for training the young lads and monitoring their progress; offering praise where it was warranted and issuing bollockings to the consistent under achievers. It was a very busy job, but predominantly I was desk based. As the chief of all stokers, I wore overalls, pretty much for appearance's sake but didn't get them dirty.

It took a few weeks for me to start to become effective in my new role, as 'Elsie' started to wind down. Gradually he handed over more and more responsibility to me before, one day, as the last act of the previous day's Officer of the Day duties, he raised the flag at 8am to say good morning to Her Majesty and then changed his epaulettes to those of a WO1. He then toured the ship, shaking hands and saying goodbye to everyone. WO1 Kent Tanner had left behind some huge boots to fill.

Unfortunately, HMS Cornwall was still sailing in the shadow of the Iranian incident of 2007, when the Iranian Navy captured two boats full of sailors and Royal Marines for allegedly straying into their territorial waters. I remembered the news coverage of the incident well, but it seemed that whatever the rights and wrongs, the navy had not forgiven the ship, dubbed the 'Ship of Shame' in the press. For this reason and, as many of the ship's company of 2007 had now moved on, HMS Cornwall was required to undergo a period of Basic Operational Sea Training, which, essentially, was eight weeks of purgatory.

Sad as it seems, I was actually looking forward to this. There were many aspects of the job that I was not completely happy with, so, what better than some intensive training, simulating peacetime and wartime fires, floods and famines, knowing that mistakes could be corrected without anyone dying?

One of my main jobs was taking charge of the Standing Sea Emergency Party, which was a small team of fire-fighters who were available twenty-four hours a day. Under my leadership at the forward control point, they would fight fires, control any flooding, and contain smoke and chemical spills. Backed by a competent leading hand, like Andy Clayton, I was to ensure that everyone knew precisely what to do, from the initial continuous and aggressive attack, which we all knew, would extinguish most fires, to sending the chaps in wearing their intermediate fire-fighting rig. These two chaps were known as the 'Attack BA' and had a bogey time of two-minutes to arrive at the scene from when the alarm was sounded.

Assuming that they would be beaten back and preparing for the worst, Andy Clayton would then coordinate the running of hoses, flaking them down with the correct nozzles on the end, so it didn't turn into a snake's wedding when they were charged with salt water, from the firemain.

Whilst Andy was doing this, the five-man support party would be getting dressed in their full fire-fighting rig, which consisted of PBI Gold fire suits, wellington boots, gloves, fire-fighters hood and EDBA. Within the eight-minutes bogey time, they would also carry out a face seal check on their breathing sets to ensure that their masks were not leaking.

My job was to stand back and oversee everything, whilst maintaining communication with the DCO in HQ1. The Logistics Officer, during emergencies at sea, took control of the incident from HQ1, which was roughly in the middle of the ship. A fire on-board a submarine is a major event and as such, the submarine always goes to Emergency Stations. On a ship, incomprehensibly, those who were not required to fight the fires could feasibly stay in bed, or continue to drink beer and watch a movie. Even now, a few years afterwards, I still cannot get to grips with that mentality, I was a submariner for far too long and that ethos stays with you forever.

Whilst I was learning how to do things the skimmer way, we exercised at least twice a week, ramping up from a minor gash bag fire to a galley fire. The exercises increased in intensity as we then tackled a more serious main machinery space fire and culminated in a helicopter crash-on-deck. Each of these exercises involved containing the fire into as small a part of the ship as possible whilst maintaining smoke boundaries and treating casualties. It was good fun. To start with, I made loads of mistakes, but with the hugely experienced Andy Clayton at my back, offering guidance, my confidence increased, as did my volume. Normally a quiet and mild mannered chap, as i/c FCP, I had a real opportunity to shout at full volume. It was amazing how quickly stuff was done, after you had shouted at someone.

After a few weeks of perfecting each exercise, as a team, we were achieving satisfactory assessments by the FOST staff and I was feeling much more confident about having to deal with shipborne fires, floods and famines.

Moving onto the wartime phase of the training, my fire-fighting responsibilities had changed completely, but nobody actually told me and during a war exercise, when a real fire occurred, I went into auto and ran off to fight the fire, completely oblivious that teams at either end of the ship were dressed and ready to tackle any eventuality. That cost me another case of beer for being a total pillock, but we live and learn. The trick is, learning from your cock-ups and not making the same mistake twice.

In week seven of BOST, things took a strange twist that made me appreciate just how political the navy had become. At the beginning, as a ship, we had started the training poorly, but over the weeks, there had been a gradual improvement. People were gelling as a ship's company and were confident in their own abilities. Therefore, it came as a bolt out of the blue when the

Captain, Commander Jeremey Woods, was relieved of his command whilst we were conducting a 'diplomatic visit' to Falmouth as part of the training. Cdr Woods was a good guy, everybody liked him, he was a people person who always had time to stop and talk to the lads and lasses under his command but, he was also in command of HMS Cornwall during the Iranian incident. Whilst this was largely forgotten about on-board, it seemed that the authorities wanted to make an example of our Captain. We were only a week away from completing BOST and now we had had the rug pulled out from under us.

The First Lt, Lieutenant Commander Simon Pink, cleared lower deck and with the ship's company mustered on the flight deck and a tear in his eye, he informed us of the hierarchy's decision to remove Commander Woods with immediate effect. As we were dismissed, nobody said a word. The whole ship's company was completely shell-shocked. Back in my office, I sat in silence for about twenty minutes unable to absorb what this meant for the ship.

A few weeks later, Commander Johnny Ley walked on-board to assume command. He was quite a young chap, but from the start, it was clear that he meant business. In his opening address to the ship's company, Cdr Ley stated that had been brought in to get the ship out of the doldrums. Like a scene from a movie, he told us that he was here to do a job and needed us to keep up with him and if we couldn't, then he invited us to knock on his cabin door and request to be removed from the ship. Very inspirational. On the flip side, he did promise "Fun in the sun," whatever that meant. I must say, I never warmed to Commander Ley, but that was not important. It was clear that he did not suffer fools or small talk, so that was me buggered from the start.

A few weeks later, the FOST staff arrived on-board again for 'BOST, The Sequel'. We still felt quite aggrieved that we had to endure it all again, but we needn't have worried. The staff knew that we were all mightily pissed off, so pretty much cut us some slack. Sure, we still needed to complete all of the required evolutions, but as we were still fresh from the last work-up, the exercises pretty much went like clockwork. As the training progressed, the exercise fires became less frequent as the staff concentrated their efforts on training the operations room and our new command team.

The routine was fairly relaxed compared with the submarine work-ups that I had experienced in the past. Whilst a submarine would carry the staff for the entire work-up, by 6pm every evening, the ship was heading back through Plymouth Breakwater to secure at a buoy for the night whilst the staff jumped on a boat and buggered off home for the night, effectively leaving us in peace and quiet for the evening.

Playing the game as it was supposed to be played, we respected the FOST staff and they largely left us alone. The daily reports started to improve, in line with the unwritten script. All of this would culminate in a massive 'Thursday war' on the final day. It all came down to this. To pass BOST, everyone needed to give maximum effort, for one last push. The FOST staff wore berets for this final inspection day and adopted an assessment role in contrast to the training role of the previous weeks. Everyone was knackered, having been up for most of the night cleaning and scrubbing, to make the ship as presentable as possible, but the end was in sight.

The 'war' started as soon as the FOST staff arrived on-board in the morning. With them safely embarked, HMS Cornwall manoeuvred through the Western Breakwater and out to sea. I was closed up at my Action Station, which coincidently was also my office, on the port side of 2-Kilo section. I was in charge of the mobile party with the new Chippie's mate, Joff Lucas, and a small handful of lads. Responsible for dealing with any incidents in the local area, we had decided amongst us that, I would fight the fires and Joff would look after shoring up any floods, but like the best laid plans of mice and men it wouldn't pan out like that and I would end the day in hospital.

Towards the end of the afternoon, we had fought off aggressors, extinguished fires, stemmed flooding in several compartments and won the war, hurrah! It had been a mega-busy day; everyone had pulled their weight and were justifiably knackered. This was the final push and nobody wanted to go through BOST, an unprecedented third time.

At around 3:30pm, the Damage Control Officer broadcast the welcome pipe, "End of exercise, end of exercise, return and stow all gear." Now, all that remained was for everybody to de-rig all of the shoring, empty and roll up all of the fire hoses and return everything back to its proper stowage before the debrief and the results of our final assessment could be learned.

Joff and I detailed off our chaps to return all of the kit in our area and to recharge the EDBA breathing sets that had recently been used. Everyone was busy doing something. There was a real desire to get back to normal. Joff went into the forward engine room, below the combined tech office, to take down some shoring, whilst I rolled up some size-3 hoses that had been used to pump flood water out of the forward auxiliary machinery room. As everyone else was busy returning stuff or cleaning up, I struggled to carry the three hoses back to the after FRPP. I was knackered and sweating buckets, but the portable submersible pump, called a Weda Pump, still needed to be hoisted out of the FAMR's bilge and returned to its circular stowage on 2 deck. This was when it all started to go pear-shaped.

Struggling to lift the Weda Pump by its lifting rope out of the bilge, I started, first of all, to feel very dizzy and experienced a feeling like I had never felt before. It was as if someone was tightening a belt around my chest. Seeing me in difficulties, one of the killicks, 'Jock' Stewart, a huge chap from Elgin, in the far north of Scotland, came to my assistance. Between us, we managed to get the pump up the ladder and out onto 2 deck. I felt very weak, I was soaked with sweat and frankly, I needed a bit of a lie down. Back in the tech office, a few of the lads had returned from stowing their kit but they were all looking at me strangely. Joff came back in and asked if I was ok. I replied that I would be, but I just needed to get my breath back. He responded with, "You've gone grey, mate," and without saying another word, he disappeared.

Within a minute, 'Jonno', the new PO medic came into the office, "You ok, chief?" "Fine," I replied. "Never mind that, let's get you down on to the deck," as the lads manhandled me down onto my office deck and started undressing me. He squirted something tingly under my tongue and started to plug me into a machine. I remember thinking to myself, shit this is bad. The First Lt, Simon Pink, then appeared in the office, which was most unusual as we were still at Action Stations. "You'll be ok, Ian," he said, "we've got a nice big blue and red helicopter coming to give you a ride home." Fuck! This *is* bad, was I dying? Well, obviously not, but it was a bit worrying all the same. When the second in command makes a special trip to see you, with the ship at Action Stations, and calls you by your Christian name, for the first time ever.

Over the main broadcast, I vaguely recall the time to the Air-sea rescue helicopters arrival being counted down before I was strapped to a stretcher and was being manhandled into a Sea King that had just managed to squeeze itself onto the end of the flight deck. I must have been drifting in and out of consciousness as the next thing I recall was the helicopter crew arguing with an ambulance paramedic about the ownership of the stretcher, not that this made any sense to me at all. Evidently, we had landed at Plymouth Airport. With sirens wailing, I was transferred to Derriford hospital, which was just around the corner, where a crash team stood by to greet me. I had never felt so important. Normally, at hospital, I am told to sit and wait for four hours, but on this occasion, I was wheeled into a cubical and connected up to a machine immediately, whilst medical people bustled about doing lots of other stuff to me. I had bits shaved and stickers attached all over the place and at some stage someone nicked some blood off me, but I don't really remember that.

Well, despite me thinking I had overdone it and just needed a bit of rest, it was clear everybody else thought I'd had a heart attack. As it turned out, I was right and everyone else was wrong. Apparently, after a heart attack, proteins are released into the blood and my blood sample showed clear, but there was some concern about what had caused my symptoms. In any event, I was finally given a GTN spray and allowed to go home, with orders to take it easy for a few days.

The following day, my boss, Lt Cdr Barrie Harvey, called to find out if I was still breathing. I assured him that I was and that I had just overdone things, before asking him how the assessment had gone. He informed me that the Admiral considered HMS Cornwall had done enough, so he had passed us fit for deployment. BOST - The Sequel was over. thank god for that.

A few days later, our new programme was published. We were off to fly the flag, sailing around the Mediterranean Sea as the flagship of the Standing NATO Maritime Group under the flag of Commodore Steve Chick. This was more like it. The Skipper had promised us some 'fun in the sun' and, it seemed as if he already knew what was on the cards. Everyone was quite excited as the programme started to firm up with more and more foreign visits to countries such as France, Gibraltar, Italy, Crete, Malta, Greece and Turkey to name but a few.

We now had a few weeks to prepare for the deployment and to get all of the stores on-board before Easter leave. Unfortunately, my heart scare had not gone away and a couple of appointments duly arrived for me to visit a hospital in Basingstoke at the same time that the ship was due to sail for Brest on the first leg of our SNMG deployment. This meant that I was going to miss the first visit. Bloody typical, do all of the hard work and miss the fun bit.

The MEO was disappointed to be sailing without his Departmental Coordinator, but told me to fly out and re-join the ship as soon as the medical people had passed me fit. Therefore, it was with a degree of sadness that I stood on the jetty in April 2009, waving my mates goodbye, as HMS Cornwall departed from Plymouth in procedure alpha, and manoeuvred her way down the Hamoaze, and turned left towards Drake's Island.

The first of my appointments in Basingstoke involved me being hooked up to an ECG machine and running on a treadmill, whilst a couple of nurses kept a watchful eye on me. This was no problem at all, apart from getting a little out of breath, running uphill on the machine. The next appointment, a week later, was far more intrusive; I had been booked in at the same hospital for an angiogram, which sounded fun, but I didn't really know what to expect.

Stripped naked on the ward, I was told to dress in a standard theatre gown and to lie on the bed. When I was ready, a pretty young nurse appeared with a cutthroat razor and some soap. After drawing the curtains, she lifted my gown and proceeded to expertly shave me, down there. God, I would have paid good money for that, as she was very gentle. She took hold of my penis and moved it to one side so as not to nick me, as she removed my pubic hair. Embarrassingly, I felt myself stiffen slightly, but she ignored it and just went about her business, until I was completely shaved. A little later, I was wheeled into the theatre and transferred to an operating table ready for the angiogram. Positioned above me were three monitors, which allowed me to see what was going on. My gown was again lifted, embarrassingly, displaying the last turkey in the shop. The doctor explained that he would first anesthetise me before inserting a tube into the side of my groin. I just laid back and looked into the eyes of the nurse who had shaved me. She was seemingly in charge of looking after me at the head end, whilst the doctor did his bits and pieces down at the other end. I must say, it did not hurt a bit. I felt a bit of tugging here and there, but was completely surprised when he eventually said, "I'm just going into the pumping chamber now," as he inserted his tube further into my artery. When he was ready, he said, "I'm going to inject some dye now and you may feel as if you've wet yourself, but don't worry, you won't have." Immediately, I experienced a very curious warmth around my groin area, which felt very pleasant, in an embarrassing sort of way. The nurse, seeing the look in my eyes simply smiled knowingly and said, "Don't worry, you haven't." Looking up at the screens, the dye briefly illuminated my arteries like the silhouette of an oak tree, which was truly amazing.

When he had finished, the doctor plugged up the hole and I was wheeled back to the ward to rest on my bed. Every ten minutes or so, my nurse would come in, lift my gown and inspect my bits to ensure I was not bleeding from the arterial hole. Eventually, I was allowed to get dressed and await my brother, Simon, who was collecting me from hospital.

Receiving an e-mail from the ship a week later, I learned that the 'fun in the sun' statement was, in fact, too good to be true. We had been re-tasked to just 'pop' through the Suez Canal, down the Red Sea and to patrol the internationally recognised transit corridor, with a load of other NATO warships. The IRTC was a potentially dangerous stretch of water from the bottom of the Red Sea, heading east through the Gulf of Aden, towards the Indian Ocean. This was an anti-piracy patrol to protect the merchant shipping and if need be, slot a few Somalian pirates along the way. Therefore, instead of travelling to Brest to re-join the ship, I was now instructed to fly to Scotland and re-join in Faslane.

A week later and I was back on the ship. With an embarked force of Royal Marines from the Fleet Protection Group and topped up with food and fuel, we sailed from Scotland and headed at high speed, via Lisbon towards Souda Bay in Crete, for more stores and two weeks of warm weather maintenance, prior to transiting the Suez Canal.

Having never been through the canal before, I was quite excited and looking forward to seeing it. As it turned out, there was a very real threat of a terrorist attack on the ship, so, for that reason, most of the upper deck was placed out of bounds to the ship's company, who just wanted to goof at the scenery. The starboard bridge wing was the only place visitors to the bridge could use as a viewing area. Interestingly, using some high-powered binoculars, I was able to see some of the old gun emplacements, camps and tanks that littered the sides of the canal.

It took quite a while for the ship to transit the waterway. All of the time we had special sea dutymen closed up, which caused me a bit of a logistical headache, trying to rotate people and keep all of the positions covered. There was a bit of respite overnight, when we entered the Great Bitter Lake and 'parked up' for the night. This allowed the northbound traffic to clear the southern part of the canal and leave the way clear for us to proceed south at first light.

Safely out of the canal and into the Red Sea for the first time in my career, the upper deck was again opened as the Officer of the Watch rang on the revs. A couple of days later, after steaming down the Red Sea, we had a need to refuel and to get the gash ditched. Once we had safely negotiated the Bab-el-Mandeb straits, at the bottom of the Red Sea, we turned right into Djibouti for the night. Having heard some nasty things about the small country, I elected not to go ashore, other than to walk onto the jetty to ditch some gash, just so I could say that I had been there.

The following morning, the patrol started in earnest. Essentially, we were running a racetrack pattern down one side of the IRTC on an easterly course and then about forty hours later on, reversing course to starboard to head back down the Gulf of Aden towards the Red Sea again. The sneaky communication chaps were continually chattering to the other ships in the area and listening in to any merchant ships transiting the area. At the same time, they were keeping a listening watch for intelligence of suspect dhow's sculling around. We had a very good chance of detecting these bad guys, as we had our Lynx helicopter flying ahead of us for most of the day and maritime patrol aircraft also investigating contacts of interest. If, of course, we heard that something was about to happen, the ship would race to the area, whilst the detachment of Royal Marines and the naval Force-Protection squad would be dressed and armed. They would be briefed and loaded into our two Pacific 22 inflatables, prior to them being lowered into the sea, shielded by the high sides of the ship. The problem was, our guys had to catch the pirates in the act of boarding a merchant vessel. Once they had hijacked the ship, our rules of engagement prevented the marines from opening fire. Of course, if the suspected pirates were still on their boat, then with the proper permission, we could stop and send the marines across to search the dhow and the skiffs that were being towed behind it. These guys could have been legitimate fishermen, but fishermen do not often go about their business with rocket-propelled grenades, AK47s and ladders with grappling hooks. It was incredibly frustrating, everybody wanted to stop these guys, but it appeared as if NATO's hands were tied. The alternative was to shoot first and ask questions later, but get that wrong and people go to jail.

After four weeks at sea and needing food, fuel and to get rid of our mountain of accumulated rubbish, we called into Salalah in Oman for a few days. What a shit hole! It might sound exotic, but it was, essentially, a container port in the desert. There was a sort of smog hanging over the port meaning that, although it was still hot, the sun wasn't shining down on us.

Logistics sorted out and with enough fresh food to sustain us, we were pleased to leave Salalah and continue with our pirate-hunting mission. It wasn't too much longer before HMS Cornwall called into Port Rashid in Dubai for our mid-deployment standoff. I had never been to Dubai before and was really looking forward to it. The couple of weeks that the ship was alongside had been split into two separate stints of leave. Many people had elected to bring wives and girlfriends out for what would turn out to be a cheap holiday. I had arranged for Anita to fly out for the second week and had booked a lovely hotel right on Jumeirah Beach. The Habtoor Grand Beach Hotel was arguably the best hotel that we had ever stayed in and with a room high up on the corner of the building overlooking the Palm Jumeirah.

I was waiting at the airport when Anita's flight touched down. There was also a Limousine and a driver already waiting to whisk us off to the hotel, which was a very pleasant surprise. I am not sure who organised that, but I certainly didn't pay for it.

We spent a fantastic week touring Dubai, marvelling at how a fishing village, barely a hundred years previously, had now risen up out of the sand into a metropolis full of gleaming glass buildings and skyscrapers. There was even a shopping mall with a real snow ski slope inside it. How mad is that, when the temperature outside was about 45°C? The most surreal experience however, was the day before Anita flew home and two days before HMS Cornwall sailed from Dubai.

We had chosen to spend our last day at the Atlantis water park, at the top of the Palm Jumeirah and spent a very enjoyable day mucking about in the water and giving myself an enema by shooting down the various water slides. It was tremendous fun but by the middle of the afternoon, a worn out Anita opted to lie on a sun bed, whilst I conquered the highest slide in the park. The slide in question was called the 'Leap of Faith' and was the nine stories high centrepiece of the 'Ziggurat', which looked like an Aztec temple. Nearing the top of the steps, I met a distinguished white-haired English chap who was clearly a bit miffed, having discovered that the top ride was closed. He was escorting his young daughter who seemed equally upset. The chap was chuntering that if this was England then they would have put a sign at the bottom to say that the ride was closed. He explained to the girl that they would have go down to the next, less scary, slide. Waiting at the end of the queue behind the chap and his daughter, I struck up the usual holiday chat. "Hiya, where are you from?" "Er Portsmouth," he replied. Taking a complete stab in the dark, I continued "You Navy?" Surprised, he countered "Er yes! You?" "Yes," I replied. He became interested in finding another matelot so far from home and asked if I was on holiday. I replied, "Sort of, I'm here on a ship." "Really? What are you in?" Alarm bells started ringing in my head. It was common knowledge amongst sailors that ratings are considered to be 'on' ships whilst officers are considered, by them, to be 'in' ships. This chap looked like an officer and spoke like an officer, but out of uniform, it didn't count. "I'm the chief stoker on HMS Cornwall," I continued. "Ah Cornwall, that's Steve Chick's flag," which was more of a statement than a question. The bells in my head rang louder. This was not going too well. This stranger was referring to my Commodore by his first name, which made him more senior than a Commodore. "Are you flag rank yourself?" I tentatively enquired "Er yes, I'm Second!" *Fuck!* Here I was, making idle holiday chitchat with Vice Admiral Sir Alan Massey, the Second Sea Lord and about a hundred ranks higher than me. I sprang smartly to attention. As luck would have it, he was a smashing bloke and asked me about how morale was in HMS Cornwall. It was not really the place to do it, but since he had asked, I mentioned a few gripes that I had about the training of my lads and the fact that they were leaving the navy after about three years as they were getting bored and not able to progress. 2SL was kind enough to listen and requested that I e-mail him with the specifics and he promised to look into it. What a nice bloke.

The following morning at the airport, preparing to wave goodbye to Anita for four months, a tall white-haired chap approached with a lady and a young girl in tow, "Good to see you again, Chief," as the Second Sea Lord introduced his wife to me. It turned out that 2SL and his family were on the same flight as our wives and girlfriends. I bet he didn't bank on spending his precious holiday with a load of sailors, but even so, what a top bloke.

Sailing from Dubai the following day, we went to Action Stations as a precaution, whilst we transited the narrow Straits of Hormuz and back out onto our stomping ground around the Indian Ocean and the Gulf of Aden.

Call me cynical, but as we were somewhere nice and sunny, we always seemed to be getting visits from high-ranking officers who desperately needed to tell us just how great we were, in order to justify them topping up their tans. In July 2009, we were visited by CinC Fleet who wanted to come to sea with us for a few days to, er... assess the tactical picture and give the lads an excuse to scrub out for Britain. Well, it took him out of the office for a bit. I thought that I would use the opportunity of his visit to my advantage and suggested to the hierarchy, that CinC Fleet present me with the bar to my Long Service and

Good Conduct Medal, representing thirty years of undetected crime. This seemed like a perfectly good plan to the Captain, so it was programmed into CinC Fleet's itinerary for an evening during his visit. On the evening in question, he popped into the chief's mess, made the presentation and after everyone had congratulated me on being an all-round good egg, I rang the mess bell and got the beers in to commemorate being the longest serving member of the ship's company.

After CinC Fleet had flown home, HMS Cornwall continued to patrol the IRTC but occasionally we got a special job, such as escorting a food ship from one Somalian port around the Horn of Africa, to another, thus ensuring that the food aid arrived safely at its destination. The deployment continued with the ship typically spending four weeks at sea followed by four or five days alongside. One of the planned visits was to Mombasa and I must say I was really looking forward to it. Anita had given me a 'shopping list' of wooden animals to barter for ashore, but due to reports of some civil unrest, we continued south, ending up in the Seychelles. Having never visited this paradise in the Indian Ocean before, I was very surprised to find that it had a distinctly West Indian feel, and considering that it was on the other side of the world, I found this quite incredible. It was very idyllic though, with crystal clear blue waters and perfect white sandy beaches but we had been away from home for several months and were starting to count down the days to when we would be home again.

Towards the end of October 2009, we received intelligence that a British married couple had been taken hostage by pirates, whilst sailing in the Indian Ocean. As we were close on a thousand miles away, frustratingly, it would have taken us days to get anywhere close and in our constant battle against the pirates, it was all about being in the right place at the right time.

Slowly working our way northwards, we stopped at Salalah again for fuel and food before heading back up the Red Sea and through the Suez Canal. Relinquished of our NATO responsibilities, the ship called into Malta at the beginning of December, to allow the lads and lasses to let their hair down and strange as it might seem, de-stress after having been at sea effectively for months. Malta was lovely, it was like being in England, only in the sun. Despite it being December and the streets lined with Christmas decorations, it felt quite surreal to be basking in the winter sun. My run-ashore oppo, Mo-Hurley, and myself found ourselves a very nice bistro overlooking Grand Harbour that offered free Wi-Fi, so we spent a very enjoyable afternoon, devouring a long lunch, washed down with a bottle of the house red whilst catching up on our e-mails.

During our visit to Malta, the ship got a visit from the Compulsory Drugs Testing team who were seemingly paying a '*random*' visit to the ship. So random was it that we happened to be in a very warm, sunny Mediterranean port. When we were freezing our nuts off in northern Norway, they were nowhere to be seen, but perhaps I'm being cynical again .

Everyone, including the Captain, needed to be tested. Surely, with a crew of two hundred and fifty, they were taking the piss. Well that is exactly what they were doing, as one by one, the girls and boys were escorted to one of the ship's toilets and asked to provide a sample. This was then tested for temperature to ensure that it was fresh, before being decanted into two sample bottles and sealed with bar codes, to avoid tampering. As a show of compliance, the Captain, Cdr Ley, went first followed by the XO, Lt Cdr Pink, so that nobody felt they could refuse. Strangely, I was asked to take some photographs of the proceedings, for a centre page spread in the February 2010 edition of the 'Navy News', before I was then asked to provide my own sample. Whilst the testing was, being carried out, nobody was allowed ashore and armed sentries stood on the flight deck guarding the gangway. I knew I had nothing to worry about, but two of the lads on-board could not say the same and they left the ship and probably the navy very shortly after they both provided positive samples.

Leaving Malta, we headed west towards the last stop of the deployment, Gibraltar. This was a welcome opportunity for a bit of last minute Christmas shopping and a post-deployment piss up in the Grand Casement Square.

Having visited Gibraltar on many occasions, I was looking forward to seeing 'The Rock' again and, like Malta and Bermuda, it was a very British country. This visit permitted me, for the first time in over twenty-five visits to the small country, to cross the border for an evening on the lash in the Spanish town of La Linea. On previous visits, the border had always been shut to visiting ships and submarines

Leaving Gibraltar, turning right into the Atlantic Ocean, the entire ship's company was excited about going home. Heading north towards Plymouth, the water and the weather started to get noticeably colder, the closer we got. The XO, Simon Pink, had been busy organising a reception for our homecoming, which included a pipe band and a huge marquee in which to shelter, whilst the families enjoyed free food and hot drinks, as they anxiously awaited our return.

After being away from home for eight months, HMS Cornwall finally entered Plymouth Breakwater on the evening of 9th December 2009 and secured to a Buoy to spend the last night of the deployment at sea, within sight of home.

The mood on-board HMS Cornwall the following morning was very buoyant, everyone was in good spirits. Even my old mate, 2SL, was popping on-board to welcome the 'Fighting 99' home from deployment. The wardroom had laid on a buffet breakfast for the Second Sea Lord, to meet some handpicked members of the crew. I was not one of them. Nil desperandum, nothing was about to ruin the day… except perhaps the weather. A thick fog had descended on Plymouth and as such, the Hamoaze was closed.

I phoned Anita from the upper deck to tell her the situation. Everybody prayed that the fog would lift sufficiently to allow the ship to safely navigate up river. I the meantime, I dressed in my best uniform, in preparation for Procedure Alpha, to celebrate our homecoming.

Suitably dressed and sat in the mess with a wobbly coffee, laced with a double measure of Pusser's rum, there was a loud knock on the door followed by a Rear Admiral brushing the door curtain to one side, "Is the chief stoker in the mess?" asked The Second Sea Lord. Startled, I stood to greet the Admiral as he thrust out his hand, "Good to see you again, chief, welcome home." Well, it's not every day, one of the most powerful men in the Royal Navy hunts you down, just to say "Hello." I made the boss a coffee as he chatted comfortably with the lads in the mess. What a nice man.

Fortunately, the fog did lift slightly, allowing HMS Cornwall to proceed slowly up river. Stood high up, on the port side of the after sea wolf deck, I could not see a thing through the mist. It was bloody freezing though, as we were all still acclimatised to the warm weather of the Med. The sounds of the pipe band drifted across the water to us, as we drew closer through the clearing fog. As we neared 6 Wharf, I tried to spot Anita amongst the hundreds of people awaiting our return, but she saw me first and started cheering and waving both of her arms high in the air. We were home, safe, at last.

I think it would be fair to say, Anita did not enjoy being home alone for eight months one little bit. However, there was already a rumour circulating of us returning to the Gulf of Aden in the summer of 2010 for another deployment. Since we married in 1985, I had never been away from home for a single patrol lasting more than twelve weeks, so this last trip had smashed all records. I wasn't too keen on leaving her again either, but this was the job that paid the bills.

Remembering what Commander Johnny Ley had said when he joined, "If at any time you are not happy on my ship, come and knock on my door and I will do all I can to get you off." Requesting to leave a ship is never going to be a very good career move, so I elected to seek council with the new MEO, Lt Cdr Mark Hamilton, who seemed a decent bloke.

The meeting actually didn't go too well, as there was seemingly a world shortage of chief stokers and although he didn't particularly want to stand in my way, he did *need* another Departmental Coordinator, so come what may, he couldn't just sanction me buggering off, just because my missus didn't want me to go to sea. He did sympathise and promised to talk to the Captain and discuss my concerns.

I wasn't privy to the conversation, but it wouldn't have made any difference, the Captain was not prepared to leave my job gapped until another chief stoker could be 'grown'. By February 2010, I was feeling decidedly backed into a corner. The rumour of a summer deployment had now been confirmed and an unprecedented third work-up had now been programmed, in preparation for the ship deploying east of Suez.

I had one final card to play. After exhausting all other options, I wrote to Vice Admiral, Sir Alan Massey, to request that I be retained in the service in a shore job. I considered, whilst carefully composing my request, that it might ruffle a few feathers, but I had tried everything else.

Still awaiting the Second Sea Lord's reply, my world suddenly fell apart. I received a phone call one afternoon in mid-March informing me of the tragic news that my dad, Lawrence Atkinson, had been fatally injured in a car accident. This made my decision to leave the service so much easier. The death of my father, as you might expect, hit me hard and immediately caused me to reflect on my own mortality. Some bright spark once said, "Nobody ever says, on their deathbed, I wish I had spent more time at work."

When the Admiral's letter of reply arrived on-board, the news was not good. It was blatantly clear that 2SL had taken the trouble to investigate my situation, as he related to personal stuff I hadn't told him about.

I didn't get what I had asked for, but the Admiral made an intelligent argument, with logic that I couldn't fault. In a nutshell, he couldn't just massage the rules when it suited as then every 'Jack Tar' or 'Jenny Wren' could come crawling out of the bunk space, demanding a shore job, using me as the precedent, and that would never do.

Instead of just saying no, the Admiral had given me some options to consider, before wishing me luck in deciding my next career move. The four options were as follows:

a) Stay as you are, and complete the job on Cornwall.
b) Submit twelve months' notice to leave the service.
c) Apply for a compassionate discharge, or
d) Apply for a swap with another Type 22 CMEM(M).

The Swap was a non-starter, as I had already investigated that. Compassionate discharge would be swift, meaning that I would probably be unemployed by the end of the week. Remaining on-board HMS Cornwall was a viable option, but I was worried about Anita's mental health issues; could she cope for another eight months alone? Probably not. With my decision made, in my office, I logged on to JPA, composed some amplifying notes and pressed the button to submit twelve months' notice to leave the Royal Navy. It would be fair to say, it was a very sad day in 'Plugsville'.

The die was now cast, I had just released the brake on a runaway train and my next ship was 'civilianship'. Twelve months may seem a long time, but trust me, when I say that it is not. There was much to do, not least applying for and getting a job. I had served in the Royal Navy almost all of my working life and the last interview I had attended was back in 1978. At the age of sixteen, anything was better than nothing, but now in my late forties, I had a mortgage, a car loan and bills up the ying yang, so I needed a job that was going to pay roughly what I earned as a chief petty officer in the navy, if only to maintain our lifestyle.

An interview with the resettlement people in HMS Drake only served to confuse me more. Apparently, I had loads of transferrable skills but still, would need to retrain for my next career. Due to my length of service, I was awarded four weeks of resettlement leave and a small pot of cash from the navy so I could retrain for my next career choice. The first suggested course was a three-day Career Transition Workshop. This course, amongst other things, was really designed to create a professional looking CV and to practice some mock interviews. The course was considered essential, and had to be worth three days of my resettlement leave.

As the ship was alongside in a maintenance period, finding the time for the course was not an issue. It was actually quite useful, and although I still had no idea what I was going to do next, the course did suggest some ideas and also a bit of financial planning, regarding the wheelbarrow full of cash that would be heading my way shortly after I had handed my ID Card back.

Back on-board the ship, the following week, my attention was focused solely towards going on draft. Another BOST was looming and I could see no point in FOST training me for a job that I was not going to be doing. It seemed far more sensible, to get someone else in post and then to train them.

After much haranguing of the MEO and the Captain, they agreed. One of my cabin buddies, CMEM(L) Paul 'Alf' Ramsey, was the chief electrician on-board, but he had long since hankered after my job, as it was considered, by some, to be a stepping-stone for promotion to warrant officer.

When it happened, it happened very quickly. I was summoned for an informal chat with the Captain who, over coffee, explained that I would be leaving the ship shortly to concentrate on my resettlement. In the meantime, with immediate effect, Chief Ramsey had assumed my responsibilities as the Departmental Coordinator. I certainly did not see that coming. With a flick of his pen, I was now, effectively, a chief stoker without portfolio. It is a very strange feeling, to suddenly go from being massively busy all day, every day to having absolutely nothing to do. No job and no responsibility, but I did try to give 'Alf' as much assistance as possible as he struggled to juggle two jobs at once.

Shortly after my meeting with the Captain, I was handed an Assignment Order to leave HMS Cornwall and join the Superintendent Fleet Maintenance team as their Manpower Coordinator. The current incumbent was apparently leaving to have a baby. Despite the state of flux that existed during this couple of months, HMS Cornwall was a fantastic last job on a great ship surrounded by some good people who, it had been my privilege to work with. However, the decision had been made.

As a swan-song, with the permission of the mess committee, Warrant Officer 'Eric' Sykes and I organised a rather splendid, black tie 'Ladies Night' at Boringdon Hall near Plymouth. We had been given a generous budget from the mess profits, which allowed us to arrange live music, a photographer, good food and an awful lot of wine, including a decanter of port on each table. From the little I remember and from what I was told afterwards, it was an excellent evening and the perfect end to my last sea-going job in the Royal Navy.

Suitably recovered, a few days later, with a degree of reluctance and a goodly amount of beer, I finally saluted and walked off the gangway of HMS Cornwall to start my last job in the Royal Navy.

Ian Atkinson

Sailor to Civvy

12th July 2010 to 12th December 2010

Having retained my coveted dockyard car pass from my time on HMS Cornwall, I was able to drive to within spitting distance of my new office and my last job in the Royal Navy. I dare say the ship would demand it back eventually, but whilst I had uniform and kit to transport, it suited me just fine to hold onto it for a while longer.

My new job was as *the* Departmental and Training Coordinator for Superintendent Fleet Maintenance. SFM was a reincarnation of the old fleet maintenance base, and during my time, it had had many names, but it had also reduced in size. As we had less ships and submarines, the navy only needed to employ a fraction of its former workforce, meaning, whilst the engineers were busy, there was much less capacity for skiving and people were required to work smarter.

The SFM workforce was divided into sections that specialised in certain areas of maintenance, such as engine changes or refrigeration maintenance. As my last job was desk based, I changed into black trousers and a white short sleeved shirt, wearing my rank badges on my epaulettes and my 'Dolphins' above my left breast pocket.

Based in Lowden Building, adjacent to the submarine 'graveyard', known as 3 Basin, the SFM Trademaster's offices were located on the second floor facing west across the river, towards Torpoint. The boss, Lt Cdr Sue Seagrave, enjoyed the luxury of her own office whilst her assistant, Warrant Officer Nick Sharland, to his continual annoyance, shared an office with WO2 Richie Smith. Richie, from the start, was mega-keen, trying to press all of the right buttons for promotion to WO1. The rest of the management team shared a huge office, which was also home to the kettle and the tea-boat. My new desk took up one corner of the office and looked quite imposing, as it had two monitors cluttering it up and a multi-layered tray of miscellaneous paperwork that I am sure was probably important to someone.

Also in the office was our pet civilian, Linda Kelly, who was employed as an admin assistant and office manager by Babcock Marine. Linda, as the only permanent resident, commanded the best desk, next to the window. If you asked Linda, she would admit that she ran the office, but this was only because the rest of the team couldn't be arsed to argue with her. Looking after the submariners was WO2 Stirling 'Spike' Way and although I had just left a skimmer, I was still a submariner at heart, which meant we were members of the same club. I had not met Spike previously, but we got along from day one. The fourth member of the office was another Warrant Officer by the name of Keith Bussell, who tended to look after the sick and medically downgraded members of SFM. Like me, Keith was counting down the days to his retirement, but he joined up when Nelson was a lad and consequently, was older than dust. Keith was a perfectly good bloke, but he didn't really have time to spend in the office as his true passion was running the Car Club up in HMS Drake.

One of my first acts, after the introductions and wetting the tea, was to stick a huge laminated wall planner behind my desk. To this, I marked out my resettlement plan. I needed to get weaving as the clock was still counting down and come what may, my naval salary would cease on the 5th April 2011, barely nine months away.

I still had no idea what I wanted to do next, and this was becoming quite a worry. One evening, my old mate, Mike Eggins, provided a potential opening. Mike had left the navy a year previously and having not really settled, he was still trying to find a job that suited his talents. He had recently interviewed for a job in Penryn with a company called Ocean Engineering who were recruiting a fire-fighting maintenance engineer. The job didn't really suit Mike, but he recommended me, which was kind of him. I subsequently had a long telephone interview with one of the directors, which went well enough for him to invite me down for a more formal chat, which would cost me another day of my precious resettlement leave.

The company, in darkest Cornwall, was based in a unit on a small industrial estate, not too far from Falmouth. The interview, as the director had promised, was quite informal followed by a tour of the factory unit. I was like a kid in a sweet shop. They had fire extinguisher components everywhere. I recognised all of the parts for what they were and felt instantly at home in the small but fully equipped workshop. The meeting concluded with the director inviting me to their stand at a corporate sailing show in Southampton where I would meet the rest of the team.

This was all starting to look very promising and I was quite excited about the possibility of building a career around maintaining fire-fighting equipment. Repairing extinguishers and breathing apparatus had been my bread and butter for nearly my entire career. The show was a typical trade fair with various stands relating to just about anything in the shipping line. This was too good an opportunity to miss, so, arriving smartly turned out, I handed out CVs to every company that looked remotely interesting to me. They were not necessarily looking for recruits, but it didn't hurt to talk to them and at this point, I hadn't been offered a job.

The Ocean Engineering stand was situated at the back of the exhibition hall, near to a door to some outside exhibits. There were four guys milling around on the stand, two directors and a couple of engineers who all seemed busy, chatting to people and very obviously drumming up business. The company was clearly going places. As I was hovering about on the stand and coincidentally wearing the same style of light blue short-sleeved shirt, visitors to the stand assumed I was on the payroll and started to ask me questions. As I knew most of the kit on display inside out, explaining what it did and offering suggestions was second nature to me. The two directors, Paul and Errol, would disappear periodically, so I didn't get much of an opportunity to speak to them until later in the afternoon when they invited me to step outside into the summer sunshine for a chat.

Unbeknown to me, they had been observing me all day and were impressed with the way that I had fitted in, so they offered me a job right there and then. They accepted that their pay offer was not great, but the opportunities for promotion and to eventually run my own office were clearly in the pipeline. The problem was, the job was in Southampton.

Driving back to Plymouth, later that afternoon, gave me the opportunity to put everything into perspective. There was much to consider, not least applying to leave the navy early and selling up and moving to Southampton, a city where I didn't know a soul. There was certainly some tough decisions to be made.

Back in the office on Monday, I was still gushing about my perfect record at job interviews. I had attended one interview and as a result, had been offered one job. Leaving the navy in August 2010, when they wanted me to start, was eight months early and this would have a detrimental effect on my pension and my final gratuity. There was also the problem about having to sell up and move to Southampton. The salary, whilst respectable, was still considerably lower than my current income and the house prices were somewhat higher in Southampton. Could I really afford to do this? The mechanics of the job sounded great, but there were too many ifs and buts. After much soul searching and talking to Anita and my family, I decided, with great reluctance, to turn down their offer. So there I was back at square one. I hoped that I wouldn't live to regret it.

Although I was concentrating on finding a second career, I still had a job to do in the navy. This largely centred on managing the SFM joiners and leavers, identifying where they were coming from and sending out letters of introduction.

Being quite a senior bunch, we used to have quite a lot of fun in the office with the new joiners. If they sauntered into the office looking somewhat dishevelled and not like smart naval ratings. This would result in either Spike or Keith, who were the closest to the door, shouting at them and being the 'bad cops'. I was always the 'good cop' and didn't shout unless I needed to, but asked them to go away, sort themselves out before coming back to complete their joining routine, so as not to upset the grumpy warrant officers. Perhaps you needed to be there, but it was funny at the time.

As the training coordinator, I had a responsibility for organising seventeenth edition wiring regulations and P.A.T testing courses for those that needed the qualifications as part of their job. It seemed to be a perk of my position that I could choose the candidates, so it became a 'jobs for the boys' type of arrangement. I intended to do the courses myself, if only to add another string to my bow and another couple of lines to my CV but, unfortunately, with everything else going on in my life and whilst still trying to find a job, I simply didn't have the time.

One of my other responsibilities, I discovered, was issuing car passes to those who were sufficiently senior. This was most definitely a perk and I wasted no time in issuing myself a full car and motorbike permit, allowing me to park almost anywhere in the dockyard. This allowed me to return my retained car pass to HMS Cornwall before they started to moan about it.

Whilst all of this was going on, I was still applying for jobs all over the place. I registered my CV with just about every recruitment agency I could find, but nothing seemed to be happening. I saw a lovely job that seemed right up my street, quite literally. It was as a supervisor fire-fighting maintenance engineer for a company that had their head office only yards from where I went to school. The job promised a company BMW and a starting salary of £40k. When do I start? Unfortunately, it wasn't quite that simple and my CV never even made it past the initial sift.

Having received no replies to my applications for a whole month, I was starting to lose faith and regret turning down my only job offer. One August afternoon in 2010, that all changed. Out of the blue, I received a telephone call from a woman, called Natalie Destie, who identified herself as a recruiter working for Matchtech in Fareham. Natalie had stumbled across my CV and had matched it to a vacancy looking for a candidate with my qualifications. After outlining the job, she asked if I was interested, as it was in Bristol. She went on to explain that the job was a permanent position and how would I feel about working in Bristol? Well, this was something that I had discussed with Anita when I had received the other job offer. The only thing that brought me to Plymouth was the Royal Navy. The only thing, apart from some good friends, keeping us in Plymouth was the Royal Navy, so we had long since decided to move house to wherever the work was. Natalie said that she would put forward my interest to the company and try to arrange an interview.

A week later, whilst I was on leave, Natalie called again with the offer of an interview at the Submarine Support Management Group in Keynsham. She told me a little more about the company and the time and place of the interview.

I was still excited about the interview twenty minutes later when the phone rang again, this time, from a number that I didn't recognise. Answering it, the voice on the other end said, "Hi Plug, it's Wal." I didn't instantly recognise the voice, but he clearly knew me well enough to address me by my naval nickname. "Who?" I asked, "Wal, the Wrecker from Turbulent," he continued. Immediately, the image of my old mate came flooding back into my head. We had been good friends for a time, but lost contact after one, or both of us, had changed our phone numbers.

After we had got the usual greeting protocol out of the way, he said, "I hear you're coming for an interview?" Having a bit of a brain fart, I replied, "Good to hear from you, mate, but what has that got to do with you?" "Apart from the fact that I'm interviewing you, nothing, mate." Fuck! Had I just buggered up my only chance of an interview in weeks? I mumbled some form of apology before he continued, asking me what I knew about the organisation and the work that SSMG did. I confessed, apologetically, that I had never heard of them. Wal then kindly offered to send me some literature and urged me to read it before the interview.

As good as his word, he quickly filled up my inbox with loads of pre-interview reading and organisational family trees, that took me a clear week to read and inwardly digest. I honestly didn't understand any of it, but I could regurgitate it, parrot fashion, if that was what it took. I learned the meanings of loads of abbreviations and who was the boss of who. I learned all about something called the Submarine Definition Database and Reliability Centred Maintenance. Hopefully this would be enough and I could wing it.

On the day of the interview, I kissed Anita goodbye and dressed smartly in my newly purchased suit, I set the satnav and left Plymouth heading for Bristol. The journey went by in a blur, as I tried to remember everything that I had tried to cram into my swede. One tiny bit of advice, from the interview techniques module of the career transition workshop, was that the interview starts from the moment that you drive into the car park. Recalling a sketch from a comedy show, where the central character has a road rage incident on the way to an interview, with a pompous chap who turned out to be his interviewer. No, that would never do. I resolved to be on my best behaviour as soon as I reached Bristol, leaving nothing to chance.

I arrived in Keynsham very early and made my introductions to the woman staffing the reception desk. Extremely nervous, I forgot one piece of advice about not drinking coffee, for fear of slopping it down my shirt and gratefully accepted the offered caffeine fix from the receptionist who tried to help me relax, making small talk.

After what seemed like an age, I was invited into a nearby interview room where, sat around a large oval table, I met Linda, a woman from HR, Ian Walton, who I knew, Adrian, another team leader and Paul who was somewhat higher up the food chain. I was asked to make myself comfortable and to relax whilst the four interviewers took turns in asking me questions. What I hadn't realised was, I was simultaneously being interviewed for one of two different positions and towards the end of the interview, Paul asked, if I was to be offered a position, which of the two jobs I would prefer? God, how do you answer that? I mumbled something to the effect that I would be grateful of any offer and I would do the job to the best of my abilities. Satisfied with that, he then snookered me with another difficult question. How much would I expect to be paid? I was not prepared for that one either. Again, I tried to think on my feet and muttered something about trying to maintain my current lifestyle by earning roughly what I was earning in the navy.

After about an hour, which seemed to fly by, it was over. I asked a few prepared questions before Wal escorted me on a tour around the building and introduced me to his team. These would be the guys that I was hoping to work with, assuming that I got the job.

Clear of Keynsham on the way home, I stopped on the A38 for petrol, a sarnie and a moment to reflect on the day. I thought that the interview had gone really well. I had fudged my way through most of the questions, dropping in the odd abbreviation every now and again, in the hope that they considered that I had done my homework.

A couple of weeks later and I hadn't heard a sausage. Wal had told me, that it might take a while, but I thought I would give him a ring anyway to see if he had heard anything. He was just as surprised as me, as they had decided to offer me the job, even before I had left the car park. He assured me though, that the job offer was on its way and sure enough, a week later, it plopped onto my doormat.

With my perfect interview record intact, I had a new bounce in my step. The offer was a decent one and I had liked the location. After first discussing the offer with Anita, I accepted the position and then set about trying to be released from the navy, as soon as possible.

The warrant officer, Nick Sharland, was completely onside and advised that, if I bundled all of my remaining resettlement leave, four weeks terminal leave and any remaining annual leave together, then it might be possible for me to start work with SSMG at the beginning of December 2010, four months prior to leaving the Royal Navy. This would mean a bit of an overlap and the potential to be paid by two jobs at the same time. I was sure that Mr Taxman would take a sizable chunk of the excess, but at least I had a job.

With my timeline now established, I had a mere ten weeks to get all of my ducks in a row and my shit, firmly in one sock, which are naval expressions for being organised. I did have some kit to return but after thirty-two years, it amounted to nothing more than my S10 gas respirator. A nice man in the Unit Personnel Office, who was hugely efficient, booked me a hotel in Keynsham for my first six weeks and issued sufficient travel warrants to pay for six return trips from Keynsham to Plymouth. He also fished around in a drawer, before making me sign for a dark blue plastic box, which turned out to be a NATO medal with an 'Africa' clasp. This was to reward my time in the Gulf of Aden with HMS Cornwall. Finally, and without fanfare or ceremony, he requested my Royal Navy identity card. He carefully transposed the details onto an A4 temporary ID card before cutting my ID card into four pieces. After laminating the temporary ID card, he handed me a small metal badge that confirmed me as an 'Armed Forces Veteran'.

It was the end of an era. Although I had heard stories of people triumphantly burning their kit and sticking two fingers up to the establishment, I was really quite sad. Somebody had been looking out for me every minute of every day, since I had left home in 1979. There was always somebody to go to for advice. My teeth and more importantly, my health had been checked on a regular basis. I had been clothed, sheltered and fed, really quite well, all of my working life, but now it was all coming to an end and although I was excited about the new challenges that lay ahead, I was frankly quite worried. It was a bit like a child riding a bike for the first time without stabilisers, would I be ok? On the other hand, would I fall? Only time would tell.

On my penultimate day at work in the Royal Navy, my section took me for a bloody big, fat boy's breakfast at a local pub. I could have requested a top table dinner, surrounded by many of my naval friends in their best uniforms and dickey bows, but that was not my style. I had had a cracking career and was rightly proud of my achievements, but all of the fuss would have embarrassed me. When I joined up in February 1979, I had no idea whether I would last a year let alone remaining for as long as I had.

My last day at work, was predictably low key. Chief petty officer Paul Dent had relieved me as the SFM departmental coordinator and all that remained was for me to bring in the cakes and to shake a few hands.

Allowing myself a week's grace before starting work, I finally walked out of the main gate of HMS Drake on Friday 3rd December 2010. After thirty-two years, man and boy, nobody could say that I didn't give the Royal Navy a bloody good try.

Abbreviations

1st Lt	First Lieutenant
2OE	Second Open Engagement
2SL	Second Sea Lord
AFFF	Aqueous Film Forming Foam
AGI	Auxiliary Gathering Intelligence Russian ship
ALARP	As Low As Reasonably Practicable
AMC	Auxiliary Machinery Course
AMEO	Assistant Marine Engineering Officer (P) Propulsion (S) Ships Systems
AS1491	The Escape Inspection checklist
AT	Adventurous Training
B13	Promotion Order
BASCCA	Breathing Apparatus Single Cylinder Compressed Air
BIBS	Built in Breathing System
BM	Bosun's Mate
BOST	Basic Operational Sea Training
BR	Book of Reference
BSQ	Basic Submarine Qualification
BSS	Basic Submarine Safety
CAF	Copper Asbestos Fibre
Capt	Captain
CBSIFTCB	Glider Pre-flight checks: **C**ontrols, **B**allast, **S**traps, **I**nstruments, **F**laps, **T**rim, **C**anopy and **B**rakes
Cdr (E)	Commander Engineering
Cdr	Commander
CDT	Compulsory Drugs Testing
CinCFleet	Commander in Chief Fleet
CMEM	Chief Marine Engineering Mechanic (M = Mechanical) or (L = Electrical)
CMEMN	Chief Mechanician (Replaced by Chief Artificers)
COGOG	**CO**mbined **G**as **O**r **G**as
COSAG	**CO**mbined **S**team **O**r **G**as
CPO	Chief Petty Officer
CSB	Courage Sparking Bitter
CSE	Certificate of Secondary Education
CSU	Craft Support Unit
CV	Curriculum Vitae
DCHQ	Damage Control Headquarters on a submarine
DCO	Damage Control Officer
DMEO	Deputy Marine Engineering Officer

DO	Divisional Officer
DRIU	Damage Repair and Instructional Unit
DTS	Dinner Time Session. A drinking term
E,D & B	Edward, Day and Baker
EBS	Emergency Breathing System
EDBA	Extended Duration Breathing Apparatus
FAMR	Forward Auxiliary Machinery Room also known as the 'FARM'
FB5X	Foam Making Branch pipe
FCP	Forward Control Point
FCS	Fleet Contingency Ship
FOST	Flag Officer Sea Training
FRC	Frigate Refit Complex
FRPP	Fire and Repair Party Post
GNK	General Naval Knowledge
GRP	Glass Reinforced Plastic
HMS	Her Majesty's Ship
HPAC	High Pressure Air Compressor
HQ1	Damage Control Headquarters on a ship
i/c FCP	The person in charge of the Forward Control Point on-board a ship
ICABA	Internal Compressed Air Breathing Apparatus
ID	Identity
INTCO	Intelligence Coordinator
IRA	Irish Republican Army
IRTC	Internationally Recognised Transit Corridor
IS Platoon	Landing Party
JPA	Joint Personnel Administration
JSHHG	Joint Services Hosanna House Group
LCVP	Landing Craft, Vehicle, Personnel
LET	Leading Engineering Technician
LHOM	Leading Hand of the Mess
LMEM	Leading Marine Engineering Mechanic
LREM	Leading Radio Electrical Mechanic
LRQC	Leading Rates Qualifying Course
LS&GC	Long Service and Good Conduct Medal
Lt Cdr	Lieutenant Commander
Lt	Lieutenant
LVA	Loud Vocal Alarm
MA	Medical Assistant
MAA	Master-at-Arms
MAA	Minor Administrative Action (A Minor Punishment)

MACCO	Manpower Allocation Office
MCP	Main Coolant Pumps
MCR	Machinery Control Room
MCTA	Maritime Commissioning Trials and Assessment
MEDEPCO	Marine Engineering Departmental Coordinator
MEM	Marine Engineering Mechanic
MIG	Metal Inert Gas welding
MMA	Manual Metal Arc welding
MoD	Ministry of Defence
MPA	Maritime Patrol Aircraft
MPA	Mount Pleasant Airport in the Falklands
MRI	Magnetic Resonance Imaging is a *scan* that is used to diagnose health conditions affecting organs, tissue and bone.
NAAFI	Navy, Army, Air Force Institutes
NATO	North Atlantic Treaty Organisation
NCO	Non Commissioned Officer
NPFS	Naval Personnel and Family Services
NPIC	Nuclear Propulsion Intermediate Course
NVQ	National Vocational Qualification
OCRS	Officer Commanding the Recruit School
OERA	Outside Engine Room Artificer (Wrecker)
OOD	Officer of the Day
OOW	Officer of the Watch
PACE	Police and Criminal Evidence Act 1984
PD	Periscope Depth
PJT	Pre-Joining Training
PLT	Practical Leadership Task
PO	Petty Officer
POLC	Petty Officers Leadership Course
POMEM	Petty Officer Marine Engineering Mechanic
PPPPPP	Prior Preparation Prevents Piss Poor Performance
PSI	Pounds per Square Inch
PT	Physical Training
PTI	Physical Training Instructor
PVR	Premature Voluntary Release
Q&A	Questions and Answers
QARRNS	Queen Alexandra's Royal Naval Nursing Service
QEWO	Qualified Educationally for Warrant Officer
QM	Quarter Master
R&R	Rest and Recuperation
RA	Resident Ashore … Someone that does not live in barracks
RAF	Royal Air Force

RC	Reactor Compartment
RFA	Royal Fleet Auxiliary
RN	Royal Navy
RNH	Royal Naval Hospital
RNR	Royal Naval Reserve
RNSH	Royal Naval Sub Harpoon
RNSMS	Royal Naval Submarine School
RTFQ	Read The Fucking Question … an examination term
SAS	Special Air Service Regiment
SCC	Systems Control Console
SETT	Submarine Escape Training Tower
SFM	Superintendent Fleet Maintenance
SG	Steam Generator
SIB	Special Investigations Branch
SLR	Self-Loading Rifle
SMIC	Submarine Introduction Course
SMICOA	Submarine Induction Course Officers Assistant
SMQ	Submarine Qualification
SNMG	Standing NATO Maritime Group
SOP	Standard Operating Procedure
SPO	Stoker Petty Officer
SRC	Submarine Refit Complex
SRE	Sound Reproducing Equipment
SSEP	Standing Sea Emergency Party
STALAG	Special Tools and Lifting Associated Gear
TA	Turbo Alternator
TG	Turbo Generator
TIC	Thermal Imaging Camera
TIG	Tungsten Inert Gas welding
TITS	Tomatoes in Tomato Sauce
TLA	Triple Letter Abbreviations
TO2	Training Officer Part Two
TSW	Television South West
TWL	Turbo Water Lubricated Feed Pump
UEL(S)	Unit Expedition Leader (Summer)
UPO	Unit Personnel Office
VM	Victualed Man … Someone that lives on the base
WAFU	Weapon And Fuel Users .. A slang term for the Fleet Air Arm
WO	Warrant Officer
WSC	Weapons Stowage Compartment
WTI	Watertight Integrity

Glossary of Terms

2nd Open Engagement
An invitation to complete a further five or ten years as the service required.
5th Watch
The landed portion of a submarines crew.
Action Stations
A wartime state when action is imminent.
Adrift
Late for work or duty.
Afternoon Watch
Midday to 4pm.
Attack BA
Fire fighters wearing intermediate fire fighting rig. They will be at the scene of an emergency within two-minutes of the alarm being sounded.
Back-Aftie
Engineer working in the after part of the submarine.
Bezzie Oppo
Best Friend.
Big Eats
Late night food
BITS
Beans in Tomato Sauce.
Boat Stopper
A defect or incident that will prevent a submarine from sailing.
Bomb Shop
Weapons Stowage Compartment.
Boot Neck
'Booties' A slang term for the Royal Marines.
Brass Razoo
A mythical coin of very low value that has its origins in the First World War.
Buffer
Chief Bosun's Mate.
Burma Road
Standard nickname for the main passageway running the length of a ship.
Cackleberries
Boiled Eggs.
Charge Chief
The second highest non-commissioned rank. Now referred to as warrant officer two.
Chuck-up
Praise for a job well done.

Clanky
Mechanic.
Club Swinger
Physical Training Instructor.
Colours
A morning ceremony of raising the White Ensign.
Coxswain
Responsible for the steering and assuming the duties, which would be performed by the master-at-arms aboard larger vessels.
Crossing the Line
Naval tradition: When a ship crosses the equator, all first time crew members must pay homage to King Neptune
Cylume Lightstick
A self-contained coloured light source that shines brightly for about a day when two chemicals are mixed together.
Dabber
Seaman.
Daily Orders
Produced by the 1st Lt or Officer of the Day to inform the crew of a ships significant events and parish notices. Unclassified and distributed on the evening of the previous day.
Defaulters
A ship borne naval court where the accused is 'tried' by the Captain and punished.
Dhoby Dust
Washing Powder.
Dhobying
Washing, Laundry or Cleaning.
Dhow
The generic name of a number of traditional sailing vessels with one or more masts with lateen sails used in the Red Sea and Indian Ocean
Diving Stations
All compartments are manned and ready to submerge the submarine.
Dog Watches
The Dog Watches are said to derive from Sirius the 'Dog Star,' on the claim that Sirius was the first star to come into view on the first dog watch.
Dolphins
The coveted submarine badge.
Double Bank
Train under an experienced watch keeper.
Draft
To leave a ship or establishment. A term for non-commissioned ratings.

Drafty
Short for Drafting Officer. The person responsible for assigning ratings to new jobs in ships or establishments.
Emergency Stations
The whole ships company are out of bed to react to an emergency such as a fire or flood.
Familygram
A forty word unclassified one way communication from a loved one to a submariner.
First Dog Watch
4pm to 6pm.
First Lieutenant
Second in Command.
First Watch
8pm to midnight.
Fleet Chief Petty Officer
The highest non-commissioned rank. Now referred to as warrant officers.
Fore-endy
Weapons Engineering Mechanic.
Forenoon Watch
8am to midday.
Freshers
A breath of fresh air usually by a submariner.
Front Cunt
A vulgar slang term for an engineer working forward of the Reactor Compartment on a submarine.
Full Fire-fighting Rig
A fully protected fire-fighter, wearing a PBI Gold fire suit, wellington boots, suede gloves, EDBA, a fire-fighter's hood and a fire-fighting helmet with built in communications.
Galley
Kitchen.
Gash
Rubbish.
Ghetto Blaster
Portable stereo Radio/Cassette recorder.
Grand Slam
To urinate, defecate and vomit simultaneously whilst fully clothed. Usually whilst drunk.
Greenie
Electrician.

Gronk Board
A mess notice board full of photographs of past female conquests.
Guzz
Plymouth. Apparently originating from the wartime call sign Golf Uniform Zulu Zulu but some believe that it has its origins as an asian word for 'yard' as in dockyard.
Harries
Tinned Tomatoes.
Heads
Toilet.
Hollywood Shower
Excessive use of fresh water whilst taking a shower on-board a submarine.
Hot Bunk
Bed sharing by sailors in opposite watches.
Hot Fog
Steam.
Inboard
A slang term meaning off the submarine.
Intermediate F/F Rig
Worn by the Attack BA and consists of working clothes such as overalls or No4's, a fire-fighter's hood, anti-flash gloves, boots and wearing EDBA.
Jimmy
An affectionate term for the First Lieutenant
(Second in Command).
Jock
Traditional nickname for any man from Scotland.
Jolly
A run ashore outside of base port.
Junior Rating
An Ordinary Seaman, Able Seaman or Leading Hand.
Killick
Leading Hand.
Killicks with ties
A derogatory term used by chief petty officers when referring to POs.
Loafing
Being Lazy.
Longcast
A restricted timeline, spanning several months, informing the crew and their immediate families of a ship's movements.
Main Drag
Main Road or passageway. Also referred to as the Burma Road.

Make and Mend
Afternoon off work.
Master-at-Arms
The on-board Policeman, referred to as 'Master'.
Max Chat
Full Speed Ahead.
Mess Cooks
A party of sailors who clean up the mess deck.
Mess Deck
Dormitory style living quarters on-board ship.
Middle Watch
Midnight to 4am.
MoD Plod
Ministry of Defence Policeman.
Morning Watch
4am to 8am.
Munro
A Scottish mountain over three thousand feet.
No 1 Uniform
A best uniform, decorated with medals, gold embroidered rank and branch badges.
No 2 Uniform
A working uniform (now discontinued) with red embroidered branch and rank badges.
No 4 Uniform
Formally referred to as No 8's, is a working uniform consisting of dark blue cortton trousers and a lighter blue cotton shirt, decorated with white embroidered branch badges and a name tally. Rank is work on the epaulettes.
No 8 Uniform
Now discontinued, this uniform is currently referred to as No 4's. Working uniform consisting of dark blue trousers and a lighter blue shirt decorated with white embroidered branch badges and a name tally. Rank is worn on the epaulettes.
No 9 Punishment
A punishment routine consisting of stoppage of leave, extra work and mustering at set times in the correct uniform.
Numpty
Idiot.
Oggie
Cornish pasty.
Old Man
An affectionate term for the Captain.

One O'clockers
A snack for the oncoming watch on a submarine, served shortly before the 1am watch change.
Oppo
Opposite number or friend.
Part 3
A historic term for a submariner under trainng that had not yet earned his 'Dolphins'.
PAS Boat
Personnel and Stores. These are small boats for transporting sailors to and from ships.
Pompey
Portsmouth.
Pongo
Slang term for British Army soldiers.
Pot Mess
A stew boiled up in the boiler room from the galley left-overs and usually enjoyed in the small hours by those on the middle watch.
Procedure Alpha
A ceremonial entry or departure of a ship with sailors lining the decks, wearing their number one uniform.
R&R
Rest and Recuperation.
Rating
A non-commissioned sailor, usually a junior rating.
Red Sea Rig
Casual evening wear at sea, consisting of a pair of black uniform trousers and a white open necked short-sleeved shirt, often with a cummerbund.
Regulating Office
The on-board Police Station.
Requestmen
A ship-borne meeting with the Captain for good reasons such as promotion.
Rig of the Day
A designated uniform for an event, thus ensuring that everyone is wearing the correct uniform.
Rig
Naval uniform.
Ring the bell
Signifies somebody celebrating and buying a round of drinks in the mess.
Rock the bubble
Manoeuvring a recently dived submarine to release air trapped under the casing.

Scran
Mealtimes or Food.
Scratcher
A slang term for a bunk or bed
Scratcher
An affectionate nickname for the 2nd Coxwain who attended to the ropes and casing maintenance.
Second or Last Dog watch
6pm to 8pm.
Senior Rating
A petty officer, chief petty officer or warrant officer.
'Ships'
AMEO(S) –Assistant Marine Engineering Officer (Ships).
Shortcast
A restricted, detailed plan of a ship's movements over a period of two weeks. This normally forms the basis for Daily Orders.
Shot through
Failed to turn up.
Skiff
The term skiff has been applied to motorised boats of small size and construction used as sea-going vessels for piracy or drug-smuggling.
Skimmer
A slang term for a sailor serving on a ship usually by a submariner.
Skipper
An affectionate term for the Captain.
Skirmish
A naval term meaning to pick up litter.
Slops
A naval slang term for uniform cash clothing.
Snorker
Sausage.
Sod's Opera
A humorous variety show, hosted by sailors at sea to entertain themselves. Not too PC.
Spinning dits
Relating experiences and telling tall tales. There is an old saying "You don't spoil a good dit with the truth."
Sprog
A young sailor or child.
Stand Easy
A morning break from about 10am for fifteen to twenty minutes.

Station Leave
Free leave, granted when the ship is in a foreign port for a length of time.
Stoker PO
A submarine petty officer marine engineering mechanic.
Stoker
Marine Engineering Mechanic
Storob
To borrow serviceable items from another vessel when naval stores could not deliver in time.
Stowed
An item put away in its proper place.
Sunset
An evening ceremony of lowering the white ensign.
Support Party
A three or five man fire team dressed in full fire-fighting rig, required to be at the scene of a fire within eight minutes of the alarm being sounded.
The Pot
A slang term for the Reactor Compartment.
The Roof
The surface of the sea for a submariner.
Thursday War
A simulated war exercise in the South Coast exercise areas.
Tiff
Artificer.
Tiller Flat
The steering gear compartment of a ship. Usually the furthest compartment aft.
TITS
Tomatoes in Tomato Sauce.
Trap
To meet and go home with a person of the opposite sex.
Trooped
Naval defaulters. Seeing the Captain or Commander for punishment.
Wardroom
Officers mess.
Warrant Officer
The highest non-commissioned rank.
Watchbill
A roster listing shifts.

Wrecker
A chief artificer, formerly known as the OERA (Outside Engine Room Artificer), who is responsible for looking after ship's systems such as HP Air and hydraulics.

Lightning Source UK Ltd.
Milton Keynes UK
UKOW04f1909060714

234615UK00001B/126/P